The

Queen

of the

South

G. P. Putnam's Sons

New York

The

Queen

of the

South

—•—

ARTURO
PÉREZ-REVERTE

TRANSLATED
FROM THE SPANISH
BY
ANDREW HURLEY

This is a work of fiction. Names, characters, places, and
incidents either are the product of the author's imagination
or are used fictitiously, and any resemblance to actual
persons, living or dead, business establishments,
events, or locales is entirely coincidental.

G. P. Putnam's Sons
Publishers Since 1838
a member of
Penguin Group (USA) Inc.
375 Hudson Street
New York, NY 10014

This is a translation of *La Reina del Sur.*

Library of Congress Cataloging-in-Publication Data

Pérez-Reverte, Arturo
[Reina del sur. English]
The queen of the South / by Arturo Pérez-Reverte ;
translated from the Spanish by Andrew Hurley.
p.   cm.
ISBN 0-399-15185-0
I. Title
PQ6666.E765R4513   2004   2003066430
863'.64—dc22

Printed in the United States of America
1   3   5   7   9   10   8   6   4   2

BOOK DESIGN BY AMANDA DEWEY

To Elmer Mendoza, Julio Bernal,
and César "Batman" Güemes.
For the friendship.
For the corrido.

The

Queen

of the

South

The telephone rang, and she knew she was going to die. She knew it with such certainty that she froze, the razor motionless, her hair stuck to her face by the steam from the hot water that condensed in big drops on the tile walls. *R-r-ring—r-r-ring.* She stayed very still, holding her breath as though immobility or silence might change the course of what had already happened. *R-r-ring—r-r-ring.* She was in the tub, shaving her right leg, soapy water up to her waist, and goosebumps erupted on her naked skin as if the cold-water tap had just gushed. *R-r-ring—r-r-ring.* Los Tigres del Norte were on the stereo in the bedroom, singing about Camelia la Tejana. *Smuggling and double-crossing,* they were singing, *were in-se-pár-able.* She'd always feared that songs like that were omens, and then suddenly they turned out to be a dark and menacing reality. Güero had scoffed, but the ringing telephone showed how wrong a man could be. How wrong and how dead. *R-r-ring—r-r-ring.* She put down the razor, slowly climbed out of the bathtub, and made her wet way into the bedroom, leaving a trail of watery footprints. The telephone was on the bed—small, black, and sinister. She looked at it without touching it. *R-r-ring—r-r-ring.* Terrified. *R-r-ring—r-r-ring.* The words to the song and the buzzing ring of the telephone mixed together, the ringing becoming part of the song. *Because smugglers,* Los Tigres sang, *are merciless men.* Güero had used the same words, laughing as only he laughed, while he stroked the back of her neck and tossed the phone into her lap. If this thing ever rings, it's because I'm dead. So run. As far and as fast as you can, *prietita*— my little dark-skinned one. And don't stop, because I won't be there anymore to help you. And if you get to wherever you're going alive, have a tequila in memory of me. For the good times, *mi chula.* For the good times . . . That was how brave Güero Dávila was, and how irresponsible. The virtuoso of the Cessna. The king of the short runway, his friends called him, as did don Epifanio Vargas, his employer— because he was a man able to get a small plane, with its bricks of cocaine and bales of marijuana, off the ground in three hundred yards, a man able to skim the water on black nights, up and down the border, eluding the radar of the Federales and those vultures from the DEA. A man able, too, to live on the knife-edge, doing runs of his own behind his bosses' backs. And a man able, in the end, to lose.

The water dripping off her body made a puddle around her feet. The telephone kept ringing, and she knew there was no need to answer—what for, to confirm that Güero's luck had run out? But it's not easy to accept the fact that a simple telephone ring can instantly change the course of a life, so she finally picked up the phone and put it to her ear.

"They wasted Güero, Teresa."

She didn't recognize the voice. Güero had friends, and some of them were loyal, bound by the code that used to apply back when they'd transport pot and bundles of cocaine inside the tires of cars they drove across the bridge in El Paso—the bridge that linked the Americas in more ways than one. It might be any one of them: maybe Neto Rosas, or Ramiro Vázquez. She didn't recognize the voice and didn't fucking need to; the message was clear. *They wasted Güero,* the voice repeated. *They got him and his cousin both. Now it's his cousin's family's turn, and yours. So run. And don't stop running.*

Then whoever it was hung up, and she looked down at her wet feet and realized that she was shivering from cold and fear, and she realized that whoever the caller was, he'd used the same words Güero had. She pictured the anonymous man sitting, nodding attentively, in a cloud of cigar smoke, amid the glasses of a cantina, Güero before him, smoking a joint, his legs crossed under the table the way he always sat, his pointed-toe snakeskin cowboy boots, his scarf around his neck under his shirt, the aviator jacket on the back of the chair, his blond hair cut short, his smile knife-sharp, self-assured. *You'll do this for me,* carnal, *if they clean my clock. You'll call and tell her to run and not stop running, because they'll want to waste her, too.*

The panic hit without warning, and it was very different from the cold terror she'd been feeling up to now. Now it was a blast of confusion and madness that made her give a quick, hard scream and put her hands to her head. Her legs couldn't hold her, and she crumpled onto the bed, where she sat stock-still. She looked around: the white-and-gold crown moldings; the garish landscapes on the walls, with couples strolling at sunset; the porcelain figurines she'd collected over the years to fill the shelves, make a pretty, comfortable home. She knew this was not her home anymore, and that in a few minutes it would be a trap. She looked at herself in the big mirror on the dresser—naked, wet, her dark hair sticking to her face, and between the strands of hair her black eyes open wide, bulging in horror. Run, and don't stop, Güero and the voice on the phone had told her. So she started running.

1. I fell off the cloud I was riding

I always thought that those narcocorridos about Mexican drug runners were just songs, and that *The Count of Monte Cristo* was just a novel. I mentioned this to Teresa Mendoza that last day, when (surrounded by bodyguards and police) she agreed to meet me in the house she was staying in at the time, in Colonia Chapultepec, in the town of Culiacán, state of Sinaloa, Mexico. I mentioned Edmond Dantès, asking if she'd read the novel, and she gave me a look so long and so silent that I feared our conversation would end right there. Then she turned toward the rain that was pittering against the windows, and I don't know whether it was something in the gray light from outside or an absentminded smile, but whatever it was, it left a strange, cruel shadow on her lips.

"I don't read books," she said.

I knew she was lying, as no doubt she'd lied countless times over the last twelve years. But I didn't want to insist, so I changed the subject.

I'd tracked her across three continents for the last eight months, and her long journey out and back again was much more interesting to me than the books she'd read.

To say I was disappointed would not be quite accurate—reality often pales in comparison with legends. So in my profession the word "disappointment" is always relative—reality and legend are just the raw materials of my work. The problem is that it's impossible to live for weeks and months obsessed with someone without creating for yourself a definite, and invariably inaccurate, idea of the subject in question—an idea that sets up housekeeping in your head with such strength and verisimilitude that after a while it's hard, maybe even unnecessary, to change its basic outline. We writers are privileged: readers take on our point of view with surprising ease. Which was why that rainy morning in Culiacán, I knew that the woman sitting before me would never be the real Teresa Mendoza, but another woman who was taking her place, and who was, at least in part, created by me. This was a woman whose history I had reconstructed piece by piece, incomplete and contradictory, from people who'd known her, hated her, and loved her.

"Why are you here?" she asked.

"I'm still lacking one episode of your life. The most important one."

"Hm. One 'episode.'"

"Right."

She'd picked up a pack of Faros from the table and was holding a plastic lighter, a cheap one, to a cigarette, after first making a gesture to stop the man sitting at the other end of the room, who was lumbering to his feet solicitously, left hand in his jacket pocket. He was an older guy, stout—even fat—with very black hair and a bushy Mexican moustache.

"The most important one?"

She put the cigarettes and the lighter back down on the table, perfectly symmetrically, without offering me one. Which didn't matter to me one way or the other, since I don't smoke. There were several other packs there, too, an ashtray, and a pistol.

"It must be," she added, "if you're here today. Must be *really* important."

I looked at the pistol. A SIG-Sauer. Swiss. Fifteen 9-millimeter cartridges per clip, in three neat staggered rows. And three full clips. The gold-colored tips of the bullets were as thick as acorns.

"Yes," I answered coolly. "Twelve years ago. Sinaloa."

Again the contemplative silence. She knew about me, because in her world, knowledge could be bought. And besides, three weeks earlier I'd sent her a copy of my unfinished piece. It was the bait. The letter of introduction so I could get what I needed and finish the story off.

"Why should I tell you about that?"

"Because I've gone to a lot of trouble over you."

She was looking at me through the cigarette smoke, her eyes slightly Mongolian, somehow, like the masks at the Templo Mayor. She got up and went over to the bar and came back with a bottle of Herradura Reposado and two small, narrow glasses, the ones the Mexicans call *caballitos,* "little horses." She was wearing comfortable dark linen pants, a black blouse, and sandals, and I noticed that she was wearing no diamonds, no stones of any kind, no gold chain around her neck, no watch—just a silver *semanario* on her right wrist, the seven silver bangles I'd learned she always wore. Two years earlier—the press clippings were in my room at the Hotel San Marcos—the Spanish society magazine *¡Hola!* had included her among the twenty most elegant women in Spain. At about the same time, *El Mundo* ran a story about the latest police investigation into her business dealings on the Costa del Sol and her links with drug traffickers. In the photo, published on page one, you could see her in a car with the windows rolled up partway, protected from reporters by several bodyguards in dark glasses. One of them was the heavyset guy with the moustache who was sitting at the other end of the room now, looking at me as though he weren't looking at me.

"A lot of trouble," she repeated pensively, pouring tequila into the glasses.

"Right."

She sipped at it, standing up, never taking her eyes off me. She was shorter than she looked in photos or on television, but her movements were still calm and self-assured—each gesture linked to the next naturally, as though there were no possibility of improvisation or doubt. Maybe she never has any doubts about anything anymore, I suddenly thought. At thirty-five, she was still vaguely attractive. Less, perhaps, than in recent photographs and others I'd seen here and there, kept by people who'd known her on the other side of the Atlantic. That included her profile in black-and-white on an old mugshot in police headquarters in Algeciras. And videotapes, too, jerky images that always ended with big gruff gorillas entering the frame to shove the lens aside. But in all of them she was indisputably Teresa, with the same distinguished appearance she presented now—wearing dark clothes and sunglasses, getting into expensive automobiles, stepping out onto a terrace in Marbella, sunbathing on the deck of a yacht as white as snow, blurred by the telephoto lens: it was the Queen of the South and her legend. The woman who appeared on the society pages the same week she turned up in the newspapers' police blotter.

But there was another photo whose existence I knew nothing about, and before I left that house, two hours later, Teresa Mendoza unexpectedly decided to show it to me: a snapshot wrinkled and falling apart, its pieces held together with tape crisscrossing the back. She laid it on the table with the full ashtray and the bottle of tequila of which she herself had drunk two-thirds and the SIG-Sauer with the three clips lying there like an omen—in fact, a fatalistic acceptance—of what was going to happen that night.

As for that last photo, it really was the oldest of all the photos ever taken of her, and it was just half a photo, because the whole left side was missing. You could see a man's arm in the sleeve of a leather aviator jacket over the shoulders of a thin, dark-skinned young woman with full black hair and big eyes. The young woman was in her early twenties, wearing very tight pants and an ugly denim jacket with a lambskin collar. She was facing the camera with an indecisive look about halfway down the road toward a smile, or maybe on the way back. Despite the vulgar, excessive makeup, the dark eyes had a look of innocence, or a vulnerability that accentuated the youthfulness of the oval face, the eyes slightly upturned into almondlike points, the very precise mouth, the ancient, adulterated drops of indigenous blood manifesting themselves in the nose, the matte texture of the skin, the arrogance of the uplifted chin. The young woman in this picture was not beautiful, but she was striking, I thought. Her beauty was incomplete, or distant, as though it had been growing thinner and thinner, more and more diluted, down through the generations, until finally what was left were isolated traces of an ancient splendor. And then there was that serene—or perhaps simply trusting—fragility. Had I not been familiar with the person, that fragility would have made me feel tender toward her. I suppose.

"I hardly recognize you."

It was the truth, and I told it. She didn't seem to mind the remark; she just looked at the snapshot on the table. And she sat there like that for a long time.

"Me, either," she finally said.

Then she put the photo away again—first in a leather wallet with her initials, then in the purse that was lying on the couch—and gestured toward the door. "I think that's enough," she said.

She looked very tired. The long conversation, the tobacco, the bottle of tequila. She had dark circles under her eyes, which no longer resembled the eyes in the old snapshot. I stood up, buttoned my jacket, put out my hand—she barely brushed it—and glanced again at the pistol. The fat guy from the other end of the room was beside me, indifferent, ready to see me out. I looked down, intrigued, at his splendid iguana-skin boots, the belly that spilled over his handworked belt, the menacing bulge under his denim jacket. When he opened the door, I saw that what I took as fat maybe wasn't, and that he did everything with his left hand. Obviously his right hand was reserved as a tool of his trade.

"I hope it turns out all right," I said.

She followed my gaze to the pistol. She nodded slowly, but not at my words. She was occupied with her own thoughts.

"Sure," she muttered.

Then I left. The same Federales with their bulletproof vests and assault weapons who had frisked me from head to toe when I came in were standing guard in the entry and the front garden as I walked out. A military jeep and two police Harley-Davidsons were parked next to the circular fountain in the driveway. Five or six journalists and a TV camera were under a canopy outside the high walls, in the street: they were being kept at a distance by soldiers in combat fatigues who were cordoning off the grounds of the big house. I turned to the right and walked through the rain toward the taxi that was waiting for me a block away, on the corner of Calle General Anaya.

Now I knew everything I needed to know, the dark corners had been illuminated, and every piece of the history of Teresa Mendoza, real or imagined, now fit: from that first photograph, or half-photograph, to the woman I'd just talked to, the woman who had an automatic lying out on the table.

The only thing lacking was the ending, but I would have that, too, in a few hours. Like her, all I had to do was sit and wait.

Twelve years had passed since the afternoon in the city of Culiacán when Teresa Mendoza started running. On that day, the beginning of a long round-trip journey, the rational world she thought she had built in the shadow of Güero Dávila came crashing down around her, and she suddenly found herself lost and in danger.

She had put down the phone and sat for a few seconds in cold terror. Then she began to pace back and forth across the room, opening drawers at random, blind with panic, knowing she needed a bag to carry the few things she needed for her escape, unable at first to find one. She wanted to weep for her man, or scream until her throat was raw, but the terror that was washing over her, battering her like waves, numbed her emotions and her ability to act. It was as if she had eaten a mushroom from Huautla or smoked a dense, lung-burning joint, and been transported into some distant body she had no control over.

Blindly, numbly, after clumsily but quickly pulling on clothes—some jeans, a T-shirt, and shoes—she stumbled down the stairs, her hair wet, her body still damp under her clothing, carrying a little gym bag with the few things she had managed to gather and stuff inside: more T-shirts, a denim jacket, panties, socks, her purse with two hundred pesos. They would be on their way to the apartment already, Güero had warned her. They'd go to see what they could find. And he did *not* want them to find her.

Before she stepped outside the gate, she paused and looked out, up and down the street, indecisively, with the instinctive caution of the prey that catches the scent of the hunter and his dogs nearby. Before her lay the complex urban topography of a hostile territory. Colonia las Quintas: broad streets, discreet, comfortable houses with bougainvillea everywhere and good cars parked in front. A long way from the miserable barrio of Las Siete Gotas, she thought. And suddenly, the lady in the drugstore across the street, the old man in the corner grocery where she had shopped for the last two years, the bank guard with his blue uniform and twelve-gauge double-barreled shotgun on his shoulder—the very guard who would always smile, or actually, leer, at her when she passed—now looked dangerous to her, ready to pounce. *There won't be any more friends anymore,* Güero had said offhandedly, with that lazy smile of his that she sometimes loved, and other times hated with all her heart. *The day the telephone rings and you take off running, you'll be alone, prietita. And I won't be around to help.*

She clutched the gym bag to her body, as though to protect her most intimate parts, and she walked down the street with her head lowered, not looking at anything or anybody, trying at first not to hurry, to keep her steps slow. The sun was beginning to set over the Pacific, twenty-five miles to the west, toward Altata, and the palm, manzanita, and mango trees of the avenue stood out against a sky that would soon turn the orange color typical of Culiacán sunsets. She realized that there was a thumping in her ears—a dull, monotonous throbbing superimposed on the noise of traffic and the clicking of her own footsteps. If someone had called out to her at that moment, she wouldn't have been able to hear her name, or even, perhaps, the sound of the gunshot.

The gunshot. Waiting for it, expecting it with such certainty—her muscles tense, her neck stiff and bowed, her head down—that her back and kidneys ached. This was The Situation. Sitting in bars, among the drinks and cigarette smoke, she'd all too often heard this theory of disaster—discussed apparently only half jokingly—and it was burned into her brain as if with a branding iron. *In this business,* Güero had said, *you've got to know how to recognize The Situation. Somebody can come over and say Buenos días. Maybe you even know him, and he'll smile at you. Easy. Smooth as butter. But you'll notice something strange, a feeling you can't quite put your finger on, like something's just this much out of place*—his fingers practically touching. *And a second later, you're a dead man*—Güero would point his finger at Teresa like a revolver, as their friends laughed—*or woman.*

"Although that's always preferable to being carried alive out into the desert," he'd added, "'cause out there, they'll take an acetylene torch and a lot of patience, and they'll ask you questions. And the bad thing about the questions is not that you know the answers—in that case, the relief will come fast. The problem is when you don't. It takes a lot to convince the guy with the torch that you don't know the things he thinks you know."

Chingale. She hoped Güero had died fast. That they'd shot down the Cessna with him in it, food for the sharks, instead of carrying him into the desert to ask him questions. With the Federales or the DEA, the questions were usually asked in the jail at Almoloya or in Tucson. You could make a deal, reach an agreement, turn state's evidence, go into the Witness Protection Program or be an inmate with certain privileges if you played your cards right. But Güero didn't play his cards right—it was just not his way of doing business. He wasn't a coward, and he didn't actually work both sides of the street. He'd only double-crossed a little, less for the money than for the thrill of living on the edge. *Us guys from San Antonio,* he'd smile, *we like to stick our necks out, you know?* Playing the narcobosses was fun, according to Güero, and he would laugh inside when they'd tell him to fly this up, fly this other stuff back, and make it fast, junior, don't keep us waiting. They took him for a common hired gun—or mule, in his case—and they'd toss the money on the table, disrespectfully, stacks of crisp bills, when he came back from the runs where the capos had collected a shitload of green and he'd risked his freedom and his life.

The problem was, Güero wasn't satisfied to just do things—he was a bigmouth, he had to talk about them. *What's the point in fucking the prettiest girl in town,* he'd say, *if you can't brag about it to your buddies? And if things go wrong, Los Tigres or Los Tucanes de Tijuana'll put you in a corrido and people'll play your song in cantinas and on the radio. Chale, you'll be a legend, compas.* And many times—Teresa's head on his shoulder, having drinks in a bar, at a party, between dances at the Morocco, him with a Pacífico and her with her nose dusted with white powder—she had shivered as she'd listened to him tell his friends things that any sane man would have kept very, very quiet. Teresa didn't have much education, didn't have anything but Güero, but she knew that the only way you knew who your friends were was if they visited you in the hospital, or the jail, or the cemetery. Which meant that friends were friends until they weren't friends anymore.

She walked three blocks, fast, without looking back. No way this was going to work—the heels she was wearing were too high, and she realized that she was going to twist an ankle if she had to take off running. She pulled them off and stuck them in the gym bag, and then, barefoot, turned right at the next corner. She came out on Calle Juárez. There she stopped in front of a café to see whether she was being followed. She didn't see anything that might indicate danger, so to buy some time to think and lower her pulse rate a little, she pushed open the door and went inside.

She sat at a table at the far end of the café, her back against the wall and her eyes on the street. To study The Situation, as Güero would have put it. Or to try to. Her wet hair was in her face; but she pushed it back only once, because she decided it was better like that, hiding her face a little. The waitress brought her a glass of nopal juice, and Teresa sat motionlessly for a while, unable to think, until she felt the need for a cigarette. In her rush to get out of the apartment she'd forgotten hers. She asked the waitress for one and held it as she lit it for her, ignoring the look on the woman's face, the glance at her bare feet; she sat there quietly, smoking, as she tried to pull her thoughts together. Ah, now. Finally. Finally, with the cigarette smoke in her lungs, she could feel her serenity returning—enough, at least, to think The Situation through with a degree of practicality.

She had to get to the other house, the safe house, before the hit men found it and she wound up with a bit part in those narcocorridos by Los Tigres or Los Tucanes that Güero was always dreaming he'd have someday. The money and the documents were there, and without the money and the documents, no matter how fast she ran, she'd never get anywhere. Güero's notebook was there, too: telephone numbers, addresses, notes, contacts, secret runways in Baja California, Sonora, Chihuahua, and Coahuila; friends, enemies—it wasn't easy to tell them apart—in Colombia, Guatemala, Honduras, and on both sides of the Río Grande—El Paso, Juárez, San Antonio. *That,* he'd told her, *you burn or hide. For your own good, don't even look at it, prietita. Don't even look at it. But if you're totally fucked, I mean you're totally in a corner and the whole thing has gone to shit, you can trade it to don Epifanio Vargas for your hide. Clear? Swear to me that you won't open that book, under any circumstances. Swear by God and the Virgin. Come here—swear by this sweet thing you're holding in your hand right now.*

She didn't have much time. She'd forgotten her watch, too, but she saw that it would be night soon. The street looked quiet—normal traffic, normal people walking normally down the street, nobody standing around. She put her shoes on. She left ten pesos on the table and got up slowly, gripping the gym bag. She didn't dare look at herself in the mirror when she left.

At the corner, a kid was selling soft drinks, cigarettes, and newspapers set out on a flattened cardboard box that read "Samsung." She bought a pack of Faros and a box of matches, stealthily looking over her shoulder, and then walked on with deliberate slowness. The Situation. A parked car, a cop, a man sweeping the sidewalk—they all spooked her. The muscles in her back were aching again, and there was a bitter taste in her mouth. The high heels were bothering her, too. If Güero had seen her, she thought, he'd have laughed. And she cursed him for that, deep inside. Laughing out the other side of your mouth now, aren't you, *pinche cabrón*? You and that macho attitude of yours, you and those fucking brass balls of yours, you and . . . She caught the smell of burned flesh as she passed a taquería, and the bitter taste in her mouth suddenly got worse. She had to stop and duck into a doorway, where she vomited up a slimy greenish thread of nopal.

I knew Culiacán. Before my interview with Teresa Mendoza, I had been there, right at the beginning, when I started researching her story and she was no more than a vague personal challenge in the form of a few photographs and press clippings. I also went back later, when it was all over and I was finally in possession of what I needed to know: facts, names, places. So I can lay it out now with no more than the inevitable, or convenient, gaps. Let me mention, too, that the seed of all this was planted some time ago, during a dinner with René Delgado, editor of the newspaper *Reforma,* in Mexico City. René and I have been friends ever since as young reporters we shared a room in the Hotel InterContinental in Managua during the war against Somoza. Now we see each other when I go to Mexico, talk over old times and new, avoid mentioning our gray hair and wrinkles. And that time, eating *escamoles* and *tacos de pollo* at the San Angel Inn, he offered me the story.

"You're a Spaniard, you've got good contacts there. Write something dynamite about her for us."

I shook my head as I tried to keep the contents of the tortilla from dripping down my chin. "I'm not a reporter anymore. Now I make it all up, and I don't write anything under four hundred pages."

"So do it your way," René insisted. "Write a fucking literary piece."

I finished off the taco and we discussed the pros and cons. I hesitated until the coffee and the Don Julián No. 1 came, just when René was threatening to call the mariachis over. But his little stratagem backfired on him: The story for *Reforma* had turned into a private book project, although our friendship didn't suffer on that account. Quite the contrary: The next day he put at my disposal all his best contacts on the Pacific coast and in the federal police force so I could fill in the dark years—the stage of Teresa Mendoza's life that was unknown in Spain, and not in the public domain even in Mexico.

"At least we'll review it," René said, *"cabrón."*

At that time, about the only things known publicly about Teresa Mendoza were that she had lived in Las Siete Gotas, a poor barrio in Culiacán, and that she was the daughter of a Spanish father and a Mexican mother. Some people also knew that she'd dropped out after elementary school and a few years later gone to work as a salesgirl in a sombrero store in the Buelna *mercado,* then become a money changer on Calle Juárez. Then, one Day of the Dead afternoon—life's little ironies—fate set her in the path of Raimundo Dávila Parra, a pilot for the Juárez cartel. In that world, he was "Güero" Dávila. "Güero" was Mexican slang for a blue-eyed, blond-headed gringo, which Güero wasn't, exactly, since he was a Chicano from San Antonio, but the name stuck.

All this latter stuff was known more from the legend woven around Teresa Mendoza than from documented sources, so to throw some light on that part of her life story I went to the capital of the state of Sinaloa, on the west coast of Mexico, at the mouth of the Gulf of California, and wandered through its streets and into its cantinas. I even followed the exact, or almost exact, route taken by Teresa on that last afternoon (or first, depending on how you look at it), when the telephone rang and she fled the apartment she'd shared with Güero Dávila. I started at the love nest they had lived in for two years: a comfortable, discreet two-story house with a patio in back, crepe myrtle and bougainvillea at the door, located in the southeast part of Las Quintas, a neighborhood that had become a favorite of middle-class drug dealers, the ones who were doing okay, but not well enough to afford a luxurious mansion in Colonia Chapultepec.

Then I walked along under the royal palms and mango trees to Calle Juárez, and in front of the little grocery store I stopped to watch the girls who, holding a cell phone in one hand and a calculator in the other, were changing money right out in the open. Or to put it another way, taking stacks of American dollars fragrant with cocaine or high-quality hashish from the sierra, and laundering it into Mexican pesos. In that city where breaking the law is often a social convention and a way of life—*It's a family tradition,* says one famous corrido, *to break the law*—Teresa Mendoza was one of those girls for a while. Until a black Bronco stopped one afternoon, and Raimundo Dávila Parra lowered the smoked-glass window and sat there and stared at her from the driver's seat. And her life changed forever.

Now she was walking down that same sidewalk, a sidewalk she knew every inch of, with her mouth dry and fear in her eyes. She dodged the girls standing around in little groups talking, or pacing back and forth, waiting for customers in front of the El Canario fruit stand, and as she did so she glanced mistrustfully at the bus-and-tram station, the taquerías in the *mercado*—the street swarming with women carrying baskets and moustached men in baseball caps and sombreros. From the music store behind the jeweler's on the corner came the words and melody of "Pacas de a Kilo"—"Kilo Bricks"—sung by Los Dinámicos. Or maybe Los Tigres—from that distance she couldn't be sure, but she knew the song. *Chale,* she knew it all too well—it had been Güero's favorite, and that *hijo de su madre* used to sing it when he shaved, with the window open to annoy the neighbors, or whisper it in her ear, just to infuriate her:

My father's friends and colleagues
Admire me and respect me
And in two or three hundred yards
I can get planes off the ground.
I can hit any bull's-eye
With a pistol or machine gun. . . .

Pinche Güero cabrón, she thought again—fucking asshole prick, and she almost said it out loud, to control the sob that suddenly rose within her.

Then she looked right and left. She was looking for a face, a presence that meant danger. They would send somebody who knew her, she thought, somebody who could recognize her. So her hope lay in recognizing him before he recognized her. Or in recognizing *them.* Because there were usually two, so one could back the other one up, and also so they could keep an eye on each other, because this was a business where nobody trusted even his own shadow.

Somebody will smile at you, she remembered. *And a second later, you'll be a dead woman.* If you're lucky, she added for him, imagining the desert and the blowtorch that Güero had mentioned.

On Juárez, the traffic was coming from behind her. She realized this as she passed the San Juan monument, so she turned left, heading for Calle General Escobedo. Güero had explained that if you ever thought you were being followed, you should take streets where the cars come toward you, so you could see them coming. She walked on down the side street, turning from time to time to look back. She came to the center of the city, passed the white edifice of City Hall, and mingled with the masses of people crowding the bus stops and the area around the Garmendia *mercado.*

Only then did she feel a little safer. The sky in the west was intense orange over the buildings—a beautiful sunset—and the store windows were beginning to light the sidewalks. They almost never kill you in places like this, she thought. Or even kidnap you. Cars and other vehicles passed by in both directions, and two brown-uniformed police officers stood on one corner. One of them had a vaguely familiar face, so she turned her own face away and changed direction. Many local cops were in the narcos' pay, as were a lot of the Judiciales and Federales and so many others, with their dime bags of smack in their wallets and their free drinks in the cantinas. They did protection work for the bosses or abided by the healthy principle of Live, collect your paycheck, and let live, if you want to stay alive. Three months earlier, a police chief who'd been brought in from outside tried to change the rules of the game. He had been shot seventy times at point-blank range with a *cuerno de chivo*—the narcos' name for the AK-47—at the door of his house, in his own car. *Rat-a-tat-a-tat.* There were already CDs out with songs about it. "Seventy Before Seven" was the most famous. *Chief Ordoñez was shot dead,* the lyrics recounted, *at six in the morning. A lot of bullets for such an early hour.* Pure Sinaloa. The album photographs of popular singers like El As de la Sierra—the Ace of the Sierra—often showed them with a small plane behind them and a .45 in their hand, and Chalino Sánchez, a local singing idol who'd been a hit man for the narcomafia before becoming a famous singer, had been shot dead over a woman or for god knew what other reason. If there was anything the guys who wrote the narcocorridos had no need for, it was imagination—the ideas for the songs came ready-made.

At the corner where La Michoacana ice cream store stood, Teresa left the area of the *mercado* and the shoe and clothing stores behind and took a side street. Güero's safe house, his refuge in case of emergency, was just a few yards away, on the second floor of an unassuming apartment building. Across the street was a cart that sold seafood during the day and *tacos de carne asada* at night. In principle, no one knew of the existence of this place except the two of them. Teresa had been here only once, and Güero himself hardly came, so as not to burn it.

She climbed the stairs, trying not to make any noise, put the key in the lock, and turned it carefully. She knew nobody could be inside, but even so, she walked through the apartment nervously, checking to make sure everything was all right. Not even that crib is completely safe, Güero had said. Somebody may have seen me, or know something, or whatever—in this fucking city, everybody knows everybody else. And even if it doesn't go down that way, say they catch me—if I'm alive, I'll only be able to keep my mouth shut for so long before they beat it out of me and I start singing rancheras. So keep one eye open, *mi chula*. I hope I can take it long enough for you to grab the money and run, because sooner or later they'll be there. But no promises, *prietita*—he kept smiling as he said that, *pinche cabrón*—I can't promise you a thing.

The little crib's walls were bare, and the only furniture was a table, four chairs, and a couch in the living room, and in the bedroom a big bed with a night table and a telephone. The bedroom window was at the back of the building, overlooking an open lot with trees and shrubs that was used for parking, and behind that were the yellow cupolas of the Iglesia del Santuario. One of the closets had a false back wall, and when she pulled the panel out, Teresa found two thick packages with stacks of hundred-dollar bills. About twenty thousand, she figured, drawing on her experience as a money changer on Calle Juárez. There was also Güero's notebook: a large one with a brown leather cover— *Don't even open it*, she remembered—a stash of white powder that weighed about three hundred grams, she estimated, and a huge Colt Double Eagle, chrome with mother-of-pearl handles. Güero didn't like weapons, and he never carried even a revolver—*What the fuck good would it do me*, he would say; *when they look for you, they find you*—but he had put this one away for emergencies. *Why should I tell you no if the answer's yes*. Teresa didn't like guns, either, but like almost every man, woman, and child in Sinaloa, she knew how to use them. And since we're talking about emergencies, this is one, she thought. So she checked to make sure the gun's clip was loaded, pulled back the slide, and released it. With a loud, sinister click a .45-caliber round was loaded into the chamber. Her hands were shaking with anxiety as she put the money, the dope, and the gun in the gym bag she had brought with her.

Halfway through the operation, she was startled by a backfire from a car down in the street. She stood very quiet for a while, listening, before she went on. With the dollars were two valid U.S. passports—hers and Güero's. She studied his photo: his hair cropped short, those gringo eyes gazing out serenely at the photographer, the beginnings of that eternal smile on one side of his mouth. After hesitating a second, she put just her passport in the bag, and it was only when she leaned over and felt tears dripping off her chin and wetting her hands that she realized she'd been crying for a long time now.

She looked around, her eyes blurry with tears, trying to think whether she was forgetting something. Her heart was beating so hard she thought it was about to burst through her chest. She went to the windows, looked down at the street that was beginning to grow dark with the shadows of nightfall, the taco cart illuminated by a naked lightbulb and the coals in the brazier. She lit a Faro and took a few indecisive steps through the apartment, puffing nervously. She had to get out of there, but she didn't know where to go. The only thing that was clear was that she had to leave.

She was at the door of the bedroom when she noticed the telephone, and a thought flashed through her head: don Epifanio Vargas. He was a nice guy, don Epifanio. He'd worked with Amado Carrillo in the golden years of runs between Colombia, Sinaloa, and the United States, and he'd always been a good padrino to Güero, always a man of his word, a man you could trust, a real professional. After a while, he invested in other businesses and got into politics, stopped needing planes. Don Epifanio had offered Güero a place with him, but Güero liked to fly, even if it was for other people. Up there you're somebody, he would say, and down here you're just a mule driver. Don Epifanio didn't take offense, and in fact he even lent Güero the money for a new Cessna when Güero's old one got fucked up in a violent touchdown on a landing strip up in the sierra, with three hundred kilos of Miss White inside, all wrapped up in masking tape, and two Federales planes circling overhead, highways green with soldiers, AR-15s firing, sirens wailing, bullhorns booming—one bad fucking afternoon, no doubt about it. Güero had escaped that one by the short hairs, with just a broken arm—broken once by the law and then again by the owners of the cargo, to whom he had to prove with newspaper clippings that everything had been nationalized, that three of the eight men on the reception team had been killed defending the landing strip, and that the one who'd fingered the flight was a guy from Badiraguato that squawked on retainer for the Federales. The loudmouth had wound up with his hands tied behind his back, suffocated with a plastic bag over his head, as had his father, his mother, and his sister—the narcomafia tended to *mochar parejo,* as they put it, wipe the slate clean. They took out the whole family, as an object lesson for anybody else who might get ideas.

Güero, cleared of suspicion, bought himself a new Cessna with don Epifanio Vargas' loan.

Teresa put out the cigarette, left the gym bag open on the floor by the headboard, and pulled out the notebook. She laid it on the bed and stared at it for a long time. *Don't even look at it.* The fucking notebook belonged to the fucking *cabrón* who was probably dancing with La Pelona right about now, and she was sitting there like a *pendeja,* docile, obedient, idiotic, not opening it. *Nor should you,* said a voice inside. *Just a little peek,* whispered another; *if this could cost you your life, you ought to see what your life's worth.* To work up the courage she took out the package of powder, stuck a fingernail through the plastic, and brought a hit to her nose, breathing deep.

Seconds later, with a new and different lucidity and her senses keen, she looked at the notebook and opened it, at last. Don Epifanio's name was there, with others that gave her cold chills just looking at them: Chapo Guzmán, César "Batman" Güemes, Héctor Palma . . . There were telephone numbers, contact points, intermediaries, numbers, and codes whose meaning she couldn't make out. She kept reading, and little by little her pulse slowed, until her blood was ice. *Don't even look at it,* she remembered, shivering. *¡Híjole!* Now she understood why. It was much worse than she'd thought.

And then she heard the door open.

L ook who we've got here, Pote. My, my . . ."
    Gato Fierros' smile gleamed like the blade of a wet knife, moist and dangerous, the smile of a killer from a gringo movie, one of those where the narcos are always brown-skinned, Latino, and bad. Gato Fierros was dark-skinned, Latino—like Juanito Alimaña, that gangster in the Hector Lavoe song—and bad. He could have been the model for the even more famous Pedro Navaja in Rubén Blades' take on "Mack the Knife." In fact, the only thing that wasn't clear was whether he cultivated the stereotype on purpose or whether Rubén Blades, Willie Colón, and gringo movies were inspired by people like him.

". . . Güero's girlfriend."

The gunman was leaning on the door frame, his hands in his pockets. His feline eyes, which had given him his nickname, never left Teresa as he spoke to his companion—twisting his mouth to the side with malignant charm.

"I don't know anything," said Teresa. She was so terrified that she hardly recognized her own voice. Gato Fierros shook his head sympathetically, twice.

"Of course not," he said, his smile broadening. Odds were, he'd lost count of the number of men and women who'd assured him they didn't know anything before he killed them, quickly or slowly, depending on the circumstances. In Sinaloa, dying violently was dying a natural death. Twenty thousand pesos for a common, run-of-the-mill hit, a hundred thousand for a cop or a judge, free if it was to help out a compadre.

And Teresa knew the score: She knew Gato Fierros, and also knew his companion, Potemkin Gálvez, whom everyone called Pote, or Pinto. They were wearing almost identical jackets, silk Versace shirts, denim pants, and iguana-skin boots, as though they shopped in the same store. They were hit men for César Güemes, "Batman," as he was called, and they had hung out a lot with Güero Dávila—coworkers, escorts for cargos airlifted up to the sierra, and also drinking buddies at parties that started at the Don Quijote in midafternoon, with fresh money that smelled like what fresh money smells like, and went on till who knew when at the table-dancing clubs in the city, Lord Black's and the Osiris, with girls dancing nude at a hundred pesos for five minutes, two hundred and thirty back in the private rooms, before the boys moved on and greeted the new day with Buchanan's and norteño music, their hangovers tempered with lines of coke while Los Pumas, Los Huracanes, Los Broncos, or some other group, paid in hundred-dollar bills, accompanied them with corridos—"Noses a Gram Apiece," "A Fistful of Powder," "Death of a Federale"—about dead men, or men as good as dead.

"Where is he?" Teresa asked.

Gato Fierros gave a low, mean laugh. "Hear that, Pote? . . . She's asking about Güero. My, my . . ."

He was still leaning on the door frame. The other gunman shook his head. He was broad and heavyset, with a solid look about him, and he had a thick black goatee and dark blotches on his skin, like a pinto horse. He didn't seem as much at ease as his companion, and he looked at his watch impatiently. Or maybe uncomfortably. When he moved his arm, he revealed the butt of a revolver at his waist, under the linen golf jacket.

". . . Güero," Gato Fierros repeated, pensive.

He'd taken his hands out of his pockets and was slowly walking toward Teresa, who was sitting motionless at the head of the bed. When he reached her he stopped and looked down at her.

"Well, you see, *mamacita*," he said at last, "your man thought he was smart."

Teresa felt the fear writhing in her intestines, like a rattlesnake. The Situation. A fear as white and cold as the surface of a gravestone.

"Where is he?" she repeated.

It wasn't her talking, it was some stranger whose unexpected, unforeseeable words startled her—a reckless stranger who didn't recognize the urgent need for silence. Gato Fierros must have sensed that, because he looked at her strangely, surprised that she could ask questions instead of sitting there paralyzed, or screaming in terror.

"He's nowhere. He died."

The stranger continued to act on her own, and Teresa was once again startled to hear her curse them: *Hijos de la chingada.* That was what she said, or what Teresa heard her say—*Hijos de la chingada*—regretting it before the last syllable had left her lips. Gato Fierros was studying her with a great deal of curiosity and a great deal of attention.

"Not nice," he said, still thoughtful. "Talking about us that way . . . That mouth on you," he added. And then he hit her in the face, knocking her full length across the bed, backward. He stood looking down at her for another while, as though taking in the view. With the blood pounding in her temples and her cheek throbbing, her head dulled by the blow, Teresa saw his eyes go to the packet of powder on the night table. He picked up a pinch and raised it to his nose.

"Hm, good stuff," the hit man said. "Been cut, but it's still good stuff." He rubbed his nose with his thumb and index finger, then offered some to his companion, but Pote shook his head and looked at his watch again.

"No hurry, *carnal*," said Gato Fierros. "None at all." He turned once more to Teresa.

"Nice piece, Güero's girlfriend . . . and now she's a widow, poor thing."

From the door, Pote Gálvez spoke his companion's name. "Gato," he said, very seriously. "Let's get this over with."

Gato raised a hand, asking for quiet, and sat down on the edge of the bed.

"Don't fuck around," Pote insisted. "The orders were to off her, not boff her. So get on with it—*no seas cabrón*."

But Gato Fierros shook his head like a man listening to the rain. "My, my," he said. "I always wanted a piece of this."

Teresa had been raped other times: at fifteen, by several of the boys in Las Siete Gotas, and then by the man who'd put her to work on Calle Juárez. So she knew what to expect when the killer's knifelike smile grew wetter and he unbuttoned her jeans. And suddenly, she wasn't afraid. It isn't happening, she thought. I'm asleep and this is just a nightmare like all the others, the ones I lived through before, something that happens to the other woman I dream about, the one who looks like me but isn't. I can wake up whenever I want to, listen to my man's breathing on the pillow, hold him to me, sink my face in his chest, and discover that none of this has ever happened. I can also die in my sleep, of a heart attack, a cerebral hemorrhage, whatever. I can die all of a sudden, and neither the dream nor life itself will have any importance anymore. Sleep, without images of anything at all, without nightmares. Rest forever from what has never happened.

"Gato," the other man repeated. He had moved at last, taking a couple of steps into the room. *"Quihubo,"* he said. "What's up? Güero was one of ours, man. A good guy. Remember—the sierra, El Paso, Río Bravo. And this was his woman." And as he was saying this, he was pulling a Python out of his waistband and pointing it at Teresa's forehead. "Get up so you don't get splattered, man, and let me put her lights out."

But Gato Fierros had other plans. "She's going to die anyway," he said, "and it'd be a waste."

He knocked the Python away, and Pote Gálvez stood looking at them, first at Teresa and then at Gato—undecided, fat, with his dark, Indian, norteño hit-man eyes, drops of sweat in his thick moustache, his finger on the trigger guard, the barrel pointing up, as though he were about to scratch his head with it. And then it was Gato Fierros who took out his gun, a big silver Beretta, and pointed it straight at the other man, at his face. Laughing, he said that Pote was either going to have a go at her, too, so they'd be in it together, or, if he was the type of guy who preferred to bat left-handed, then he needed to step aside, *cabrón*, because if he didn't he was having lead for lunch.

Pote Gálvez looked at Teresa with resignation and embarrassment; he stood a few seconds more, and then he opened his mouth to say something but then didn't. Instead, he slowly stuck the Python back into his waistband and walked slowly to the door, without turning around. The other killer kept his pistol pointed at him, saying, "I'll buy you a Buchanan's afterward, *mi compa,* to make you feel better about being a *maricón.*"

And as Gálvez disappeared into the other room, Teresa heard a crash, the sound of wood splintering—maybe the hit man putting his fist through the closet door—which for some reason made Teresa very grateful. But she didn't have time to think about that anymore, because Gato Fierros was already taking off her jeans, or rather ripping them off, raising her T-shirt, and pawing at her breasts, and as he did so he stuck the barrel of the pistol up between her legs as though he were going to blow her away from down there. She let him, without a scream or even a whimper, her eyes very open, looking up at the white ceiling, praying to God for it to all happen fast, and when it was over, for Gato Fierros to kill her fast, before it all stopped being a nightmare and turned into the naked horror of *pinche* fucking life.

I t was the same old story. Winding up like that. How could it be otherwise, even though Teresa Mendoza never imagined that The Situation would smell like sweat, like rutting macho, like the shot glasses of tequila that Gato Fierros had knocked back before coming up those stairs looking for his prey. I wish it was over, she thought in her moments of lucidity. I wish it was just fucking over and done with, and I could rest. She thought that for a second and then she sank again into her void without emotions, without fear. It was too late for fear, because fear was what you felt before things happened, and the consolation when they finally did happen was that it all came to an end. The only true fear was that the end would take too long to come.

But Gato Fierros was not going to be *that* case. He was pushing violently, with the urgency to finish and empty himself. Quiet. Short. He was pushing cruelly, without looking at her, shoving her little by little to the edge of the bed. Teresa emptied her mind as she suffered his thrusts. She let her arm drop, and it touched the open gym bag on the floor.

The Situation can go two ways, she suddenly discovered. It can be Your Situation or the Other Guy's. She was so surprised to realize this, that if the man holding her down had let her, she would have sat straight up in bed, one finger held up, very serious and reflective, to think it through. Let's see, let's just consider this variant. . . . But she couldn't sit up, because the only part of her that was free was her arm and hand, which, falling accidentally into the gym bag, was now stroking the cold metal of the Colt Double Eagle inside it, among her clothes and the stacks of bills.

This is not happening to me, she thought. Or maybe she never really thought anything, but instead just observed, passively, while that other Teresa Mendoza thought in her place. Whatever—before she became conscious of it, her or the other woman's fingers had closed around the butt of the pistol. The safety was on the left, next to the trigger and the button to release the clip. She touched it with her thumb and felt it slide down, to the vertical, freeing the hammer. There's a bullet in the chamber, she remembered, there's a bullet there because I put it there—she remembered the metallic *click-click*—although maybe she just *thought* she'd loaded the chamber, but hadn't, and the bullet wasn't ready. She considered all this with dispassionate calculation: Safety, trigger, hammer. Bullet. That was the right sequence of events—if, that is, that *click-click* had been real and not the product of her imagination. Because if it hadn't been real, the hammer was going to hit nothing, air, and Gato Fierros would have time to take it badly. Of course, whatever happened, things couldn't be that much worse than they were now. There might be a little more violence, or rage, in the last moments. Nothing that wouldn't be over within a half-hour or so—for her, for that woman watching her, or for both at once. Nothing that wouldn't stop hurting in a little while. And as she thought all this, she stopped looking up at the white ceiling and realized that Gato Fierros had stopped moving, and that he was looking at her. That was when Teresa raised the pistol and shot him in the face.

There was an acrid smell, the smell of gunpowder, and the report of the gunshot was still echoing off the walls of the room when Teresa pulled the trigger the second time—but the Double Eagle had jumped at the first shot, recoiling so much that the new bullet only took a chunk of plaster out of the wall. By that time, Gato Fierros was lying against the night table, gasping for air, covering his mouth with his hands, while through his fingers gushed streams of blood that also spattered his eyes, which were wide open with surprise. He was stunned by the blast that had singed his hair, eyebrows, and eyelashes, but Teresa couldn't tell whether he was screaming or not, because the noise of the gunshot so close had deafened her.

She'd gotten up on her knees in the bed, her T-shirt bunched up over her breasts, naked from the waist down, holding her right hand with her left so she could aim the third shot more accurately, when she saw Pote Gálvez appear in the doorway, stupefied, his mouth agape. She looked at him again, as though in a slow-motion dream, and Pote, whose revolver was still stuck in the waistband of his pants, put both hands up in front of him, as though to protect himself, looking in fear at the Double Eagle that Teresa was now pointing at him. Under the black moustache his mouth opened to pronounce a silent "No," like a plea for mercy—although what may have happened was that Pote Gálvez actually said "No" aloud and she simply couldn't hear it because she was still deaf from the gunshots. She finally decided that that must be it, because Pote kept moving his lips, fast, his hands out in front of him, looking at her apologetically, conciliatorily, speaking words she couldn't hear. Even so, Teresa was about to pull the trigger when she remembered the fist through the closet door, the Python pointed at her forehead, the "Güero was one of us, man, *no seas cabrón.*" And the "She was Güero's woman, man."

She didn't shoot. That sound of splintering wood kept her finger motionless on the trigger. Her naked belly and legs were beginning to feel cold when, never taking the gun off Pote Gálvez, she backed up on the bed and with her left hand threw the clothes, the notebook, and the coke into the gym bag. As she did this, she watched Gato Fierros out of the corner of her eye. He was still slowly writhing on the floor, his bloody hands on his face. For a second she thought of turning the gun on him and finishing the job, but the other killer was still at the door, his hands outstretched and his revolver at his waist, and she knew with absolute certainty that if she stopped pointing the gun at him, the next bullet fired would be for her.

She grabbed the gym bag, and holding the Double Eagle firmly in her right hand, stood up and stepped away from the bed. First Pote, she decided, and then Gato Fierros. That was the right order, and the noise of splintering wood—which she was truly grateful for—was not enough to change that. Just then she saw that the eyes of the man standing before her had read her own. The mouth under the moustache suddenly stopped, interrupted itself in mid-sentence—now it was a confused murmur in Teresa's ears—and by the time she fired a third time, Potemkin Gálvez, with an agility surprising in a man as heavy as he was, had leapt to the front door and was clambering downstairs, pulling his gun as he ran.

She shot a fourth and a fifth time, before realizing that it was useless and that if she wasn't smart, she could wind up without ammunition. Nor did she run after him, because she knew that he wouldn't just let this go, that he was going to come back for her, soon, and finish what the two of them had started.

Two stories, she thought. Although it's not any worse than what I've already been through. So she opened the bedroom window, looked down at the back yard, and saw a few stubby trees and some bushes in the darkness. I forgot to finish off that *cabrón* Gato, she thought too late, just as she was jumping. Then the branches and the bushes were scratching her legs, thighs, and face as she fell into them, and she felt a sharp pain in her ankles as she hit the ground. She got up, limping, surprised to be alive, surprised that nothing seemed broken, and she ran,

barefoot, and naked from the waist down, through the parked cars and
shadows in the lot.

Finally, out of breath, far away, she stopped, squatting next to a half-
ruined brick wall. Besides the sting of the scratches and the cuts to her
feet from running, she felt an uncomfortable burning in her thighs and
sex. The memory of what had just happened to her now hit her, because the other Teresa Mendoza had just abandoned her, left her with
nobody to attribute sensations and emotions to. She felt a violent urge
to urinate, and she did so just as she was, squatting motionless in the
darkness, shivering as though she had a high fever. A car's headlights illuminated her for a second; she clutched the gym bag in one hand and
the pistol in the other.

2 . They say the law spotted him, but they got cold feet

I mentioned earlier that I had been in Culiacán, Sinaloa, at the beginning of my research, before I met Teresa Mendoza personally. There, where drug trafficking had come out from underground a long time ago and become an objective social fact, a few well-placed dollars opened doors for me into certain exclusive worlds, places where a curious foreigner without any references might, overnight, turn up floating in the Humaya or the Tamazula with a bullet in his head. I also made a couple of good friends: Julio Bernal, head of the city's office of cultural affairs, and the Sinaloan writer Elmer Mendoza—no relation to Teresa—whose splendid novels *A Lonely Murderer* and *The Lover of Janis Joplin* I'd read for background. It was Elmer and Julio who acted as my guides through that underworld and filled me in on all the local eccentricities.

Although neither of my friends had had any personal dealings with Teresa Mendoza in the beginnings of this story—she was nobody back then—they did know Güero Dávila and some of the other characters who in one way or another pulled the strings of the plot, and they and their contacts set me on the track to knowing a good deal of what I know now. In Sinaloa everything is a question of trust; in a hard, complex world like that one, the rules are simple and there's no place for mistakes. You're introduced to somebody by a friend somebody trusts, and that somebody trusts you because he trusts the friend who vouched for you. Then, if anything goes wrong, the voucher pays with his life, and you pay with yours. *Bang bang.* The cemeteries of northwest Mexico are full of graves of people somebody trusted.

One night of music and cigarette smoke in the Don Quijote, drinking beer and tequila after listening to the disgusting jokes of the comedian Pedro Valdez—who'd been preceded by the ventriloquist Enrique and his cokehead dummy Chechito—Elmer Mendoza leaned over the table and pointed to a heavyset, dark-skinned man in glasses who was drinking at a table in one corner, surrounded by a large group of the kind of guys that leave their sport coats or jackets on, as though they were cold no matter where they were—snake- or ostrich-skin boots, thousand-dollar belts with leather-laced edging, panama hats or baseball caps with the insignia of the Culiacán Tomateros, and a lot of heavy gold at their necks and wrists. We'd seen them get out of two Ram Chargers and walk in like they owned the place, right past the bouncer, who greeted them obsequiously, forgoing the ritual pat-down that all the other customers were subjected to.

"That's César 'Batman' Güemes," Elmer said softly. "A famous narco."

"Got any corridos to him?"

"Several." My friend laughed in mid-sip. "He killed Güero Dávila."

My jaw dropped as I looked at the group: brown faces and hard features, lots of moustache and obvious danger. There were eight of them; they'd been there fifteen minutes and had already downed a case of beer—twenty-four tall ones. Now they'd just ordered two bottles of Buchanan's and two of Rémy Martin, and the dancers—this was unheard-of in the Don Quijote—were coming over to sit with them when they left the runway. A group of bottle-blond gays—the place filled with gays late at night, and the two worlds mixed without any problems—had been giving the table insinuating looks, and Güemes smiled sarcastically, very macho, and called the waiter over to pay for their drinks. Pure peaceful coexistence.

"How do you know?" I asked.

"Me? Everybody in Culiacán knows."

Four days later, thanks to a friend of Julio Bernal's who had a nephew in the business, Batman Güemes and I had a strange and interesting conversation. I was invited to a cookout at a house in San Miguel, in the hills above the city. There, the junior narcos—the second-generation guys, less ostentatious than their fathers who'd come down from the sierra, first to the barrio of Tierra Blanca and later assaulting the spectacular mansions of Colonia Chapultepec—began to invest in more discreet houses, in which the luxury was reserved for the family and guests, inside. The nephew of this friend of Julio's was the son of a historic narco from San José de los Hornos—one of those legendary bandidos who in his youth had traded bullets with the police and rival bands and was now serving a comfortable sentence in the prison at Puente Grande, Jalisco; the son was twenty-eight, and his name was Ernesto Samuelson. Five of his cousins and an older brother had been killed by other narcos, or the Federales, or soldiers, and he had quickly learned the lesson: law school in the United States; businesses abroad, never on Mexican soil; money laundered through a respectable Mexican company whose holdings included big transport rigs and Panamanian shrimp farms. He lived in an unassuming house with his wife and two children, drove a sober Audi, and spent three months a year in a simple apartment in Miami, with a Golf in the garage. You live longer that way, he would say. In this business, envy kills.

It was Ernesto Samuelson who, under the bamboo-and-palm palapa in his garden, introduced me to Batman Güemes, who was standing with a beer in one hand and a plate of burnt meat in the other. "He writes novels and movies," Ernesto told Batman, by way of introduction, and then he left us.

Batman Güemes spoke softly, with long pauses that he employed so he could study you from head to toe. He'd never read a book in his life, but he loved movies. We talked about Al Pacino (*Scarface* was his favorite movie of all time) and Robert De Niro (*Goodfellas, Casino*), and how Hollywood directors and scriptwriters, those *hijos de la chingada,* never portrayed a blond, blue-eyed, gringo drug dealer; they all had to be named Sánchez and be born south of the Río Grande. His remark about the blond, blue-eyed drug runner was my cue, so I dropped the name Güero Dávila, and while Batman Güemes looked at me through his dark glasses very carefully and very quietly, I stuck my neck out by following that up with the name Teresa Mendoza. I'm writing her story, I added, aware that in certain circles and with a certain kind of man, lies always explode under your pillow. And Batman Güemes was so dangerous, I'd been warned, that when he went up into the sierra the wolves lit bonfires to keep him away.

"One shitload of years has passed since then," he said.

I figured him for younger than fifty. His skin was very dark, and he had an inscrutable face with strong norteño features. I later learned that he was not from Sinaloa but from Alamos, Sonora, the homeland of María Félix, and that he had started out as a coyote and a burro, using a truck that belonged to him to run undocumented workers, marijuana, and cocaine for the Juárez cartel over the border. He rose in the hierarchy, starting as an operator for the Lord of the Skies and finally becoming the owner of a transport company and a private aviation business that ran contraband between the sierra and the western United States—Nevada and California—until the gringos tightened up the airspace and closed almost all the gaps in their radar system. Now he was living a relatively quiet life off the savings he'd invested in safe businesses and a few other investments, mainly opium villages up in the sierra, on the border with Durango. He had a nice ranch over in El Salado, with four thousand head: Do Brasil, Angus, Bravo. He also raised thoroughbreds for the *parejeras,* which is a two-horse race they run in Mexico, and fighting cocks that brought him sackfuls of money every October or November from the cockfights at the livestock fairs.

"Teresa Mendoza," he murmured after a while.

He shook his head as he said this, as though remembering something funny. Then he took a swig of his beer, chewed on a piece of meat, and drank again. He was still looking at me hard from behind the dark glasses, a little sneer on his lips, perhaps, letting me know that he had no problem talking about something so old, and that the risk of asking questions in Sinaloa was entirely mine. Talking about dead men didn't cause problems—the narcocorridos were full of real names and stories; what was dangerous was asking questions about live men, because you might get taken for a bigmouth and a snitch. And I, accepting the rules of the game, looked at the gold anchor—only slightly smaller than the *Titanic*'s—hanging from the thick gold chain that gleamed under the open collar of his plaid shirt, and without beating around the bush asked the question that had been burning my mouth since Elmer Mendoza had pointed this man out to me four days earlier. I asked what I needed to ask, and then I raised my eyes, and the guy was looking at me just like before. Either he likes me, I thought, or I'm going to have problems.

After a few seconds, he took another drink of his beer, still watching me. He must have liked me, because he finally smiled a little, just a hint. "Is this for a novel or a movie?" he asked. I told him I didn't know yet; it could be either, or both. At that, he offered me a beer, went to get another one for himself, and started to tell the story of Güero Dávila's two-timing.

He wasn't a bad guy, Güero. Kept his word, a lot of heart—brave, really brave. He was good-looking, a little like Luis Miguel, but thinner—and tougher. Great sense of humor. Easygoing. Raimundo Dávila Parra spent money as fast as he made it, or almost, and he was generous with his friends. He and Batman Güemes had been up until dawn lots of nights, partying with music, alcohol, and women, celebrating successful operations. At one time they were even close friends—bro's, or *carnales,* as the Sinaloans put it. Güero was a Chicano—he'd grown up in San Antonio. And he started young, transporting grass in cars to the U.S. They'd made more than one run together up through Tijuana, Mexicali, or Nogales, until the gringos offered him a stay in a jail up there somewhere.

After that, Güero didn't want anything to do with cars—all he wanted to do was fly. He had a pretty good education, high school anyway, and he took pilot's classes in the old flying school on Zapata. He was a good pilot—the best, Batman Güemes acknowledged, nodding emphatically—one of those that aren't afraid of anything: the right man for clandestine takeoffs and landings on the little hidden runways up in the sierra, or for low-altitude flights to avoid the Hemispheric Radar System that scanned the air routes between Colombia and the U.S. The Cessna was like an extension of his hands and his courage: he would land anywhere and at any hour, and that brought him fame, respect, and green. The guys in Culiacán called him the king of the short runway, and for good reason. He was so famous that Chalino Sánchez, who was also a close buddy of his, promised to write a corrido for him using that exact name—"The King of the Short Runway." But Chalino got taken out before he could do it—Sinaloa was not a healthy place to live, depending on the neighborhood—and Güero never got his song.

Anyway, with or without his corrido, he never lacked for work. His *padrino* was don Epifanio Vargas, a narco boss who was a veteran of the sierra, a guy with real balls, tough and straight-shooting in every sense of the word. Epifanio Vargas' cover was Norteña de Aviación, a company he owned that sold and leased Cessnas and Piper Comanches and Navajos. And on Norteña's payroll, Güero Dávila did runs of two or three hundred kilos, before the big deals of the golden age, when Amado Carrillo earned himself the title Lord of the Skies by organizing the biggest air bridge in the history of drug trafficking between Colombia, Baja California, Sinaloa, Sonora, Chihuahua, and Jalisco. A lot of the missions that Güero flew back in the early days were diver-sionary—he was a decoy for both the land-based radar screens and those Orions crammed with technology and manned by mixed gringo and Mexican crews. And they were for diversion meaning "fun," too, because he loved it. So he made a fortune risking his skin on flights to the limit, day and night: fancy-as-hell maneuvers, takeoffs and land-ings on forty feet of runway and in places you wouldn't think a plane could ever manage, diverting attention from the big Boeings, Car-avelles, and DC-8s—bought during the period when the cartels were all pooling together—that would transport eight and ten tons in one trip. And all this with the complicity of the police, the Ministry of De-fense, and even the President of the Republic. Because those were the good times—the high times—of Carlos Salinas de Gortari, with narcos running drugs under the protection of the presidency itself. They were good times for Güero Dávila, too: empty planes, no cargo to be respon-sible for, playing cat and mouse with adversaries that it wasn't always possible to completely buy off. Flights where you risked your life on a roll of the dice, pure chance whether they popped you or not—or threw your ass in jail for a long stay if they caught you on the gringo side.

Back then, Batman Güemes, who had his feet on the ground figura-tively as well as literally, was beginning to do pretty well in the Sinaloa narcomafia. The Mexicans were beginning to declare their indepen-dence from the providers in Medellín and Cali, raising the stakes, be-ing paid with greater and greater amounts of coca, and commercializ-ing the Colombian drug that they'd only transported before. That made Batman's rise in the local hierarchy easier, after some bloody set-tling of scores to stabilize the market and the competition—some days, there would be twelve or fifteen bodies, your side and theirs. He had put as many cops, military men, and politicians on the payroll as pos-sible—including Customs officers on the Mexican side and INS offi-cers, the *migras,* on the U.S. side—and in a very short time, packages with his trademark, a little bat, started to cross the Río Grande in eigh-teen-wheelers. Sometimes hashish, what they called *goma de la sierra,* rubber from up in the mountains, and sometimes coke or weed—mar-ijuana. There was a song, a corrido they say somebody commissioned from a norteño group on Calle Francisco Villa, and the lyrics summed it up: *Vivo de tres animales—mi perico, mi gallo y mi chiva.* I make my living from three animals: my parakeet, my rooster, and my goat—which in Mexican slang was coke, marijuana, and heroin.

At about this same time, don Epifanio Vargas, who until then had been Güero Dávila's employer, began to specialize in drugs of the future like crystal meth and ecstasy. He had his own laboratories in Sinaloa and Sonora, and also on the other side of the border. "The gringos want to ride," he would say, "I saddle the horse for 'em." In not very many years, and with not many shots fired or trips to the cemetery—practically what you'd call a white-collar operation—Vargas managed to become the first Mexican magnate of precursors for designer drugs like ephedrine, which he could import problem-free from India, China, and Thailand, and one of the main producers of methamphetamines north or south of the border. He also started looking into politics. With legal businesses in plain view and the illegal ones well camouflaged behind a pharmaceutical company with state backing, the cocaine and Norteña de Aviación were unnecessary. So he sold the airplane business to Batman Güemes, and with that, Güero Dávila got a new boss in the drug-running game. Güero wanted to fly even more than he wanted to make money. By then he'd bought a two-story house in Las Quintas, was driving a brand-new black Bronco instead of the old one, and was living with Teresa Mendoza.

And that's when things started getting complicated. Raimundo Dávila Parra was not a discreet fellow. Living forever didn't interest him particularly, so he seems to have decided to blow it all fast. He was one of those guys that don't give jack shit about much of anything, as his daredevil antics with the Cessna showed all too clearly, but in the end he basically let his mouth get the better of him—which happens even to sharks, so the saying goes. He got careless—and things got ugly—when he bragged about what he'd done and what he was going to do next. Better, he used to say, five years on your feet than fifty on your knees.

So little by little, rumors began reaching Batman Güemes. Güero was sandwiching his own cargo into flights full of other people's, taking advantage of the runs he was making to do his own deals. The drugs, he got from an ex-cop named Guadalupe Parra, aka Lupe the Chink, or Chino Parra, who was Güero's first cousin and had contacts. Usually it was cocaine confiscated by Judiciales who grabbed twenty, reported five, and sold the rest down the line. This was the worst thing you could do—not on the part of the Judiciales, but Güero, doing his own deals—because he was charging a shitload of money for his work, rules were rules, and doing private deals, in Sinaloa and behind your employers' back, was the quickest way to get yourself in very ugly trouble.

"When you live crooked," Batman Güemes said that afternoon, a beer in one hand and the plate of meat in the other, "you've gotta work straight."

So in summary: Güero talked too much, and the asshole cousin was no brain surgeon. Stupid, sloppy, a real mouth-breather: Chino Parra was one of those guys you sent out for a shipment of coke and he came back with Pepsi. He had debts, he needed a snootful every half-hour, he loved big cars, and he had bought his wife and three kids a mansion in the most ostentatious part of Las Quintas. It was a disaster waiting to happen: the dollars went out faster than they came in. So the cousins decided to set up their own operation, and big-time: a shipment of a certain cargo that the Judiciales had confiscated in El Salto, Durango, and found buyers for in Obregón. As usual, Güero flew solo. Taking advantage of a flight to Mexicali with fourteen fifty-gallon drums of lard, each containing twenty kilos of smack, he made a detour to pick up fifty keys of White Horse, all neatly shrink-wrapped in plastic. But somebody fingered him, and somebody else decided to clip Güero's wings.

"Which somebody?"

"What the fuck. Somebody."

The trap, Batman Güemes went on, was laid on the runway at six in the afternoon—the precision of the hour would have been perfect for that corrido Güero wanted and Chalino Sánchez, R.I.P., never quite composed—near a place up in the sierra known as El Espinazo del Diablo. The runway was just 312 yards long, and Güero, who flew over without seeing anything suspicious, had just touched down, with the flaps on his Cessna 172R on the last notch, the plane having come down so vertical it looked like he was dropping in on a parachute, and he was rolling down the first stretch of the runway at about forty knots when he saw two trucks and a bunch of people that shouldn't have been there, camouflaged under the trees. So instead of hitting the brakes he gave it the gas and pulled up on the stick.

He might have made it, and somebody later said that by the time they started emptying their AR-15s and AK-47s at him, he'd already gotten the wheels off the ground. But all that lead was a lot of weight to lift, and the Cessna crashed about a hundred yards beyond the end of the runway. When they got to him, Güero was still alive among the twisted wreckage of the cabin; his face was bloody, his jaw smashed by a bullet, and splinters of broken bones were sticking out of the flesh of his legs; he was breathing weakly. He couldn't last long anyway, but the instructions had been to kill him. So they took the smack out of the plane, and then, like in the movies, they threw a lighted Zippo into a trickle of the hundred-octane aircraft fuel that was leaking out of the gas tank. *Fluhm!* The fact is, Güero hardly knew what hit him.

W hen you live crooked, Batman Güemes repeated, you've got no choice but to work straight. This time he said it as a kind of conclusion, pensively, setting his empty plate down on the table. Then he clucked his tongue, held up the beer bottle to see how much was left, and looked at the yellow label: Cervecería del Pacífico, S.A. All this time he had been speaking as though the story he'd just told me had nothing to do with him, as though it was just something he'd heard here and there. Something in the public domain. And I figured it was.

"What about Teresa Mendoza?" I chanced.

He looked at me suspiciously from behind his dark glasses, wordlessly querying, *What about her?* So I asked straight out whether she'd been implicated in Güero's operations, and he shook his head instantly. No way, he said. Back then she was just another girl, like all the rest: young, quiet, a typical *morra*—a narco's girlfriend. The only difference was that she didn't dye her hair blond and she wasn't one of those bitches who liked to show it all off. The *morras* here just do girl things: they get their hair done, they watch the telenovelas on TV, they listen to Juan Gabriel and norteño music, and then they go on little $3,000 shopping sprees to Sercha's and Coppel, where their credit's even better than their cash. You know—when the hunter comes home, the little woman's there to massage his worries away. Teresa had heard things, sure, but she didn't have anything to do with the deals.

"Why go for her, then?"

"Why're you asking me?" he said, turning serious.

Once again I feared he was going to cut off the conversation. But after a moment he shrugged.

"There are rules," he said. "You don't get to pick the ones you like, you follow the ones they give you when you come in. It's all about reputation, and respect. Like piranhas. You go chicken or bleed, the others are all over you. You make a pact with life and death: so many years as a king, and then . . . Say what you will, dirty money spends as green as clean. Plus, it gives you luxuries, music, wine, and women. Then you die fast, and rest in peace. Not many narcos retire, and the natural way out is jail or the cemetery. Cases of really lucky guys, or really smart ones who get off the horse in time, like Epifanio Vargas, are rare. People here don't trust anybody that's been too long in the business and is still active."

"Active?"

"Alive."

He let me chew on that for three seconds. "They say," he went on then, "those who are in that line of business"—he stressed the third-person, distant aspect of all this—"that even if you're good at your business and you're straight with people—no funny stuff, you know—you come to a bad end. You come, slide in easy, you're preferred for some reason over others, you move up before you even know it, and then the competitors come after you. That's why any false step, you pay. Plus, the more people you care about, the more vulnerable you are. Take the case of that other famous gringo, corridos and the whole thing, Héctor Palma. The story goes that he and a former associate of his had a falling-out, so this former associate of his kidnapped and tortured his family. So they say, you understand. And on his birthday this former associate sends him a box with his wife's head in it. *Happy birthday—to—you.*

"Living on the edge like that, nobody can afford to forget the rules. It was the rules that took Güero down. He was a good guy, I give you my word. A fine fellow to work with, that *compa.* Brave—the type who'll risk his soul and die wherever he's supposed to die. A little talkative, you know, and ambitious, but not much different from the best we've got around here. I don't know if you understand that. But as for Teresa Mendoza, she was his woman, and innocent or not, the rules went for her, too."

Santa Virgencita. Santo Patrón. The little Malverde Chapel was in shadow. A single light glowed in the portico, whose doors were open night and day, and through the windows filtered the reddish flicker of four or five candles lighted before the altar. Teresa had been sitting motionless in the dark a long time, hidden by the wall between Avenida Insurgentes—deserted at this hour—and the railroad tracks and the canal. She tried to pray, but couldn't; other things occupied her mind.

It had taken her a long time to decide whether to make the phone call. Calculate the possibilities. Then she'd walked here, watching her surroundings carefully, and now she was waiting, a lighted cigarette cupped in her hand. Half an hour, don Epifanio had said. Teresa had forgotten her watch, so she had no way to know how much time had passed.

She got a hollow feeling in the pit of her stomach, and she hurried to stub out the cigarette when a patrol car passed by slowly, headed toward Zapata: silhouettes of two cops in the front seats, the face of the one on the right slightly illuminated, seen and not seen, by the light on the porch of the chapel. Teresa scooted back, seeking more darkness. It wasn't just that she was outside the law. In Sinaloa, as in the rest of Mexico, from the patrolman looking to get his back scratched—wearing his jacket zipped up so you couldn't see his badge number—to his superior who received a stack of bills every month from the narco-mafia, crossing paths with the law could often mean stepping into the lion's den.

That useless prayer that never ended. *Santa Virgencita. Santo Patrón.* She'd started it six or seven times, and never finished. The chapel to the bandido Malverde brought back too many memories linked to Güero Dávila. That may have been why when don Epifanio Vargas agreed over the phone to the meeting, she named this place almost without thinking. At first don Epifanio had suggested she go to Colonia Chapultepec, near his house, but that meant crossing the city and a bridge over the Tamazula. Too risky. And although she didn't mention any details about what had happened, just that she was running and that Güero had told her to get in contact with him, he understood immediately that things were bad, or even worse than that. He tried to reassure her: *Don't worry, Teresita, I'll come to see you, just calm down and don't move. Hide and tell me where to find you.* He always called her Teresita when he saw her with Güero on the *malecón,* in the restaurants on the beach at Altata, at a party, or eating mussels or shrimp ceviche and stuffed crab on Sunday at Los Arcos. He would call her Teresita and give her a kiss, and he had even introduced her to his wife and children once. And although don Epifanio was an intelligent, powerful man, with more money than Güero had ever had in his life, he was always nice to Güero, and he kept calling him his godson, just like in the old days. And once, around Christmas, the first Christmas that Teresa was Güero's girlfriend, don Epifanio sent her flowers and a pretty Colombian emerald on a gold chain, and an envelope with $10,000 inside, so she could buy her man something, a surprise, and with the rest buy herself whatever she wanted.

That was why Teresa had phoned him that night, and was intending to give him that notebook of Güero's that was burning a hole in her gym bag. *Santa Virgencita. Santo Patrón.* Because don Epi is the only one you can trust, Güero had always told her. He's a gentleman, and a stand-up guy—he was a good boss when he was boss, and he's my godfather. *Pinche* Güero. He'd said that before everything went to shit and that telephone rang. . . . Now she knew she couldn't trust anyone, not even don Epifanio. Which was probably why she'd asked him to come there, almost without thinking, although actually thinking about it pretty well.

The chapel was a quiet place she could get to by skulking along the train tracks that ran along the canal. From here, she could watch the street on both sides in case Güero had been wrong in his calculations and the man who called her Teresita—and who gave her $10,000 and an emerald at Christmas—didn't come alone. Or in case she got cold feet and—in the best of cases, if she was still able—took off running again.

She struggled with the temptation to light another cigarette. *Santa Virgencita. Santo Patrón.* Through the windows she could see the candles that threw flickering light across the walls and pews of the chapel. During his mortal life, St. Malverde had been Jesús Malverde, the good bandit who stole from the rich, they said, to help the poor. The priests and church authorities never recognized him as a saint, but the people canonized him on their own. After his execution, the government had ordered that the body not be buried, as an object lesson for other would-be Robin Hoods, but people who passed by the place would put down stones, one each time—religiously, you might say—until they'd given him a Christian burial. The chapel grew out of that devotion. Among the gruff people of Culiacán and all of Sinaloa, Malverde was more popular and had done more miracles than God Himself, or Our Lady of Guadalupe. The chapel was filled with little signs and ex votos placed there in gratitude to Malverde for the miracles: a lock of a child's hair for a successful childbirth, shrimp in alcohol for a good catch, photographs, kitschy religious prints.

But above all, St. Malverde was the patron saint of the Sinaloa narcos, who came to the chapel to offer their lives up to him, and to give thanks, with offerings and hand-lettered signs after each successful return and each profitable deal. *Gracias for getting me out of jail,* one might read, stuck up on the wall next to an image of the saint—dark-skinned, moustached, dressed in white with an elegant black neckerchief. Or *Gracias for you know what.* The toughest of them, the worst criminals, murderers from the sierra and the plains, had his likeness on their belts, on scapulars, on their baseball caps, in their cars; when they spoke his name they would cross themselves, and many mothers would go to the chapel to pray when their sons made their first run or were in jail or some other trouble. There were gunmen who glued a picture of Malverde to the butts of their pistols, or on the shoulder stocks of their AK-47s. And even Güero Dávila, who said he didn't believe in that sort of thing, had a photo of the saint on the instrument panel of his plane; it was in a leather frame, with the prayer *God bless my journy and allow my return,* misspelling and all. Teresa had bought it for him at the shop at the chapel, where, early in their relationship, she'd often go, secretly, to light candles whenever Güero didn't come home for several days. She did this until he found out and forbade her. Superstitions, *prietita.* Idiotic. *Chale,* I don't like my woman being ridiculous.

But the day she brought him the photo with the prayer, he didn't say a word, didn't even make fun of it—he just put it up on the Cessna's instrument panel.

By the time the headlights went out, after illuminating the chapel with two long sweeps, Teresa was aiming the Double Eagle at the car. She was scared, but that didn't keep her from weighing the pros and cons, trying to foresee the appearances under which danger might present itself. Her head, as the men who gave her a job as a money changer had discovered years before, was good at figures: A plus B equals X, plus Z probabilities backward and forward, multiplications, divisions, additions and subtractions.

And that brought her once again face to face with The Situation. At least five hours had passed since the telephone rang, and maybe two since that first shot fired into Gato Fierros' face. Her dues in horror and confusion had been paid; all the resources of her instinct and her intelligence were now committed to keeping her alive.

Which was why her hand didn't tremble. Which was why she'd wanted to pray, but couldn't. Instead she recalled with absolute clarity that she had fired five shots, that there was one in the chamber and ten in the clip, that the Double Eagle's recoil was very powerful, and that the next time, she needed to aim slightly below the target if she didn't want to miss. Her left hand was not under the butt of the gun, like in the movies, but rather on top of her right wrist, to steady it. This was her last chance, and she knew it. If her heart beat slowly, her blood circulated quietly, and her senses were on alert, it would make the difference between being alive and lying dead on the ground. Which was why she'd taken a couple of quick sniffs from the package in the gym bag. And which was why, when the white Suburban pulled up, she'd instinctively turned her eyes away from the headlights, so as not to be blinded. She looked over the top of the weapon again, finger on the trigger, holding her breath, alert to the first possible sign that something wasn't quite right. Ready to shoot anybody, no matter who.

The doors slammed. She held her breath. One, two, three. *¡Híjole!*—shit. Three male silhouettes standing alongside the car, backlighted by the streetlamps. Choose. She'd thought she could be safe from this, on the sidelines, while somebody did it for her. *You just take it easy, pri-etita*—that was at the beginning—*you just love me, and I'll take care of the rest.* It was sweet and comfortable. It was deceptively safe to wake up at night and hear her man's—any man's?—peaceful breathing. There was not even any fear back then, because fear is the child of the imagination, and back then there were only happy hours that passed like a pretty love song, or a soft stream. And the trap was easy to fall into; his laughter when he held her, his lips traveling over her skin, his mouth whispering tender words, or dirty words down below, between her thighs, very close and very far inside, as though it were going to stay there forever—if she lived long enough to forget, that mouth would be the last thing that she forgot. But nobody stays forever. Because nobody is safe, and all sense of security is dangerous. Suddenly you wake up with proof that it's impossible to just live—you realize that life is a road, and that traveling it entails constant choices. Who you live with, who you love, who you kill. Whether you want to or not, you have to walk the road by yourself. . . . The Situation . . . What it came down to was choosing.

After hesitating a second, she aimed the gun at the broadest and biggest of the three silhouettes. It was the best target, and besides—he was the boss.

"Teresita," said don Epifanio Vargas.

That familiar voice stirred something inside her. Suddenly, tears blurred her vision. Unexpectedly, she'd turned fragile; she tried to understand why, and in the effort it was too late to avoid it. Stupid bitch, she told herself. *Pinche* fucking stupid baby. If something goes wrong, you had your chance. The distant lights from the street blurred and wavered before her eyes, and everything became a confusion of liquid lights and shadows. Suddenly there was no one to aim at.

So she lowered the pistol. All because of one fucking tear, she thought, resigned to what awaited. Now they're going to kill me, and all because of one *pinche* tear.

I t's bad times."
Don Epifanio Vargas took a long puff of his cigar and stood looking at the ember, pensive. In the semidarkness of the chapel, the candles and altar lights illuminated his Aztec profile, his thick, combed-back jet-black hair, his norteño moustache, all those stereotyped features that Teresa had always associated with Emilio Fernández and Pedro Armendáriz in the old Mexican movies on TV. He was probably

somewhere around fifty, and he was big and wide, with huge hands. In his left hand he held a cigar, and in his right, Güero's notebook.

"In the old days, at least there was some respect for women and children."

He shook his head sadly, remembering. Teresa knew that "the old days" referred to the time when, as a young campesino from Santiago de los Caballeros, tired of being hungry, Epifanio Vargas traded in the brace of oxen and the little field of corn and beans for marijuana plants. He'd screened out the seeds for a clean product, he'd put his life on the line selling it and taken the lives of everybody else he could, and finally he'd come down from the sierra to the flatland, settling in Tierra Blanca. That was when the networks of Sinaloa drug smugglers had first been moving north not just their bricks of Mexican gold but also the first packages of white powder that came in by boat and plane from Colombia.

The men of don Epifanio's generation—men who had once swum the Río Grande with cargos on their backs—now lived in mansions in Colonia Chapultepec. They had pliant rich-kid offspring who went to high school in their own cars and to American universities. But they'd had their long-ago days of big adventures, big risks, and big money made overnight: a lucky operation, a good crop, a big cargo that got to the right place. Years of danger and money, living a life that up in that sierra would have been scarcely more than a miserable getting-by. Intense and short, because only the toughest of men managed to survive, make a life for themselves, and mark off the territory of a large drug cartel. Those had been years when the lines were still being drawn. When nobody held a place without pushing out somebody else, and if you fucked up, you paid the price.

But the price was *your* life, not anybody else's with you. Just yours.

"They went to Chino Parra's house, too," he said. "I heard it on the news a little while ago. Wife and three kids." The ember of his cigar glowed bright again. "Chino was found in the driveway, in his Silverado."

He was sitting beside Teresa on the pew to the right of the little altar. When he moved his head, the candles made patent-leather glints in his thick, stiff-combed hair. The years that had passed since he first came down from the sierra had refined his appearance and his manners, but under the handmade suits, the Italian ties, and the $500 silk shirts, there was still the campesino from the mountains of Sinaloa. And you could see that not just because of the norteño ostentation—pointed-toe boots, huge silver belt buckle, gold centenary medal on the keychain—but also, and especially, because of the eyes, which were sometimes impassive, sometimes distrustful or patient. They were the eyes of a race that for generations, hundreds of years, had been forced, time and time again, by a hailstorm or a drought, to start over again, from scratch.

"Apparently they caught Chino in the morning and spent the day with him, talking. . . . From what the radio said, they took their time with him."

Teresa could imagine, and it didn't take much effort: Hands tied with wire; cigarettes; razor blades. Chino Parra's screams muffled by the plastic bag or the strip of duct tape, in some basement or warehouse, before they finished him off and went for his family. Maybe Chino himself had ratted out Güero. Or his own family. Teresa had known Chino well, his wife, Brenda, and the three kids—two boys and a girl. She remembered them playing, running around on the beach at Altata, the previous summer: their warm little brown bodies in the sun, covered by towels, sleeping as they drove back in that same Silverado their father's remains had been found in. Brenda was a petite woman, very talkative, with pretty brown eyes, and on her right ankle she wore a gold chain with her man's initials on it. She and Teresa had gone shopping together many times in Culiacán—getting expensive manicures, buying tight leather pants, spike heels, Guess jeans, Calvin Klein, Carolina Herrera . . . She wondered whether they'd sent Gato Fierros and Potemkin Gálvez, or some other gunmen. Whether it had happened before or at the same time as they were coming after her. Whether they killed Brenda before or after the kids. Whether it had been fast, or whether they'd also taken their time with them. *Pinche hombres puercos.*

She inhaled and then breathed out slowly, so that don Epifanio wouldn't see her sob. Then she silently cursed Chino Parra, after cursing that *cabrón* Güero Dávila even more. Chino was brave the way so many that killed or ran drugs were—out of pure fucking ignorance, because he didn't think. He got into jams because he was fuck-stupid, unaware that he was putting not just himself but his whole family in danger. Güero had been different: he was smart. He knew all the risks, and he'd always known what would happen to her if they got him, but he couldn't care less. That fucking notebook. *Don't read it,* he'd said. *Take it, but don't even look at it.* Damn him, she muttered again. God damn him, *pinche Güero cabrón.*

"What happened?" she asked.

Don Epifanio Vargas shrugged. "What had to happen," he said.

She looked at the bodyguard standing at the door, AK-47 in hand, silent as a shadow or a ghost. Just because you'd traded in drugs for

pharmaceuticals and politics didn't mean you didn't take the usual precautions. The other backup was outside, also armed. They'd given the
night watchman two hundred pesos to take off early. Don Epifanio
looked at the gym bag Teresa had set on the floor, between her feet, and
then at the Double Eagle in her lap.

"Your man had been tempting fate a long time, Teresita. It had to
come sooner or later."

"Is he really dead?"

"Of course he's dead. They caught him up in the sierra. . . . It wasn't
soldiers, or Federales, or anybody. It was his own people."

"Who?"

"What difference does it make? You know what kind of deals Güero
was doing. He got caught playing both sides. And somebody finally
blew the whistle on him."

The cigar's ember glowed red again. Don Epifanio opened the notebook. He held it in the candlelight, turning pages randomly.

"You read what's in here?"

"I just brought it to you, like he told me. I don't know anything
about these things."

Don Epifanio nodded, reflectively. He seemed uncomfortable. "Poor
Güero got what he'd been looking for," he concluded.

She was staring straight ahead, into the chapel's shadows, where ex
votos and dry flowers were hanging. "Poor Güero my ass," she suddenly
said. "That pig never thought about what would happen to me."

She'd kept her voice from shaking. Still staring into the shadows, she
sensed that don Epifanio had turned to look at her.

"You're lucky," she heard him say. "For the time being, you're alive."

He sat like that a while longer. Studying her. The smell of the cigar
mingled with the fragrance of the candles and the cone of incense
burning slowly in a censer next to the bust of the sainted bandit. "What
do you plan to do?" he asked at last.

"I don't know." Now it was Teresa's turn to shrug. "Güero said you'd
help me. 'Give it to him and ask him to help you.' That's what he said."

"Güero was always an optimist."

The hollow feeling in her stomach got worse. The waxy smell of candles, the flickering lights before St. Malverde. Humid, hot. Suddenly
she felt an unbearable sense of anxiety, and of trepidation. She repressed the urge to jump up, knock over the burning candles, get out,
get air. Run again, if they'd still let her. But when she looked up, she saw
that the other Teresa Mendoza was sitting across from her, watching
her. Or maybe it was she herself sitting there, silently, looking at the

frightened woman leaning forward on the pew next to don Epifanio, with a useless pistol in her lap.

"He loved you," she heard herself say.

Don Epifanio moved uneasily in his seat. A decent man, Güero had always said.

"And I loved him." Don Epifanio was speaking very softly, as though he didn't want the bodyguard at the door to hear him talk about emotions. "And you, too . . . but those stupid runs of his put you in a tough spot."

"I need help."

"I can't get mixed up in this."

"You have a lot of power."

She heard him cluck his tongue in discouragement and impatience. In this business, don Epifanio explained, still speaking softly, power was relative, ephemeral, subject to complicated rules. And he had kept his power, he said, because he didn't go sticking his nose in other people's business. Güero didn't work for him anymore; this was between him and his new bosses. And those people *mocharon parejo*— they took out everybody, wiped the slate clean.

"They don't have anything personal against you, Teresita. You know these people. But it's their way of doing things. . . . They have to make an example when people fuck with them."

"You could talk to them. Tell them I don't know anything."

"They already know you don't know anything. That's not the issue . . . and I can't get involved. In this country, if you ask for a favor today, tomorrow you've got to pay it back."

Now he was looking at the Double Eagle on her lap, one hand lying carelessly on the butt. He knew that Güero had taught her to fire it, and that she could hit six empty Pacífico bottles one after another, at ten paces. Güero had always liked Pacífico and liked his women a little tough, although Teresa couldn't stand beer and jumped every time the gun went off.

"Besides," don Epifanio went on, "what you've told me just makes things worse. If they can't let a man get away, imagine a woman. . . . They'd be the laughingstock of Sinaloa."

Teresa looked at his dark, inscrutable eyes. The hard eyes of a norteño Indian. Of a survivor.

"I can't get involved," she heard him repeat.

And don Epifanio stood up. So it was useless, she thought. It all ends here. The hollow feeling in the pit of her stomach grew until it included the night that awaited her outside, inexorable. She gave up, but the woman watching her from the shadows refused to.

"Güero told me that you'd help me," she insisted stubbornly, as though talking to herself. "'Take him the book,' he said, 'and trade it for your life.'"

"Your man liked his little jokes."

"I don't know about that. But I know what he told me."

It sounded more like a complaint than a plea. A sincere and very bitter complaint. Or a reproach. She was silent for a moment, and then she raised her face, like the weary prisoner waiting to hear the sentence. Don Epifanio was standing before her; he seemed even bigger and more heavyset than ever. His fingertips were drumming on Güero's notebook.

"Teresita . . ."

"*Sí, señor.*"

He kept drumming. She saw him look at the saint's portrait, at the bodyguard at the door, and then at her. Then his eyes fell again on the pistol.

"You swear you didn't read anything?"

"I swear to you."

A silence. Long, she thought, like dying. She heard the wicks of the candles at the altar sputtering.

"You've got just one chance," he said at last.

Teresa clung to those words, her mind as keen as though she'd just done a line of coke. The other woman faded into the shadows. "One's enough," she said.

"Have you got a passport?"

"Yes, with a U.S. visa."

"And money?"

"Twenty thousand dollars and a few pesos." She opened the gym bag at her feet to show him, hopefully. "And a ten- or twelve-ounce bag of snow."

"Leave that. It's dangerous to travel with it. . . . Do you drive?"

"No." She had stood and was looking straight at him, following his every word. Concentrating on staying alive. "I don't even have a license."

"I doubt you'd be able to get across anyway. They'd pick up your trail at the border, and you wouldn't be safe even among the gringos. . . . The best thing is to get away tonight. I can loan you the car with a driver you can trust. . . . I can do that, and have him drive you to Mexico City. Straight to the airport, and there you catch the first plane out."

"To where?"

"Anywhere. If you want to go to Spain, I've got friends there. People that owe me favors . . . If you call me tomorrow morning before you get on the plane, I'll give you a name and telephone number. After that, you're on your own."

"There's no other way?"

"Heh." The laugh was mirthless, flat. "It's this way or no way. You get led by the rope or it hangs you."

Teresa looked around the chapel, gazing into the shadows. She was absolutely alone. Nobody made decisions for her now. But she was still alive.

"I have to go." Don Epifanio was growing impatient. "Decide."

"I've already decided. I'll do whatever you say."

"All right." Don Epifanio watched as she put the safety on and stuck the pistol into the waist of her jeans, between the denim and her skin, and then covered it with her jacket. ". . . And remember one thing— you won't be safe over there, either. You understand? . . . I've got friends, but these people do, too. Try to bury yourself deep enough so they don't find you."

Teresa nodded again. She'd pulled the coke out of the gym bag, and she set it on the altar, under the statue of Malverde. She lighted another candle. *Santa Virgencita*, she prayed a moment in silence. *Santo Patrón*. God bless my journy and allow my return. She crossed herself almost furtively.

"I'm truly sorry about Güero," don Epifanio said behind her. "He was a good man."

Teresa had turned to hear this. Now she was so lucid and cool she could feel the dryness of her throat and the blood running very slowly through her veins, heartbeat by heartbeat. She threw the gym bag over her shoulder, smiling for the first time all day—a smile that registered on her lips as a nervous impulse, unexpected. And that smile, or whatever it was, must have been a strange one, because don Epifanio's expression changed—that smile gave him something to think about. Teresita Mendoza. *Chale.* Güero's *morra*. A narco's old lady. A girl like so many others—quieter, even, than most, not too bright, not too pretty. And yet that smile made him study her thoughtfully, cautiously, with a great deal of attention, as though suddenly a stranger stood before him.

"No," she said. "Güero was not a good man. He was *un hijo de su pinche madre*."

3. When the years have passed . . .

S he was nobody," said Manolo Céspedes.
"Explain that to me."

"I just did." My interlocutor pointed at me with two fingers, between which he held a cigarette. "Nobody means *nobody*. The lowest of the low. When she got here she had nothing but the clothes on her back, like she was trying to crawl into a hole and disappear. . . . It was just chance."

"And something else, too. She was a smart girl."

"So what? . . . I know a lot of smart girls that have wound up on a street corner."

He looked up and down the street, as though trying to see whether there might be an example he could show me. We were sitting under the awning on the terrace of the Café California, in Melilla, the Spanish town that sits across the strait from its country on the Moroccan coast. A noonday African sun turned the modernist façades of Avenida

Juan Carlos I yellow. It was the hour when everyone in Melilla stopped for *aperitivos,* and the sidewalks and terraces were filled with pedestrians, idlers, lottery vendors, and shoeshine boys. European dress mixed with North African jihabs and djellabas, accentuating the cultural-frontier atmosphere of this place spanning two continents and several races. In the background, around the Plaza de España and the monument to those killed in the colonial war in 1921—a young soldier in bronze with his face turned toward Morocco—the high fronds of the palm trees indicated the nearness of the Mediterranean.

"I didn't know her back then," Céspedes went on. "Actually, I don't even remember her. A face behind the bar at the Yamila, maybe. Or not even that. It was only much later, when I began hearing things here and there, that I finally associated that girl with the other Teresa Mendoza. . . . Like I said. Back then she was nobody."

Former police chief, former head of security at Moncloa, the seat of the Spanish presidency, former parliamentary delegate from Melilla—fate and life had made Manolo Céspedes all those things, although they might have made him a wise, seasoned bullfighter, a happy-go-lucky Gypsy, a Berber pirate, or an astute Rifeño diplomat. He was an old man as dark, lean, and canny as a hophead Legionnaire, with a lot of experience and a lot of under-the-table dealings. We had met twenty years earlier, during that period of violent incidents between the European and Muslim communities that had put Melilla on the front pages of newspapers across the continent, back when I was still earning a living as a reporter. And back then, Céspedes, a Melillan by birth and the highest civilian authority in the North African enclave, knew everyone. He would stop in for drinks at the bar frequented by officers from the Spanish army brigade stationed there, the Tercio; he controlled an efficient network of informers on both sides of the border; he would have dinner with the governor of Nador; and on his payroll he had everyone from street beggars to members of the Moroccan Gendarmerie Royale. Our friendship dated back to that: long conversations, lamb with Middle Eastern spices, gin and tonics until the wee hours of the morning. Between us there was always an unspoken agreement: You scratch my back, I'll scratch yours. Now, retired from his official post, Céspedes was bored and peaceful, growing old, devoted to local politics, his wife, his children, and the noon *aperitivos.* My visit was a welcome interruption of his daily routine.

"I tell you, it was pure chance," he insisted. "And in her case, the chance was named Santiago Fisterra."

My glass froze in its upward track; I caught my breath.

"Santiago López Fisterra?"

"Sure." Céspedes took a drag on his cigarette, gauging my interest. "El Gallego"—the Galician.

I exhaled slowly, took a sip of my drink, and leaned back in my chair, delighted to have picked up a lost trail, while Céspedes smiled, assessing the new balance of our back-scratching account. That name had brought me to Melilla, in search of a period of obscurity in Teresa Mendoza's biography. Until that day on the terrace of the California, I had had only conjectures, or reports that were doubtful at best: This might have happened; they say that such-and-such went on; somebody had been told, or someone thought he remembered. . . . Rumors. The rest—the concrete facts—were few; in the immigration files of the Ministry of the Interior there was only an entrance date—Iberia airlines, Barajas Airport, Madrid—with her real name: Teresa Mendoza Chávez.

Then the official trail went cold for two years, until police report 8653690FA/42, containing fingerprints and one mugshot from the front, one in profile, had allowed me to follow her footsteps with a little more certainty from then on. The report was an old one, kept in an actual manila file folder, before the Spanish police computerized their documents. I'd had it before me on a desk a week earlier, in the police headquarters in Algeciras, thanks to a call from another old friend of mine: the police chief of Torremolinos, Pepe Cabrera. Among the bare facts on the report were two names: a person's and a city's. The person was Santiago López Fisterra. The city was Melilla.

That afternoon Céspedes and I paid two visits. One was brief, sad, and almost useless, although it served to add another name to my list and a face to one of the characters of this story. Across the street from the yacht club, at the foot of the old city's medieval wall, Céspedes pointed out a filthy man with thin, ashy-colored hair who was "watching" parked cars—making sure nothing happened to them, you understand—in exchange for a few coins from the cars' charitable drivers. He was sitting on the ground near a mooring post, staring at the dirty water under the pier. From a distance I took him for an older man, battered by time and life, but as we approached I realized that he was probably not yet forty. He was wearing a pair of old pants torn and crudely sewn back together, an astoundingly clean white T-shirt, and filthy, stinking tennis shoes. The bright sunlight did nothing to hide the matte gray tone of his skin, which was covered with blotches. His face was cavernous; there were hollows at his temples.

Half his teeth were missing, and it occurred to me that he resembled the sea wrack thrown up at high tide or by storms.

"His name is Veiga," Céspedes told me as we approached him. "And he knew Teresa Mendoza."

Without pausing to observe my reaction, he said, "*Hola*, Veiga, how are you," and gave him a cigarette and a light. There were no introductions, no other words between them, and we stood there awhile, silent, looking at the water, the fishing boats tied up, the old mineral barge on the other side of the harbor, and the horrific twin towers built to commemorate the five-hundredth anniversary of the Spanish conquest of the city. I saw scabs, scars, marks on the man's arms and legs. He'd gotten to his feet to light the cigarette—clumsily, muttering disconnected words of thanks. He smelled like stale wine and stale misery. He limped when he walked.

"Ask him, if you want to," Céspedes finally said.

I hesitated and then spoke the name Teresa Mendoza. I detected no sign of recognition, or of memory. Nor did I have any better luck when I mentioned Santiago Fisterra. This Veiga, or what remained of him, had turned back toward the oily water of the pier.

"Try to remember, man," Céspedes urged him. "This friend of mine has come to talk to you. Don't tell him you don't remember Teresa and your partner. Don't make me look bad, all right? . . ."

But Veiga still didn't answer, and when Céspedes insisted, the most he got was a puzzled, indifferent look as the man scratched lazily at his arms. And those blurred, distant eyes, their pupils so dilated they occupied the entire iris, seemed to slide across people and things from a place there was no returning from.

"He was the other Gallego," Céspedes said as we walked away. "Santiago Fisterra's crew . . . Nine years in a Moroccan jail did that to him."

Night was falling by the time we paid the second visit. Céspedes introduced the man as Dris Larbi—"My friend Dris," he said, patting him on the back—and I found myself standing before a Rifeño with Spanish citizenship who spoke Spanish perfectly. We met in the Hippódromo section of the city, in front of the Yamila, one of the three nightspots Dris Larbi owned in Melilla—I later learned that and several other things. He stepped out of a shiny Mercedes sports coupe: medium height, very curly black hair, carefully trimmed beard. A hand that extended to shake yours cautiously, to see what you were carrying.

"My friend Dris," Céspedes repeated, and the way the other man looked at him, cautiously and deferentially at the same time, made me wonder what biographical details about the Rifeño might justify his prudent respect for the former congressman.

It was my turn to be introduced. "He's investigating the life of Teresa Mendoza."

Céspedes said it like that, straight out, as the other man offered me his right hand and with his left aimed his car-security control toward the Mercedes, the beeps from the car—*bip-bip,* fast—confirming activation. But when the words registered, Dris Larbi studied me with great deliberation and great silence, to the point that Céspedes broke out laughing.

"Relax," Céspedes said. "He's not a cop."

The noise of shattering glass made Teresa Mendoza's brow furrow. It was the second glass the party at table four had broken that night. She exchanged looks with Ahmed, the waiter, and he walked over with a broom and dustpan, taciturn as always, his black bow tie bobbing loose under his Adam's apple. The lights swirling across the empty dance floor cast bright dots on his striped vest.

Teresa went over the tab being run up by a customer at the far end of the bar. He'd been there a couple of hours, and the tab was respectable: five White Label and waters for him, eight splits of champagne for the girls—most of which had been discreetly made to disappear by Ahmed, under the pretext of changing the glasses. It was twenty minutes to closing, and Teresa could overhear the animated conversation the customer was having with the girls. It was the usual exchange: I'll wait for you outside. One or both of you. Preferably both. Et cetera. Dris Larbi, the boss, was inflexible when it came to the establishment's official morality. It was a bar that served drinks, period. Outside working hours, the girls were free to do whatever they wanted. Or in principle they were, because there was still strict control: Fifty percent for the house, fifty for the girl. With the exception of trips and parties, when the rules were modified depending on who, what, how, and where. I'm a businessman, Dris would say. Not a pimp.

A Tuesday. Slow night. On the empty dance floor, Julio Iglesias was singing to no one. *Caballero de fina estampa,* he sang. Teresa's lips moved silently, following the lyrics, her mind on her paper and ballpoint pen in the cone of light from the lamp next to the cash register. A soft night, she saw as she added the numbers. Almost bad. Pretty different from Fridays and Saturdays, when they had to bring in girls from other places because the Yamila filled to capacity: government officials, businessmen, wealthy Moroccans from the other side of the border, soldiers from the base. A middle-level crowd generally, not too much rough trade except for the inevitable. Girls young and clean, respectable-looking, the work force renewed every six months with Arab girls Dris recruited in Morocco or the marginal neighborhoods of Melilla, or with European girls from the Peninsula. Payments made punctually—that was the key—to the right authorities: Live and let live. Free drinks for the assistant chief of police and the plainclothes detectives—"inspectors," they were called here. An exemplary business, permits all in order. Almost no problems.

Certainly nothing Teresa didn't remember a thousand—or infinite—times from her still-recent days in Mexico. The difference was that people here, though more gruff, less courteous, settled their scores with lead from a pencil, not a gun, and everything happened under the table. There were even people—and this took her a while to get used to—who simply could not be bought off. *I'm sorry, miss, you're mistaken.* Or in the more strictly Spanish version: *Why don't you just shove that up your ass.* It made life hard, sometimes. But just as often, it made life easier. You could relax a lot if you didn't have to fear every cop. Or fear every cop all the time.

Ahmed came back with his dustpan and broom, slipped behind the bar, and struck up a conversation with the three girls who were free. From the table with the broken glasses came the sounds of laughter, toasts, the clinking of glasses. Ahmed calmed Teresa with a wink. Everything all right there. That tab was going to be a good one, she noted, looking down at the pad next to the cash register. Spanish and Moroccan businessmen celebrating some deal, jackets on the backs of their chairs, collars unbuttoned, ties in their jacket pockets. Four middle-aged men and four girls. The supposed Moët et Chandon in the ice buckets disappeared quickly: five bottles, and there'd be another one killed before closing. The girls—two Moors, one Jew, one Spaniard—were young, and professional. Dris never slept with the employees—you don't stick your dick in the cash register, he would say—but sometimes he would have one of his friends act as a kind of quality-control inspector. Top drawer, he would later crow. In my places, only the best. If the report was less than excellent, he would never mistreat the girl; he would fire her, and that would be that. Pink slip. There was no lack of girls in Melilla, with illegal immigration and the crisis and all that. Some dreamed of making it to the Peninsula, becoming models, TV stars, but most were happy with a work permit and legal residency.

Only a little more than six months had passed since Teresa Mendoza's conversation with don Epifanio Vargas in the Malverde Chapel. But she realized how long it had been only when she looked at the calendar—most of the time she'd spent in Melilla seemed static, unmoving. It might just as well have been six years as six months.

This was her destiny, but it could have been any other when, newly arrived in Madrid, with a room in a *pensión* near the Plaza de Atocha, her only luggage a gym bag, she had a meeting with the contact to whom Epifanio Vargas had sent her. To her disappointment, there was nothing for her in Madrid in the way of a job. If she wanted someplace out of the way, as far as possible from any potentially unpleasant encounters, and also a job to justify her residency until the papers establishing her dual nationality came through—the Spanish father whom she'd barely known was going to be of some use to her for the first time—she had to make one more trip.

The contact, a rushed young man of few words whom she met in the Café Nebraska on the Gran Vía, offered just two choices: Galicia or southern Spain. Heads or tails, take it or leave it. Teresa asked whether it rained much in Galicia, and the young man smiled a little, just enough—it was the first time he'd smiled in the entire conversation—and said it did. It rains like hell, he said.

So Teresa chose the south, and the man took out a cell phone and went to another table to talk for a while. When he came back, he wrote a name, a telephone number, and the name of a city on a paper napkin. There are direct flights from Madrid, he told her, handing her the napkin. Or from Málaga. To Málaga, trains and buses. There are also boats from Málaga and Almería. And when he saw the puzzled look on her face—boats? planes?—he smiled for the second and last time before explaining that the place she was going belonged to Spain but was in North Africa, sixty or seventy kilometers from the Andalucían coast, near the Strait of Gibraltar. Ceuta and Melilla, he explained, are Spanish cities on the Moroccan coast.

Then he laid an envelope full of money on the table, paid the bill, stood up, and wished her good luck. He said those words—"Good luck"—and was leaving when Teresa, grateful, tried to tell him her name. The man interrupted, saying he didn't want to know it—couldn't care less what it was, in fact. He was just helping out some Mexican friends of his by helping her. He indicated the envelope on the table, and said she should use the money well. When it ran out and she needed more, he added in a tone of objectivity clearly not intended to give offense, she could always use her cunt. That, he said in farewell, apparently regretting he didn't have one of his own, is the advantage you women have.

She was nothing special," said Dris Larbi. "Not pretty, not ugly. Not particularly quick, not particularly stupid. But she was good at numbers. . . . I saw that right away, so I put her at the register." He remembered a question I'd asked before, and shook his head before continuing. "And no, the fact is she didn't work on her back. At least not when she worked with me. She was recommended by friends, so I let her choose. One side of the bar or the other, your choice, I told her. . . . She chose to stay behind it, as a waitress at first. She didn't make as much, of course. But that was fine with her."

We were walking along the border between the neighborhoods of Hippódromo and Real—straight streets that ran down to the ocean, colonial-style houses. The night was cool, and filled with the fragrance of the flowers in window boxes.

"She may have gone out now and then. Two, three times, maybe. I'm not sure." Dris Larbi shrugged. "It was her decision, you understand? . . . A couple of times she went off with somebody she wanted to go with, but not for money."

"What about the parties?" Céspedes asked.

The Rifeño looked away, suspicious. Then he turned to me before he looked over at Céspedes again, like a man who prefers not to talk about delicate matters in front of strangers.

But Céspedes didn't care. "The parties," he repeated.

Dris Larbi looked at me again, scratching his beard.

"That was different," he conceded after thinking it over. "Sometimes I organized meetings on the other side of the border. . . ."

Now Céspedes laughed sarcastically. "Those famous parties of yours," he said.

"Yeah, well. You know . . ." The Rifeño was looking at him as though trying to remember how much Céspedes really knew, and then, uncomfortable, he turned his eyes away again. "People over there . . ."

"'Over there' is Morocco," Céspedes noted for my information. "He's referring to important people: politicians and police chiefs." He smiled foxily. "My friend Dris always had good contacts."

The Rifeño smiled uneasily as he lit a low-nicotine cigarette. I asked myself how many things about him and his contacts had wound up in Céspedes' secret files. Enough, I figured, for Dris Larbi to grant us the privilege of this conversation.

"She went to these meetings?" I asked.

Larbi made a gesture of uncertainty. "I don't know. She may have been at some. And, well . . . You should ask *her*." He appeared to reflect for a while, studying Céspedes out of the corner of his eye, and then at last he nodded unhappily. "The fact is, toward the end she went a couple of times. I didn't want to know, because these particular meetings weren't to make money with the girls—they were another kind of business. I just threw in the girls for free. Compliments of the house, you might say. But I never told Teresa to come. . . . She came because she wanted to. She asked to."

"Why?"

"No idea. Like I told you—you should ask *her*."

"And she was going out with the Gallego then?" Céspedes asked.

"Yeah."

"They say she did certain things that he needed done," Céspedes prodded.

Dris Larbi looked at him. Looked at me. Looked at him again. Why is he doing this to me? his eyes said. "I don't know what you're talking about, don Manuel."

Céspedes laughed maliciously, arching his eyebrows. He was clearly enjoying this. "Abelkader Chaib," he said. "Colonel. Gendarmerie Royale . . . That sound familiar?"

"I swear I don't get it."

"Don't get it? . . . Bullshit, Dris. I told you, this man is a friend of mine."

We walked a few steps in silence while I tried to figure all this out. The Rifeño smoked, silently, as if unhappy about the way he'd told the story.

"While she was with me she didn't get involved in anything," he suddenly said. "And I didn't have anything to do with her, either. I mean I never fucked her." He lifted his chin toward Céspedes, tacitly saying, *Ask him.*

It was, as I said, public knowledge that Dris never got involved with any of his girls. And he had said that Teresa was good at keeping the books. The other girls respected her. La Mexicana, they called her. La Mexicana this and La Mexicana that. She clearly was a good-tempered girl, and although she hadn't gone to school much, her accent made her sound educated, with that big imposing vocabulary Latin Americans have, that makes them sound like members of the Royal Academy. Very reserved about her private life. Dris Larbi knew she'd had problems back in Mexico, but he never asked. Why should he? Nor did Teresa talk about Mexico; when somebody brought up the topic, she'd say one or two words, as little as possible, and change the subject. She was serious at work, lived alone, and never allowed customers to be confused about what her role was in the bar. She didn't have any girlfriends, either. She minded her own business.

"Everything was fine for . . . I don't know . . . six or eight months. Until the night the two Gallegos turned up." He turned to Céspedes, gesturing at me. "Did he see Veiga? . . . Well, that one didn't have much' luck. But the other one had less."

"Santiago Fisterra," I said.

"Right. And I can still see him: a dark-skinned type, with a big tattoo here." He shook his head disapprovingly. "Something of a troublemaker, like all Gallegos. One of those that you never know what they'll do next. . . . They came and went through the Strait in a Phantom— Señor Céspedes knows what I'm talking about, right? . . . Winstons from Gibraltar and chocolate from Morocco . . . Back then they weren't working the smack, although it was right around the corner. . . . So . . ."

He scratched his beard again and spit straight at the ground, bitterly. "So what happened was, one night those two came into the Yamila, and that's when I began to lose the Mexicana."

Two new customers. Teresa glanced at the clock beside the register. Less than fifteen minutes to closing time. She saw that Ahmed was looking at her questioningly, and without raising her head she nodded once. A quick drink before they turned on the lights and threw everybody out. She went on with her numbers, finished balancing the cash drawer. These two probably wouldn't change the bottom line much. A couple of whiskies, she thought, sizing them up. A little chat with the girls, who were already swallowing their yawns, and maybe a date outside, a while later. Pensión Agadir, half a block down the street. Or maybe, if they had a car, a quick trip to the pine groves, alongside the walls of the Tercio headquarters. Anyway, none of her business. Ahmed kept the list of dates in another book.

The two new customers sat at the bar, leaning on their elbows, next to the beer pulls, and Fatima and Sheila, two of the girls that had been talking to Ahmed, went over to sit with them while the waiter poured two putative twelve-year-old Chivases with a lot of ice, no water. The girls ordered splits of champagne, with no objection from the customers. The men at the broken-glasses table were still toasting and laughing, after having paid the tab without so much as blinking. The guy at the end of the bar couldn't quite reach an agreement with his companions; they could be heard arguing softly, through the sound of the music. Now it was Abigaíl singing for nobody on the deserted dance floor, whose only sign of life was the monotonous spinning of the disco ball. *I want to lick your wounds*, she was singing. *I want to hear your silences.* Teresa waited for the last line of the final stanza—she knew all the songs of the Yamila's repertoire by heart—and looked again at the clock beside the register. Another day down. Identical to yesterday's Monday and tomorrow's Wednesday.

"Closing time," Teresa said.

When she raised her eyes, she found herself looking into a quiet smile. And into a pair of light-colored eyes—green or blue, she thought after a second—looking at her with amusement.

"So soon?" asked the man.

"We're closing," she repeated.

She returned to the books. She was never friendly with the customers, especially at closing time. In six months she'd learned that was the best way to keep things in their places and avoid misunderstandings. Ahmed turned on the lights, and the scant charm that the semidarkness had given the place vanished: threadbare fake velvet on the chairs and barstools, stains on the walls, cigarette burns on the floor. Even the smell—of rancid cigarette smoke, of musty upholstery that never saw the light of day—seemed stronger. The men who had broken the glasses pulled their jackets off the backs of their chairs, and after reaching a quick agreement with their female companions, they left, to wait for them outside. The other customer had already left, alone, refusing to pay the price for a double-header. I'd rather jerk off, he muttered as he walked out.

The girls gathered up their things. Fatima and Sheila, without touching their champagne, were lingering, hanging on the newcomers, but the two men didn't seem interested in becoming any closer acquainted. A look from Teresa sent the girls off to join the others.

She put the check down on the bar, in front of the dark-skinned one. He was wearing a khaki work shirt, the sleeves rolled up to his elbows, and when he reached for the check she saw that he had a tattoo that covered his entire forearm: a crucified Christ in a design of sailing symbols. The man's friend was blond and thinner, with light skin. Almost a kid. Twenty-something, maybe. The dark one, thirty-something.

"Can we finish our drinks?"

Teresa once again met with the man's eyes as she raised her head. In the light, she saw that they were green. Playful. Maybe mocking. She saw that they weren't just serene, they were also smiling, even when the mouth below them wasn't. His arms were strong, a dark beard was be-

ginning to show on his chin, and his hair was tousled. Almost good-
looking, she thought. Or strike that "almost." She also thought he
smelled of clean sweat and salt, although she was too far away to know
that. She just thought so.

"Sure," she said.

Green eyes, a tattoo on his right arm, a skinny blond friend. One of
those things that happen in a bar. Teresa Mendoza, far from
Sinaloa. One day like another, until one day, something happens. The
unexpected that pops up—no fanfare, no signs on the horizon, no
warning, just sneaking up on you, easy, so quiet it might be nothing at
all. Like a smile or a look. Like life itself, or—that other thing that
sneaks up on you—death. Which may have been why, the next night,
she expected him to come in again. But he didn't. Each time a customer
entered, she looked up, hoping it was him. But it wasn't.

After she locked up she walked along the nearby beach, where she lit a
cigarette—sometimes she would spike it with a few grains of hashish—
and looked at the lights on the breakwater and in the Moroccan port of
Nador, on the other side of the dark stretch of sea. When the weather
was good, she did that, strolled along the sea walk until she found a taxi
to take her to her little apartment near the Polígono—bedroom, tiny
living room, kitchen, and bathroom rented to her by Dris Larbi, who
deducted it from her salary. Dris wasn't a bad sort, she thought. He
treated the girls pretty well, tried to get along with everybody, and was
violent only when circumstances left him no choice. I'm not a whore,
she had told him that first day, straight out, when he met with her in the
Yamila to explain the kinds of jobs that were possible in his business. I'm
glad for you, he'd said—and left it at that.

At first he took her in as something inevitable, neither a bother nor
an advantage, an arrangement he was forced into by personal commitments—the friend of a friend of a friend—that had nothing to do with
her. A certain deference, due to obligations that Teresa knew nothing
about, the chain that joined Dris Larbi to don Epifanio Vargas through
the man at the Café Nebraska, led Dris to let her work behind the bar,
first with Ahmed, as bartender girl, and later as cashier, beginning the
day there was an error in the figures and she caught it and set the books
straight in fifteen seconds. Dris asked whether she'd studied for that.
She answered that she'd never gone beyond the sixth grade, and Dris
stood looking at her thoughtfully and said, "You've got a head for numbers, Mexicana, you seem like you were born to add and subtract."

"I did some of that back in Mexico," she answered. "When I was younger."

So Dris told her that the next day she'd be earning the salary of a cashier, and Teresa took over the place, and they never mentioned the subject again.

She walked on the beach for a while, until she had finished her cigarette, absorbed in the distant lights that seemed almost to have been strewn over the quiet black water. Finally she looked around and shivered, as though the cold of the late hour had just penetrated the jacket she wore buttoned all the way up, its collar raised around her neck and chin. *Híjole.* Back in Culiacán, Güero Dávila had often told her that she didn't have what it took to live alone. No way, he would say. You're not that kind of girl. You need a man to take charge. While you stay—why, just like you are—sweet and tender. Unbelievably pretty. Soft. Treated like a queen or not treated at all, *mi vida.* You don't even have to make enchiladas—that's what restaurants are for. Plus you like that, *mi vida,* you like what I do to you and how I do it, and when I get mine, *bang,* you'll be so sad. He laughed as he whispered, that *pinche Güero cabrón,* his lips between her legs, So come here, *prietita.* Come down here, to my mouth, and hang on to me and don't let me get away, and hold me tight because one day I'll be dead and nobody will ever hold me again. How sad for you, *mi chula.* You'll be so alone in the world when I'm not here anymore and you remember me, and miss all this, and know that nobody will ever do this to you again, not the way I do it.

So all alone. How strange and at the same time how familiar that word was now: *alone.* Every time Teresa heard it, or said it down deep inside, the image that came to her was not of herself, but of Güero. Or maybe the image *was* of herself: Teresa watching him. Because there had also been dark times, black doors that Güero would close behind him, and he would be miles away, as though he hadn't come down from wherever he'd been up there. Sometimes he would come back from a mission or one of those runs that he never told her about—but that all Sinaloa seemed to know about—and he would be mute, silent, without his usual swaggering and bravado. He'd dodge her questions from an altitude of five thousand feet, evasive, more self-absorbed than usual, as though he were deeply thoughtful, or preoccupied, or worried. And Teresa, bewildered, not knowing what to say or do, would hover around him like some clumsy animal, in search of the word or gesture that would bring him back to her. Scared.

Those times, he would leave the house and head downtown. For a while, Teresa suspected that he had another woman—he had them, no question, like all these men did, but she resented the fact that he might have one in particular. That thought drove her crazy with shame and jealousy, so one morning, mixing in with the flow of people, she followed him to a place near the Garmendia *mercado,* where she saw him enter a cantina called La Ballena. "Vendors, beggars, and minors not allowed"—the sign on the door didn't mention women, but everyone knew that that was one of the unspoken rules of the place: Nothing but beer and nothing but men.

So she stood out on the street for a long time, more than half an hour in front of a shoe store window, doing nothing but watching the swinging doors of the cantina and waiting for him to come out. But he didn't, so at last she crossed the street and went into the restaurant next door, which connected to the cantina through a bead curtain toward the middle of the room. She ordered a soft drink, walked to the curtain, looked through, and saw a large room full of tables, and in the rear a Rock-Ola from which Los Dos Reales were singing "Caminos de la Vida." And the strange thing about the place, at that hour, was that at every table there was a single man with a bottle of beer. One of each per table. Almost all the men looked down-and-out or old—straw hats or baseball caps on their heads, dark-skinned faces, big black or gray moustaches—each drinking in silence, lost in his own thoughts, speaking to no one, like some weird convention of isolated, downcast philosophers, and some of the beer bottles still had a paper napkin stuck in the neck, the way they'd been served, as though a white carnation came with each longneck. The men sat silently, drinking and listening to the music, and once in a while one of them would get up and put a few coins in the jukebox and select another song. And at one of the tables sat Güero Dávila with his aviator jacket over his shoulders, completely alone, his blond head unmoving, staring into space. He sat there minute after minute, breaking his trance only to pull the paper carnation out of the neck of the seven-peso Pacífico and put the bottle to his lips. Los Dos Reales fell silent and were relieved by José Alfredo singing "Cuando los Años Pasen"—"When the Years Have Passed."

Teresa stepped back slowly from the curtain and walked out of the restaurant, and on the way home she cried for a long time. She cried and cried, incapable of stopping the tears, yet not quite knowing why. Maybe for Güero, and maybe for herself—and maybe for *them.* Maybe for the years that pass.

She *had* done it. But just twice the whole time she was in Melilla. And Güero was right. Not that she'd expected any big deal. The first time was out of curiosity. She wanted to know what it felt like after so long, with the distant memory of her man and the more recent and painful memory of Gato Fierros, his cruel smile, his violence, still clear on her flesh and in her memory. She had chosen with a certain amount of care—though care not altogether free of chance—so that there'd be no problems and no consequences. He was a young soldier, a *mili*, who had approached her outside the Cine Nacional, where she had gone to see a Robert De Niro movie on her day off—a movie about war and friends, with a stupid ending, soldiers playing Russian roulette the way she'd seen Güero and his cousin, out of their minds on tequila, play once, acting like idiots with a revolver until she yelled at them and took the weapon away and sent them to bed, while they just laughed, the miserable, irresponsible drunks. The Russian roulette scene had made her sad, remembering, and maybe that was why, as she was leaving, when the soldier approached her—plaid shirt like Sinaloa men wore; tall, friendly, dirty-blond hair and haircut like Güero's—she let him take her for a soft drink to Anthony's and listened to his trivial conversation, then ended up with him at the wall of the old city, naked from the waist down, her back against the stone, a cat sitting a few yards away looking at them with interest, its eyes glowing in the moonlight. She hardly felt a thing, because her mind was too intent on watching herself, comparing sensations and memories, as though she had split into two people again and the other woman were the cat over there looking on, as dispassionate and silent as a shadow. The soldier wanted to see her again, but she was clear—Another day, *mi vida*. She knew she would never see him again, or that even if one day she should run into him somewhere—Melilla was a small place—she would barely recognize him, or would pretend not to. She didn't even remember his name.

The second time was a practical, and police, matter. The processing of her temporary-residence papers was going slow, and Dris Larbi advised her on a way to speed things up. The guy was named Souco. He was a middle-aged inspector, reasonably presentable, who did favors for immigrants. He'd been to the Yamila a couple of times—Teresa had instructions not to charge him for his drinks—and they vaguely knew each other. She went to see him and he put the question to her straight. Like in Mexico, he said, though Teresa couldn't figure out what that *hijo de puta* could possibly know about customs in Mexico. The options were money or the other thing. With regard to money, Teresa was saving her last peseta, so she opted for the other. Out of some odd machista dedication that almost made her laugh out loud, this Souco managed to acquit himself admirably during the encounter in room 106 of the Hotel Avenida—Teresa had made it more than clear that this was a one-time thing, no follow-ups—and he even asked for the verdict as they lay panting, cigarettes lit, him with his self-esteem on the line and still wearing the condom. I came, she answered, dressing slowly, her body covered in sweat. That means orgasm? he asked. Of course, she replied.

Back in her apartment, she sat in the bathroom washing herself slowly, pensively, for a long time, then stood at the mirror, smoking a cigarette, looking apprehensively at each of the marks of her twenty-three years of life as if afraid of seeing them morph before her eyes into some strange mutation. Afraid that one day she might see her own image, alone at the table, with the men in that cantina in Culiacán, and not cry, and not recognize herself.

But Güero Dávila had been wrong, too. Solitude was not hard to take. It was unaltered even by small accidents and concessions, because something had died with Güero. A certain innocence, perhaps, or an unjustified sense of security. Teresa came in out of the cold very young, leaving the rough streets, the poverty, the apparently harshest aspects of life behind. She had thought she had escaped all that forever, not knowing that the cold was still out there, lurking just beyond the door, waiting to squeeze in through the cracks and make her shiver again. The minute you think the horror can never get close again, it pounces. She was just a girl—a narco's *morra*, all set up with a house, collecting videos and figurines and pretty landscapes to hang on the wall. Attentiveness to her man repaid in luxury. With Güero, it had been all laughing and screwing.

Later, she had seen the first signs of trouble from afar, without paying them much attention. Bad signs that Güero laughed off or, to be more precise, didn't give jack shit about. He was very quick, very cunning, and he'd just decided to try to pull off something big, and not wait. Not wait even for her, the *cabrón*. And as a result, one day Teresa found herself out in the cold again, running to save her life, carrying nothing but a gym bag and a pistol.

Now, on this side of the long journey, she would never be able to forget the cold, sinister wind that blew out there on the outside. Not even if she had her skin and her sex available for men who weren't Güero anymore. Not even if—the idea always made her smile a strange smile—she should fall in love again, or think she had. But, she thought, perhaps the correct sequence might be: first fall in love, then think you've fallen in love, and finally stop loving, or love a memory.

Now she knew—this frightened her and, paradoxically, calmed her at the same time—that it was possible, even easy, to live in solitude as though in an unfamiliar city, in an apartment with an old television set and a bed that creaked when you turned over, unable to sleep. Possible, even easy, to get up to pee and sit there quietly, a cigarette between your fingers. To get in the shower and caress your sex with your soapy hand, your eyes closed, remembering a man's mouth. And to recognize that a life like that could last forever, and that you could, strangely enough, get used to it. You could resign yourself to growing old, bitter, and alone, stuck in this godforsaken place, while the earth kept turning, just as it always had, even though you never realized it before—impassive, cruel, indifferent.

She saw him again a week later, near the little market on the Montes Tirado hill. She had gone to the Kif-Kif import store to buy spices— in the absence of Mexican chiles, her taste for spicy foods had adapted to the strong Moroccan flavors. Now she was walking home, uphill, a bag in each hand. She kept close to the storefronts that offered the most shade, to avoid the hot sun of the morning, which wasn't humid as in Culiacán, but dry and harsh—a North African heat of dry riverbeds, cactus, low hills, and naked rocks. She saw him coming out of an electrical-parts store with a box under his arm, and she recognized him at once: the Yamila, several days earlier, the man who had finished his drink while Ahmed mopped the floor and the girls said their *Hasta mañanas*.

And he recognized her, because when he passed by her, stepping aside so as not to bump into her with the box he was carrying, he smiled the same way he had when he asked permission to finish the whisky at the bar, more with his eyes than with his mouth, and he said hello. She said hello, too, and kept walking, while he put the box in a van parked at the curb, and without turning around she knew that he was still looking at her, until, near the corner, she heard his footsteps behind her, or thought she did.

Then Teresa did something strange, which she herself was unable to explain: instead of walking on straight up to her house, she turned to the right and entered the market. She wandered here and there aimlessly, as if seeking protection among the people, although she wouldn't have known what to answer if she'd been asked protection from what. But for whatever reason, she roamed among the animated stalls of fruits and vegetables, the voices of vendors and customers resonating under the glass ceiling of the navelike space, and after wandering through the fish stalls left the market by the door that opened into the café on Calle Comisario Valero. And so, not looking back once during the entire long walk, she came at last to her house. The entrance was at the top of a whitewashed stairway, on a narrow street that climbed up past Polígono between wrought-iron gates and bars at windows with pots of geraniums and green shutters—it was good exercise, walking up and down the street two or three times a day—and from the stairs you could look out over the rooftops of the city, the red and white minaret of the central mosque, and, in the distance, in Morocco, the dark shadow of Mount Gurugú. As she was trying to find the keys in her pocket, she looked behind her, and she saw him at the corner of the narrow street, quiet, calm, as though he hadn't moved from that spot the whole morning. The sun reverberated on the whitewashed walls and on his shirt, gilding his arms and neck and projecting a neat, crisp shadow on the ground. A single gesture, a word, an ill-timed smile would have made her turn on her heel and open the door and close it behind her and leave the man outside, far from her house and her life. But when their eyes met, all he did was stand the way he was standing, motionless on the corner in all that light off the white walls and his white shirt. And his green eyes seemed to smile at a distance, as they had when she had said "Closing time" at the Yamila, and they seemed also to see things that Teresa had no knowledge of. Things about her present and future. That may have been why, instead of opening the door and closing it behind her, she set the bags down, sat on one of the steps, and took out a pack of cigarettes. She took it out very slowly, and without raising her eyes she sat there while the man came up the stairs. For a moment, his shadow blocked the sun, and then he sat down beside her, on the same step, and still without raising her eyes she saw a pair of blue cotton pants, washed many times. Gray tennis shoes. The cuffs of his shirt rolled up to his elbows, his thin, strong arms tanned by the sun. A waterproof Seiko with a black band on his left wrist. The tattoo of the crucified Jesus on his right forearm.

Teresa lit her cigarette, leaning over it, and her loose hair fell over her face. As she did so, she came a little closer to the man, without intending to, and he leaned away a bit, just as he'd done on the street when he was carrying the box, so they wouldn't bump into each other. She didn't look at him, and she knew that he wasn't looking at her, either. She smoked in silence, serenely analyzing the emotions and physical sensations her body was feeling. The conclusion was surprisingly simple: Better near than far. Suddenly he moved a bit, and she found herself fearing that he was about to leave. *Why would I tell you no,* she thought, *if the answer's yes.* She raised her face, pushing back her hair so she could look at him. He had a pleasant profile, a bony chin, tanned face, forehead furrowed from the light, which made him avert his eyes. Everything *bien padre*. He was looking into the distance, toward Gurugú and Morocco.

"Where were you?" she asked.

"On a trip." His voice had a slight accent that she hadn't noticed the first time, a pleasant, soft modulation, clipped a little, different from the Spanish that people spoke here. "I got back this morning."

It was like that, as though they had picked up an interrupted conversation. Two old acquaintances running into each other, neither particularly surprised. Two friends. Perhaps two lovers.

"I'm Santiago."

He had finally turned. You're either very smart, she thought, or you're a dream. Which, she realized, amounted to the same thing. His green eyes were smiling again, self-assured and quiet, studying her.

"Teresa."

He repeated her name softly. *Teresa*, he said reflectively, as though, for some reason neither of them understood, he needed to get used to saying it. He continued to look at her while she inhaled cigarette smoke before suddenly blowing it out again, apparently having come to a decision, and when she dropped the butt and stood up, he remained seated on the step. She knew that he would stay there, not forcing things, if she didn't open the way to what came next. Not out of insecurity or shyness, of course. She was sure he wasn't one of those. His calm seemed to say that this was fifty-fifty, and that they had to meet halfway.

"Come in," she said.

He was different from Güero, she found. Less imaginative, less fun. With him, unlike Güero (the young *mili* and the cop didn't even enter the equation), there were no jokes, no laughter, nothing daring, no dirty words spoken as prologue or spice. In fact, that first time there were hardly any words at all; the man said almost nothing the whole time, as he moved very seriously, very slowly. Painstakingly, she'd almost call it. His eyes, which even then were calm, didn't move from her for an instant. They never turned away, never looked up. And when a shaft of light came in through the shutters, making tiny droplets of sweat gleam on Teresa's skin, his green eyes seemed to become even lighter—they were fixed, alert, as serene as the rest of the thin, strong body that did not mount her impatiently, as she had expected, but firmly, slowly, self-assuredly. Unhurriedly. He was as watchful of the sensations the woman showed on her face and in the quivering of her flesh as of his own control, each kiss, each caress, each situation drawn out to the limit. The entire complex chain of gestures, vibrations, and responses repeated over and over: the smell of wet, naked, tense sex. Saliva. Warmth. Softness. Pressure. Peace. Causes and effects that became new causes, identical sequences, seemingly endless.

And when she grew dizzy with lucidity, as though about to fall from some place she was lying or floating in, and she thought she was awakening, she tried to do her part, repay him somehow, by accelerating the rhythm, or taking him where she knew—or thought she knew—that all men want to be taken, he would shake his head, and the smile would grow brighter in his eyes, and he would softly say almost inaudible words—once he even raised his finger to gently warn her: Wait, he whispered, be still, don't move, don't even blink—and after pulling back and freezing for a second, the muscles in his face rigid, his mind concentrating on recovering control—she could feel him between her thighs, hard and wet with her—suddenly he plunged in again, softly, even more slowly and deeply, until he was deep inside. And Teresa muffled a moan and everything began again, while the sun through the chinks in the shutters dazzled her with flashes of light as quick and warm as knife wounds. And thus, panting, her wide eyes looking at him in such close-up that she seemed to have his face and lips and eyes inside her, her flesh imprisoned between that body and the wet, tangled sheet beneath her, she squeezed him more intensely with her arms and legs and mouth as she suddenly thought: *Dios mío, Virgencita, Santa Madre de Cristo,* we're not using a condom.

4. Let's go where no one will judge us

Dris Larbi didn't like to stick his nose into his girls' private lives. Or that, at least, is what he told me. He was a quiet man, concerned about his business, a believer in letting people live the way they thought best, so long as they didn't pass the bill on to him. He was so even-tempered, he said, that he had even let his beard grow to please his brother-in-law, a boring-as-spit fundamentalist who lived in Nador with his wife—Dris' sister—and their four kids. He had the Spanish National Identity Document and the Moroccan *neqwa* (as Rifeños called the *waraqa*, or identity card), he voted in the elections, he killed his lamb on Aid el-Adha, and he paid tax on the declared income from his official business: not a bad biography for a man who'd crossed the border at the age of ten with a shoeshine box under his arm and fewer papers than a rabbit.

It was precisely that point—business—that had led Dris Larbi more than once to consider the situation of Teresa Mendoza. Because La

Mexicana had turned out to be special. She kept the Yamila's books and knew some of the business' secrets. Plus she had a head for numbers, and that was very useful in another sphere. Bottom line, the three hostess clubs that the Rifeño owned in the city were part of a more complex enterprise, which included facilitating the flow of illegal immigrants—he called it "private transport"—into Melilla and the Peninsula. That meant border crossings, safe apartments in Cañada de la Muerte or old houses in Real, bribing the police on guard at the control posts, and sometimes more complicated expeditions, twenty or thirty people at a time, with clandestine disembarkations on Andalucían beaches, aided by fishing boats, launches, or other small craft that sailed from the Moroccan coast.

Dris Larbi had been approached by someone seeking to take advantage of this infrastructure to transport something more profitable, but besides being a good citizen and a good Muslim, Dris Larbi was prudent. Drugs were all right, and it was fast money, but working that line when you were a well-known businessman with a certain position on this side of the border implied, sooner or later, getting hauled into court. And it was one thing to grease the palms of a couple of Spanish cops so they wouldn't ask the girls or the immigrants for too many papers, but a very different thing to buy off a judge. Prostitution and illegal immigration implied less ruin in police proceedings, when it came to that, than fifty keys of hashish. Fewer hassles. The money came in slower, but you enjoyed the freedom to spend it, and not on lawyers and other bloodsuckers. So no thanks.

He had followed her a couple of times, not even concealing himself particularly, sometimes pretending he'd just bumped into her. He'd also made inquiries about that individual: Galician, trips to Melilla every week or ten days, a Phantom speedboat painted black. You didn't have to be an enologist or ethnologist or whatever they were called to figure out that liquid in green bottles with a cork had to be wine.

Two or three questions in the right places allowed Dris to discover that the person in question lived in Algeciras, that his speedboat was registered in Gibraltar, and that he was named, or was called—in that world, it was hard to know which—Santiago Fisterra. No police record, Dris was told confidentially by a corporal in the National Police, a fellow who was, coincidentally, quite a fan of getting blowjobs from Dris Larbi's girls in his patrol car while on duty. All these inquiries allowed Teresa Mendoza's boss to make a rough appraisal: Santiago Fisterra was inoffensive as a Yamila customer, but uncomfortable as a close, even intimate friend of La Mexicana's. Uncomfortable for Dris, that is.

He thought about all this as he observed the couple. He'd spotted them as he was driving down near the docks, in the area of Mantelete, alongside the walls of the old city, and after driving on for a hundred yards or so, he turned around and came back, parked, and went to the corner, to the Fisherman's Retreat, for a beer. In the little plaza, under one of the fortress' ancient arches, Teresa and the Gallego were sitting at one of three rickety tables in front of a food stall, eating kebabs. Dris Larbi could smell the heavily spiced meat on the coals, and he had to control himself—he hadn't had lunch—not to go over and join them. The Moroccan side of him loved kebabs.

Underneath, these girls are all alike, he said to himself. No matter how calm and serene they look, when a good screw comes along they listen to their hormones, not their heads. He sat for a while, watching from a distance, holding his Mahou, trying to make the young woman he knew, La Mexicana, efficient and discreet behind the cash register, jibe with this other woman, dressed in jeans, very high heels, and a leather jacket, her hair parted in the middle and pulled back tight, the way they wore it in Mexico, talking with the man sitting next to her in the shadow of the wall. Once again the thought struck him that she was not especially pretty—just one of many—but that depending on the moment, or how she fixed herself up, she could be striking. Her big eyes, that jet-black hair, the white teeth, the young body that so easily wore tight jeans, the sweet way she talked, and above all the way she listened when you spoke to her—quiet and serious, like she was thinking, so you felt you were the center of her attention, almost important. In the right circumstances, all that made her *very* attractive.

He knew the essentials of Teresa's past, and he didn't want to know more: She'd had serious problems in Mexico and some influential person had found her a place to hide. He'd seen her get off the ferry from Málaga with her bag and a confused look about her—banished to a strange world whose rules she was totally unfamiliar with. That little pigeon'll be eaten alive in two days, he'd thought at the time. But La Mexicana had shown a remarkable ability to assess the lay of the land and adapt to it, like those young soldiers from the country, accustomed to working in the sun and the cold, who later, during the war, stand up to anything, are able to bear up under fatigue and privation and to face every situation as though they had spent their lives in it.

That was why he was surprised by her relationship with the Gallego. She wasn't one of those to get mixed up with a customer or just anybody—she seemed to have learned her lesson. Seemed to be one of those that thought about things. Yet there she was, eating kebabs without taking her eyes off Fisterra. She might have had a future ahead of her—Dris Larbi was proof that a person could get ahead in life—but for the time being she didn't have a pot to piss in, and the most likely fate for her in the near future was ten years in some Spanish or Moroccan prison, or a razor blade on some corner.

Why, he was even sure that the Gallego was involved in Teresa's recent, unprecedented requests to attend some of the private parties that Dris Larbi organized on both sides of the border.

"I want to go," she'd said, with no further explanation, and he, surprised, couldn't, or wouldn't, refuse.

Okay, all right, why not. But you'd have had to be there to believe it—the way the girl that walked the straight and narrow behind the bar in the Yamila was now all dolled up, wearing lots of makeup, really attractive, with that same hairdo, the part down the middle and pulled back tight, and a black dress, very short skirt, very deep cleavage—one of those dresses that cling to a body that turned out to be not bad at all—with good legs, shown off by very high heels. Dressed to kill, he thought the first time, when he picked her up with a couple of cars and four European girls he carried to the other side of the border, beyond Mar Chica, to a luxurious place on the beach at Karia da Arkeman. Later, when the party got under way—a couple of colonels, three high-ranking government officials, two politicians, and a rich Nador businessman—Dris Larbi had not let Teresa out of his sight; he was curious to find out what she was up to. While the four European girls, aided by three very young Moroccans, entertained the guests in the way typical of such gatherings, Teresa chatted with almost everyone, in Spanish and also in an elementary English that until then he had not known she spoke. He himself knew only the words "good morning," "good-bye," "fuck," and "money."

All night, he observed disconcertedly, Teresa was attentive, charming, conversing here and there, as though calculatedly feeling out the territory. After fending off the advances of one of the local politicians, who by that hour was pretty full of everything ingestible in solid, liquid, and gaseous form, she chose a colonel in the Gendarmerie Royale, one Chaib. And Dris Larbi—who, like those efficient maître d's in hotels and restaurants, remained discreetly distant yet always at hand, a touch here and another there, a nod or a smile, making sure that everything was to his guests' taste, and who had a nice bank account and three puti-clubs to run, plus dozens of illegal immigrants waiting for the green light to be transported to Spain, and who therefore was a master of public relations—had to take his hat off to the ease with which La Mexicana swept the gendarme off his feet. Nor was this gendarme, Dris Larbi noted with concern, some mere soldier. Because any drug runner that wanted to move hashish between Nador and Al Hoceima had to pay an additional tax, in U.S. dollars, to Colonel Abdelkader Chaib.

Teresa attended another party, a month later, where she rendezvoused again with the Moroccan colonel. And while Dris Larbi watched them conversing alone and in low voices on a sofa just inside the door to the terrace—this time the setting was a luxurious penthouse in one of the best buildings in Nador—he began to get nervous, and he decided there wouldn't be a third time. He even considered firing her, but he was bound by certain commitments. In that complex chain of friends of friends, the Rifeño had no control over the first causes or the intermediate links, and in such cases it was best to be cautious and not upset anybody. Nor could he deny a certain personal fondness for La Mexicana—he really did like her. But that didn't mean he was going to pimp for the Gallego or her with his Moroccan contacts. Not to mention that Dris Larbi tried to stay at arm's length from the cannabis plant in any of its shapes or transformations. So never again, he swore to himself. If she wanted to give Abdelkader Chaib or anybody else a blowjob to help Santiago Fisterra get ahead, that was fine, but he wasn't going to provide the bed to do it in.

He warned her the way he tended to do those things—without much fuss. Letting a word drop. They were leaving the Yamila together, walking down toward the beach and talking about a delivery of gin that was supposed to arrive the next morning. When they reached the corner of the sea walk, Dris Larbi saw the Gallego sitting on a bench waiting, and without any transition, between some remark about the cases of gin and paying the supplier, he said, "He's not the type who'll stay around."

That was all. Then he didn't say anything for a few seconds before returning to the gin, and also before realizing that Teresa was looking at him with a very serious expression. Not as if she hadn't understood, but more as if she were defying him to go on. The Rifeño felt obliged to shrug and add something—"They either leave or get killed."

"What would you know about that," she'd said—a statement, not a question.

She had said it with a tone of superiority and a degree of scorn that made Dris Larbi feel a bit insulted. Just who does this stupid Apache think she is, he thought. He opened his mouth to say something coarse, or perhaps—he hadn't decided—to tell this little Mexican tramp that he knew a few things about men and women, after spending a third of his life trafficking in men and women and cunts, and that if she didn't like it, there was still time to find herself another boss. But he said nothing, because he suspected that she wasn't referring to that—to men and women and the ones that screw you and move on—but to something more complicated, something that he wasn't fully aware of, something that showed in this woman's silences.

And that night, on the seaside where the Gallego was waiting, Dris Larbi sensed that Teresa's remark had less to do with men who move on than with men who get killed. Because in the world she came from, getting killed was a way of dying as natural as any other.

Teresa had a photograph in her purse. She had been carrying it in her wallet for a long time—since Chino Parra took it, of her and Güero Dávila on his birthday: Güero wearing his aviator jacket, one arm over her shoulders. He looked great, laughing for the camera, that tall, thin gringo look of his, his other hand hanging from his thumb on his belt buckle. His smiling, sunny expression contrasted with Teresa's—she could manage only an uneasy smile, half innocent, half disconcerted. She was barely twenty then, and besides looking young she looked fragile, with her eyes very wide open at the flash, and on her lips that tense smile, almost forced, that couldn't quite manage to catch the contagious happiness of the man embracing her. The expression, as is often the case in snapshots, may well have been coincidental: just another moment, chance caught on film. But why not venture an interpretation now, with the lesson learned. Because often images and situations and snapshots are not fully understood until later events fully reveal them—they hang in suspense, provisional, to be confirmed or disproved further down the line.

We take photos not so we can remember, but so we can flesh them out later with the rest of our lives. That's why there are snapshots that are true, that hit the mark directly, and snapshots that aren't, that don't. Snapshots are images that time sets in their right place, giving significance to some and denying it to others, which fade on their own, like colors that fade over time.

That snapshot that she kept in her wallet was the kind that takes on meaning later. No one knew it when the picture was made, but in that photo one might now read, or interpret, everything that had happened so far. Everything, now, looked so obvious in Güero's attitude, Teresa's expression, her confused smile motivated by the presence of the camera. She was smiling to please her man, just enough—*Come over here, prietita, look into that lens there and think about what you love about me, mi chula*—while the dark premonition took refuge in her eyes. The foreboding.

Now, sitting next to another man at the foot of the walled city of old

Melilla, she thought about that photograph. She thought about it because hardly had they gotten there that afternoon, while Santiago was
ordering kebabs from the Moor at his charcoal brazier, when a street
photographer with an old Yashica around his neck had approached
them. Even though they told him no, thanks, she wondered what future
might be read someday in the photo they weren't going to have taken,
if someone should look at it years later, when everything had been
played out. What signs might one be able to see in that scene next to
the medieval wall, with the sea a few yards away, the waves battering the
rocks behind the arch through which showed a piece of intensely blue
sky—you'd almost be able to smell the algae and centuries-old stone
and beach litter mixing with the smell of spicy kebabs on the coals. Because Teresa's most recent past gave that old snapshot an inexorable future, which was not yet revealed, either.

"I'm leaving tonight," Santiago said.

It was the sixth time they had been together. Teresa counted a few
seconds before she looked at him, and she nodded as she did.

"Where?"

"Doesn't matter where." He looked at her gravely, assuming it was
bad news for her. "It's a job."

Teresa knew what the job was. It was on the other side of the border,
because she herself had seen to what would be there. They had the
word of Abdelkader Chaib—the colonel's secret bank account in
Gibraltar had just gotten a little bigger—that there'd be no problems
with the shipment. Santiago had been in his room in the Hotel Anfora
for eight days, waiting for word, with Lalo Veiga watching the boat in a
cove on the Moroccan coast, near Punta Bermeja. Waiting for the
cargo. And now word had come.

"When will you be back?"

"I don't know. A week at the outside."

Teresa nodded slightly again, as though a week was about right for
what he had to do. She would have made the same gesture if he had
said a day, or a month.

"The dark of the moon is coming," he noted.

Maybe that's why I'm sitting here with you. The new moon is coming and you've got a job, and it's like I've been sentenced to play the
same role all over. The question is whether I want to play it again or
not. Whether it's good for me or not.

"I want you to be faithful to me," he—or his smile—said.

She looked at him as if returning from someplace far away. So far
away that she had to make an effort to understand what the fuck he was
talking about.

"I'll try," she said at last, when she understood.

"Teresa."

"What."

"You don't have to stay here."

He looked her straight in the eye, almost faithful. All of them looked you straight in the eye, almost faithful. Even when they lied, or made promises they were never going to keep, even if they didn't know it.

"Bullshit. We've talked about that."

She had opened her purse and was looking for her cigarettes and lighter. Bisontes. Harsh, unfiltered cigarettes, which she had gotten used to almost accidentally; there were no Faros in Melilla. She lit one, and Santiago kept looking at her the same way.

"I don't like your job," he said after a while.

"Oh, I love yours."

It sounded like the reproach it was, and there were many things said in four words. He looked away. "What I meant was that you don't need that Moor."

"But you need other Moors . . . and you need me," she said.

She remembered without wanting to. Colonel Abdelkader Chaib was about fifty, and not a bad sort. Just ambitious and egotistical like any man, and as reasonable as any intelligent one. He could also, when he wanted to, be polite and friendly. He had treated Teresa very courteously, never demanding more than she had planned to give him, and without confusing her with the woman she wasn't. He kept his eye on business and respected the limits. Respected them to a certain point.

"Never again," he said.

"Of course."

"I swear. I've thought about it a lot. Never again."

He was still frowning, and she half turned away. Dris Larbi was on the other side of the plaza, on the corner at the Fisherman's Retreat, with a cold one in his hand, watching the people and cars pass by. Or the two of them. She saw him raise the bottle, greeting her, and she responded by bobbing her head.

"Dris is a good man," she said, turning back to Santiago. "He respects me and he pays me."

"He's a pimp and a *cabrón* and a Moor."

"And I'm a *puta* Indian *cabrona.*"

He said nothing, and she smoked silently, ill humored now, listening to the murmur of the sea. Santiago toyed with the metal skewers on the plastic plate, crossing and uncrossing them. He had strong, harsh, dark-skinned hands, which she knew well. He was wearing the cheap, reliable waterproof wristwatch he always wore—no gold, no chains, no rings. The light reflecting off the whitewashed walls of the plaza gilded the hairs on his forearm, over the tattoo. And made his eyes brighter.

"You can come with me," he said at last. "It's nice in Algeciras. . . . We'd see each other every day. Far from this."

"I don't know if I want to see you every day."

"You're a strange girl. I didn't know Mexican girls were like that."

"I don't know what Mexican girls are like. I know what I'm like." She thought about it. "Well, some days I think I know."

She threw the cigarette down and crushed it under her shoe. Then she turned to see whether Dris Larbi was still at the bar across the plaza. He wasn't. She stood up and said she'd like to take a walk. Still seated, while he dug in his back pocket for money, Santiago stared at her, but his expression was different now. He was smiling. He always knew when to smile, to make the dark clouds pass and her mood brighten. To make her mood brighten, or make her do other things. Abdelkader Chaib included.

"Jesus, Teresa."

"What?"

"Sometimes you look like a teenager, and I like that." He stood up, leaving a few coins on the table. "I mean when I watch you walk, you know, and all that. You swing your ass, you turn, and I'd eat you alive if I could . . . and those tits."

"What about them?"

Santiago tilted his head, trying to find a good definition.

"They're pretty," he said, seriously. "The best tits in Melilla."

"¡Híjole! That's the way a Spaniard pays a compliment?"

"I wouldn't know." He waited for her to stop laughing. "That's what came into my head."

"Just that?"

"No. Also that I like the way you talk. Or don't talk. It makes me . . . I don't know . . . lots of things. One of the things it makes me is . . . maybe the word is 'tender.'"

"Okay. I'm glad you sometimes forget my tits and get all tender."

"I don't have to forget anything. Your tits and me being tender are compatible."

She took off her shoes and they started walking through the dirty sand, and then among the big rocks at the water's edge, under the walls of ocher stone through whose loopholes protruded the barrels of rusty cannons. In the distance rose the blue-gray silhouette of Cabo Tres Forcas. From time to time the spray wet their feet. Santiago was walking with his hands in his pockets, pausing now and then to make sure that Teresa didn't slip on the moss-covered wet rocks.

"Other times," he added suddenly, as if he hadn't stopped thinking about it, "I look at you and all of a sudden you look older, a lot older. . . . Like this morning."

"What happened this morning?"

"Well, I woke up and you were in the bathroom, and I got up to look at you and I saw you standing in front of the mirror, splashing water on your face, and you were looking at yourself like you were having a hard time recognizing yourself. And you had the face of an old woman."

"Ugly?"

"Horrible. Which was why I wanted to make you pretty again, so I swept you up in my arms and carried you to the bed and we screwed for over an hour."

"I don't remember."

"Being in bed?"

"Being ugly."

She remembered perfectly, of course. She had waked up early, with the first gray light. Roosters crowing at daybreak. The voice of the muezzin in the minaret. The tick-tock of the clock on the night table. Unable to get back to sleep, she had watched the light gradually grow brighter, more golden, on the ceiling, with Santiago asleep on his stomach, his hair tousled, half his face sunk into the pillow, the rough shadow of his beard grazing her shoulder. His heavy breathing and his almost perfect motionlessness, so like death. And the sudden panic that made her jump out of bed, go to the bathroom, turn on the faucet, and splash water on her face over and over again, while the face looking out at her from the mirror resembled that woman with wet hair who had stared back at her the day the phone rang in Culiacán. And then Santiago reflected behind her, his eyes swollen with sleep, naked like her, embracing her before he carried her back to bed to make love between the wrinkled sheets that smelled of them both, of semen, and of the warmth of entwined bodies. And then the ghosts fading away into the new order once again, with the shadow of the dirty dawn—there was nothing in the world as dirty as that undecided lead-gray light just before dawn—that the sunlight, now streaming in through the shutters, was banishing once more to the underground.

"With you, sometimes, I feel like I'm a little outside, you know?" Santiago was gazing out at the blue ocean, the waves rising and falling, splashing among the rocks—an experienced look, almost technical. "I've got you all controlled and then—*bam!*—all of a sudden you seem to go off somewhere."

"To Morocco."

"Stop it. I told you that's over."

Again the smile that erased everything else. Handsome as hell, she thought again, *bien padre*. Fucking smuggling *hijo de su puta madre*.

"You seem far away sometimes, too," she said. "God knows where you are, but it's fucking far."

"That's different. There are things that worry me . . . I mean things now. But you're different."

He didn't say anything else for a while. He seemed to be searching for an idea that was hard to pin down. Or express.

"You . . ." he said at last, "it's that there are things that were there before I met you."

They walked on a little farther before returning to the arch. The old kebab man was cleaning off the table. He and Teresa smiled at one another.

"You never tell me anything about Mexico," Santiago said.

She leaned on him as she put on her shoes. "There's not much to tell," she replied. ". . . Some guy fucks over another guy because of drugs or a few pesos, or because he says you're a Communist, or a hurricane comes and *everybody* gets fucked."

"I was talking about you."

"I'm Sinaloan. A little wounded in my self-esteem lately. But stubborn as hell."

"What else?"

"That's it. I don't ask you questions about your life. I don't even know whether you're married."

"I'm not." He waggled his finger, negative, before her eyes. "And it pisses me off that you've never asked till now."

"I'm not asking. I'm just saying what I don't know. That was the deal."

"What deal? I don't recall any deal."

"No stupid questions. You come, I'm there. You leave, I stay."

"What about the future?"

"We'll talk about the future when it gets here."

"Why do you sleep with me?"

"Who else is there?"

"Why me?"

She halted before him, hands on her hips, as though she were about to sing him a ranchera.

"Because you're a good-looking guy," she said, appraising him, her eyes traveling up and down him slowly, appreciatively. "Because you've got green eyes, a great ass, strong arms . . . Because you're an *hijo de la chingada* without being totally fucking selfish. Because you can be hard and sweet at the same time . . . That enough?" She could feel the muscles in her face grow tense, without her realizing it. "And because you look like somebody I once knew."

Santiago looked at her. An awkward expression on his face now, naturally. The flattered expression had gone, and she could predict what he was about to say.

"I don't like the idea of you remembering another man."

Fucking Gallego, she thought. *Pinches hombres de mierda.* So easy, all of them, and such assholes. She had to end this conversation.

"Jesus Christ. I didn't say I remember another man. I said you looked like somebody."

"And you don't want to know why I sleep with you?"

"Besides my usefulness at Dris Larbi's parties?"

"Besides that."

"Because you have a great time in my dark little cave down there. And because sometimes you feel alone."

She watched him run his hand through his hair, confused. Then he took her by the arm.

"What if I slept with other women? Would you care?"

She pulled her arm away gently, until she felt free again. "I'm sure you sleep with other women."

"In Melilla?"

"No. Not that I know of. Not here."

"Say you love me."

"*Órale.* I love you."

"That's not true."

"What do you care? I love you."

It was not hard for me to trace the life of Santiago Fisterra. Before I went to Melilla, I supplemented the Algeciras police report with another document, a very detailed Customs report that had dates and places, including Fisterra's birth in O Grove, a fishing village on a tidal inlet, the Ría de Arosa. Which is how I learned that when he met Teresa, Fisterra had just turned thirty-two. His was a classic case: He had shipped on fishing boats starting at age fourteen, and after military service in the navy had worked for the *amos do fume,* which in Galician is the "tobacco bosses," the capos of the smuggling rings that operated in the Galician *rías*—Charlines, Sito Miñanco, the Pernas brothers. Three years before he met Teresa, the Customs report had him in Villagarcía as the owner of a speedboat working for the Pedrusquiños, a well-known clan of tobacco smugglers who were then expanding into Moroccan hashish.

At that point, Fisterra was a hired man, so much per run; his work consisted of piloting speedboats that offloaded tobacco and drugs from mother ships and fishing boats sitting just outside Spanish waters, taking advantage of the complicated geography of the Galician coastline. That led to dangerous duels with the coast guard, Customs, and the Guardia Civil. On one of those incursions, when he was eluding pursuit by a turbocraft by making tight zigzags through the mussel barges just off the island of Cortegada, Fisterra or his copilot—a young man from Ferrola named Lalo Veiga—turned a spotlight on their pursuers in the middle of a maneuver, and the Customs men crashed into a barge. Result: One dead.

The police reports gave only a rough outline of what happened, so I fruitlessly dialed several telephone numbers until Manuel Rivas, a writer friend of mine who happened to be Galician and happened to live in the area—he had a house on the Costa de la Muerte—made a couple more calls and confirmed the episode. What Rivas told me was that no one could actually prove that Fisterra had a hand in the incident, but the local Customs officers, who were as tough as the smugglers—they'd been raised in the same small towns and sailed on the same boats—swore to send him to the bottom at the first opportunity. An eye for an eye.

That had been enough to make Fisterra and Veiga leave the Rías Bajas in search of less insalubrious air: Algeciras, in the shadow of the Rock of Gibraltar, with its Mediterranean sun and blue waters. And there, profiting from the permissive British laws, the two Galicians registered, through a third party, a powerful speedboat twenty-four feet long and packing a Yamaha PRO six-cylinder engine that put out 225 horsepower, tweaked to 250, on which they made runs between the colony, Morocco, and the Spanish coast.

"Back then," Manolo Céspedes explained to me in Melilla, after I'd seen Dris Larbi, "cocaine was still for the super-rich. Most of the illegal trafficking consisted of moving Gibraltar tobacco and Moroccan hashish: two harvests and twenty-five hundred tons of cannabis illegally exported to Europe every year. . . . And all of it came through here, of course. Still does."

We were putting away a dinner remarkable for both quality and quantity as we sat at a table in La Amistad, a bar-restaurant better known by Melillans as Casa Manolo. It was across the street from the headquarters of the Guardia Civil, which Céspedes himself had had built during his time in power. The owner of the place was actually not named Manolo, but rather Muhammad, although he was also known as Juanito's brother—Juanito being the owner of the restaurant Casa Juanito, though his name was not Juanito, but rather Hassan. Labyrinths of names, all very much in keeping with a city, like Melilla, of multiple identities. As for La Amistad, it was a decidedly working-class place, with plastic chairs and tables and a tapas bar frequented by both Europeans and North Africans; people often ate standing up, even dinner. The quality of the food was memorable, as I said: a menu of fresh shellfish and crustaceans brought in from Morocco that Manolo/Muhammad himself bought every morning at the central market. That night, Céspedes and I were having clams, langostinos from Mar Chica, chunks of halibut, pollack kebabs, and a bottle of cold Barbadillo. And enjoying it, of course. With the Spanish trawlers that fishermen used nowadays, it was getting harder and harder to find anything like this in the waters off the Peninsula.

"When Santiago Fisterra came here," Céspedes continued, "almost all the major traffic was handled in speedboats. He came because that was his specialty, and because a lot of Galicians were setting up in Ceuta and Melilla and along the Andalucían coast. . . . The contacts were made here or in Morocco. The busiest part of the whole Strait was the fourteen kilometers between Punta Carnero and Punta Cires—small-time drug runners in the Ceuta ferries, big consignments in yachts and fishing boats, speedboats. . . . The traffic was so intense that that strip of water started being called Hashish Boulevard."

"What about Gibraltar?"

"Well, right over there, in the middle of everything." Céspedes pointed to the pack of Winstons in front of him on the table, and with a fork he drew a circle around it. "Like a spider in its web. Back then it was the main base for smuggling in the western Mediterranean. . . . The Brits and the locals from the colony left the mafias' hands free. Invest here, sir, trust us with your dough, your financial contacts, and your port facilities. . . . The shipment of tobacco would go directly from the warehouses on the docks to the beaches of La Línea, a thousand meters or so over there. . . . The fact is, it's still going on." He pointed toward the cigarettes again. "These are from there. Tax-free."

"You're not ashamed to smoke them? . . . A former delegate to parliament defrauding Tabacalera, S.A., and the government?"

"Yeah, right. I'm on a pension, don't forget. Any idea how many packs I smoke a day?"

"So what about Santiago Fisterra?"

Céspedes chewed his halibut a moment, savoring it. Then he took a sip of his Barbadillo and looked at me.

"I don't know whether that particular individual smoked or not, but he never moved tobacco. One run with a cargo of hashish was worth a hundred bringing in Winstons or Marlboros. Hashish was a hell of a lot more profitable."

"And more dangerous, I imagine."

"Much more." After painstakingly sucking them, Céspedes was arranging the langostino heads along the rim of his plate, as though lining them up in formation for inspection. "If you didn't have the Moroccans well greased, you were fucked. Look at poor Veiga. . . . But with the English there was no problem—they acted according to their usual double standard. As long as the drugs didn't touch British soil, they looked the other way. . . . So the traffickers came and went with their consignments, and everybody knew who they were. And when they were surprised by the Guardia Civil or Spanish Customs, they hightailed it to Gibraltar for shelter. The only condition was that first they had to throw their cargo overboard."

"It was that easy?"

"That easy." He pointed to the pack of cigarettes with his fork again, this time tapping it. "Sometimes the drug runners would post accomplices up on top of the rock with night-vision binoculars and walkie-talkies—monkeys, they called them—to keep track of the Customs boats. . . . Gibraltar was the hub of an entire industry, and billions, billions were moved through it. Moroccan, Gibraltar, Spanish cops, everybody was on the take. . . . They even tried to buy me." He laughed out loud at the memory, the glass of wine in his hand. "But how could they? Back then it was me who bought off other people!"

After that, Céspedes sighed.

"Now," he said as he polished off the last langostino, "things are different. In Gibraltar, money moves in another way now. Take a walk down Main Street and look at the mailboxes, count the number of ghost corporations. You won't believe it. They've discovered that a financial paradise is more profitable than a pirates' den, even if it's the same thing, underneath. And customers, add it up: the Costa del Sol is a gold mine, so the foreign mafias move in and set themselves up in everything you can think of. Plus, from Almería to Cádiz there's heavy surveillance of the Spanish waters because of illegal immigration. And although the hashish business is still good, coke is catching on, too, and the methods are different. . . . Let's just say that the old days of independent operators—the heroic days—are over, and now there are suits instead of old sea wolves. Everything is decentralized. The smugglers' speedboats have changed hands, tactics, and bases. And the dough is different, too."

Having said all this, Céspedes leaned back in his chair, signaled Manolo/Muhammad for a coffee, and lit up a tax-free cigarette. That old cardsharp's face of his smiled nostalgically; he raised his eyebrows. They can't take that away from me, he seemed to be saying. And I realized that the former parliamentary delegate missed not just the old days, but a certain kind of men as well.

"What happened," he concluded, "is that when Santiago Fisterra appeared in Melilla, the Strait, if not the world, was his oyster. It was a golden age, as the locals in Gibraltar would say. Whew . . . Round-trip runs, balls out. Every night was a game of cat and mouse between the drug runners on the one hand and the Customs guys, police, and Guardia Civil on the other. . . . Sometimes you won and sometimes you lost." He took a long drag on his cigarette, and his sly eyes narrowed, remembering. "And out there—jumping out of the frying pan so she could land directly in the fire—is where Teresa Mendoza wound up."

People say it was Dris Larbi who ratted out Santiago Fisterra, and that he did it despite Colonel Abdelkader Chaib, or maybe even with Chaib's knowledge. That would have been easy in Morocco, where the weakest link was the small-time smugglers that weren't protected by money or politics: a name dropped here and there, a few bills changing hands, and the police would have some big new numbers to add to their statistics. At any rate, no one could ever prove that Dris Larbi dropped the dime. When I raised the subject—I had saved it for our last meeting—he clammed up like an oyster and there was no way to get another word out of him. It's been a pleasure. End of confidences, bye-bye, and never again.

But Manolo Céspedes, who was still a delegate to parliament in Melilla when the events took place, maintains that it *was* Dris Larbi who, intending to run the Gallego off so as to keep Teresa behind the bar, passed the word to his contacts on the other side. Generally, the motto was, Pay up and the Strait's yours, and go with God. *Iallah bismillah.* And that motto applied to a vast network of corruption that ran from the mountains where the cannabis was harvested to the border or the Moroccan coast. The payments rose according to rank: cops, soldiers, politicians, high-level officials, and members of the government. To justify themselves to public opinion—after all, the Moroccan minister of the interior had observer status at the antidrug meetings of the European Union—gendarmes and soldiers would carry out periodic antidrug operations; there would be dragnets, raids, arrests. But it would always be on a pretty small scale, and the guys arrested would never belong to the big official mafias, so nobody would care much one way or another if they got hauled in. People as often as not were ratted out, or pushed out, by the same contacts that got the hashish for them.

Commander Benamú of the Moroccan Gendarmerie Royale's coast guard division had no hesitation in telling me about his role in the Cala Tramontana episode. He did so on the terrace of the Café Hafa, in Tangiers, after a mutual friend, police inspector José Bedmar—veteran of the Central Brigade and intelligence agent in the days of Céspedes— located him and made an appointment; all this came about after a great deal of fax- and phone-praise of my work, to soften the commander up.

Benamú was a nice fellow—elegant, with a small, neatly trimmed moustache that gave him the look of a Latin lover from the 1950s. He was wearing civilian clothes, a jacket and white shirt, no tie, and he spoke to me for easily half an hour in French, without the slightest hesitation, until, feeling more at ease, he switched to almost flawless Spanish. He was a born storyteller and had a certain dark sense of humor; once in a while he would gesture out toward the ocean that lay before our eyes, below the cliff, as though it had all happened right out there, just off the terrace where he was sipping his coffee and I my mint tea.

When the events took place, he was a captain, he said. Routine night patrol in an armed cutter—he spoke the words "routine night patrol" looking out at an indefinite spot on the horizon—with radar contact to the west, at Tres Forcas, all perfectly normal. By pure chance there was another patrol on land, connected via radio—he was still looking out at the horizon when he spoke the word "chance." Between them, within Cala Tramontana—like a little bird in its nest—a speedboat in Moroccan waters, very near the coast, loading a cargo of hashish off a skiff pulled up directly alongside.

They issued the warning to halt, a parachute-descending flare lighting the rocks off Charranes Island against the milky water, the standard shouts and warnings and a couple of shots in the air as a sign they were serious. As far as they could see, the speedboat—low, long, as thin as a needle, painted black, outboard motor—was having some problems with the engine, because it took some time to start moving. By the spotlight and the flare, Benamú saw two figures aboard the speedboat. One was in the pilot's seat, the other running toward the stern to release the line from the skiff, on which two more men were at that very second throwing overboard the bales of the drug that hadn't been loaded onto the speedboat. The starter ratcheted, but the engine wouldn't catch, and Benamú—following orders, he noted between sips

of coffee—ordered his sailor on the bow to fire off a burst from his
12.7, shooting to kill. Noisy, of course. Scary, according to Benamú.
Then another flare.

The men on the skiff raised their hands. Just then the bow of the
speedboat reared up out of the water, the propeller kicked up a fountain of spray behind it, and the man that was standing in the stern toppled into the water. The patrol boat's machine gun was still firing—*rat-
a-tat-tat, rat-a-tat-tat*. The gendarmes on land followed its lead,
timidly at first—*bam, bam, bam*—but then more enthusiastically. It
sounded like war. There was a last flare, and the spotlight illuminated
the ricochets and strikes in the water, and suddenly the sound of the
speedboat deepened, and the boat took off, roaring, growling, in a
straight line, so that by the time they looked off to the north it had disappeared in the darkness. They approached the skiff, detained its occupants—two Moroccans. They fished out of the water three bales of
hashish and a Spaniard with a 12.7 round in his thigh; Benamú indicated the circumference of his coffee cup. "A hole that big."

Interrogated while being given the appropriate medical attention,
the Spaniard told them that his name was Veiga and that he was the
crew on a smuggling boat captained by one Santiago Fisterra; it was
this Fisterra, he told them, who had slipped through their fingers at
Cala Tramontana. "And left me in the water," Benamú recalled his prisoner complaining. The commander also he recalled that this
Veiga, tried two years later in Al Hoceima, got fifteen years in the
prison at Kenitra—his look told me not to consider this spot among
the possibilities for a summer residence—and that he had served out
half the sentence.

Had Fisterra and Veiga been ratted out? I asked.

Benamú repeated the phrase a couple of times, as if it were totally
unknown to him. Then, looking out at the cobalt-blue expanse of
ocean that separated us from the Spanish coastline, he shook his head.
He recalled nothing along those lines. Nor had he ever heard of any
Dris Larbi. The Gendarmerie Royale had a competent intelligence service of its own, and its coastal surveillance was very effective. Like your
own Guardia Civil, he noted. Or more so. The Cala Tramontana operation had been completely routine, a brilliant catch like so many others. The war against crime, and all that.

It took him almost a month to come back, and the fact is, she had
never expected to see him again. Her Sinaloan fatalism led her to
think of him as gone forever—"He's not the type who'll stay around,"

Dris Larbi had said—and she had accepted his absence the same way she now accepted his reappearance.

In the last few years, Teresa had come to the conclusion that the world worked by its own incomprehensible laws, which played out through chance events such as coincidences, appearances and disappearances, presences and absences, lives and deaths. And the best she could do was accept those rules as her own, float along, allow herself to be part of a huge cosmic joke as she was swept downstream by the current—dog-paddle sometimes to stay afloat rather than exhaust herself by swimming upstream. To struggle for anything but the concrete moment, the act of inhaling and exhaling, the sixty-five heartbeats a minute—her heart had always beat slowly and regularly—that kept her alive was absurd. God was busy with other, more important matters.

As for her religious beliefs—those that had survived the routine of her new life—Teresa was still going to mass on Sunday, mechanically reciting her prayers before she went to sleep, *Padre Nuestro, Ave María,* and she sometimes surprised herself by asking Christ or the Virgin (a couple of times she also invoked St. Malverde) for this or that. For example, that Güero Dávila be in heaven, amen. Although she knew very well that despite her good wishes, it was unlikely that Güero was in fucking heaven. He was almost surely burning in hell right now, the son of a bitch *cabrón,* just like in the songs of Paquita la del Barrio—*Are you burning, you worthless son of a gun?* As with all her prayers, the prayer for Güero was spoken without conviction, more out of protocol than anything else. Or perhaps in the case of Güero, out of loyalty. Whatever, she did it the way you'd take a request to a powerful government minister—without much hope that the plea would be heard, much less that it would be granted.

But she didn't pray for Santiago Fisterra. Not once. Neither for his well-being nor for his return. She kept him at arm's length deliberately, refusing to see him as officially linked to the problem. No repetitions, no dependency—she'd been down that road once. Never again.

And yet the night he returned to her house and she found him sitting on the steps as though he'd left just hours earlier, she felt an incredible relief, and a happiness, almost a joy, that shook her between her thighs, in her womb, and in her eyes, and that made her open her mouth and breathe deep. It was a brief second, and then she found herself calculating exactly how many days it had been since that last time, figuring out how long it took to go there and back, miles and hours—enough time for telephone calls, enough time for a letter or a postcard to have gone from point A to point B, so she'd know he was all right. She thought about all that, although she uttered not a word of reproach, while he kissed her, and they went into the house together without a word, straight for the bedroom. And she was still thinking of the same thing when he lay quietly at last, relieved, atop her, and his labored breathing began to grow softer against her throat.

"They got Lalo," he said at last.

Teresa lay even more still. The light from the hall fell over the male shoulder in front of her mouth. She kissed it.

"They nearly got me," he added.

He lay motionless, his face huddled into the hollow of her throat. He was speaking very softly, and his lips brushed her skin with every word. Slowly, she put her arms around him.

"Tell me about it, if you want to."

He shook his head a little, and Teresa didn't insist, because she knew she didn't need to. She knew that he'd talk when he felt calmer, if she maintained the same attitude and the same silence. And she was right. After a while, he began to talk. Not as though telling a story, but rather in short phrases, like images or memories. He was actually recalling it aloud, she realized. In all those days, this may have been the first time he had talked about it.

And so she learned, and so she imagined. And above all, she realized that life plays nasty tricks on people, and that those tricks mysteriously link up into chains with other nasty tricks that are played on other people, and that you might even be able to see yourself at the center of some absurd network of links, like a fly in a spider's web. And so she listened to a story that she knew beforehand, a story in which only the places and characters were different—and she decided that Sinaloa wasn't as far away as she had thought. She, too, saw the spotlight from the Moroccan patrol boat cutting through the night like cold sweat, the white flare in the air, Lalo Veiga's face with its mouth open, calling out in shock and fear—*The Moros! The Moros!* And there they were, with the stupid grinding of the starter, Lalo's silhouette in the spotlight as he ran back to the stern to free the mooring rope, the first shots, the muzzle flashes near the spotlight, the water kicked up by the gunfire, the *zi-i-ing, zi-i-ing* of the bullets flying past, and more muzzle flashes from the shore. And suddenly the engine roaring to life, the bow of the speedboat rising toward the stars, and more bullets, and Lalo's cry as he fell overboard—first one cry and then many—*Santiago, wait, wait, Santiago, don't leave me, Santiago, Santiago, Santiago.* And then the powerful rumble of the engine at full throttle, and the last glance over his shoulder to see Lalo falling behind in the water, framed in the cone of light from the patrol boat, one arm raised to grasp, futilely, at the speedboat as it ran, leapt, fled, its keel slapping the dark waters.

Teresa listened to all that while the lips of the naked, motionless man on top of her continued to brush the skin of her throat. He did not raise his face, did not look at her. And did not let her look at him.

The crowing of roosters. The chant of the muezzin. Once again, the dirty-gray hour, the undecided limbo between night and day. This time Santiago was not asleep, either; she could tell from his breathing that he was still awake. All that night she had felt him moving restlessly in the bed next to her, jerking when he managed to fall asleep for a few minutes. Teresa was lying on her back still, controlling her desire to get up or smoke a cigarette, her eyes open, looking first at the darkness of the ceiling and then at the gray stain that crept in from outside like some malignant slug.

"I want you to come with me," he whispered, out of nowhere.

She was absorbed in the beating of her own heart. Every morning, every dawn, it seemed slower and slower, like that of an animal hibernating. One day I'm going to die at this hour, she thought. That dirty light that always comes at this hour is going to kill me.

"Yes," she said.

That same day, Teresa searched in her purse for the snapshot she had saved from Sinaloa: her with Güero Dávila's protective arm around her, gazing out on the world in amazement, without a clue about what was lurking there. She contemplated the photo a good while, and then went to the bathroom and looked at herself in the mirror, still holding the snapshot. Comparing herself to herself. Then, carefully and very slowly, she tore it in two, kept the half that she was in, and lit a cigarette. With the same match she lit a corner of the other half of the photo and stood motionless, the cigarette between her fingers, watching the image sputter and burn away. Güero's smile was the last thing to disappear, and she told herself that was just like him—laughing at everything right up to the end, not giving jack shit. The same man in the flames of the fucking photo as in the flames of the Cessna.

5. What I planted up there in the sierra

The wait. The ocean dark, and millions of stars clotting the sky. The shadowy expanse infinite to the north, limited on the south by the black silhouette of the coastline. Everything around so still, the water looked like oil. And a light, barely perceptible offshore breeze that brushed the water and stirred tiny sparkles of phosphorescence.

Sinister beauty, she concluded. That was the word for it.

She was not good at expressing that sort of thing. It had taken her forty minutes. But anyway, that was what this seascape was—beautiful and sinister, and Teresa Mendoza was contemplating it in silence. Since the first of those forty minutes she had sat motionless, her lips never parting, and had felt the damp night air soak her cotton sweater and the legs of her jeans. Listening attentively to the sounds of both land and water. To the muffled murmur of the radio, channel 44—the volume so low she could hardly hear it.

"Give a look," Santiago said.

He spoke in a barely audible whisper. The ocean, he had explained the first few times, transmits sounds and voices differently at different times. If the moment was right, you could hear things said a mile away. Same thing with lights, which was why the Phantom was running dark, camouflaged in the night, on the water, by the black matte paint that covered its fiberglass hull and the engine casing. And which was also why she was not smoking and the two of them were sitting silently, unspeaking, hardly moving. Waiting.

Teresa put her face into the rubber cone that hid the screen of the Furuno eight-mile radar. At each sweep of the antenna, the dark line of the Moroccan coast was redrawn with perfect neatness on the bottom of the screen, with the arch of the cove down, between Punta Cruces and Punta Al Marsa. The rest was clean—not a blip on the entire surface of the ocean. She hit the zoom button twice, widening the surveillance radius from one to four miles. With the next sweep, the coast appeared smaller and longer, and toward the east included the precise outline of Perejil Island. Everything clean there, too. No boats. Not even the false echo of a wave. Nothing.

"*Esos cabrones*," she heard Santiago mutter.

Waiting. That was part of the job, but in the time she had been on the job, going out to sea with Santiago, Teresa had learned that the bad part was not the waiting itself, but the things your imagination did while you waited. The sound of water against the rocks, the murmur of the wind that could be confused with a Moroccan patrol—the Moros, in Strait slang—or the Spanish Customs helicopter were not as unsettling or disquieting as that long calm during which your thoughts became your worst enemy. Even concrete danger, the hostile echo that suddenly appeared on the radar screen, the roar of the engine struggling to achieve speed and freedom and life, the fifty-knot run-for-it with a patrol boat glued to your stern, the slaps of the boat's keel on the water, the violent alternating discharges of adrenaline and fear were for her preferable to the uncertainty of the calm, the imagination. How terrible lucidity was. And how perverse the terrifying, coldly assessed possibilities that lurked in the unknown. That unending wait as you tried to pick up a signal from land, a contact on the radio, was like the gray dawns that still found her awake every morning, and that now had followed her onto the sea, with the night growing light in the east, and the cold, and the wetness that made the deck slippery and soaked her clothes, her hands, and her face. *Chale.* No fear is unbearable, she concluded, unless you've got time on your hands and a healthy imagination.

Five months already. Sometimes, the other Teresa Mendoza she would catch sight of in the otherworld of a mirror, on some corner, in the dirty light of dawn, was still hovering, still spying on her, apparently curious to see the changes gradually being registered on her. That was why it was interesting, almost educational, to come and go from her own body, her own mind that way, and to be able to see herself from outside as well as from inside. Now Teresa knew that everything—fear, uncertainty, passion, pleasure, memories, her own face, which looked older now than it had only a few months ago—might be contemplated from that double point of view, and with a mathematical lucidity that belonged not to her but rather to that other woman that throbbed in her. The aptitude for this uncanny out-of-body experience, which had been discovered, or rather intuited, the afternoon (not even a year earlier) that the telephone rang in Culiacán, was what now allowed her to cast a cold eye on the motionless motorboat in the darkness of the sea that was becoming so familiar to her. She stood, once more, alongside the silent shadow of a man whom she didn't love—or perhaps just thought she didn't love—but with whom she was out here on this boat, at the risk of spending the rest of her life rotting in jail. It was an idea (the ghost of Lalo Veiga was the third crewman accompanying them on every run) that made her shiver.

But it was better than Melilla, better than anything she had expected. More personal and cleaner, somehow. At times she even thought that it was better than Sinaloa, but then the image of Güero Dávila would come to her mind like a reproach, and she would feel guilty, deep inside, for betraying his memory that way. Nothing was better than Güero, and that was true in more than one sense. Culiacán, the pretty house in Las Quintas, the restaurants on the *malecón*, the music of the *chirrines*, the street musicians that only Sinaloa in all of Mexico had, the drives to Mazatlán, the beaches at Altata, everything that she had believed to be the real world, and that had made her happy with life, was based on a mistake.

Now, however, there was something new, something indefinable and not altogether bad in the darkness of the night, and in the quiet, resigned fear she felt when she looked around her, despite the nearby shadow of a man who—this she had learned in Culiacán—would never be able to persuade her to deceive herself again, allow herself to believe that she was somehow protected against horror, pain, and death. And strangely, that sensation, far from intimidating her, excited her and goaded her on. It forced her to analyze herself and other things more intensely, with a thoughtful curiosity not altogether free of respect. Which was why she sometimes stood looking at the snapshot that she and Güero had been in, glancing back and forth at the mirror, taking note of the ever greater distance between the three women: the young woman with the surprised eyes in the snapshot, the Teresa who was now living on this side of life and the passage of time, and the stranger who observed the other two from her—increasingly less precise—reflection.

Chíngale, she'd come a long way from Culiacán. Between two continents, with the Moroccan coast just ten miles from Spain: the waters of the Strait of Gibraltar and the southernmost limit of a Europe she had never in her life dreamed of visiting.

Here, Santiago Fisterra ran a transport operation for other people. He rented a little house on a beach in the Bay of Algeciras, on the Spanish side, and kept his speedboat tied up at Sheppard's marina, under the protection of the British flag that flew over the Rock. The boat was a 24-foot Phantom able to go 160 miles on its gas tanks, with a 250-horsepower engine that could go from zero to fifty-five knots in twenty-two seconds. Santiago was a mercenary. Unlike Güero Dávila in Sinaloa, he had no one boss, did not work for a single cartel. His employers were the Spanish, British, French, and Italian drug traffickers who ran their business on the Costa del Sol. Aside from that, though, it was more or less the same: transport shipments from one place to another. Santiago charged so much per delivery, and he paid for losses or failures with his life. But that would be only in the most extreme case. This smuggling—almost always hashish, sometimes tobacco from Gibraltar warehouses—had nothing to do with what Teresa Mendoza had known before. The world of these waters was hard, the people gruff, but both the world and the people were less hostile than in Mexico. There was less violence, fewer deaths. People were not shot down over one drink too many, nor did they carry AK-47s, like in Sinaloa. Of the two sides of the Strait, the northern, Spanish side was more easygoing, even if you fell into the hands of the law. There were lawyers, judges, rules that applied to the criminals as well as to their victims.

But the Moroccan side was different: there, it was a nightmare. Corruption at every level, human rights virtually unrecognized, prisons you could rot in. With the added problem of being a woman, and what that meant if you fell into the inexorable machinery of a Muslim society like that.

At first, Santiago had refused to let her take Lalo Veiga's place. Too dangerous, he had said, nipping the discussion in the bud. Or thinking that he had. It was one thing for her to come with him and stay onshore, but ride with him? Never. Real serious, totally macho, the Gallego, with that odd accent he sometimes had, less brusque than other Spaniards, who were so contemptuous, so rude when they talked.

But after a night Teresa spent with her eyes open, staring first at the darkness of the ceiling and then at the familiar gray light, she woke Santiago up to tell him that she'd made a decision. And that was that. She was never going to wait for anybody again, watching telenovelas in some house in some city somewhere—so he could choose: Either take her on the boat, or she would leave him then and there, forever, nice knowing you.

Santiago, his chin unshaven, his eyes red with sleep, scratched his tousled hair and asked her if she was crazy or had turned into a bitch or what. Until she got out of bed, naked, and still naked took down her suitcase and began to throw her things into it, trying not to look in the mirror or at him or think about whether she was sure she would truly leave. Santiago let her pack, watching her for a minute and a half without opening his mouth.

Finally convinced that she was actually leaving, he said, All right, you win, okay. Fuck it. It's not my cunt the Moros are going to rip open if they catch you. Just try not to fall overboard like Lalo.

There they are."
A *click-clack,* three times, barely audible on the radio. A small shadow, leaving a wake of phosphorescence on the black, quiet surface. Not even an engine, just the muffled splash of oars. Santiago was watching with the Baigish-6U night-vision binoculars. Russian. The Russians had flooded Gibraltar with them during the Soviet liquidation. Any boat, submarine, or fishing boat that came into port sold off everything that could be unscrewed.

"Those *hijos de puta* are an hour late."

Teresa heard his whispers while her face was cradled in the rubber cone of the radar. All clear outside, she said, whispering also. Not a sign of the Moros. The speedboat rocked when Santiago stood up to move toward the stern with a rope.

"*Salaam aleikem.*"

The cargo was well packed, in plastic shrink-wrap with handles for easier handling. Pills of hashish oil, seven times more concentrated, seven times more valuable than the conventional resin. Twenty kilos per bundle, Teresa calculated while Santiago passed them to her and she stowed them in rows in the hold. Santiago had taught her to fit one pack tightly against another so they wouldn't shift during the run across the open sea. This underscored the importance that good stowage had on the Phantom's speed—as much importance as the propeller's revolutions or depth in the water. One package, badly stowed, might mean a difference of two knots, two nautical miles per hour. And in this line of work two nautical miles, two and a third land miles, was not a distance to be sneezed at. It often meant the difference between prison and freedom.

"Anything on the radar?"

"Everything clean."

Teresa could make out two dark silhouettes on the little rowboat. Sometimes she could hear a few words in Arabic, spoken softly, or an expression of impatience from Santiago, who was still tossing bundles on board. She looked at the gray line of the coast to see if she could make out any lights. Everything was dark except a few distant dots on the black bulk of Mount Musa and on the steep profile she could distinguish from time to time toward the west, under the light from the Punta Cires lighthouse, where she could see a few fishermen's and smugglers' houses. She looked at the screen again, then clicked down the scale from four miles to two, then back up to eight. There was a blip at almost the outer limit. She looked through the 7X50 binoculars but saw nothing, so she picked up the Russian pair: a very distant light, moving slowly toward the west, no doubt a big boat on its way to the Atlantic. Still peering through the binoculars, she turned toward the coast. Now any point of light could be seen clearly in the green landscape, its rocks and shrubs neatly defined, and she could even see the slight undulations of the water. She turned the lenses on the two Moroccans in the rowboat: one young, in a leather jacket, and the other an older man, wearing a wool beret and a dark windbreaker. Santiago was on his knees next to the big outboard-motor housing, stowing away the last bundles in the stern: jeans, boat shoes, black T-shirt, his stubborn profile turning from time to time for a cautious look around. Through the night-vision lenses, Teresa could make out his strong arms, his muscles tense as they lifted the cargo. Even here, the *cabrón* was fine.

The problem with working as an independent runner, unconnected with the big narcomafias, was that somebody could get upset with you and whisper a few dangerous words in the wrong person's ear. Just like in *pinche* Mexico. That might explain the capture of Lalo Veiga—Teresa had her ideas about that, and Dris Larbi was one of them. But Santiago had apparently learned his lesson, and now he was trying hard to keep the unexpected to a minimum with more money spread around in Morocco through an intermediary from Ceuta. That lowered his profits but at least in principle lowered the risk. Of course his modest means would never be enough to buy off everybody. Not to mention that there might always be some agent for the Moros, some Moroccan cop or gendarme that wasn't happy with his cut, some competitor that could pay more than Santiago could and blow the whistle on him, some influential fucking leech lawyer that needed clients to bleed. Or the Moroccan authorities might organize a roundup of little fish so they could have something to show at some big international narcocop convention. In any case, Teresa had acquired enough experience to know that the real danger, the concrete threat, came later, when they entered Spanish waters, where Customs and the Heinekens of the Guardia Civil—their colors were just like the beer's—patrolled night and day, looking for smugglers. The advantage with them was that un-like the Moroccans, the Spaniards never shot to kill, because if they did, the judges and courts would be all over them—in Europe certain things were taken more seriously than in Mexico or the United States. That gave you the chance to get away, if your boat could outrun them, although it was not easy to shake the Customs' powerful HJ turbocraft or their helicopter—the bird, Santiago called it—with its powerful de-tection systems, its veteran captains, and its pilots able to fly just feet above the water, forcing you to go throttle-out in dangerous evasive maneuvers, with the inevitable risk of engine or steering problems, the risk of being captured before you could reach the lights of Gibraltar. In those cases, the bales were thrown overboard—*adiós* forever to the cargo, and *hola* to another kind of problem, maybe worse than the cops, because the people that shipped the hashish were not always un-derstanding mafiosi, and you ran the risk that after all the books were balanced there might be a couple of sombreros too many. All that with-out taking into account the possibility of a bad bounce on the waves, a leak in the hull, a crash between your boat and the boats pursuing you, a submerged rock that would rip out the guts of the boat and its crew, running aground on the beach.

"That's it. Let's go."

The last package had been stowed. Exactly three hundred kilos. The men in the rowboat were now rowing toward shore, and Santiago, af-ter coiling the rope, jumped into the cockpit and sat down in the pilot's seat, on the starboard side. Teresa moved to let him pass as she, like him, pulled on a life jacket. Then she gave another look at the radar screen: everything clean ahead, toward the north and the open sea. End of the immediate precautions. Santiago turned the key, and the weak light of the instruments illuminated the dash: compass, tachometer, oil pressure gauge. Throttle levers to the left of the pilot, trim-tab lever to the right. *Rrrr. Roarrr.* The needles moved, startled, as though they'd suddenly been shaken awake. *Roaaarr.* The propeller whipped up a froth of spray, and the Phantom's twenty-four feet began to move, faster and faster, cutting through the oily water as cleanly as a well-sharpened knife: 2,500 rpms, twenty knots. The vibration of the engine was transmitted to the hull, and Teresa could feel the power pushing them forward, making the fiberglass of the hull, which suddenly felt as light as a feather, quiver. 3,500 rpms, thirty knots, and hydroplaning. The sensation of power, of freedom, was almost physical, and as she felt it once again, her heart beat as though to the rush of the third drink of the night. Nothing, she thought once more, is like this. Or almost nothing.

Santiago, concentrating on the boat's reactions, leaning slightly into the wheel, his jaw reddish from the instrument panel lights, eased the throttle forward: 4,000 rpms, forty knots. The windshield was no longer enough to protect them from the wind, which was now wet and cutting. Teresa zipped up the life jacket and pulled on a wool cap; she tucked her hair, which was whipping into her eyes, under it. Then she gave another look at the radar and swept the channels on the Kenwood radio—the Customs agents and Guardia Civil used scramblers to talk back and forth, but even if she couldn't understand their transmissions, the intensity of the signal let her know whether they were close by. Once in a while she raised her face, looking for the menacing shadow of the helicopter against the cold lights of the stars. The firmament and the dark circle of the sea around them seemed to run with them, as though the speedboat were at the center of a sphere traveling swiftly through the night. Now, on the open sea, the slight swell made them bounce over the surface of the water, and in the distance she could begin to make out the lights of the coast of Spain.

How alike and how different they were, she thought. How much they resembled one another in some things—she had sensed this since the night at the Yamila—yet what different ways they had of facing life and the future. Like Güero, Santiago was quick, smart, determined, and very cold in his work, one of those men that never lose their head even when they're getting beat to shit. He also was good for her in bed—generous, thoughtful, always controlling himself very calmly, attentive to her reactions. Less fun, maybe, but more tender than Güero. Sweeter, sometimes. And there the similarities ended. Santiago was a man of few words, didn't spend money, had few friends, and distrusted everybody.

"I'm a Celt from Finisterre," he would say. "In Galician, *fisterra* means end, the end of the earth. I want to live to be an old man and play dominoes in a bar in O Grove, and have a big *pazo*"—the Galician word for a country house or villa—"with a mirador, all glassed-in, that I can see the ocean from, with a telescope to watch the boats going in and out, and my own sixty-foot schooner beached down at the mouth of the river. But if I spend my money, or have too many friends, or trust too many people, I'll never live to be an old man or have any of that— the more links in the chain, the less you can trust it."

Santiago never smoked tobacco or hashish or anything else, and he would have as much as a glass of wine only now and then. When he got up in the morning he would run for a half-hour on the beach, through water up to his ankles, and then do push-ups, pull-ups, sit-ups—Teresa counted, and it was always fifty of each. His body was lean and hard, with skin that was light but tanned dark on the arms and face, with his tattoo of the crucified Christ on his right forearm and another mark on his left shoulder, a circle with a Celtic cross and the initials I.A., whose meaning—she suspected they stood for the name of a woman— she always refused to ask. He also had an old scar, about three inches long, diagonal, at kidney level, on his back.

"A knife," he said, when Teresa asked. "A long time ago. When I was selling Turkish tobacco in bars and the other kids were afraid I'd take their customers away." And as he said this he smiled ruefully, melancholy, as though he missed those days when somebody could stab you in the back with a knife.

She would almost have been able to love him, Teresa thought sometimes, had everything not happened in the wrong place at the wrong time in her life. Things always happen too soon or too late. But she liked being with him, really liked it, watching TV as she leaned on his shoulder, looking through romance magazines, lying in the sun with a Bisonte laced with hashish between her fingers—she knew that Santiago didn't approve of her smoking the stuff, but she never heard him say a word against it—or watching him out on the porch, his torso naked, the sea in the background, as he worked on his wooden boat models. She loved to watch him build those little boats, because he was so very patient and painstaking, and incredibly skillful at constructing fishing boats that looked exactly like the real ones—painted red, blue, and white—and sailboats with every sail, line, and cable in its place. It was strange about those boats, and the speedboat, too, because she had discovered that Santiago didn't know how to swim. Not even paddle along like she did, clumsy strokes that Güero had taught her in Altata—with almost no style, but at least swimming.

"I could never even float," he confessed once, a parenthesis while they were talking about something else. "It makes me feel weird."

And when Teresa asked him why, then, he risked his life in a speed-boat, all he did was shrug fatalistically, with that grin of his that seemed to emerge after many twists and turns through his insides.

"Half of us Galicians don't know how to swim," he said at last. "We sink, we die—with resignation." He grinned.

And at first she didn't know whether he was altogether joking, or altogether serious.

One afternoon, over tapas at Kuki's—Casa Bernal, a *tasca* in Campamento—Santiago introduced her to a man he knew, Óscar Lobato, a reporter for a Cádiz newspaper. Dark-skinned, fortyish, his face marked and scarred like a ruffian, which he wasn't, and loquacious—a born talker—Lobato moved as easily (like a fish in water, thought Teresa) among smugglers as among Customs agents and members of the Guardia Civil. He read books and he knew something about everything, from engines to geography to music. He also knew everybody, wouldn't reveal his sources even if you held a .45 to his head, and had moved in this murky world for some time, with his telephone book full of contacts. He always lent a hand when he could, no matter which side of the law you were on, partly out of an instinct for public relations and partly because despite the bitter aftertaste of his trade, people said, he was not a bad guy. Not to mention that he liked his work.

These days he was hanging out in La Atunara, the old fishing neighborhood of La Línea, where a strike had turned fishermen into smugglers. Boats from Gibraltar would pull up onto the beach in broad daylight and be unloaded by women and children who painted their own pedestrian crosswalks on the highway so they could carry the packages and bales of contraband across the road. The kids played at being drug traffickers and Civil Guardsmen along the water, chasing each other with empty Winston cartons on their heads; only the youngest and most gullible of them could be persuaded to be the cops. And every enforcement operation ended in tear gas and rubber bullets, with real bullets only between the inhabitants and the riot police.

"Picture the scene," Lobato was saying. "The beach at Puente Mayorga, at night, a speedboat from Gibraltar with two guys unloading tobacco. A patrol from the Guardia Civil, old corporal and young private. 'Halt, who goes there,' et cetera. The guys on the beach take off running. The engine won't start, the young guardsman jumps in the water and climbs on the speedboat. The engine finally catches, and there goes the speedboat for the Rock, one drug trafficker at the helm and the other one beating the living shit out of the guardsman. . . . Now picture that speedboat stopping in the middle of the bay. . . . The conversation with the guardsman. 'Listen, kid,' they tell him. 'If you stay on this boat all the way to Gibraltar we'll be fucked, and you'll get screwed over for chasing us into British waters. So let's think this over, all right?' . . . Bottom line: Speedboat returns to the beach, guardsman climbs off. *Adiós, adiós, buenas noches.* And peace on earth, goodwill to men."

As that combination of Galician and drug runner that he was, Santiago distrusted journalists. But Teresa knew that he considered Lobato an exception: he was objective, discreet, didn't believe in bad guys and good guys, knew how to get along, paid for the drinks, and never took notes in public. He also told good stories and even better jokes, and he never spoke ill of those who weren't present. He had come into Casa Bernal with Toby Parrondi, a speedboat pilot from Gibraltar, and some of Toby's friends. They were all young: long hair, tans, tattoos, gold rings in their ears, cigarettes and gold lighters on the table, high-powered cars with dark-tinted windows that they drove around in playing the music of Los Chunguitos or Javivi or Los Chichos as loud as it would go—songs that reminded Teresa a little of Mexican narcocorridos. *At night I don't sleep, in the daytime I don't live,* went the lyrics to one, *in these four walls, this miserable prison.* Songs that were part of the local folklore, like those songs in Sinaloa, and with equally picturesque titles: "The Moorish Girl and the Legionnaire," "I'm a Stray Dog in the Street," "Fists of Steel," "To My Colleagues." The smugglers from the Rock differed from the Spaniards only in that more of them had blond hair and light skin, and they mixed English words into their Andalucían-accented Spanish. Otherwise, they were cut from the same cloth: gold chains with crucifixes around their necks, medals to the Virgin or the inevitable image of Camarón. Heavy-metal T-shirts, expensive jogging suits, Adidas and Nike sneakers, faded designer jeans with wads of bills in one back pocket and the bulge of a knife in the other. Very tough guys, as dangerous at times as their Sinaloan cousins. Nothing to lose and a lot to gain. Their girlfriends stuffed into stretch pants that showed off their tattooed asses and short T-shirts that showed off their navel-piercings, with lots of makeup and perfume, and all that gold. They reminded Teresa of the girls that ran with the narcos from Culiacán. And in a certain way they reminded her of herself—and realizing that made her think that too much time had passed, and too many things had happened.

In this group there was the occasional Spaniard from La Atunara, but most of the kids were from Gibraltar—Brits with surnames inherited from Spain, England, Malta, and every other corner of the

Mediterranean. As Lobato said with a wink, including Santiago in the gesture, "the best of every country."

"So, Mexican, eh?"

"*Órale.*"

"You've come a long way."

"Life's like that."

The journalist's smile was flecked with beer foam.

"That sounds like a song by José Alfredo."

"You know José Alfredo?"

"A little."

And Lobato started humming "The Drunk Came In Drunk" as he signaled the waiter for another round. "The same for my friends and me," he said. "And for those gentlemen at that table, and their ladies."

Calling for five tequilas,
and the bartender told him
that'd be all for tonight.

Teresa sang a few lines with him, and they laughed at the end. He was *simpático,* she thought. And he wasn't a know-it-all. Being a know-it-all with Santiago and those guys over there was bad for the health. Lobato was studying her, trying to guess her weight, so to speak. Eyes that knew which side of his mouth the iguana chewed on.

"A Mexican and a Gallego. Never thought I'd live to see the day."

That was good. Don't ask questions, but open the door so the other person could tell his story, if he wanted to. Smooth as silk, this one.

"My father was Spanish."

"From where?"

"I never knew."

Lobato didn't ask whether that was true or not, that she'd never known, or whether she was just closing that door. Giving up on the family questions, he sipped at his beer and gestured toward Santiago.

"They say you ride over to Morocco with this guy."

"Who says that?"

"People. There are no secrets here. Ten miles—not a lot of water, you know."

"End of interview," said Santiago, taking Lobato's half-drunk beer out of his hand, in exchange for another one from the new round that the blond guys at the next table had just sent over.

The reporter shrugged.

"She's pretty, your girl. And that accent."

"I like her," said Santiago.

Teresa let herself be hugged tight in Santiago's arms. Kuki, the owner, set out some tapas on the bar—*gambas al ajillo,* roast beef, meatballs, tomatoes drenched in olive oil. Teresa loved to eat this way, the way the Spaniards did, from a dozen little plates of all sorts of food, eating standing at the bar, going from one bar to another—sausages, cold cuts, wonderful things from the kitchen. Tapas. She saw the beef, and dipped a piece of bread in the juice. She was famished, and she didn't worry about gaining weight; she was naturally thin, and for years she had been able to allow herself to indulge. Overindulge. Stuff herself, in fact. Kuki had a bottle of Cuervo behind the bar, so she ordered a tequila. In Spain they didn't use the tall, narrow *caballitos* that were so common in Mexico, so she always drank it from sherry glasses, which weren't a bad substitute. The problem was that you got a double with every drink.

More customers came in. Santiago and Lobato, at the bar, were discussing the advantages of Zodiac-type rubber speedboats for crossing the sea in high swells, and Kuki was taking part in the conversation. Stiff hulls took a beating during chases, and for a while now Santiago had been toying with the idea of a semi-rigid with two or three engines, a boat big enough to stand up to the ocean and run as far as the eastern coast of Andalucía and Cape Gata. The problem was money—too much investment and too much risk. Even assuming that these ideas could be confirmed on the water.

Suddenly the conversation halted. The Gibraltar boys at their table had fallen quiet, too, and their eyes were turned toward the group that had just taken seats at the far end of the bar, next to an old poster announcing the last bullfight before the civil war—*Feria de La Línea—19, 20 y 21 de julio de 1936.* The group consisted of four young men, clean-cut and good-looking. A blond in sunglasses and two tall, athletic types wearing polo shirts, hair cropped short. The fourth man was attractive, dressed in an impeccably ironed blue shirt and a pair of jeans so clean and starched they looked new.

"And here I am once more," Lobato sighed ironically, "between the Achaeans and the Trojans."

He excused himself a moment, winked at the Gibraltar boys, and went over to say hello to the newcomers, pausing especially at the man in the blue shirt. When he returned, he laughed softly.

"All four of them are with Customs Surveillance."

Santiago regarded them with professional interest. One of them, when he realized he was being inspected, inclined his head a bit in greeting, and Santiago lifted his glass a couple of inches. It might be a reply, or might not. The codes and the rules of the game they all played:

hunters and prey in neutral territory. Kuki set out sherry and tapas as though nothing were happening—which in a way it wasn't; this kind of encounter happened every day.

"The movie star," Lobato went on, "is the pilot of the bird."

The bird was the Customs' BO-105, equipped for tracking and hunting at sea. Teresa had seen him harrying the smugglers' boats. He flew well—low, and well. Took risks. She examined him: thirty-something, dark hair, deep tan. Could pass for Mexican. Looked good, maybe even fine. A little shy.

"He told me somebody fired a flare at him and hit a blade." Lobato looked at Santiago. "That wouldn't have been you, would it?"

"I didn't go out last night."

"Must have been one of these guys."

"Must have been."

Lobato looked at the Gibraltar boys, who were now talking exaggeratedly loud, and laughing. "I'm gonna ram eighty kilos tomorrow," one of them was crowing, "right up your ass." One of them, Parrondi, told Kuki to serve a round to the gentlemen from Customs. "It's my birthday and it will be my pleasure," he said with obvious sarcasm, "to buy them a drink." From the end of the bar, the four men turned down the gesture of appreciation, if it could be called that, although one of them held up two fingers in the sign of victory as he wished Parrondi happy birthday. The blond in sunglasses, Lobato informed them, was the captain of an HJ turbocraft. And a Galician, of course. From La Coruña.

"As for the bird," Lobato added for Santiago's sake, "it's in the shop, so there's a week of clear air, no vultures on your back. So . . ."

"I don't have anything going these days."

"Not even tobacco?"

"Nope."

"That's a shame."

Teresa was still watching the pilot. He looked so calm, well behaved, inoffensive. With that ironed shirt and gleaming hair it was hard to tie him to the helicopter that was every smuggler's nightmare. Maybe, she thought, it was like in that movie that she and Santiago had seen in La Línea: Dr. Jekyll and Mr. Hyde.

Lobato, who had noticed where her eyes were turned, smiled more broadly.

"He's a good-looking young man. From Cáceres. And they throw the wildest things you can imagine at him. Once somebody threw an oar. It broke a blade and almost killed him. And when he landed on the beach, the kids almost stoned him to death. . . . Sometimes, I swear, La Atunara is like Vietnam. 'Course out on the water, it's different."

"Yeah," said Santiago, sipping at his beer. "Out there it's those *hijos de puta* that have the advantage."

That was how she and Santiago filled their free hours. Other times they would go shopping, or run errands at the bank in Gibraltar, or walk along the beach in the afternoon, enjoying the long, glorious Andalucían sunset, with the lights on the Rock coming on one by one in the background. The bay would be full of ships under many flags— Teresa could now identify most of them—and their lights, too, would come on one by one as the sun sank in the west. The house was a little place about ten yards from the water, at the mouth of the Palmones River, where there were also a few fishermen's houses, in the middle of the bayshore between Algeciras and Gibraltar. She liked this area, whose sandy beaches and blue and red fishing skiffs beside the calm river reminded her a bit of Altata.

In the morning they would have coffee—very black, just a drop of milk; *café cortado,* it was called, coffee cut in this case with rich whole milk—and bread toasted on a grill with oil, at El Espigón or the Estrella del Mar. On Sunday, Spanish omelettes at Casa Willy—thick, potato-rich plates with onions and, in Willy's case, shrimp. Sometimes, between cargo runs across the Strait, they would take Santiago's Cherokee and head up toward Seville on the Ruta del Toro, to eat at Casa Becerra or stop at roadside stands for spicy sausage or hard, gamy slices of ham from hogs fed only on nuts. They might drive up the Costa del Sol to Málaga, or in the opposite direction, through Tarifa and Cádiz to Sanlúcar de Barrameda and the mouth of the Guadalquivir—Barbadillo wine, langostinos, discos, outdoor cafés, restaurants, bars (sometimes with karaoke), until Santiago would pull out his wallet, look inside, and say, "Let's go, we're running on the reserve tanks already. Gotta go back and earn some more—nobody's giving it away." Sometimes they would spend days on the Rock, covered with oil and grease, getting roasted by the sun and eaten by flies on the dry dock at Sheppard's marina, breaking down and then reassembling the Phantom's engine—words once Greek to Teresa, like "pistons," "hemi heads," "bearings," no longer held any mystery—and then they would take the boat out for a test run through the bay. They'd race along at planing speeds, watched over by the chopper and the HJs and the Heinekens that that very night might well meet them again in the cat-and-mouse game they played south of Punta Europa. And every afternoon on those calm days in port or dry dock, when the work was done they would go to the Olde Rock to sit at their usual table, under an engraving depicting the death of an English admiral named Nelson, and have a drink.

So during those almost happy months—for the first time in her life she was conscious of being happy—Teresa became a pro. The little Mexican girl that little more than a year earlier had taken off running in Culiacán was now a woman experienced in midnight runs and scares, in sailing skills, in boat mechanics, in winds and currents. She knew the course and activity of boats by number, color, and positioning of their lights. She studied Spanish and British nautical charts of the Strait and compared them with her own observations until she knew soundings, coastal profiles, references by heart—things that later, at night, would make the difference between success and failure. She stowed tobacco in the hold from the Gibraltar warehouses and unloaded it a mile farther on, in La Atunara, and stowed away hashish on the Moroccan coast and then unloaded it in coves and on beaches from Tarifa to Estepona. Wrench and screwdriver in hand, she checked refrigeration pumps and cylinders, changed electrodes, oil, and spark plugs, and learned things that she never imagined would be useful, such as, for example, that the fuel consumption per hour of a souped-up engine is calculated by multiplying the maximum horsepower by 0.4—an extremely valuable rule of thumb when fuel is being burned at high speeds on the open sea, where there are no gas stations.

She also learned to guide Santiago by tapping him on the shoulder during super-fast chases, so that the proximity of the turbocraft or helicopter wouldn't distract him when he was running at dangerously high speeds. She even learned to steer a speedboat herself at over thirty knots, giving it gas or slacking off in bad seas so the hull wouldn't suffer unnecessarily, raising the tail of the outboard motor in swells or lowering it for planing, camouflaging the boat near the coast, taking advantage of moonless nights, running close in to a fishing boat or big cargo ship in order to throw off the radar signal. And also evasive tactics: using the Phantom's short turning radius to keep the more powerful but less maneuverable turbocraft from boarding them, circling behind the pursuit boat, turning its bow or cutting across its wake, taking advantage of gasoline over the adversary's diesel. And so, run by run, she went from fear to euphoria, from victory to failure, and she learned, once again, what she already knew: that sometimes you win, sometimes you lose, and sometimes you call it a draw. She would throw bundles of cargo into the sea, with her pursuers' spotlight right on her, or offload them to fishing boats or black shadows that scurried out of the underbrush onto deserted beaches and waded waist-deep into the water, with the murmur of the waves as background noise.

On one occasion—the only one so far, and in the course of an operation with people you couldn't trust too much, anyway—she offloaded the cargo while Santiago looked on from the rear deck. He was standing in the darkness with an Uzi under his coat, not as a precaution should Customs or the Guardia Civil show up—that was against all the rules—but as a precaution against the people he was delivering the stuff to: some French guys with a bad reputation and worse manners. And then, that same dawn, on their way back to the Rock, the cargo offloaded, Teresa herself, with great relief, had thrown the Uzi into the sea.

Now she was far from feeling that sense of relief, despite the fact that they were hydroplaning empty, on their way back to Gibraltar. It was four-forty in the morning, and just two hours earlier they had loaded three hundred kilos of hashish resin on the Moroccan coast—enough time to travel the nine miles between Al Marsa and Cala Arenas and offload the cargo with no problems. But as the Spanish saying had it, until the tip of the tail goes by, it's still a bull. And to confirm that, a little before Punta Carnero, just after they entered the lighthouse's red zone and could see the lighted mass of the Rock on the other side of the Bay of Algeciras, Santiago, looking up, had muttered a curse. And an instant later, over the sound of the engine, Teresa heard a purring sound approaching from one side and then taking up a position on the stern, seconds before a blinding light suddenly lit up the boat.

"The bird," Santiago growled. The fucking bird. The helicopter's blades were raising a tornado of wind and spray around the Phantom when Santiago moved the trim-tab lever, shoved the throttle lever forward—the needle jumped from 2,500 to 4,000 rpms—and the speedboat took off, its nose high, hydroplaning, slapping lightly over the water. But no luck—the spotlight was still on them, moving from one side of the boat to the other and from bow to stern, its white curtain of light illuminating the spray raised by 250 horsepower of finely tuned engine. Bounced by the slaps of the hull against the water, stung by the spray, holding tight so she wouldn't fall overboard, Teresa did what she had to do: forget about the relative threat of the helicopter—it was flying, she calculated, about twelve to fifteen feet above the water, and like them, at about forty knots. She needed to worry about another threat that was no doubt close by, and certainly, because they were so close to land, more dangerous: the Customs Surveillance HJ that must be even now racing toward them at full speed, trying to cut them off or force the speedboat in toward the shore. Toward the rocks on the sandbar at La Cabrita, which was somewhere forward and to port.

She glued her face to the rubber cone of the Furuno, banging her forehead and nose each time the hull hit the water, and punched the buttons to reduce the range to a half-mile. *Dios, dios. In this business, if you're not in good with God, you're cooked,* she thought. The antenna sweep on the screen seemed to take forever, an eternity through which she held her breath. *Get us out of this, sweet God,* she prayed. She even remembered St. Malverde, that black night in Sinaloa. They were running without any cargo that might send them to prison, but the Customs people were hard, even if they wished you happy birthday in the bars in Campamento. At this hour, and on this course, they could use any pretext they felt like to seize the boat, or to ram it "accidentally" and sink it. The blinding glare of the spotlight fell on the screen, making it hard to see. She noticed that Santiago had revved the engine higher, despite the fact that with the sea raised by the wind out of the west, they were at the limit already. But the Gallego was not one to roll over and play dead, or to gift-wrap his boat for a fucking Customs seizure. So the speedboat gave a leap longer than the others—*Don't let the engine seize up,* she prayed silently, imagining the propeller whirling in space, out of the water—and when the hull hit the water again, Teresa, holding on the best she could, her face striking the radar cone, finally saw on the screen, among the countless little echoes of the wave swell, another green blip, a different kind—a long, sinister shape approaching rapidly from off the starboard stern, less than five hundred yards away.

"Five o'clock!" she cried, shaking Santiago's right shoulder. "Three cables!"

To make herself heard above the roar of the engine and the wind, she held her mouth against his ear. Santiago gave a futile look in that direction, lowering his eyes against the brightness of the spotlight from the helicopter, which was still right on their tail, and then he turned the radar screen toward him, to see for himself. The sinuous green line of the coast was drawn uncomfortably close with each sweep of the antenna—about three hundred yards to port. Teresa looked back. The lighthouse at Punta Carnero was still red. On this course, when they passed into the white zone there would be no way to avoid the sandbank at La Cabrita. Santiago must have been thinking the same thing, because at that very second he reduced the boat's speed and turned the wheel hard right, then accelerated again and made several zigzags, seaward, looking alternately at the radar screen and the helicopter's spotlight, which at every zig or zag seemed to shoot ahead, losing them momentarily but then fixing on them again, framing them in its light. Whether this was the guy in the blue shirt or another one, Teresa thought admiringly, he certainly had balls. *Why should I tell you no, if the answer's yes.* And he knew what he was doing. Not just anybody could fly a helicopter at night four yards above the water. The pilot must be as good as Güero was in his time. Or better. She'd like to shoot a fucking flare at him, if they had any flares aboard. Watch him go down in flames. *Whoof.*

Now the blip off the HJ was nearer, and closing fast. Running at full throttle over a flat sea, the speedboat was untouchable, but with swells it suffered, and the pursuers had the advantage. Teresa looked back and to starboard, using her hands to shield her eyes against the light from the helicopter, expecting to see the HJ at any second. She was still holding on as well as she could, ducking each time a splash of spray came over the windshield, and her kidneys hurt from the banging of the hull against the waves. Every now and again she looked up at Santiago's stubborn profile, his tense features dripping salt water, his wide eyes peering through the night. His hands gripped the Phantom's wheel tightly, steering the boat with short, skillful turns, getting the most out of the souped-up engine's extra 500 rpms, the inclination of the stern, and the flat keel that during some long leaps seemed to fly, as though the propeller were touching the water only intermittently, then other times slapped down hard, the hull creaking as if it were about to splinter.

"There it is!"

And there it was: a ghostly shadow, sometimes gray, sometimes blue and white, approaching in the field of light projected by the helicopter, throwing off a broad wake—its hull was dangerously close. It went into and out of the light like some enormous wall or monstrous cetacean on the surface of the water, and a spotlight was being trained on them now from the turbocraft as well, flashing blue as the police lights spun, like some malignant eye. Deafened by the roar of the engines, soaked by the spray, Teresa hung on where she could, not daring even to rub her eyes, which were burning from the salt water, for fear of being thrown out of the boat. She saw that Santiago had opened his mouth to yell something that she couldn't understand, and then she saw him ease back on the throttle and move his right hand to the trim-tab lever and the stern thruster. He turned the wheel sharply to starboard and pushed the throttle forward, hard and fast, the boat's bow now pointed straight at the lighthouse on Punta Carnero. The maneuver allowed them to evade the helicopter and the HJ, but Teresa's relief lasted only the brief seconds it took her to realize that they were headed straight for land between the red and white zones of the lighthouse, toward the four hundred yards of rocks and reefs at La Cabrita. *Don't screw this up,* she whispered. The turbocraft's spotlight was now trained on them from the rear, and the helicopter was practically on top of them again. And then, as Teresa, her hands clutching the bits on the side of the boat, was still calculating the pros and cons, she saw the lighthouse in front of them and above, too close, go from red to white. She didn't need the radar to know that they were less than a hundred yards from the rocks, and that the depth was lessening rapidly. *This is bad,* she told herself. *Either he backs off or we crash.* When she looked around, she saw the HJ's spotlight falling farther and farther back, as its crew gave the sandbar a wide berth. Santiago remained on the same course a few seconds longer, shot a look over his shoulder at the HJ, glanced at the depth finder and then ahead, where the distant lights of Gibraltar silhouetted the darker La Cabrita.

I hope he doesn't do it, Teresa thought fearfully. I hope he doesn't try to thread the channel through those rocks; he did it once, but it was in daylight, and we weren't going as fast as we are now.

Just then, Santiago let up off the gas again, turned hard right, and passing under the belly of the helicopter, whose pilot pulled up fast to miss the Phantom's radar antenna, shot not through the channel but over the outer point of the sandbar, with the black mass of La Cabrita so close that Teresa could smell the algae and hear the echo of the engine off the rocky walls of the cliff face.

And suddenly, her mouth still open and her eyes popping out of their sockets, she found herself on the other side of Punta Carnero: the sea much calmer than outside the bar, and the HJ a couple of cables away because of the arc it had had to make to slow down. The helicopter was about to glue itself to their stern again, but now it was little more than undesired company, no big deal, while Santiago revved the engine to the maximum, 6,300 rpms, and the Phantom crossed the Bay of Algeciras at fifty-five knots, planing over the flat sea toward the opening in the harbor at Gibraltar. Fucking incredible! Four miles in five minutes, with a slight maneuver to avoid an oil barge anchored halfway in. And when the HJ peeled away and abandoned the pursuit and the helicopter began to fall back and gain altitude, Teresa stood up in the middle of the speedboat and, still illuminated by the spotlight, lifted a triumphant single finger. *Adiós, cabróooon.*

6. I'm staking my life on it, I'm staking my luck on it

I located Óscar Lobato with a telephone call to the Cádiz newspaper. Teresa Mendoza, I said. I'm writing a book. We agreed to meet the next day at the Venta del Chato, an old restaurant on the beach at Cortadura.

I had just parked the car, with the ocean across the street, the city in the distance, sunny and white at the end of its sandy peninsula, when Lobato got out of a banged-up Ford full of old newspapers, a press card half visible on the dashboard. Before coming over to me he stood talking with the parking attendant and then gave him a pat on the back, for which the young man thanked him as profusely as if it had been a tip. Lobato was *simpático*, a talker, with an inexhaustible supply of anecdotes and information.

Fifteen minutes later, we were best friends, and I had broadened my knowledge: of the inn, an authentic smugglers' inn, with two hundred years of history; of the composition of the sauce the inn served with its

venison; of the name and usefulness of each and every one of the hun-
dred-year-old (at least) tools, instruments, and appliances decorating
the walls of the restaurant; and of *garum,* the sauce for fish that was the
favorite of the Romans when Cádiz was called Gades and tourists traveled in triremes. Before the second course I had also learned that we
were near the San Fernando Naval Observatory, through which the
Cádiz meridian passes, and that in 1812, Napoleon's troops laying siege
to the city—they didn't reach the land gate, Lobato pointed out—had
pitched one of their camps there.

"Did you see that movie *Lola la Piconera?*"

I said no, I hadn't, so he then narrated the story, from beginning to
end. Juanita Reina, Virgilio Teixeira, and Manuel Luna. Directed by
Luis Lucia in 1951. According to the legend, false of course, Lola the
Picador was shot by a frog firing squad on this very spot. National
heroine et cetera. And there was that song—*Long live happiness and
down with grief, Lola, Lolita, the Picador.* He looked at me as I put on
my interested-as-all-hell face, winked at me, refreshed his glass of
Yllera—we had just uncorked the second bottle—and with no transition whatsoever, started talking about Teresa Mendoza. Very willingly.

"That Mexicana. That Gallego. That hashish back and forth and up
and down, like fucking ring-around-the-rosie. Epic times," he sighed,
with a drop of nostalgia in my honor. "Dangerous times, too, of course.
Hard people. But there was none of the grudges and fuck-you-for-the-
fun-of-it there is nowadays."

He was still a reporter, he said. Like back then. A fucking infantry-
man reporter. But with honor. The truth was, he didn't know how to
do anything else. He liked his job, although it still paid the same ratshit
salary as ten years back. But thank goodness his wife brought home a
second check. And there were no kids to say, "Papi, I'm hungry!"

"That," he concluded, "gives you more *liberté, egalité,* and *frater-
nité.*"

He paused to return the greeting of some local politicos in dark suits
who were just sitting down at a nearby table—a low-level minister of
culture and another one of urban affairs, he whispered. "Never even
graduated from college." And then he went on with Teresa Mendoza
and the Gallego. He would run into them from time to time in La Línea
and Algeciras, her with her Indian-looking face, kind of pretty, really,
very dark-skinned . . .

". . . And those big eyes . . . vengeance in those eyes. She was not
what you'd call a knockout, she was a little thing, no bigger than this,
but when she fixed herself up she was good-looking. With good tits, by
the way. Not big, but . . ." Here Lobato brought his hands together and

extended his index fingers, like the horns of a bull. "A little tacky in the wardrobe department, same style as the molls of the other hashish and tobacco runners: skintight pants, T-shirts, high heels, all that. Good hair, good makeup, good nails, but the rest . . . slutty, you know? But she didn't mix much with the other girls. She had just enough class, although it was hard to say why, exactly. Maybe the way she talked, because she spoke softly, with an accent that was sweet and cultured. With those nice archaisms that Mexicans use. When she pulled her hair back into a bun, with a part down the middle, you could see the class even clearer. Like Sara Montiel in *Veracruz*. Twenty-something, probably."

It had struck Lobato that she never wore gold, only silver. Long dangling earrings, bracelets. All silver, and not much of it. Sometimes she would wear seven bangles on one arm—a *semanario,* he thought she called it. *Cling, cling.* He remembered her by that clinkling.

"In the street she started earning respect—little by little at first, you know. First, because the Gallego had a reputation, people respected him. And second, because she was the only one of those girls that went out shoulder to shoulder with her man. Early on, people thought it was a joke—Whoa, look at that, you know. Even the Customs agents and the Guardia Civil had their little laugh. But when word got out that she had the same balls as any man, things changed."

I asked him why Santiago Fisterra had such a good reputation, and Lobato made a circle with his index finger and thumb, as though indicating he was okay. "He was straight with people. Quiet, dependable. Very much the Gallego, in the good sense of the word. I mean, he wasn't one of those callous, dangerous *cabrones,* or one of those guys you could never depend on, or some fucking ghost—appearing out of nowhere and vanishing just as fast—dabbling in hashish running. He was discreet, never made trouble. Straight-shooting. Not one of these fucking wise guys, and no fooling around. *Not* an amateur. He went about his business like he was working in a bank or an insurance office or something. The other guys, the guys from Gibraltar, would tell you tomorrow at three, and tomorrow at three they'd be screwing their girlfriend or off drinking in some bar, and you'd be leaning against a lamppost with spiderwebs up and down your back, looking at your watch. But if the Gallego told you, Tomorrow I'll be there, that was it. He'd be out there, with his sidekick, even if there were fifteen-foot waves. A man of his word. A professional. Which was not always a good thing, because he made certain other . . . entrepreneurs look bad.

"His dream was to save enough money to go into something else. And that may have been why he and Teresa got on so well. They looked like they were in love, of course. Holding hands, hugging each other, you know. Standard stuff. But there was something about her that wouldn't allow her to be completely controlled. I don't know if I'm explaining myself. Something that forced you to ask yourself whether she was sincere—and I'm not talking about hypocrisy or anything like that. I'd put my hand in the fire and swear she was an honest girl. . . . I'm talking about something else. I'd say that Santiago loved her more than she loved him. *Capisce?* . . . because Teresa was always kind of distant. She'd smile, she was discreet and a good woman, and I figure they fucked like rabbits. But there was that something, you know? . . . Sometimes, if you looked carefully—and looking carefully is my job, my friend—there was something in the way she looked at all of us, even at Santiago, that implied that she wasn't in it for the whole ride. Like she had some bread and ham wrapped in wax paper, and a bag with a few clothes and a train ticket ready somewhere up in the closet. You'd see her laugh, drink her tequila—she loved tequila, of course— kiss her man, and all of a sudden there'd be something in her eyes, a strange expression . . . like she was thinking, This can't last."

This can't last, she thought. They had made love almost all afternoon, like there was no tomorrow, and now they were walking under a medieval arch in the old city walls of Tarifa. Won from the Moors—Teresa read on a tile set into the archway—during the reign of King Sancho IV the Brave, September 21, 1292.

"An appointment, work," Santiago had said. "Half an hour by car. We can take advantage of the trip to have a drink, take a walk through the town. And then have pork ribs at Juan Luis."

So there they were, with the sunset almost gray from the salt spray raised by the wind blowing in from the east, across from the beach at Los Lances, on the Atlantic, with the Mediterranean on the other side and Africa hidden in the haze that the setting sun was slowly darkening in the east. Slowly—the way they were walking, their arms about each other's waist, wandering through the narrow whitewashed streets of the town where the wind always blew, from whatever direction, almost every day of the year. That afternoon it was blowing hard, and before walking into the town proper they had sat in the Cherokee and watched the waves break on the rocks along the edge of the parking lot at the foot of the old wall, alongside the Caleta, the shattered water spattering the windshield. And sitting there, comfortable, happy, listening to music from the radio, her head resting on Santiago's shoulder, Teresa saw, in the distance, a sailboat sail out of the harbor, its three

masts looking like something out of an old movie. It was sailing slowly
out toward the Atlantic, its bow plunging into the high waves as the
strongest gusts overtook it, the boat blurred in the gray curtain of wind
and spray like some ghost ship from another time, one that had been
sailing for centuries. Then they'd gotten out of the car and walked
down the most protected streets toward the center of Tarifa, looking
into shop windows. The summer season was over, but the terrace under the awning and the interior of Café Central were still full of sun-
tanned, athletic-looking foreigners. Lots of blond, blue-eyed types, lots
of gold earrings, lots of T-shirts with company logos and city names.
Windsurfers, Santiago had said the first time they were there. The latest craze. People will do the strangest things.

"I wonder if you'll make a mistake someday and tell me you love
me."

She turned to look at him when she heard his words. He was not upset with her, or in a bad mood. It was not even a reproach. "I love you,
cabrón."

"Of course you do." He was always making this joke. In his easygoing way, watching her, inciting her to talk, provoking her.

"You'd think it cost you money," he would say. "You're so cool. . . .
You've got my ego, or whatever you call it, beat to a pulp." And then
Teresa would hold him, kiss his eyes, say I love you, I love you, I love
you, over and over. *Pinche Gallego piece of shit.* And he would laugh as
though it didn't matter to him, as though it were nothing but a simple
pretext for conversation, a joke, and she were the one that should be re-
proaching him. Stop, stop. Stop! And in a minute they would stop
laughing and stand facing each other, and Teresa would feel powerless
at all the things that she couldn't do, while the male eyes would look at
her fixedly, resignedly, as if crying a little inside, silently, like some kid
running after the older boys that were leaving him behind. A dry, unspoken grief that made her feel so tender, and then she would be almost sure that maybe she did really, actually love this man. And each
time this happened, Teresa would repress the impulse to raise her hand
and caress Santiago's face in some way hard to know, explain, feel, as if
she owed him something and could never repay him.

"What are you thinking about?"

"Nothing."

I wish this would never end. I wish this existence somewhere between life and death, suspended above some strange abyss, might go on
until one day I could say words that are true again. I wish his skin and
his hands and his eyes and his mouth could erase my memory, and I
could be born again, or die once and for all, so that I could say old

words as though they were new, as though they didn't sound to me like
betrayal or a lie. I hope I have—I wish I had, we had—enough time for
that.

They never talked about Güero Dávila. Santiago was not one of
those men that can talk about other men, nor was she one of those
women that does. Sometimes, when he lay breathing quietly beside her
in the darkness, very close, Teresa could almost hear the questions.
That still happened, but for a long time the questions were just habit,
the routine whisper of silences. In the beginning, during those first
days when men, even the ones just passing through, try to make obscure—inexorable—demands that go beyond mere physical intimacy,
Santiago asked some of those questions aloud. In his own way, of
course. Not particularly explicit, or not explicit at all. He circled like a
coyote, attracted by the fire but not daring to come in. He had heard
things. Friends of friends that had friends. And, well . . .

She'd had a man, she summarized one day, tired of seeing him slink-
ing around the same old topic when the unanswerable questions left
unbearable silences.

"I had a man that was good-looking and brave and stupid," she said.
"A great guy. A *pinche cabrón* like you—like all of you, but this one in
particular got me when I was just a kid, without a world, and in the end
he screwed me good, and I had to run because of him, and you can see
how far I had to run if I came all the way to fucking Spain or whatever
the fuck this place is. But it's no business of yours if I had a man or not,
because this man I'm talking about is dead—very, very dead. He got
taken out, and he died, the way we all die, but early. And what that man
was or was not in my life is my business, not yours."

And after all that, one night when they were screwing, clutching
each other for dear life, and Teresa's mind was deliciously blank,
stripped of memory or future—nothing but dense, thick present, a
warm intensity to which she abandoned herself without remorse—she
opened her eyes and saw that Santiago had stopped and was looking at
her very close in the semidarkness, and she also saw that he was moving his lips, and when she finally came back to where they were and
paid attention to what he was saying, the first thing she could think
was, Stupid Gallego, stupid, stupid, stupid, like all men, with those
questions at the absolutely worst fucking time—him or me, him better, me better, love me, loved him. As though it were that easy, just sum
everything up that way, life in black and white, good and bad, one better than the other, one worse. And she felt a dryness in her mouth and
in her soul and between her legs, a new anger bursting inside, not because he was asking questions again but because he was elementary,

and awkward, and was seeking confirmation for things that had nothing to do with him, and it wasn't even jealousy, but habit, self-image,
some absurd stupid male thing, the hang-ups of a macho that takes the
woman out of the herd and refuses to allow her any life but the life that
he plants in her womb. Which was why she wanted to insult him, and
hurt him, and she shoved him away as she spat out Yes, the truth, of
course—to see what he would think, this idiotic Gallego. What did he
think—that life started with him and his fucking prick?

"I'm with you because I've got no better place to go, or because I
learned that I don't know how to live alone, without a man—which
could be one man or another, no big deal—and I couldn't care less why
he chose me or I chose the first one that came along." And getting up,
naked, still not free of him, she slapped him, hard, a slap that made
Santiago turn his face. And she tried to hit him again, but this time it
was him that hit her, kneeling above her, returning the slap with a violence that was calm, dry, without anger—she was surprised, perhaps—
and then he stood there above her, still on his knees, unmoving, while
she cried and cried, tears that sprang not from her eyes but from her
chest and throat, as she lay still, on her back, insulting him—*Pinche
gallego cabrón de la chingada, pendejo, hijo de puta, hijo de tu pinche
madre, cabrón, cabrón, cabrón.* Then he tumbled down beside her and
lay there awhile not saying anything, not touching her, ashamed and
confused, while she lay on her back, also not moving but growing
calmer little by little, until she felt her tears drying on her face. And that
was all, and it was the only time. Neither one ever again raised a hand
against the other. Nor were there, ever again, any questions.

Four hundred kilos," said Cañabota in a half-whisper. "First-quality
oil, seven times purer than the normal stuff. The cream of the
crop."

He had a gin and tonic in one hand and an English cigarette with a
gold filter in the other, and he alternated puffs at the cigarette and sips
at his drink. He was short and fat, and his head was shaved, and he
sweated all the time, to the point that his shirts were always wet under
the arms and at the collar, where there gleamed an inevitable gold
chain. Maybe, thought Teresa, it was his job that made him sweat that
way. Because Cañabota—she had no idea if that was his surname or
some kind of nickname—was what in professional slang was called *un
hombre de confianza,* a man of trust: a local agent, a go-between, an intermediary between two groups of drug traffickers. Specializing in logistics, in organizing the shipment of hashish from Morocco and en-

suring its delivery. That included hiring runners like Santiago, and also seeing to the complicity of certain local authorities. The sergeant of the Guardia Civil—thin, fiftyish, dressed in civilian clothes—who accompanied him that afternoon was one of the many instruments that had to be played to make the music. Teresa knew him from other times, and she knew that he was posted somewhere around Estepona. There was a fifth person in the group: a Gibraltar attorney named Eddie Alvarez, a small man with thin, kinky hair, very thick glasses, and nervous hands. He had a modest law office located down by the harbor in the British colony, with ten or fifteen front operations with their signs on the door. He was in charge of controlling the money that Santiago was paid in Gibraltar after each run.

"This time we have to send notaries," Cañabota added.

"No way." Santiago shook his head, very calmly. "Too many people on board. What I've got is a Phantom, not a fucking ferryboat."

Notaries were witnesses that drug traffickers put on speedboats to ensure that everything went according to plan: one for the providers, who were usually Moroccan, and another for the buyers. Cañabota didn't seem to like this new wrinkle.

"She"—he tilted his head toward Teresa—"can stay on land."

Santiago didn't take his eyes off the *hombre de confianza* as he shook his head. "I don't see why she should. She's my crew."

Cañabota and the guardsman turned to Eddie Alvarez disapprovingly, as though they blamed him for the refusal. But the lawyer shrugged. It's useless, his gesture said. I know the story, and besides, I'm just here to watch. What the fuck do I care.

Teresa ran her finger over the condensation on the outside of her glass. She had never liked going to these meetings, but Santiago always insisted. "You take the same risks I do," he would tell her. "You have a right to know what goes down and how it goes down. Don't talk if you don't want to, but it can't hurt you to pay attention. And if these guys don't like you being there, fuck 'em. Fuck all of 'em. I mean, their women are playing with themselves at home, watching TV, they're not risking their cunts against the Moros five or six times a month."

"Usual payment?" Eddie Alvarez asked, looking out for number one.

Payment would be made the day after the delivery, Cañabota confirmed. One-third direct to a BBV account in Gibraltar—the Spanish banks in the colony were branches not of the main bank in Madrid, but rather the bank in London, and that made for delightful financial blindspots—and two-thirds in hand. The two-thirds in *dinero B,* as the Spaniards called money that was never reported on tax forms. Although they'd need some fake invoices for the bank. The usual red tape.

"Make the arrangements with her," Santiago said. And he indicated Teresa.

Cañabota and the guardsman exchanged an uncomfortable glance. What a fucking thing, their silence said. Bringing a chick into this. Lately, Teresa had been increasingly involved in the bookkeeping side of the operation. That included control of expenses, doing the books, telephone calls in code, and periodic visits to Eddie Alvarez. And also dealing with a corporation headquartered in the lawyer's office, the bank account in Gibraltar, and the justifiable money invested in low-risk ventures—something without too many complications, because Santiago was not used to having his life exposed too much to banks. He'd opted for what the lawyer called a minimal infrastructure. A conservative portfolio, he also called it, when he was wearing a tie and decided to get technical. Until recently, and despite his mistrustful nature, Santiago had depended almost blindly on Eddie Alvarez, who charged him a commission even for simple monthly payments when he invested legal money. Teresa had changed that, suggesting that everything be used for safer and more profitable investments, and even that the lawyer make Santiago a partner in a bar on Main Street, to launder part of their income. She didn't know anything about banks or finance, but her experience as a money changer on Calle Juárez in Culiacán had given her some very clear ideas. So gradually she took over the money end of the business, putting papers in order, finding out what could be done with the money instead of immobilizing it in some hiding place or checking account. Skeptical at first, Santiago finally had to yield to the evidence: she had a good head for numbers, and was able to foresee possibilities that never entered his mind. Above all, she had incredible common sense. Unlike him—the son of the Galician fisherman was one of those people who keep their money in plastic bags in the back of the closet—Teresa always saw the possibility that two and two made five. So despite Eddie Alvarez' initial reticence, Santiago put it to him clearly: She had a say in the money.

"Cunt hair ties tighter knots than hemp rope," was the lawyer's verdict when he got Santiago alone. "I hope you don't wind up making her co-owner of all your holdings, too: Gallego-Aztec Transport, Inc., or whatever. I've seen stranger things. Because women . . ." He shook his head as his voice trailed off. ". . . And these quiet little mousy types, worse yet. You start out screwing them, then you get them to sign papers, then you put everything in their name, and in the end they run off and leave you without a penny."

"That," replied Santiago, "is my business. Read my lips: Mine. . . . And by the way, fuck yourself."

He said this with an expression that made the lawyer almost drop his glasses in his drink. After that he very meekly drank down his whisky—they were on the terrace of the Rock Hotel, with the Bay of Algeciras spread out below them—and never again expressed any reservations about the matter. *I hope you learn your lesson, you pendejo*, the lawyer thought to himself, however. *Or that that slut two-times you like they all wind up doing.* But he didn't say it.

Now Cañabota and the Guardia Civil sergeant were looking at Teresa, the atmosphere tense, and it was clear that the same thoughts were going through their minds. *Skirts stay home and watch TV,* their silence said. Uncomfortable, Teresa averted her eyes. "Trujillo Fabrics," read the glazed-tile sign on the building across the street. "Notions." It was not pleasant, being studied that way. But it occurred to her that the way they were looking at her was an insult to Santiago, too, and at that she turned her face, now angry, toward them and locked unblinkingly on their gaze. *You don't know who you're fucking with,* she seemed to be telling them.

"Well, when all is said and done," the lawyer was saying—he never missed a thing—"she's in pretty deep already."

"Notaries are good for what they're good for," said Cañabota, still looking at Teresa. "And both sides want guarantees."

"I'm the guarantee," Santiago shot back. "They know me."

"This shipment is important."

"As far as I'm concerned, they all are, so long as somebody's paying. And I'm not in the habit of having people tell me how to do my job."

"Rules are rules."

"Cut the crap. This is a free market, I'm a free agent, and I have my own rules."

Eddie Alvarez shook his head in discouragement. Useless to argue, he appeared to be saying, when there's tits involved. Just wasting your time.

"The boys over in Gibraltar don't make such a fuss about it, Santiago," Cañabota insisted. "Parrondi, Victorio . . . They take on notaries and anything else that's asked of them."

Santiago took a drink of his beer, staring over the rim of the glass at Cañabota. That fat fuck has been in the business ten years, he had once remarked to Teresa. And never been in jail. Makes me resent him, you know?

"You don't trust the Gibraltar boys as much as me."

"That's what you say."

"So do the thing with them and stop busting my balls."

The guardsman was watching Teresa, with an unpleasant smile on his face. He was badly shaven, and a few white hairs bristled on his chin and under his nose. He wore his clothes awkwardly, like a man who's more used to a uniform, a man whose plainclothes cover is never quite comfortable. I know your type, thought Teresa. I've seen you a thousand times in Sinaloa, in Melilla, everywhere. You're always the same. "Let me see your documents," et cetera. "And tell me how we can get you out of this problem." Oh, the cynicism of it. The excuse that you can't quite make it on your salary, with all your expenses, till the end of the month. Shipments of drugs intercepted and half the seizure reported, fines you collect but never put in your reports, free drinks, hookers, made men. And those official investigations that never get to the bottom of anything, everybody covering for everybody else, live and let live, because everybody has a stash of something in the closet or a dead man buried under the floor. The same thing here as over there, except that the Spaniards aren't to blame for what goes on over there, because they left Mexico two hundred years ago, so . . . Less brazen about things here, of course, more suave. Europe and all that. Teresa looked across the street. That "less brazen" applied only sometimes. The salary of a sergeant in the Guardia Civil, or a cop, or a Spanish Customs officer wasn't enough to pay for a brand-new Mercedes like the one this asshole had parked, brazenly, in front of the Café Central. And he probably—no, surely—went to work in that same car, to his fucking police station, and nobody was surprised, and all of them, chiefs included, pretended they didn't see a thing. Yeah. Live and let live.

The discussion—almost an argument—went on in lowered voices, while the waitress came and went with more beers and gin and tonics. Despite Santiago's firmness about the notaries, Cañabota wasn't giving in just yet. "If they jump you and you have to throw the shipment overboard," he said, "let's see how you justify that without witnesses. X number of kilos overboard and you coming back without a scratch. Plus this time they're Italians, and they're bad boys—trust me, I deal with these guys. Mafiosi cabroni. Bottom line, a notary is a guarantee for you as well as for them. For everybody. So just this once, leave the little lady on land and don't be so fucking stubborn. Stop fucking around and don't be so fucking stubborn and you don't get fucked."

"If they jump me and I throw off the bundles," Santiago replied, "everybody knows that it's because I had to. . . . . It's my word. And anybody that hires me knows that."

"Jesus fucking Christ. I'm never going to convince you?"

"No. No, you're not."

Cañabota looked at Eddie Alvarez and passed his hand over his shaved head, declaring himself beaten. Then he lit another of those cigarettes with the weird filters. And if you ask me, thought Teresa, this one bats left-handed. His shirt was sopping wet, and a rivulet of sweat ran down one side of his nose, to his upper lip. Teresa still said nothing, her eyes fixed on her own left hand on the table. Long red nails, seven bangles of Mexican silver, a thin silver cigarette lighter, a gift from Santiago for her birthday. With all her heart she wanted this conversation over. Wanted to get out of there, kiss her man, lick his lips, dig her red nails into his kidneys. Forget about all this for a while. All of *them.*

"One day something bad is going to happen to you," the guardsman muttered.

They were the first words he had spoken, and he spoke them directly to Santiago. He stared at him deliberately, as though engraving his features in his memory. A gaze that promised other conversations in private, in the privacy of a jail cell, say, where no one would be surprised to hear quite a few screams.

"Well, you make sure it's not you that makes it happen."

They studied each other a few seconds longer, wordlessly, and now it was Santiago's expression that promised things. For example, that there might be jail cells where a man might be beaten to death, but there were also dark alleys and parking lots where a corrupt Civil Guardsman might find six inches of knife rammed up his crotch, right about where the femoral runs. And five quarts of blood spurting out before he knew what was happening. And that the man you push past going up the stairs, you might trip over real bad on the way down. Especially if he's a Galician—and hard as you try, you never really know whether you're on the way up or on the way down.

"Okay, then, that's settled." Cañabota clapped his hands together softly in a gesture of reconciliation. "Your fucking rules. Let's not quibble . . . we're all in this together, right?"

"All of us," added Eddie Alvarez, who was cleaning his glasses with a Kleenex.

Cañabota leaned toward Santiago. Notaries or not, business was business. "Four hundred kilos of oil in twenty kits of twenty," he said, tracing out imaginary numbers and drawings on the table. "Delivered Tuesday night, dark of the moon . . . You know the place—Punta Castor, on the beach near the rotunda, right at the end of the Estepona loop, where the highway to Málaga begins. They'll be waiting for you at one sharp."

Santiago thought about it for a second. He looked at the table as though Cañabota had actually drawn the route there.

"Seems a little far to me, if I have to go down to Al Marsa or Punta Cires for the shipment and then deliver it so early . . . From Gibraltar to Estepona it's forty kilometers as the crow flies. I'll have to load while it's still light, and it's a long return."

"There's no problem." Cañabota looked around at the others, encouraging them to confirm his words. "We'll put a monkey up on the Rock with binoculars and a walkie-talkie to watch for HJs and the bird. There's an English lieutenant up there that we've got eating out of our hand, plus he's fucking a stripper that works for us in a titty club in La Línea. . . . As for the kits, no problem there, either. They'll pass them over to you from a fishing boat, five miles east of the Ceuta lighthouse just after dark. The *Julio Verdú,* from Barbate. Channel 44 on the marine band: you say 'Mario' two times, and they'll guide you in. At eleven you come alongside the fishing boat and load up, then head north hugging the coast, nice and easy, no hurry, and you unload at one. At two, the kids are in bed and you're in your warm little love nest."

"That easy," said Eddie Alvarez.

"Yep." Cañabota was looking at Santiago, and the sweat ran down his nose again. "That easy."

She woke before dawn, and Santiago wasn't there. She lay for a while between the wrinkled sheets. September was on the way out, but the temperature was the same as on the summer nights that were behind them. A humid heat like the heat in Culiacán, softened just at dawn by the breeze through the open windows: an offshore breeze that came down the river in the early morning, just before sunrise. She got up, naked—she always slept naked with Santiago, as she had with Güero Dávila—and when she stood in front of the window she felt the coolness of the breeze. The bay was a black semicircle dotted with lights: the boats anchored off Gibraltar, with Algeciras on one side and the Rock on the other, and nearer in, at the end of the beach the house sat on, the towers of the refinery reflected in the motionless water close to the shore. It was all very lovely, and still, and the sun had not yet begun to turn the horizon blue and pink, so she picked up the pack of Bisontes on the night table and lit one as she leaned on the windowsill. She remained there awhile, doing nothing, just smoking and looking at the bay while the breeze cooled her skin and her memories. The time that had passed since Melilla. Dris Larbi's parties. Colonel Abdelkader Chaib's smile when she laid the thing out for him. A friend would like to do some business, et cetera. And you will be a part of it? the Moroccan had asked—or said—in his friendly voice, the first time. I make my own deals, she replied, and the man's smile intensified. An intelligent type, the colonel. Cool and correct. Nothing, or almost nothing, had happened with respect to the personal margins and limits set by Teresa.

But that had nothing to do with anything. Santiago hadn't asked her to go, nor did he forbid it. He, like all of them, was predictable in his intentions, in his awkwardness, in his dreams. He was also going to take her with him to Galicia, he said. When all this was over, they'd go to O Grove. It's not as cold as you think, and the people don't say much. Like you. Like me. There'll be a house you can see the ocean from, and a roof you can hear the rain and wind on, and a fishing skiff tied up on the shore, you'll see. With your name on the bow. And our kids will play among the mussel barges with radio-controlled model speedboats.

By the time she put out the cigarette, Santiago was still not back. He wasn't in the bathroom, so Teresa pulled the sheets off the bed—her fucking period had started during the night—put on a T-shirt, and crossed the darkened living room toward the sliding doors that opened onto the beach. She saw a light, and she stopped, still inside the house, to look out. *Híjole.* Santiago was sitting on the porch, in shorts, his torso naked, working on one of his model boats. A gooseneck lamp on the table illuminated the skillful hands that sanded and fit the wood pieces before gluing them. He was building an antique sailboat. Teresa thought it was beautiful: the hull formed by strips of different-colored wood made even more striking by the varnish, all perfectly curved—he wet them and curled them with a soldering iron—and tin nails; the deck like the real thing; and a miniature wheel, built stick by tiny stick, now positioned very near the stern, alongside a small hatch with a door and everything. Whenever Santiago saw a photograph or drawing of an old boat in a magazine, he would cut it out carefully and put it in a thick file, which was where he got ideas for his models, all perfect down to the last detail. From the living room, very quietly, so he wouldn't know she was there, she watched him—his profile as he leaned over the pieces, the way he picked them up to study them closely, in search of imperfections, before applying a drop of glue and setting them in place. So neat—so wonderful, she meant. It seemed impossible that those hands Teresa knew so well—hard, rough, with nails always stained with grease—possessed that remarkable dexterity. Working with your hands, she had heard him say once, makes you a better man. It gives you back things you've lost or you're about to lose. Santiago was not much of a talker, or one to make fine-sounding phrases, and he had not much more culture than even she did. But he had common sense, and since he was almost always so quiet, he looked and learned and had time to turn ideas over in his head.

She felt a deep tenderness for him as she watched from the dark living room. He seemed both a child busy playing with a toy and a man loyal to his dreams. There was something in those wooden models that Teresa didn't fully understand, but that she sensed was close to profundity, the hidden keys to the silences and ways of life of the man whose woman she now was. Sometimes she would see Santiago stop, sit motionless, not opening his mouth, looking at one of those models that he had invested weeks or even months of work on, and that were now everywhere—eight in the house, or nine, counting the one he was working on—in the living room, the hall, the bedroom. Studying them with a strange look on his face. It gave the impression that working on them for so long was the equivalent of having sailed on them in imaginary times, on imaginary seas, and that now he found in their small painted and varnished hulls, under their miniature sails and lines, echoes of storms, boardings, desert islands, long journeys he had experienced in his mind as those little ships took form. All human beings dream, Teresa concluded. But not in the same way. Some go out to risk their necks on the ocean in a Phantom, or in the sky in a Cessna. Others build models as compensation. Others just dream, period. And some build models, risk their necks, *and* dream. All at once.

As she was about to step out onto the porch she heard the roosters crowing in the yards down in Palmones, and suddenly she was cold. Since Melilla, the crowing of roosters had been linked in her memory with the words "sunrise" and "solitude." A band of brightness lay low in the east, silhouetting the towers and smokestacks of the refinery, and that part of the view was turning from black to gray, the same color as the water along the shoreline. Soon it will be day, she told herself. And the gray of my grimy sunrises will be illuminated first with golds and reds and then with blue, and sunlight will spread across the beach and the bay, and I will once more be safe, until tomorrow's dawn.

Those were her half-thoughts when she saw Santiago raise his head to the lightening sky, like a hunting dog sniffing at the air, and then sit there absorbed, his work suspended, for a long time. Finally he stood up, stretching his arms to wake himself a bit, turned off the light, and removed his shorts, stretched his shoulders and arms, tensed his muscles as though he were about to embrace the whole bay, and walked down to the shore, wading out into water that the breeze made hardly a ripple on—water so still that the concentric circles in it could be seen from far away. He toppled forward and waded out slowly, to where the water was too deep to stand in, and then he turned and saw Teresa, who had pulled off her T-shirt as she stepped off the porch and was now wading out into the water, because it was much colder back there, alone in the house or on the sand that the sunrise had turned steely gray. And so they met, the water up to their chests, and her naked, goosebump-covered skin grew warm at its contact with the man, and when she felt his hard member press first against her thighs and then her belly, she opened her legs, holding it between them while she kissed his mouth, felt his salty tongue, and, half weightless, put her legs around his hips as he entered her, deeply, and emptied himself inside her slowly, unhurriedly, as Teresa stroked his wet hair and the bay grew lighter around them and the whitewashed houses of the shore turned gold in the morning light and a few early-rising seagulls flew in circles above them, cawing, as they came down from the marshes. And then it struck her that life was sometimes so beautiful that it didn't seem like life at all.

It was Óscar Lobato who introduced me to the helicopter pilot. The three of us met on the terrace of the Hotel Guadacorte, very close to the place where Teresa Mendoza and Santiago Fisterra had lived. There were a couple of first communions being celebrated in the banquet rooms, and the lawn was full of well-dressed children chasing each other under the oaks and pines.

"Javier Collado," the reporter said. "Helicopter pilot for Customs. Born hunter. From Cáceres. Don't offer him a cigarette or alcohol, because he doesn't smoke and all he drinks is orange juice. He's been at this for fifteen years and he knows the Strait like the palm of his hand. Serious, but a good guy. And when he's up there, as heartless as the mother that bore him. He does things with that whirlygig that I've never seen anybody else do in my whole goddamn life."

The pilot laughed. "Don't listen to him," he said. "He exaggerates." Then he ordered a lemon slush. He was tanned, good-looking, forty-something, thin but broad-shouldered, a little reserved—introverted, I wanted to say. "Exaggerates like hell." He seemed uncomfortable at Lobato's praise. At first, when I made an official request through Customs headquarters in Madrid, he had refused to talk to me. "I don't discuss

my work," was his reply. But the veteran reporter was a friend of his—
I asked myself whether there was a man, woman, child, or stray dog in
the province of Cádiz that Lobato didn't know—and he offered to put
a word in. "I'll bring him around," Lobato had said. And there we were.

As for the pilot, I'd made inquiries, so I knew that Javier Collado was
a legend in his world—one of those guys who could walk into a bar full
of smugglers and they'd elbow each other, mutter, "Jesus fuck, look
who's here," under their breath with a mixture of resentment and respect. The modus operandi of smugglers had changed some over the
last few years, but he was still flying six nights a week, on the prowl for
hashish like some big-eyed owl after mice. A professional—that word
made me think that sometimes it all depends on which side of the
fence, or the law, fate has put you on.

"Eleven thousand hours of flight time in the Strait," Lobato said.
"Chasing bad guys. Including, of course, your Teresa and her Gallego.
In illo tempore."

And so we talked about that. Or to be more precise, about the night
that *Argos,* the Customs BO-105, was flying at surveillance speed over
a reasonably flat sea, scanning the Strait with its radar. A hundred and
ten knots. Pilot, copilot, observer. Routine flight. They'd taken off from
Algeciras an hour earlier, and after patrolling a sector off the Moroccan
coast known in Customs slang as the Econo-Mat—the beaches between Ceuta and Punta Cires—they were now flying without lights
toward the northeast, far off the coast but following the Spanish shoreline. There were warships, Collado remarked, NATO maneuvers west
of the Strait. So the patrol that night centered on the eastern side,
watching for a target to pass off to the turbocraft, which was also running without lights, fifteen hundred feet below. A night of hunting like
any other.

"We were five miles south of Marbella when the radar picked up a
couple of blips down below, without lights," Collado said. "One lying
motionless and the other headed for land. . . . So we gave their position
to the HJ and started to drop down on the one that was moving."

"Where was it going?" I asked.

"It was headed toward Punta Castor, near Estepona," Collado said,
turning to look east, beyond the trees that hid Gibraltar, as though he
could see it from there. "A good place to beach, because the Málaga
highway passes by there. No rocks, and you can put the bow right up
on the sand. . . . With guys waiting for you on the beach, you can unload in three minutes."

"You said there were two blips."

"Yeah. The other one was sitting farther out, about fifteen hundred yards offshore. Like it was waiting. But the one that was moving was almost to the beach, so we decided to go for it first. The infrared was giving us a wide blast every time it hit the water. . . . " When he saw the confused look on my face, Collado laid his hand on the table, then raised and lowered it to imitate the movement of a speedboat. "A wide splash indicates that the boat is loaded. If they're not loaded, they hit easier, so the spray doesn't spread out so wide—all that hits the water is the tail of the engine. . . . So anyway, we went for that one."

I saw that he was showing his teeth, the way a predator draws back its lips and shows its fangs when there's prey in sight. *This guy,* I thought, *is enjoying this—he gets off remembering that night.* Suddenly, somehow, he was different, transformed. "Just leave it to me," Lobato had said. "He's okay, and if you trust him, he relaxes."

"Punta Castor," Collado went on, "was a regular drop-off point. Back then the smugglers didn't have GPS, so they steered by sightlines. The spot was easy to hit because you left Ceuta on a course of seventy or ninety, and when you lost sight of the lighthouse light you just turned north-northwest, sailing by the glow of La Línea, which lies abeam—straight out perpendicular. . . . Out front you'll immediately spot the lights of Estepona and Marbella, but there's no way to get confused, because you see the Estepona lighthouse first. Pushing it, you're on the beach in an hour.

"Ideally, you catch 'em in the act, along with the accomplices waiting for them onshore. . . . I mean, when they're right on the beach. Because before that, they'll throw the bales overboard and then run like hell."

"Run like hell," Lobato echoed, nodding—he had ridden along on several of these pursuits.

"Yeah. And it's as dangerous for them as it is for us." Now Collado was smiling a little, and this accentuated the air of hunter about him—the danger seemed to spice up the chase for him. "That's the way it was back then, and that's the way it still is."

He enjoys this, I decided. This *cabrón* enjoys his work. That's why he's spent the last fifteen years going out on night hunts, and has those eleven thousand hours Lobato was talking about. There's really not much difference between the hunter and the hunted, after all. Nobody jumps into a Phantom just for the money, and nobody hunts it down just out of a sense of duty.

That night, Collado went on, the Customs chopper dropped down slow and easy, heading for the blip closest to the coastline. The HJ— Chema Beceiro, the skipper, was an efficient guy—was closing in on it at fifty knots, and would be there in about five minutes. The chopper descended to five hundred feet. It was getting set to maneuver over the beach, to drop the copilot and observer if it came to that, when all of a sudden, lights came on down below. There were vehicles illuminating the beach, and they could see the Phantom for a second right along the shoreline, black as a shadow, before it cut hard to port and took off like lightning, leaving a cloud of white spray. So Collado put the chopper right on his tail, turned on the spotlight, and took off after him, three feet off the surface of the water.

"Did you bring the picture?" Óscar Lobato asked Collado.

"What picture?" I asked.

Lobato didn't answer; he was looking at Collado tauntingly. The pilot was playing with his glass of lemon slush, twirling it in half-circles, as though he hadn't quite made up his mind.

"Come on," Lobato insisted, "it was ten years ago."

Collado still hesitated. Then he laid a brown envelope on the table.

"Sometimes," he explained, gesturing toward the envelope, "we photograph the people in the speedboats during the pursuits, so we can identify them later. . . . It's not for the police or the press—just for our files. And it's not always easy, with the spotlight swinging back and forth and up and down, and the water and all that. Sometimes the shots come out and sometimes they don't."

"This one came out," Lobato said, laughing. "Go on, show it to him."

Collado took the photograph out of the envelope and put it on the table, and when I saw it my mouth went dry. Eighteen by twenty-four, black-and-white, and the quality not perfect: very grainy, and a little out of focus. But the scene was clear enough, given that the shot had been taken from a helicopter flying three feet above the water at fifty knots, in the midst of the cloud of spray raised by a speedboat going full-out—a helicopter skid in the foreground, darkness all around it, white spots and splatters multiplying the flash. And through all that you could see the central part of the Phantom from port, and in it the image of a dark-skinned man, his face dripping water, looking out into the darkness over his bow, leaning over the wheel. Behind him, kneeling on the deck of the speedboat, her hands on his shoulders as though indicating the movements of the helicopter that was chasing them, was a young woman dressed in a dark windbreaker or slicker that gleamed from the water running off it, her hair pulled back into a ponytail and wet from the spray, her eyes very wide, the light reflected in them, her lips clenched and firm. The shutter had snapped just as she was turning to look to one side and up slightly, toward the chopper, and her face was whitened by the nearness of the flash, her expression startled by the burst of light. Teresa Mendoza at twenty-four.

It had stunk from the beginning. First the fog, as soon as they left the Ceuta lighthouse behind. Then the delay in the arrival of the fishing skiff they were waiting for out on the open sea, in the middle of the hazy darkness with no references, no landmarks, nothing to tell them where they were, and the screen of the Furuno covered with blips from merchantmen and ferries, some dangerously close. Santiago was antsy, and although Teresa couldn't see anything of him but a dark mass in the darkness, she could tell he was not his usual calm self by the way he moved from one side of the Phantom to the other, checking to see that everything was in order. The fog covered them enough for her to dare to light a cigarette, so she ducked under the dashboard, cupped the lighter in her hands, and made sure to hide the lit end of the cigarette in her palm. And she had time to smoke three more.

Finally the *Julio Verdú,* a long shadow on which silhouettes were moving about like ghosts, materialized out of the darkness, just as a glow from the east shredded the fog into long cottony tatters. And then the cargo wasn't right—as the men on the fishing boat passed them the twenty bales wrapped in plastic and Teresa stowed them in the hold, Santiago remarked how surprised he was that they were larger than he'd expected. They're the same weight, but more bulk, he said. And that means that they're not the good stuff, they're the other—regular chocolate, lousy quality, instead of hashish oil, which was purer, more concentrated, more expensive. And in Tarifa, Cañabota had talked about oil.

After that, everything was normal until they got to the coast. They were running behind and the Strait was as flat as a dinner plate, so Santiago raised the nose and ran the Phantom north at full speed. Teresa sensed that he was uncomfortable, forcing the engine brusquely, harshly, hurriedly, as though he especially wanted this thing over with that night. Nothing's wrong, he replied when she asked whether anything was wrong. Nothing at all. He was far from being a loquacious type, but to Teresa this silence seemed more worried than at other times. The lights of La Línea were glowing in the west, off the port side, when the twin glows of Estepona and Marbella appeared over the bow, more visible each time the speedboat bounced off the water, and the light of the lighthouse at Estepona very clear to port—one flash followed by two more, every fifteen seconds. Teresa put her face into the rubber cone of the radar to see whether she could calculate the distance to land, and then, shocked, she saw a blip on the screen, motionless, a mile to the east. She looked through the binoculars in that direction, and when she saw no red or green lights she feared it was an HJ lurking, waiting to pounce. But when the echo disappeared on the second or third sweep of the antenna, she felt calmer. Maybe the crest of a wave, she thought. Or another speedboat waiting to run in to the coast.

Fifteen minutes later, on the beach, the trip turned *really* bad. Spotlights everywhere, blinding them, and shouts—Halt! Halt, halt!—and blue lights flashing up on the highway. The men standing in water to their waists, unloading, froze with the bales in midair or dropped them and took off running, in vain, high-kneed through the surf. She saw Santiago lit from behind, crouching without a word—not a groan, not a curse, not anything—absolutely silent, resigned and professional, backing the Phantom off. Then, with the hull just barely not grazing the sand, turning the wheel hard to port and slamming the throttle all the way forward—*roooaaarr!*—running parallel to the beach in no more than eight or nine inches of water. At first, the speedboat reared up like an ICBM, then it made short bounces along the quiet water—*swooosh, swooosh*—pulling away diagonally from the beach and the lights, seeking the protection of the dark ocean and the distant brightness of Gibraltar, twenty miles to the southwest. At the same time, Teresa grabbed the four bales that were still aboard, lifted them one by one and tilted them overboard, the roar of the engine drowning out each splash as the bale sank in the boat's wake.

It was then that the chopper dropped down on top of them. She heard the *whump whump whump* of the blades above her and to the rear and she raised her head, but she had to close her eyes and turn away because in that instant she was blinded by the white glare of a spotlight, and the end of a skid lighted by that glare was swinging back and forth just above her head, forcing her to crouch down with her hands on Santiago's shoulders. Under his clothes she felt his tense muscles, his back bowed over the wheel, and she saw his face illuminated in brief bursts from the spotlight swinging above them, all the bursts of spray that wet his face and hair—he looked better than ever this way, she thought; he was even better-looking than when they were screwing and she was looking at him up close and could have eaten him alive and then licked her lips. When he was this way, stubborn and sure of himself, totally concentrated on the wheel and the ocean and the Phantom's gas tanks, doing what he knew how to do best in the world, fighting the way he knew how to fight against life and fate and that *pinche* light that was chasing them like the eye of some evil giant, he was fucking irresistible, *bien padre, padrísimo*. There are two kinds of men, she thought suddenly: Those who fight and those who don't. Those who take life the way it comes and say, Oh well, what the fuck, and when the spotlights come on put up their hands and say, Take me. And those who don't. Those who sometimes, in the middle of a pitch-dark ocean, make a woman look at them like she was looking at him now.

And women, she thought. There are two kinds of women, she started to say to herself, but she couldn't complete the thought, because she stopped thinking.

The skid of the *pinche* fucking bird, less than a yard above their heads, was swinging closer and closer. Teresa tapped Santiago's left shoulder to warn him, and he nodded once, intent on steering the boat. He knew that no matter how close the helicopter came, it would never hit them, except by accident. Its pilot was too good to let that happen, because if it did, pursuers and pursued would go down together. This was a pursuit maneuver, to confuse and frighten them and make them change course, or make mistakes, or accelerate until the engine, already at its limit, flamed out. It had happened before, many times. Santiago knew—and Teresa did, too, although that skid so close scared her—that the chopper couldn't do much more, and that the purpose of its maneuver was to force them closer to shore, so the straight course the speedboat had set for Punta Europa and Gibraltar would turn into a long curve that would string out the chase and make the speedboat crew lose their nerve and run aground on some sandbank, or give the Customs HJ time to arrive and board them.

The HJ! Santiago lifted his chin toward the radar, gesturing for Teresa to give it a look, and she walked over on her knees, feeling the boat's bounces off the water through the thin skin of the hull, and put her face to the rubber cone. Holding on to a rib of the hull and Santiago's seat, the intense vibration of the engine through the hull numbing her hands, she watched the dark line of the coast that the sweep outlined to port, closer and closer, and the clean expanse on the other side. At a half-mile everything was clear, but when she doubled the range, she found the expected dark shadow coming in quickly at fifteen hundred or so yards, on a course that would cut them off. She put her mouth to Santiago's ear to shout at him over the roar of the engine, and she saw him nod again, unspeaking, his eyes fixed on the course. The chopper dropped a little more, the skid almost touching the deck on the port side, and then lifted again, without making Santiago swerve even a degree off the course he'd set. He remained hunched over the wheel, fixed on the darkness ahead, while the lights of the coast ran swiftly off starboard: first Estepona with the streetlights along the long avenue and the lighthouse at one end, then Manilva and the port of

Duquesa, with the speedboat at forty-five knots slowly gaining the open sea. And it was then, when she looked for a second time at the radar, that Teresa saw the black blip of the HJ too close, and closing faster than she'd thought—about to cut them off on the left. When she looked in that direction she saw, through the mist of the spray, despite the white glare of the chopper's spotlight, the HJ's rotating blue lights coming ever closer. That presented the eternal alternative in these cases: run the boat up on the beach, or try your luck while the menacing flank of the cutter growing more and more visible in the night skimmed up alongside, taps from its bow trying to break your hull, stop your engine, throw you into the water. There was no longer any need for the radar, so moving again on her knees—she could feel the violent bounces in her kidneys—Teresa took a place again behind Santiago, her hands on his shoulders to warn him of the movements of the helicopter and the cutter, to right and left, near and far, and when she shook his left shoulder four times because the fucking HJ was now a sinister wall looming over them, charging at them, Santiago pulled back on the throttle, slowing the engine 400 rpms; he lowered the hydraulic-powered trim tabs with his right hand, hit the stern thruster, furiously whirled the wheel to port, and the Phantom, in the cloud of its own spray, made a tight circle, incredible, that cut through the wake of the Customs cutter, leaving it a bit behind in the process.

Teresa felt like laughing out loud. *Jesus!* They all bet everything they had in these strange hunts that made your heart beat a hundred and twenty times a minute—aware that the advantage you had over your adversary was in the narrow margin that defined that limit. The chopper was flying low, feinting with the skid, threatening to tap the boat and knock it over, and marking their position for the HJ, but most of the time it was acting as a headlight, because it couldn't make real contact. The HJ, in turn, was cutting back and forth across the bow of the speedboat, making it bounce in the wake it left, making its engine whine as the propeller whirled in air; or it pursued, ready to nudge the speedboat, the cutter's skipper knowing he could do that only with the cutter's bow, because lifting the bow meant killing the occupants of the Phantom instantly, in a country where you had to explain a lot to the judges when that sort of thing happened. And Santiago knew all this, too, the smart *cabrón de mierda* that he was, and he was willing to put all his chips on the table—zigzag, or run in the wake of the HJ until it slowed down or turned back, cut across its bow to stop it. Even slow down suddenly, cold-bloodedly when he was leading—trusting in the reflexes of the skipper of the other boat to stop the cutter in time, not run right over them—and then five seconds later accelerate, gaining precious distance, with Gibraltar closer and closer. All on a knife-edge. And a single error in his calculations would be enough to tip that precarious balance between hunter and hunted, and send them all to hell.

"We're fucked," Santiago shouted.

Teresa looked around, disconcerted. Now the HJ was on their left again, outside, pressing inexorably in toward land, with the Phantom running at fifty knots in less than fifteen feet of water and the chopper right on top of them, its white spotlight trained on them tight. The situation looked no worse than five minutes earlier, and Teresa put her mouth to Santiago's ear and told him that. "We're not so bad," she shouted. But Santiago moved his head as though he hadn't heard, absorbed in piloting the speedboat, or in what he was thinking. "That cargo," she heard him say. And then, before he stopped talking altogether, he added something, but Teresa could make out only one word: *decoy*. He's probably saying they suckered us, she thought. Then the HJ sideswiped them with its bow, and the spray from the two boats running alongside each other at full speed turned into foam, water beaten into a meringue that drenched them, blinded them, and Santiago was forced to yield a notch, to take the Phantom in toward the beach, so that now they were running in the current, between the breakers and the beach itself, with the HJ off to port and a little more open, the chopper above them, and the lights from land flying by just a few meters away, it seemed. In six inches of water.

Jesus, there's no water here, thought Teresa. Santiago was taking the speedboat in as close as he could, to keep the cutter off them, but the other boat's skipper took every opportunity to run them in to the coast. Even so, she calculated, it was much less probable that the HJ would run aground, or suck in a rock that would totally fuck the engine, than that the Phantom would touch the sand with its propeller in the middle of a bounce, and then the bow would go straight in and the two of them would be sucking at Faros until the resurrection of the flesh. Jesus God. Teresa clenched her teeth and gripped Santiago's shoulders when the cutter closed in again, spray flying, then pulled away, ahead of them, to blind them again with its spray and then tacked in to starboard just a touch, to press them tighter against the beach. That skipper was something, no denying that, she thought. A guy that takes his job seriously. Because no law demanded this much out of him. Or maybe it did, when things got personal between two macho fucking *cabrones* who turned any spat into a cockfight to the death.

The HJ was close—its flank looked so big and dark that the excitement the race had produced in Teresa started to turn to fear. She had never run in this close, in the shore current, so close to the shoreline in such shallow water, and every so often the helicopter's spotlight showed her the undulations of the sand, pebbles, seaweed on the bottom. There's hardly enough draft for the propeller, she thought. We're plowing this *pinche* beach. And suddenly she felt ridiculously vulnerable there, soaked through, blinded by the light, shaken, rocked by the bounces on the water. *Fuck the law,* she told herself. *These two are just testing each other. The first one who blinks, loses, that's all. These two are doing a little dick-measuring here, and I'm in the middle, fucked. Sad, dying for this.*

And that was when she remembered the León Rock. It was a boulder, not very high, that sat a few yards off the beach, halfway between Duquesa and Sotogrande. It was named after a Customs agent who had smashed the hull of the cutter he was using to chase down a speedboat—*craaccck!*—and was forced to run ashore. And that rock, Teresa now remembered, was directly on the course they were following now. The thought gave her a jolt of panic. Forgetting the closeness of their pursuers, she looked out to the right for references, to locate herself by the land lights flashing past the Phantom. It had to be, she decided, very, very fucking close.

"The rock!" she shouted to Santiago, leaning over his shoulder. "We're close to the rock!"

In the light of the pursuing helicopter she saw him nod, never taking his attention off the wheel and the course, glancing over now and again at the cutter and the shore to calculate the distance and depth they were running at. Just then the HJ pulled away a bit, the helicopter closed in, and as she looked up, shielding her eyes with her hand, Teresa could make out a dark figure in a white helmet descending to the skid, which the pilot was maneuvering just over the Phantom's engine. She was fascinated by that incredible image: a man suspended between sky and water, one hand grasping the door of the helicopter and the other holding an object that it took her a second to recognize as a pistol. He won't shoot at us, she thought, befuddled. They can't do that. This is Europe, goddammit, and they have no right to treat us like that, just shoot us, *bam!* The speedboat gave a long leap and she fell backward, and when she sat up, dazed, ready to scream at Santiago— "They're going to kill us, *cabrón,* slack off, stop, stop before they shoot us!"—she saw that the man in the white helmet was pointing the pistol at the engine head and was emptying the clip into it, one shot after another, orange flashes in the glare of the spotlight and the thousands of dots of shattered water, with the blasts—*blam! blam! blam!*—almost drowned out by the roar of the engine and the blades of the chopper and the sound of the ocean and the chops of the Phantom's hull against the shallow water of the shoreline. And then the man in the white helmet disappeared into the helicopter, and the bird gained some altitude, though its spotlight never wavered from them, and the HJ once more veered in dangerously close while Teresa looked in shock and stupefaction at the black holes in the casing of the engine, which went on working as though nothing had happened, not even a wisp of smoke, just the way Santiago coolly held his course, without ever having turned around to look at what was happening, without asking Teresa if she was all right, without doing anything but running that race he seemed willing to run till the end of time, or his life, or their lives.

The rock, she remembered again. The León Rock had to be right there, a few yards ahead of them. She stood up behind Santiago to peer out ahead, trying to see through the curtain of droplets illuminated by the white light of the helicopter, trying to make out the rock in the darkness of the shoreline that snaked before them.

I hope he sees it in time, she said to herself. *I hope he sees it in time to maneuver and dodge it, and that the fucking HJ lets us.* She was hoping all this when she saw the rock ahead, black and menacing, and without needing to look to the left she knew that the Customs cutter had swerved to miss it at the same second that Santiago, water pouring off his face, his eyes averted from the blinding light that never lost them for an instant, hit the trim-tab lever and turned the Phantom's wheel, a burst of spray covering them in its luminous white cloud, the boat dodging the danger just as Santiago accelerated and resumed his course again, fifty knots, flat water, once again inside the breakers, almost no draft. Then Teresa looked back and saw that the rock wasn't the *pinche* rock—it was a boat at anchor that in the darkness had looked like the rock—but the rock was still ahead of them, waiting. She opened her mouth to yell at Santiago, to tell him it wasn't behind them, be careful, it's still up there ahead, when she saw that the helicopter had turned off the spotlight and lifted almost straight up, and that the HJ was pulling away with a violent jerk seaward. And she also saw herself, as though from outside, very quiet and very alone in that boat, as if everyone were about to abandon her in some wet, dark place.

She felt a wave of intense, familiar fear, because she had recognized The Situation. And then the world exploded.

7. They marked me
with the Seven

*A*t this moment, Dantès felt himself being thrown into a huge *void, flying through the air like a wounded bird, then falling, falling, in a terrifying descent that froze his heart. . . .*

Teresa Mendoza read those words again and sat suspended, the book open on her knees, looking at the prison yard. It was still winter, and the rectangle of light that moved in a direction counter to the sun warmed her half-knitted bones under the cast on her right arm and the thick wool sweater that Patricia O'Farrell had lent her.

It was nice out there in the late-morning sun, before the bell for lunch. Around her were fifty or so women, gathered in circles, talking, sitting in the sun like she was. Some lay back smoking, trying to get some color, while others paced in groups from one side of the yard to the other, in that walk typical of inmates forced to move within the limits of their surroundings: two hundred thirty paces across and then back, one, two, three, four . . . then a half-turn when they got to the wall crowned by a guard tower and rolls of razor wire between them and the men's unit . . . two hundred twenty-eight, two hundred twenty-nine, two hundred thirty paces exactly to the basketball court, another two hundred thirty back to the wall, and so on, eight, ten, twenty times a day. After two months in El Puerto de Santa María, Teresa had become familiar with those daily paces, and she herself, hardly noticing, had come to adopt that way of walking, with the fast, slightly elastic bounce one saw especially in the veteran prisoners—as fast and direct as though they were actually going somewhere.

It was Patricia O'Farrell who had pointed it out to her after she'd been inside a few weeks. You ought to see yourself, she told Teresa, you've already got the prisoner walk. Teresa was convinced that Patricia, who was now lying on her back near her, her hands under her neck, her very short gold hair gleaming in the sun, would never walk that way, even if she spent another twenty years in this place. In her Irish-Jerez blood, she thought, there was too much class, too many good habits, too much intelligence.

"Gimme a nail," Patricia said.

She was lazy or capricious, depending on what day it was. She smoked American-style filter cigarettes, with blond tobacco, but if she didn't feel like getting up for one of her own she would smoke one of Teresa's unfiltered, black-tobacco Bisontes, often taken apart and rerolled with a few grains of hashish. Nails, without. Joints or *basucos,* with.

Teresa pulled a cigarette out of the pack next to her on the ground, half of them laced with hash, half straight, lit it, and leaning over Patricia's face, put it between her lips. She saw Patricia smile before she said, "Thanks," and inhaled without removing her hands from behind her neck, the cigarette dangling from her mouth, her eyes closed in the sun that gave a glow to her hair and the light dusting of golden hairs on her cheeks, around the slight wrinkles at the corners of her eyes. Thirty-four years old, Patricia had said, without anybody's asking, Teresa's first day in the cell—the rack, in the jail slang that Teresa now knew so well—that the two women shared. Thirty-four on her National Identity Document, and nine on her sentencing sheet, "of which I've served two. With good behavior, work credits, a third off just because . . . I figure I've got one or two more, max."

Teresa started to tell her who she was—"My name's Teresa and . . ."—when the other woman cut her off. "I know who you are, sweetheart. Here, we know everything about everybody real fast—sometimes even before they get here. So let *me* tell *you*. There are three basic types: bitches, dykes, and pussies. By nationality, aside from the Spaniards we've got Moors, Romanians, Portuguese, Nigerians—with AIDS and everything, you want to stay away from them, they're in bad shape, poor things—a group of Colombian girls that practically run the place—they get any fucking thing they want, and sometimes get away with murder, so watch out—a French girl or two, and a couple of Ukrainians—whores that offed their pimp because he wouldn't give back their passports. Then there are the Gypsies—don't mess with them. The young ones with the Lycra pants, long hair, and tattoos deal in pills and chocolate and whatever, and they're the toughest ones. The older ones, the fat ones with the big tits and the long skirts and their hair in buns, they've taken the fall for their men—who've got to stay on the street because they've got a family to feed, so they come to pick up their Rosarios in a big Mercedes when they get out—and they're pretty peaceable, but they look out for each other. Except for the Gypsies, among themselves, the inmates look out for number one and only number one, which means that the ones you see in groups are there out of self-interest, or survival—the weak ones looking for a ride on the strong ones.

"If you want a piece of advice, don't make friends, don't mix. Try to get a good gig: laundry, kitchen, commissary—which also takes time off your sentence. And don't forget to wear flipflops in the shower and never sit your ass down on the toilet in the latrines in the yard—you could catch god knows what. Never say anything against Camarón or Joaquín Sabina or Los Chunguitos or Miguel Bosé, or ask to change the channel when the soaps are on, or take drugs from anybody without knowing what it's going to cost you in return. Your rap, if you stay out of trouble and do what you're told to do, will keep you here a year—obsessing about getting out, like all of us, thinking about the family, or remaking your life, or the drink you're going to have, or the screw, whatever it is. Year and a half max, with the papers and the reports from Corrections and the shrinks and all those other bastards that open the doors or close them on us, depending on their digestion or whether you make a good impression on them or whatever other bug happens to be up their ass that day. So take it easy, keep that nice sweet expression on your face, say Yes sir, Yes ma'am to everybody, don't pull my chain, and we'll get along fine, Mexicana. I hope you don't mind if people call you Mexicana. Everybody's got some name here. Some girls like them, some don't. Mine is Lieutenant O'Farrell. And I like it. Maybe one day I'll let you call me Patty."

P atty."
      "What."
   "This book is great."

"I told you."

Patty's eyes were still closed, the lighted cigarette dangling from her lips, and the sun accentuated little spots, like freckles, on the tip of her nose. She had been attractive once, and in a certain way still was. Or maybe more pleasant-looking than actually attractive, with her blond hair and her five feet eight inches and her bright eyes that made it seem she was always laughing inside. Her mother was a Miss Spain 1950-something, married to the O'Farrell of sherry and thoroughbred-horse fame, a man you saw from time to time in the magazines: an elegant, raisin-wrinkled old man photographed with beautiful horses and barrels of wine in the background, or in a house with tapestries, paintings, and shelves filled with ceramics and books. There were more children; Patricia was the black sheep. Something to do with drugs on the Costa del Sol, with the Russian mafia and a couple of dead men. A boyfriend with three or four noble last names shot dead at point-blank range, and her making it out alive by a miracle, with two gunshots that had kept her in the ICU for a month and a half. Teresa had seen the scars in the showers and when Patricia took off her clothes in the rack: two star-shaped areas of drawn and puckered skin on her back, under her left shoulder blade, about two inches apart. The exit wound from one had left a slightly bigger scar, under her clavicle. The second bullet, smashed flat against a bone, had been removed in the operating room.

"Full metal jacket," was Patricia's comment the first time Teresa stared at the scars. "If it had been a dum-dum or a hollow-point we wouldn't be talking right now." And then she closed the matter with a silent, comic grimace. On humid days that second wound bothered her, as Teresa ached from the fresh fracture of her arm.

"How do you like Edmond Dantès?"

"Edmond Dantès is me," Teresa replied, almost seriously, and she saw the wrinkles around Patricia's eyes deepen, the cigarette quiver as she smiled.

"Me, too," Patricia said. "And all of us," she added, gesturing toward the yard without opening her eyes. "Innocent and virginal and dreaming of a treasure that awaits us all when we get out."

"Abbé Faria died," Teresa said, looking down at the book's open pages. "Poor old man."

"You see? There are times when some people have to buy it so others can live."

A group of inmates passed by, walking the two hundred thirty steps toward the wall. They were tough, mean-looking, a half-dozen girls led by Trini Sánchez, also known as Makoki III: a small, masculine, aggressive, tattooed dark-skinned woman, always scrapping with the other inmates, or shivving them—dangerous, and a regular in the Hole. She'd gotten fourteen years for stabbing her girlfriend over half a gram of horse. "Those dykes like fresh bait," Patricia had warned Teresa the first time they met in the module corridor, when Trini said something that Teresa didn't catch and the others laughed, sharing the code. "But don't worry, Mexicanita. They'll only eat your cunt if you let them." Teresa hadn't let them, and after a few tactical advances in the showers, the stalls, and the yard—including one attempt at social interchange via smiles and cigarettes and condensed milk at a table in the dining room—they went on their way. After all, her rackmate was Lieutenant O'Farrell. And with her, the word was, La Mexicanita was taken care of.

"Hey, Lieutenant."

"How's it goin', bitches?" Patricia hadn't even opened her eyes. And her hands were still crossed behind her neck. The others laughed harshly—a couple muttered some good-humored obscenity—and continued pacing the yard. Teresa watched them pass and then looked over at her friend. It had not taken her long to see that O'Farrell enjoyed certain privileges among the inmates: she had access to money far above the legal amount of available funds, she received packages from the outside, and with these goods, people on the inside were disposed to help her. Even the guards and prison officers treated her better than the rest.

But there was also an air of authority about her that had nothing to do with money or packages from the outside. First of all, she was a girl with culture, which made an important difference in a place where very few inmates had gone as far as high school. She expressed herself well, read books, knew people at a certain level of society. It was not unusual for other inmates to come to her for help in filling out forms—requests or official documents that should have been filed by their lawyers—appointed by the court, the motherfuckers disappeared the minute the sentence was handed down, or even before.

O'Farrell could also get her hands on drugs, from pills of any color to pot or chocolate, which was what they called hash, and she always had rolling paper or aluminum foil for those who needed to light up.

Plus, she wasn't one to let anybody get to her. The story was that one day when she was still new, a longtime inmate had raped her, and that O'Farrell had taken it without opening her mouth. But the next morning, when she and the rapist were both naked in the showers, she had come up to the bitch and held a shiv—made from the frame of a fire-extinguisher box—to her throat. Never again, sweetheart, were her words as she looked into the woman's eyes, the water from the shower running off her, the other inmates standing around like they were watching the TV, although later they all swore on their most recently departed loved ones that they hadn't seen a thing. And the trouble-maker, an alpha bitch everyone called La Valenciana, with a reputation as one mean cunt, was in complete agreement.

Lieutenant O'Farrell. Teresa saw that Patricia had opened her eyes and was looking at her, and she slowly turned her eyes away so that the other woman wouldn't read her thoughts. Sometimes the youngest and most defenseless inmates bought the protection of a respected, danger-ous alpha bitch—"respected" and "dangerous" meant the same thing—in exchange for favors that in this prison without men included the ob-vious. Patricia never suggested anything like that to Teresa, but sometimes Teresa caught her watching her in that fixed, slightly reflec-tive way, as though she were looking at her but thinking about some-thing else. She had felt herself looked at that way when she arrived at El Puerto, with the noise of locks and thick bars and heavy doors—*clang, clang*—and the echo of footsteps and the impersonal voices of the guards and that smell of locked-up women, dirty clothes, musty mattresses, foul-smelling food, sweat, and lye. As Teresa undressed the first night, or went to the toilet—hard at first, until she got used to it, because of the lack of privacy, her jeans and underwear down around her ankles—Patricia would sometimes look at her from her bunk with-out a word. She'd lay the book she was reading—she had a bookcase full—facedown on her stomach and study Teresa from head to toe. She'd done this for days, weeks, and once in a while she still did. Like now, for example.

Teresa went back to the book. Edmond Dantès, tied in a sack and with a cannonball attached to his feet to weigh him down, had just been thrown over a cliff—his captors thought it was the body of the dead abbé. *The sea is the graveyard of the Château d'If . . .* she read avidly. I hope he gets out of this, she thought, quickly turning the page, to the next chapter. *Though stunned and almost suffocated, Dantès still had the presence of mind to hold his breath. . . . ¡Híjole!* I hope he can get out of that sack and go back to Marseilles and get his boat and take his revenge on those three sons of bitches that sold him out like that.

Teresa had never imagined that a book could absorb her attention to the point that she could sit down and pick it up right where she'd left off, with a scrap of torn paper for a bookmark so as not to lose her place. Patricia had given her this book after talking about it a lot—Teresa had been marveling to see her sit so quietly for so long, looking at the pages of her books. To think of her getting all those things in her head and preferring that to the telenovelas—she herself loved the ones from Mexico, with their accents of her homeland—and movies and game shows that the other inmates would crowd around the television for.

"Books are doors that lead out into the street," Patricia would tell her. "You learn from them, educate yourself, travel, dream, imagine, live other lives, multiply your own life a thousand times. Where can you get more for your money, Mexicanita? And they also keep all sorts of bad things at bay: ghosts, loneliness, shit like that. Sometimes I wonder how you people that don't read figure out how to live your lives." But she never said, You ought to read such-and-such, or Look at this, or that; she waited for Teresa to come to it herself, after catching her several times rummaging around among the ever-changing twenty or thirty books that she kept on the shelves in the rack, some from the prison library and others that some relative or friend on the outside would send her, or that she would have other inmates, with third-degree permits, order for her.

Finally, one day Teresa said, "I've never read a whole book before, but I'd like to read one." She was holding something called *Tender Is the Night,* or some such title, which had drawn her attention because it sounded so incredibly romantic, plus it had a lovely picture on the cover, a slender, elegant girl in a garden hat, very, very twenties. But Patricia shook her head, took it from her, and said, "Wait, all things in good time—first you ought to read something that you'll like even better." And the next day they went to the prison library and asked Marcela Rabbit, the inmate in charge—Rabbit was her nickname, of course; she had put that brand of lye in her mother-in-law's wine—for the book that Teresa now held in her hands. "It's about a prisoner like us," Patricia explained when she saw Teresa worried about having to read such a thick book. "And look—Porrúa Publishers, Mexico City. It came from over there, like you. You were meant for each other."

There was a scuffle at the far end of the yard—Moors and young Gypsies cursing each other, some hair-pulling. From there you could see the barred windows of the men's unit, where the male inmates would often exchange messages—yells and signs—with their "girlfriends" or female buddies. More than one jailhouse idyll had been hatched in that corner—one prisoner doing some cement work had managed to knock up a female inmate in the three minutes the guards took to find them—and the place was frequented by women with male interests on the other side of the wall and the razor wire. Now three or four inmates were arguing, and it had reached the point of slapping and scratching—jealousy, maybe, or a dispute over the best spot in the improvised observatory, while the guard in the guardhouse leaned over the wall to watch.

Teresa had seen that in prison the women had more balls than some men did. They might wear makeup, have their hair fixed by other inmates who'd been hairdressers on the outside, and like to show off their jewelry, especially when they went to mass on Sunday—Teresa, not thinking about it, stopped going to mass after the death of Santiago Fisterra—or when they were working in the kitchen or areas where some contact with men was possible. That, too, gave rise to jealousy, ripoffs, and settling of scores. She'd seen women beaten to within an inch of their lives over a cigarette or a bite of omelette—eggs weren't on the official menu and you could get shivved for one—or an insult or even a "What" spoken in the wrong tone of voice. She'd seen women stabbed, or kicked until they bled from their nose and ears. Thefts of food or drugs also caused fights: jars of preserves, cans of meat or other delicacies, heroin or pills stolen from the racks while the inmates were in the dining hall at breakfast and the cells were open. Or breaking the unwritten rules that governed life on the inside. A month earlier, a snitch that cleaned the guardhouses and blew the whistle once in a while on her sister inmates had been beaten to a bloody pulp in the yard latrine when she went to pee. She'd hardly gotten her skirt up when four inmates rushed inside, while others, who later turned out to be deaf and blind and mute, stood outside to block the door. The bitch was still in the infirmary with several broken ribs and her jaw held together with wires.

Teresa watched the commotion at the end of the yard. Behind the bars, the guys in the men's unit were throwing fuel on the fire, and the shift sergeant and two other guards were running across the quadrangle to take charge. After her distracted glance, Teresa returned to Edmond Dantès, with whom she was madly and frankly in love. And as she turned the pages—the fugitive had just been rescued from the sea by fishermen—she could feel Patricia O'Farrell's eyes fixed on her, looking at her the same way that other woman did, the woman she'd caught so many times stalking her from the shadows and in mirrors.

She was awakened by rain on the window, and she opened her eyes, terrified in the gray light, because she thought she was out on the ocean again, near the León Rock, in the middle of a black sphere, falling into the void the same way Edmond Dantès had in Abbé Faria's shroud. After the rock and the impact and the night, the days that followed her awakening in the hospital with one arm immobilized on a splint to the shoulder, her body covered with bruises and scratches, she had gradually—from comments by doctors and nurses, the visit from the police and a social worker, the flash of a photograph, her fingers stained with ink after an official fingerprinting—reconstructed the details of what had happened. Still, whenever somebody pronounced the name Santiago Fisterra, her mind went blank. All that time, the sedatives and her own emotions had kept her in a state of semi-consciousness that prevented any real thought. Not for a moment during those first four or five days did she allow herself to think about Santiago, and when the memory came to her unbidden, she would push it away, sink back into that voluntary stupor. Not yet, her subconscious and her body would say to her. You'd better not face that yet.

Until one morning, when she opened her eyes and saw Óscar Lobato sitting there, the reporter from the Cádiz paper who was a friend of Santiago's. And beside the door, standing, leaning against the wall, another man whose face was vaguely familiar. It was then, while that second man listened without saying a word—at first she took him for a cop—that she heard from Lobato's lips what on some level she already knew, or guessed. That night the Phantom had crashed at fifty knots into the rock, shattering into a million pieces, and Santiago had died instantly. Teresa had lived only because she had somehow been thrown out of the speedboat. But her right arm had broken when she hit the surface of the water, and she had sunk fifteen feet to the bottom.

"How did I make it?" she wanted to know. And her voice sounded strange, no longer her own. Lobato smiled in a way that softened the hard features of his face, the marks of time around his eyes, and his tone lightened. He gestured toward the man leaning on the wall, not saying a word, looking at Teresa with curiosity and a hint of shyness, as though not daring to come any closer.

"He pulled you out," Lobato said.

Then he told her what had happened after she was knocked unconscious—that after the impact she floated for a minute before she sank, with the helicopter spotlight illuminating her. The pilot had passed the controls to his copilot and jumped into the water from ten feet above, and in the water he had taken off his helmet and self-inflating life jacket and dived to the bottom, where she was drowning. He brought her to the surface, in the midst of the spray raised by the chopper's blades, and from there swam with her in to the beach. While the HJ was looking for the remains of Santiago Fisterra—the largest pieces of the Phantom were no more than eight or ten inches across—the lights of an ambulance approached along the highway. And while Lobato was recounting all this, Teresa was looking at the face of the man leaning against the wall, the man who was still not saying a word or nodding or anything, as though what the reporter was describing had happened to somebody else. And finally she recognized the man as one of the Customs officers she'd seen in Kuki's that night, the night the smugglers from Gibraltar had been celebrating that guy's birthday.

"He wanted to come with me to see your face," Lobato explained. And she looked at the other man's face, too, the Customs helicopter pilot who'd killed Santiago and saved her. Thinking: I need to remember this man later, so when I'm all right again I can decide whether to kill him, if I can—or say, Peace, brother, *cabrón*, shrug and let it go.

She finally asked about Santiago, where his body was, and the man leaning against the wall looked away, and Lobato frowned a bit, in grief, when he told her that the casket was on its way to O Grove, the Galician town where he'd been born. "A good guy," he added, his face solemn, and it struck Teresa that he may have been sincere, that the two men had spent time together, and that maybe Lobato had really liked him. That was when she started to cry, quietly, because now, now she was thinking about Santiago dead, and she could see his motionless face with his eyes closed, like when she'd slept with her head on his shoulder. And she thought: What am I going to do now with that fucking model sailboat that's sitting on the table at the house in Palmones, half done, with nobody to finish it. And she realized that she was alone for the second time, and in a certain way forever.

It was O'Farrell who really changed her life," María Tejeda repeated. She had spent the last forty-five minutes telling me how and why. When she finished, she went to the kitchen, came back with two glasses of herbal tea, and sipped at one while I went over my notes and digested the story. The former prison social worker at El Puerto de Santa María was a chubby, vivacious woman with long, dark hair streaked with gray, kindly eyes, and a firm set to her mouth. She wore round gold-rimmed glasses and gold rings on several fingers—at least ten of them, I counted. I figured her for somewhere around sixty. For thirty-five of those years she had worked for Corrections in the provinces of Cádiz and Málaga. It had not been easy to find her, since she had recently retired, but once again, Óscar Lobato had come to my aid and tracked her down.

"I remember them both very well," she said when I phoned. "Come to Granada and we'll talk."

She greeted me in a jogging suit and tennis shoes from the balcony of her apartment in the low-lying Albaicín section of the city, with all of new Granada and the plain of the Darro on one side, and the Alhambra, gold and ocher in the morning sun, perched among trees up on the hill, on the other. Her house was filled with light, and there were cats everywhere: on the couch, in the hall, on the balcony. At least half a dozen live cats—it smelled like hell, despite the open windows—and some twenty more in paintings, porcelain figurines, woodcarvings. There were rugs and pillows embroidered with cats, and among the things hung out to dry on the balcony was a towel with Sylvester on it. While I read over my notes and savored the mint tea, a tabby observed me from the top of a wardrobe closet, as though she'd known me somewhere before, and a fat gray cat slunk toward me over the carpet, as though my shoelaces were legal prey. The rest were lying or walking about the house in various postures and attitudes. I hate these creatures, which are much too quiet and intelligent for my taste—there is nothing like the stolid loyalty of a stupid dog—but I girded my loins and soldiered on. Work is work.

"O'Farrell made her see things about herself," my hostess was saying, "that she had never imagined existed. And she even started to educate her a little, you know . . . in her own way."

On the table she had stacked several notebooks, in which for years she had kept records of her interviews. "I was looking over these before you came," she said. "To refresh my memory." She showed me some pages written in a round, tight hand: individual entries, dates, visits, interviews. Some paragraphs were underlined. Follow-up, she explained. "It was my job to evaluate their rehabilitation, so to speak, help them to find something for afterward. On the inside, some women sit with their hands folded, while others prefer to stay busy. I made staying busy possible.

"Teresa Mendoza Chávez and Patricia O'Farrell Meca," she went on. "Classified as SFIs: special follow-up inmates. They gave people lots to talk about in their time, those two."

"They were lovers?"

She closed the notebooks and gave me a long, evaluating look. No doubt considering whether that question stemmed from sick curiosity or professional interest.

"I'm not certain," she replied at last. "Among the girls there were rumors, of course. But there are always rumors like that. O'Farrell was bisexual. At least, no? . . . And the truth is, she had had relationships with some inmates before Mendoza came. But about those two specifically, I can't say for sure."

After biting at my shoelaces, the fat gray cat was rubbing against my pants, covering them with cat hairs. I bit the end of my ballpoint stoically.

"How long were they together?"

"A year as cellmates, and then they got out a few months apart. . . . They were both clients of mine—that's what we call them. Mendoza was soft-spoken and almost shy, very observant, very cautious in a way, with that Mexican accent that made her seem so prim and proper. . . . Who'd have known what was coming, no? . . . O'Farrell was just the opposite: amoral, uninhibited, always with an attitude—superior and frivolous at the same time. Worldly. A society girl who condescended to live in the real world. Irreproachable conduct, hers. Not a black mark in the three and a half years she spent on the inside, you know? Despite the fact that she purchased and consumed narcotics . . . I'll tell you, she was too intelligent to get into trouble. She seemed to consider her stay in prison an unavoidable interruption in her life, and she was just waiting for it to pass—she wasn't about to make trouble for herself or anybody else."

The cat that was rubbing up against my pants leg sank its claws into my sock, so I pushed it away with a discreet kick that earned me a brief censorious silence from my hostess.

"Anyway," she went on after the uncomfortable pause, calling the cat up to her lap, "Come here, Anubis, precious thing—O'Farrell was a woman, not a child, with a personality, a character, you know? She was already formed, and the newcomer was very much influenced by her— the good family, the money, the name, the culture. . . . Thanks to her cellmate, Mendoza discovered the usefulness of an education. That was the positive part of the influence—it gave her the desire to better herself, to change. She read, studied. She discovered that you don't have to depend on a man. She was good at figures, and she found the opportunity to get even better at them in the prison education program, which allowed inmates to get time off their sentences for taking classes. She took an elementary mathematics course and a course in Spanish, and her English improved tremendously as well. She became a voracious reader, and toward the end you might find her with an Agatha Christie novel or a book of travel writing or even something scientific. And it was O'Farrell, definitely, who inspired all that.

"Mendoza's lawyer was a Gibraltar fellow who dropped her just after she came to the prison, and so far as I could see he also kept the money, which may have been a little or a lot, I really couldn't say. In El Puerto de Santa María she never had any male visitors, no 'conjugal visits'—some of the inmates managed to get false marriage certificates so men could visit them—or any other kind of visitor, for that matter. She was completely alone. So O'Farrell did all the paperwork for her parole hearing.

"Had it been anyone else, all of that would have probably led to real rehabilitation. When she got out, Mendoza could have found a decent job: she was a quick study, you know, she had good instincts, a cool head and an IQ"—the social worker had consulted her notes again— "in the high one thirties. Unfortunately, her friend O'Farrell was too far gone. Certain tastes, certain friends, you know . . ." She looked at me as though she doubted that I really did know. "Certain vices. Among women," she went on, "some influences or relationships are stronger than among men. And then there was the matter of the lost cocaine that everyone has talked about. . . . Although in the prison"—Anubis was purring as she ran her hand over his neck and back—"there are hundreds of such stories. So no one actually believed that this one was true. . . . Absolutely no one," she insisted after a thoughtful silence, still petting the cat. Even now, years later and despite everything that had been published about it, the social worker was still convinced that the story of the cocaine had been a myth.

"But you see how things are. First it was O'Farrell who changed the Mexican girl, and then the Mexican girl completely took over O'Far-rell's life. . . . You never know about those quiet kind of girls. . . ."

As for myself, I can still see the young soldier with his pale skin and black eyes. When the angel of death comes down to take me, I am certain I shall recognize Selim. . . .

The day she turned twenty-five—they had taken the cast off her arm a week earlier—Teresa paused and put a bookmark on page 740 of the novel that held her in its spell. Never before, she reflected, had she thought that a person could project herself, as she had, so intensely, into what she was reading, so that reader and protagonist became one. And O'Farrell was right: More than the movies or TV, novels let you live so many things you'd never otherwise be able to live—more than you could ever fit into a single life. That was the strange magic that kept her glued to that volume whose pages were so old they were coming unsewn. But Patty had insisted it be repaired, because, as she said, "It's not a question of just reading books, Mexicana, it's also the physical pleasure and inner peace you get from holding them in your hands." To intensify that pleasure and inner peace, Patty went with the book to the inmates' bookbinding shop, and she had the book taken apart and carefully resewn and then rebound with stiff covers, good paste, Flo-rentine paper for the endpapers, and a lovely cover of brown leather with gold letters on the spine: *Alejandro Dumas, El conde de Monte Cristo.* And under it all, with smaller gold letters, the initials TMC, for Teresa Mendoza Chávez. So after five days of impatient waiting, with

Teresa's reading interrupted at Chapter XXXVII—"The Catacombs of Saint Sebastian"—Patty presented it to her once again, all new.

"It's my birthday present for you."

It was the hour for breakfast, just after the day's first head count. The book was very nicely wrapped, and when she held the book again, Teresa felt that special pleasure her companion had spoken about. It was heavy and soft, with the new cover and those gold letters. And Patty looked at her, elbows on the table, a cup of chicory in one hand and a cigarette in the other, enjoying her happiness. "Happy birthday," she repeated, and the other girls also congratulated Teresa. "To the next one on the street," one of them said. "With a stud to wake you up in the morning," another added, "and me there to watch!"

That night, after the fifth head count, instead of going down to the dining hall for dinner—the usual disgusting breaded halibut and overripe fruit—Patty had made arrangements with the guards for a little private party in the rack. They played cassettes of old torch songs by Vicente Fernández, Chavela Vargas, and Paquita la del Barrio, and after closing the door Patty pulled out a bottle of tequila she'd gotten god knows how—an authentic Don Julio some prison officer had probably smuggled in, after payment of a sum five times its price—and they put it away delightedly, enjoying how great it was. Some other girls joined the party, sitting on the bunks and in the chair and on the toilet in the case of Carmela, a big, older Gypsy, a shoplifter by profession, who cleaned for Patty and washed her sheets—Teresa's clothes, too, while her arm was in a cast—in exchange for Lieutenant O'Farrell's depositing a small sum of money into her account each month. Rabbit, the lye-pouring librarian, was there, as was Charito, who was in for picking pockets at the Rocío and Abril fairs (not to mention a hundred or so others). And also Pepa Trueno, aka Blackleg, who'd killed her husband with a knife they used for slicing ham in the bar they ran on National Highway 4, and who bragged that her divorce had cost her twenty years and a day, but not a penny.

Teresa put the silver *semanario* on her right wrist, to inaugurate her new arm, she said, and the bangles clinked happily with every drink. The party lasted until the eleven-o'clock head count. There was parcheesi, which was the slammer game par excellence, and tinned meat, and "perk-up-your-cunt" pills, as Carmela called them, and *basucos* made with thick rolls of hashish, and jokes, and laughter. *Here we are in Spain,* Teresa thought, *in big-deal Europe for god's sake, with its rules and its history and the way these people look down their noses at corrupt Mexicans, and look at us. Pills and chocolate and a bottle once in a while—nobody goes without if they find the right guard and have the money to pay for it.*

And Patty O'Farrell had money. She presided over the celebration, sitting off to one side, watching Teresa through a cloud of smoke the whole time, with a smile on her face and in her eyes. With her rich-girl attitude, it was as though she was just looking on, not really part of any of this—like some mommy who takes her little girl to a birthday party with hamburgers and clowns.

Meanwhile Vicente Fernández was singing about women and cheating, Chavela's breaking voice reeked of alcohol as she sang of bullets and cantinas, and Paquita la del Barrio belted out that song about *a dog, loyal and unquestioning, lying always at your feet, all day and all evening, and in your bed at night.* Teresa felt the embrace of the nostalgia, the music, and the accents of her homeland—the only thing lacking were *chirrines* strolling down the prison corridors making music, and a case of long-necked Pacíficos—although she was a bit befuddled by the hashish burning between her fingers. "Don't bogart that joint, there, Mexicanita." "I've smoked worse, girl— 'cause you go down to the Moors to score, you are definitely going to smoke some nasty shit." "To your twenty-fifth, my darling," toasted Carmela the Gypsy. And when Paquita started singing that old one about *Three times I cheated,* and she came to the chorus, all of them, now gloriously buzzed, joined in: *The first time out of anger, the second just because, and the third for pure damn pleasure*—"Three times I cheated, you motherfucker," shouted Pepa Trueno, no doubt in honor of her dearly departed.

They went on like that until one of the guards came around in a foul mood to tell them the party was over, but the party went on, in the same vein, later, when the cells were closed and the iron doors clanged shut all over the prison. Patty and Teresa were alone now in the rack, almost in darkness, the gooseneck lamp on the floor next to the washbasin, the shadowy magazine clippings—movie stars, singers, landscapes, a tourist map of Mexico—decorating the green-painted wall, the window with its lace curtains made by Charito the pickpocket, who had good hands. It was then that Patty took a second bottle of tequila and a little bag out from under her bunk and said, "This is just for us, Mexicana—I mean, giving is better than receiving, but you do need to keep something back for yourself!"

And with Vicente Fernández singing "Mujeres Divinas" for the umpteenth time, and Chavela, slurring her words, warning, *Don't threaten me, don't threaten me,* they passed the bottle back and forth and made little white lines on the cover of a book called *The Leopard.*

And later, Teresa, powder on her nose from the last sniff, said, "It's awesome. Thank you for this birthday, Lieutenant, never in my life . . ."

Patty shook her head, it was nothing, and as though she were thinking of something else, she said, "I'm going to masturbate a little now, if you don't mind, Mexicanita." She lay back on her bunk and took off her slippers and skirt, a very pretty dark full skirt that she looked good in, keeping on just her blouse. Teresa sat a little stunned with the bottle of Don Julio in her hand, not knowing what to do or where to look. Then Patty said, "You could help me, girl—it works better with two." But Teresa gently shook her head. "*Chale*. You know I'm not into that," she whispered.

And although Patty didn't insist, Teresa got up slowly after a minute or so, still clutching the bottle, and went and sat on the edge of her cellmate's bunk. Patty's legs were open and she had a hand between them, moving it slowly and softly, and she was doing all this while gazing at Teresa out of the green shadows of the rack. Teresa passed her the bottle, and Patty drank with her free hand, then returned the bottle as she continued to gaze at Teresa's face, into her eyes. Then Teresa smiled and said, "Thanks again for the birthday, Patty, and the book, and the party." And Patty never took her eyes off her as she moved her fingers between her naked thighs. Then Teresa leaned down close to her friend, repeated, "Thanks," very softly, and kissed her softly on the lips, just that, and for only a second. And she felt Patty hold her breath and tremble several times under her mouth, and moan, her eyes suddenly very wide, and afterward she lay without moving, still looking at her.

O'Farrell woke her up before dawn.
    "He's dead, Mexicanita."
    They hardly spoke about him. About *them*. Teresa was not one to open up too much, share confidences. Dropped words here and there, casual remarks: one time this, another time that. She really tried to avoid talking about Santiago, or Güero Dávila. Or even thinking very long about either one of them. She didn't have any photographs—the few with the Gallego, who knew where they were now?—except, of course, for the one of her and Güero torn in half. Sometimes the two men merged in her memory, and she didn't like that. It was like being unfaithful to both of them at once.
    "That's not it," Teresa replied.
    They were in darkness, and the sky had not yet begun to turn gray outside. It was still two or three hours before the guard would start banging on the doors with her key, waking the inmates up for the first

head count, giving them time to wash up before they rinsed out their underwear—the panties and T-shirts and socks that they would hang up to dry on broom handles stuck into the wall. Teresa heard her cellmate turning over, moving about in her bunk. A while later she changed positions, too, trying to sleep. Very far away, behind the metal door, down the module's long corridor, a woman's voice cried out. *I love you, Manolo,* she screamed. *I love you, I tell you,* another called back, closer, provocatively. *So do I,* a third voice chimed in. Then there were the footsteps of a guard, and silence once again. Teresa lay on her back, in a nightshirt, her eyes open in the darkness, waiting for the fear that would inevitably come, as regular as clockwork, when the first glow appeared in the window, through the lace curtains sewn by Charito the pickpocket.

"There's something I'd like to tell you," said Patty.

Then she fell silent, as though that were all, or as though she weren't sure she should tell, or perhaps waiting for some response from Teresa. But Teresa didn't say anything—not *Tell me,* not *Don't.* She lay motionless, looking up at the night.

"I've got a treasure hidden on the outside," Patty finally said.

Teresa heard her own laugh before she realized she was laughing. *"¡Híjole!"* she said. "Just like Abbé Faria."

"Yeah." Patty laughed too. "Except I don't intend to die in here. . . . In fact, I don't intend to die anywhere."

"What kind of treasure?" Teresa was curious.

"Something that got lost and everybody looked for, but that nobody found because the people who hid it are dead. . . . Like in the movies, huh?"

"I don't think it's like the movies. It's like life."

The two were silent for a while. I'm not sure, thought Teresa. I'm not totally convinced that I want to hear your secrets, Lieutenant. Maybe because you know more than I do and you're smarter than I am and older and everything, and I always catch you looking at me that way you look at me. Or maybe because I'm not crazy about the fact that you come when I kiss you. If a person's tired, there are things that shouldn't be talked about. And tonight I'm very tired, maybe because I drank and smoked and snorted too much, and now I can't sleep. This *year* I'm very tired. Hell, this *life.* For the moment, the word "tomorrow" doesn't exist. My lawyer only came to see me once. Since then all I've gotten from him is a letter telling me he invested our money in paintings whose value has dropped to almost nothing and there's not even enough left to pay for a coffin if I kick the bucket. But the truth is, I don't care about that. The one good thing about being in here is that this is all there is. And that keeps you from thinking about what you left outside. Or what's waiting for you out there.

"That kind of treasure is dangerous," Teresa said.

"Of course it is." Patty was speaking slowly, very softly, as though she were weighing every word. "I've paid a high price myself . . . got shot, you know. Bang bang. And here we are."

"So what *about* this fucking treasure, Lieutenant O'Farrell?"

They laughed again in the darkness. Then there was a quick burst of light at the head of Patty's bunk—she had just lit a cigarette.

"Well, I'm going to go look for it," she said, "when I get out of here."

"But you don't need that. You've got money."

"Not enough. What I spend in here is not mine, it's my family's." Her voice turned sarcastic when she pronounced that last word. "And the treasure that I'm talking about is real money. A lot of it. The kind that sometimes makes lots more, and more, and more."

"You really know where it is?"

"Sure."

"But somebody owns it. . . . I mean somebody besides you. Who owns it?"

The ember of the cigarette glowed. Silence.

"That's a good question."

"*Chale*. That's *the* question."

They fell silent again. You may know a lot more things than I do, thought Teresa—you've got education, and class, and a lawyer that comes to see you once in a while, and a good chunk of money in the bank, even if it belongs to your family. But what you're talking to me about—*that*, I know about, and it's very possible that I know quite a bit more about it than you do. Even if you've got two scars like little stars and a boyfriend in the cemetery, you're still like above it all. But me, I've seen it from down below. I've had mud on my bare feet when I was a kid, in Las Siete Gotas, where the drunks knocked on my mother's door in the middle of the night. I've also seen Gato Fierros' smile. And the León Rock. I've thrown fortunes overboard at fifty knots, with a chopper on my ass. So let's cut the crap.

"That question is hard to answer," Patty finally said. "There are people that were looking for it, sure. They thought they had a certain right to it, you know. . . . But that was a while back. Now nobody knows that I know."

"So why are you telling me about it?"

The red glow of the cigarette grew brighter a couple of times before the reply came. "I don't know. Or maybe I do."

"I never figured you for such a talker," said Teresa. "I could turn out to be the kind of girl who can't keep a secret. I could rat you out."

"Uh-uh. We've been in here together for a while, and I've been watching you. You aren't like that."

Another silence. This time longer than the others.

"You keep your mouth shut. You're loyal."

"You are too," Teresa replied.

"No. I'm other things."

Teresa saw the cigarette go out. She was curious, but she also wanted this conversation to be over. *Let's get this behind us,* she thought. I don't want you to wake up tomorrow and regret having said things you shouldn't have. About things that I don't need to know, places where I can't follow you. Or better yet, if you go to sleep now, we can always forget this happened, blame it on the party and the tequila and the coke.

"One day I may get you to help me recover that treasure," Patty suddenly concluded. "You and I, together."

Teresa held her breath. Oh shit, she said to herself. Now we can never pretend that this conversation never took place.

"Why me?" Teresa asked. She couldn't just say nothing. But she couldn't say flat-out yes or no, either. So that question was her only possible reply.

She heard Patty turn over in her bunk, toward the wall, before she answered.

"I'll tell you when the moment comes. If it does."

8. Kilo bricks

T here are people whose good luck derives from misfortunes," Eddie Alvarez concluded. "And that was the case of Teresa Mendoza."

The lenses of his glasses made his wary eyes look smaller. It had taken me time and a couple of intermediaries to get him to this point, sitting in front of me, but there he was, putting his hands in his jacket pockets and pulling them out again, after offering me just the tips of his fingers to shake. We were chatting on the terrace of the Rock Hotel in Gibraltar, with the sun filtering in through the ivy, ferns, and palms of the hanging garden on the face of the Rock itself. Down below, on the other side of the white balustrade, lay the Bay of Algeciras, bright and blurry in the blue haze of the afternoon: white ferries at the end of long straight wakes, the coast of Africa a hint of gray out beyond the Strait, the boats at anchor with their bows all pointing east.

"Well, I understand that at the beginning *you* helped her," I said. "By which I mean, you made some of those 'misfortunes' possible."

The lawyer blinked twice, twirled his glass on the table, and looked at me again.

"You shouldn't talk about things you don't know anything about." It sounded like reproach, and advice. "I did my job. That's how I make my living. And back then, she was nobody. No one could possibly have imagined . . ."

His face underwent two or three changes of expression, almost involuntarily, and there was displeasure, discomfort, a squirming quality there, as though somebody had told him a bad joke, one that it took a while to get. "Couldn't possibly . . ." he mused.

"Perhaps you're mistaken. Perhaps somebody *could* have imagined how things would go."

"We're often mistaken." Alvarez seemed to console himself with that plural. "Although in that chain of mistakes, I was the least of them."

He passed a hand across his sparse, curly hair, which he wore too long and which gave him an air of seediness. Then he touched the broad-mouthed glass again: his whisky was an unappetizing chocolaty color.

"In this life, everything comes with a price," he said after thinking for a moment. "Some pay in advance, others during, and still others afterward. . . . In the case of the Mexicana, she paid in advance. . . . She had nothing to lose, and everything to gain. And that's what she did."

"People say that you abandoned her in prison. Without a penny."

He looked truly offended. Although in a guy like him, with his background—I had taken the trouble to look into it—that meant absolutely nothing.

"I don't know what these 'people' might have told you, but that's not quite accurate. I can be as practical as the next man, understand? . . . It's perfectly normal in my profession. But that's not the point. I didn't abandon her."

With that out of the way, he gave a series of more or less reasonable justifications. Teresa Mendoza and Santiago Fisterra had, in fact, entrusted a certain amount of money to him. Not an extraordinary amount, just some funds that he proceeded to discreetly launder. The problem was that he invested almost all of it in paintings: landscapes, seascapes, and so on. A couple of nice portraits. Yes. And this happened to be just after the Gallego's death, when Teresa was in prison. And the painters were not very well known. Their parents may not even have claimed them—he smiled—which was why he invested in them. Appreciation, of course. But then the crisis came along and he'd had to sell off everything, to the last canvas, plus their small interest in a bar on Main Street and a few other things. From all that he deducted his fees—there were late payments and other matters—and the rest of the money went toward Teresa's defense. That entailed a considerable amount of money in expenses, of course—an arm and a leg, you might say. And after all was said and done, she'd spent only a year in prison.

"They say," I told him, "that that was thanks to Patricia O'Farrell, because it was her lawyers who did the paperwork."

He started to put a hand over his heart, once again offended. But he stopped in mid-gesture.

"They say a lot of things. The fact is, there came a moment when, well . . ." He looked at me the way a Jehovah's Witness looks at a doorbell. ". . . I had other concerns. The Mexicana's case was at a standstill."

"You mean the money had run out."

"The little there was, yes. Run out."

"And so you stopped representing her."

"Look . . ." He showed me the palms of his hands, raising them slightly, as though that were a guarantee. "This is how I earn my living. I couldn't afford to work for free—that's what court-appointed lawyers are for. Besides, I repeat that it was simply not possible to know . . ."

"I understand. She didn't come around to settle the score later?"

He became lost in the contemplation of his glass on the glass top of the table. My question did not seem to call up pleasant memories. Finally he shrugged in reply, and sat looking at me.

"But later," I insisted, "you *did* work for her again."

Once more he put his hands in his jacket pockets and took them out again. A sip from the glass, and the hands again.

"Maybe I did," he finally admitted. "For a short period of time, and a long time ago. Then I refused to go on. I'm clean."

My information said otherwise, but I didn't argue. What I'd been told was that when she got out of prison, the Mexicana had grabbed him by the balls and squeezed them till Eddie did what she wanted him to do, and then she threw him out once he was no longer useful. Those were the words of the police chief of Torremolinos, Pepe Cabrera. "Mendoza had that bastard shitting bricks. To the last." And that phrase fit Eddie Alvarez like a glove. You could perfectly imagine him so scared he was shitting bricks, or anything else Teresa Mendoza told him to shit. "Tell him I sent you," Cabrera had said while we were eating in the sporty port city of Benalmádena. "That piece of shit owes me big-time, and he won't be able to say no. That affair of the container from London and the robbery at Heathrow, for example—just mention that and he'll be eating out of your hand. What *you* get out of *him* is your business."

"She wasn't upset or anything, then," I persisted.

He looked at me with professional caution. "Why do you say that?" he asked.

"Punta Castor."

I figured he was calculating exactly how much I knew about what had happened. I didn't want to disappoint him. "The famous trap," I prodded.

The word seemed to have a laxative effect.

"Bullshit," he said, squirming in his rattan-and-wicker chair, making it creak. "What do you know about traps? . . . That word is an exaggeration."

"That's why I'm here. So you can set the record straight."

"At this late stage of things, it can hardly matter," he replied, picking up his glass. "In that mess at Punta Castor, Teresa knew I had nothing to do with what Cañabota and that sergeant in the Guardia Civil were planning. Afterward, she took the trouble to find all that out. And when my turn came . . . Well, I convinced her that I'd been an innocent bystander. And the fact that I'm still alive proves that I convinced her."

He turned thoughtful, tinkling the ice in his glass. He took a drink. "Despite the money lost on the paintings, Punta Castor, and all the rest . . ." he insisted, and he himself seemed surprised, "I'm still alive."

He took another drink. And then another. Apparently, all this remembering made him thirsty.

"Actually," he said, "no one ever went specifically after Santiago Fisterra. No one. Cañabota just needed somebody to use as a decoy while the real cargo was unloaded someplace else. That was standard practice: they used the Gallego the way they might have used anybody else. Bad luck is all it was. He wasn't the type to flip if somebody slapped a pair of handcuffs on him. Plus he was from outside, he had that attitude of his, and he had very few friends in the Strait. . . . And there was that sergeant in the Guardia Civil that had got the idea in his head of doing the Gallego in. So they picked him."

"And her," I suggested.

He squirmed and made the chair creak again, looking at the stairs to the terrace as though Teresa Mendoza were about to appear on them. A silence. Another drink. Then he straightened his glasses and said, "Unfortunately." Then he fell silent again. Another drink. Unfortunately, no one could have imagined the Mexicana would get where she got.

"So what happened to them afterward? . . . To Cañabota and this Sergeant Velasco?"

The defiance lasted three seconds. He folded. *You know as well as I do,* his eyes said distrustfully. Anybody that reads the newspapers knows. But if you think it's me that's going to explain it to you, you've got another think coming.

"I don't know anything about that." He made the gesture of zipping his mouth closed, looking mischievous and self-satisfied—the expression of a man who has remained standing longer than others of his acquaintance. I ordered coffee for me and another chocolate-colored whisky for him. From the city and the port came sounds muted by distance. An automobile was climbing the highway below the terrace, with a great deal of noise from its muffler, toward the peak of the Rock. I thought I saw a blond woman at the wheel, and a man in a sailor's jacket.

"Anyway," Eddie Alvarez went on, after considering the matter for a while, "all of that was later, when things changed and she decided to collect on her outstanding debts. . . . And listen, when she got out of El Puerto de Santa María, I figure all she was thinking about was disappearing from the world. I don't think she was ever ambitious, or a dreamer. . . . I'll wager she was never even truly vengeful. She just wanted to stay alive, that's all. Thing is, sometimes luck, after slapping you around for a while, decides to smile on you."

A group of men and women from Gibraltar occupied a neighboring table. Alvarez knew them, and he went over to say hello. That gave me the opportunity to study him from some remove: the obsequious way he smiled, shook hands, listened—like a man listening for clues to what he ought to say. A survivor, I told myself. The kind of slimy son of a bitch who survives, as another Eddie had described him—in this case Eddie Campello, also from Gibraltar, an old friend of mine and publisher of the local weekly *Vox.* "Doesn't even have the balls to double-cross you, our friend," said Campello when I asked about the relationship between the lawyer and Teresa Mendoza. "What happened at Punta Castor was Cañabota and that sergeant from the Guardia Civil—Alvarez wasn't involved. He just pocketed the Gallego's money, and money didn't mean shit to that woman. The fact that she rescued that asshole and put him to work for her again is proof of that."

"And let me tell you"—Eddie Alvarez was back at our table—"I'd say that the Mexicana is still not vengeful. She's more . . . I don't know. Maybe just practical, you see? . . . In her world, you don't leave loose ends."

Then he told me something interesting. "When they threw her into El Puerto, I went to the house that she and the Gallego had in Palmones, to liquidate everything and close it up. And you know what? She had gone to sea that night like so many other times, not knowing that it would be the last time. But she had everything all in order, in boxes, drawers, everything in its place. Even in the closets. That house could have passed an army inspection.

"More than cold-blooded calculation, ambition, or thirst for revenge"—Alvarez nodded, looking at me as though the drawers and boxes and closets explained everything—"I think it was a sense of symmetry."

She finished sweeping the wooden walkway, poured herself half a glass of tequila and filled the rest with orange juice, and then went to smoke a cigarette out on the end of the walk, shoeless, her feet half buried in the warm sand. The sun was still low, and its diagonal rays covered the beach with shadows from each wave or footprint, making the sandy expanse look like a landscape on the moon. Between the kiosk and the shoreline everything was clean and neat, awaiting the swimmers who would begin to arrive at mid-morning: two lounge chairs under each umbrella, carefully aligned by Teresa, with their blue-and-white-striped cushions shaken out and straightened. The air was calm, the sea was quiet, the water at the shore silent, and the early-morning sun shimmered with metallic orange splendor between the black silhouettes of the few passersby: retirees on their morning walks; a young couple with a dog; a solitary man looking out at the ocean, a fishing pole stuck into the sand beside him. And down toward the end of the beach and the orange glow, toward the east, behind the pines and the palm trees and the magnolias, Marbella, with the red-tile rooftops of its villas and its concrete-and-glass towers rising in the golden haze.

She savored her cigarette, undone and rerolled, as usual, with a little hashish. Tony, the manager of the stall, didn't like her to smoke anything but tobacco when he was around, but at this hour Tony hadn't arrived and the swimmers would be a while yet—it was the first few days of the season—so she could smoke in peace. And that tequila with orange juice, or vice versa, was terrific. She'd been here since eight this morning—coffee, no sugar, a piece of bread with olive oil, a donut—setting out the lounge chairs, sweeping the walkway, straightening tables and chairs, and ahead of her she still had a day of work identical to yesterday's and the day before's: dirty glasses behind the counter, and at the bar and the tables lemon slushes, juices, iced coffees, Cuba libres, mineral waters, her head splitting and her shirt drenched with sweat, under the palm-thatch roof the sun filtered through. The heavy, humid atmosphere reminded her of Altata in the summer, but with more people and more smell of suntan lotion.

And she had to be alert, too, to the demands of the customers: I ordered this with no ice, Listen, hey, I ordered this with lemon and ice, Don't tell me you don't have any Fanta, You gave it to me sparkling and I ordered it still. *Chíngale.* These fucking Spaniards and gringos summering here with their flowered shorts and red greasy skins and sunglasses, their screaming kids and their bodies spilling out of their bathing suits and T-shirts and pareos—they were much worse, much more self-centered and inconsiderate, than the customers that frequented Dris Larbi's puti-clubs. Teresa spent twelve hours a day with these people, back and forth, with no time even to sit down for ten minutes, the recently healed fracture in her arm aching from the weight of the drink-laden tray, her hair in two braids and a kerchief around her forehead to keep the sweat out of her eyes. And always with Tony watching her suspiciously.

But it wasn't all bad. There was that period in the morning when she'd finished straightening the kiosk and lining up the lounge chairs and could sit quietly and look out at the ocean, waiting, at peace. Or at night when she walked down the shore toward the modest *pensión* in the old part of Marbella, just like in the old days—centuries ago—in Melilla, when she closed up the Yamila. The hardest thing to get used to when she got out of El Puerto had been the bustle of the outside world, the noises, the traffic, the beaches full of people, the deafening music from the bars and discotheques, the flocks of people all along the coast from Torremolinos to Sotogrande. After a year and a half of strict routine and order, Teresa sometimes felt more uncomfortable on the outside than she'd felt behind bars. In prison, they told stories about inmates with long sentences who got out and then tried to find a way—that is, a crime—to get back into that single place in the world where they felt at home. Teresa never believed that, until one day, sitting in the same place where she was sitting now, smoking, she was suddenly swept by homesickness, if it could be called that, for the order and routine and silence of the life behind bars. Jail is home for nobody but the unfortunate of the earth, Patty had said once. For people who don't have any dreams.

Abbé Faria—Teresa had finished *The Count of Monte Cristo* and many other novels, and she was still buying books, which sat in piles around her room in the *pensión*—was not one of those who considered prison home. On the contrary: the old prisoner had yearned to get out so that he could recover the life that had been stolen from him. Like Edmond Dantès, but too late. After thinking a lot about this, Teresa had come to the conclusion that the treasure that belonged to the two men was simply a pretext for staying alive, dreaming of escape, feeling that

they were free despite the locks and bars and chains and walls of the
Château d'If. And in the case of Lieutenant O'Farrell, the story of the
cache of lost coca was also, in its way, a means of staying free—which
may have been why Teresa never entirely believed it. Although now,
when she was finally living in a world with real days, not just numbers
on a calendar, she found that she *wanted* to believe in something. She
wanted to have something just that clear-cut to live for.

Now what? she had asked herself as she'd stepped into the street outside the prison. The answer had come from O'Farrell, who sent her to
some friends who owned kiosks on the beaches at Marbella. "They
won't ask questions or exploit you too much," she'd said. "Or fuck you
if you don't want them to." The job made Teresa's parole possible—she
still had more than a year of her debt to society to pay off, and the only
limitation on her was that she stay in one place and make an appearance once a week at the local police station. The job also paid enough
for a room in a *pensión* on Calle San Lázaro, some books and clothes,
food, tobacco, a few sniffs of coke from time to time—and the packages of Moroccan chocolate for spiking the Bisontes she smoked in her
room at night or during slow hours on the beach, like now.

A seagull dropped down, watchfully gliding near the shore. It
skimmed the surface of the water and flew out seaward without finding anything. Fuck you, thought Teresa, inhaling, as she watched it fly
away. Fucking wolf with wings. She'd once liked seagulls; she had considered them romantic, until she got to know them on the trips back
and forth across the Strait in the Phantom, and especially one afternoon, in the early days, when something went wrong with the engine
in the middle of the ocean. They had both tried to get the engine
started, and Santiago stayed at it while she lay down to rest, watching
the gulls circle lazily nearby. He warned her to cover her face, because
gulls were known, he said, to peck at people if they fell asleep. The
memory came back with crystal-clear images: the quiet water, the seagulls floating on the water around the drifting speedboat or gliding
and fluttering above it, and Santiago aft, working on the engine, covered with grease to his elbows, his naked torso with the tattoo of Christ
on one arm, on the other those initials—whose, she never found out.

She inhaled several times more, letting the hash spread slowly
through her veins, toward her heart and brain. She tried not to think
much about Santiago, just as she tried to keep her headaches at bay by
taking a couple of aspirin before it was too late and the pain moved in
for hours, shrouding her in an exhausting cloud of queasiness and un-
reality.

Generally she managed not to think too much, period, about Santiago or anybody or anything. She had discovered too many uncertainties and horrors lurking in every thought that went beyond the here and now, or the practical. Sometimes, especially when she was lying awake at night, she couldn't keep herself from remembering. But as long as she didn't actually think, the remembering would give her no more than a sensation of movement toward nowhere, like a boat adrift. That was why she now smoked hashish. The smoke in her lungs—which may have traveled with me in twenty-kilo bundles from Morocco, she sometimes thought, amused by the paradox, when she scraped around in her pocket to pay for a miserable little bag of it—accentuated that sense she had of drifting off, drifting away. It brought with it not consolation or indifference, but rather a gentle stupor. It made her unsure that it was she herself she was remembering, as though there were several Teresas lurking in her memory, none with any direct relation to the Teresa of today.

Maybe it's that this is life, she would tell herself, confused and puzzled. Maybe old age, when it comes, is about looking back and seeing the many strangers that you have been and in whom you can't quite recognize yourself. With that idea in her head, sometimes she took out the torn photograph and looked at it, realizing that the features of the man that had been torn from the photo mixed in her memory with those of Santiago Fisterra, as though the two of them had been one. It was the opposite of what happened with the girl in the photo, the one with the big black eyes, who had shattered into so many different women that it was no longer possible to recompose her into just one.

These were Teresa's thoughts from time to time, until she realized that they were, or could be, the trap. So from then on she seized at the recourse of keeping her mind blank—allowing the smoke to run slowly through her blood and the tequila to calm her with its familiar taste. Those women who resembled her, those other Teresas, were falling into the past, floating like dead leaves on water.

That was also why she read so much, now. Reading, she'd learned in prison, especially novels, allowed her to inhabit her mind in a new way—as though by blurring the boundaries between reality and fiction, she might witness her own life as if it were happening to somebody else. Besides teaching her things, reading helped her think differently, or think better, because on the page, others did it for her. Although it was also true that with novels you could apply your point of view to every situation or character. Even to the voice that told the story: sometimes it would be that of a narrator, either with a name or anonymous, and sometimes it would be your own. She had discovered with surprise and pleasure that as she turned each page, the book was written, as though for the first time, all over again.

When she got out of El Puerto, Teresa had continued to read, and her choices were guided by intuitions, titles, first lines, cover illustrations. So now, in addition to her leather-bound *Monte Cristo,* she had her own books, which she bought one by one, cheap editions that she found at street markets or in used-book shops, or pocket books that she bought after giving spin after spin to those revolving racks. She would read novels written long ago by men and women whose portraits were sometimes on the back cover or the flap of the dust jacket, and also modern novels about love, adventure, travel. Of all she had read, her favorites were *Gabriela, Clove, and Cinnamon,* by a Brazilian writer named Jorge Amado; *Anna Karenina,* about the life of a Russian aristocrat, written by another Russian; and *A Tale of Two Cities,* which made her cry at the end, when the brave Englishman—Sydney Carton was his name—consoled the frightened young woman by taking her hand as she walked toward the guillotine. She also read that book about a doctor married to a millionaire that Patty had suggested she leave till later, and another, very strange one, hard to understand, that had drawn her in because from the first moment she recognized the land and the language and the soul of the characters that ran through its pages. The book was called *Pedro Páramo,* and although Teresa never fully unlocked its mysteries, she returned to it over and over again, opening it at random to reread a few pages. The way the words flowed fascinated her, as though she had peered into an unknown, shadowy, magical place that was related to something she herself possessed—she was sure of that—in some dark part of her blood and memory: *I came to Comala because I was told that my father, a certain Pedro Páramo, was living there. . . .*

So after a great deal of reading in El Puerto de Santa María, Teresa went on adding books to her inner library, one after another, on her free day each week, on nights when sleep would not come. Even the familiar fear of the gray light of dawn could be held at bay, sometimes, if she opened the book that always lay on the night table.

Tony arrived. Still young, with a beard, a ring in each ear, his skin tan from many Marbella summers. A T-shirt with the Osborne bull on it. A beach professional—or beach bum, perhaps, living off tourists, with no apologies. No apparent emotions at all. In the time she'd been there, Teresa had never seen him angry or in a particularly good mood, excited or disappointed, and certainly never cheery. He managed the kiosk with dispassionate efficiency, earned good money, was courteous with the customers and inflexible with the bores and troublemakers. Under the counter, he kept a baseball bat for emergencies, and he served the municipal police that patrolled the beaches snifters of cognac in the morning and gin and tonics when they were off duty. When Teresa came to meet him, shortly after getting out of El Puerto, Tony looked at her long and hard and said he'd give her a job because a friend had asked him to. "But no drugs, no alcohol in front of the customers, no picking them up or letting them pick you up, no sticking your hand in the cash drawer, or I'll throw you out on the fucking street. And if you stick your hand in the cash drawer, I'll also bust your face. The hours are eight to eight, plus the time it takes you to pick up after we close. Take it or leave it."

Teresa had taken it. She needed a legal gig in order to satisfy the conditions of her parole, and eat, and sleep under a dry roof. And Tony and his kiosk were as good or bad as anything else.

She finished smoking the *basuco,* burning the tips of her fingers, and then finished off the tequila and orange juice in one long gulp. The first swimmers were beginning to arrive, with their towels and their suntan lotion. The guy with the fishing rod was still down on the shoreline, and the sun was rising higher and higher, warming the sand. A nice-looking man was doing exercises down past the lounge chairs, gleaming with sweat like a horse after a long race. She could almost smell his skin. Teresa stood watching him for a while—his flat stomach, his back muscles flexing with each push-up or twist of his torso. Once in a while he would pause to catch his breath, looking down at the ground as though he were thinking, and she watched him with her own thoughts running around and around in her head. Flat stomachs, back muscles. Men with bronzed, weather-beaten skin smelling of sweat, jealous under their pants. *Chale.* It was so easy to catch them, and yet so hard, despite everything, despite how predictable they were. And so simple to become a mere "girlfriend," an appendage, a nothing, when you thought with your pussy, or even when you just thought so much that finally it was all the same, you were stupid from being so fucking smart. Since she'd been on the outside again, Teresa had had only one sexual encounter: a young waiter at a kiosk on the other end of the beach, one Saturday night when instead of heading off for her room she stayed around, drinking a few drinks and smoking a couple of joints while she sat on the sand and watched the lights of the fishing boats in the distance and dared herself not to remember. The waiter's timing when he came up to her was perfect, and he was cute, clever, and funny enough to make her laugh, so they wound up a couple of hours later in his car, parked in an abandoned lot near the bullring. It was an encounter that just happened, and Teresa went into it with more curiosity than real desire—she watched herself, absorbed in her own reactions and emotions. The first man in a year and a half—something many of the girls in the prison would have given months of freedom for.

But she picked the wrong place and the wrong company. Those lights out on the black ocean, she later decided, were to blame. The waiter, a kid who resembled the man doing exercises down by the lounge chairs—no doubt why this memory had come to her now—was selfish and clumsy, and the condom that she made him put on after looking for a good long time for a pharmacy open at that hour didn't make things any better. It was so uncomfortable inside the car that she had to struggle even to unzip her jeans. When they finished, the kid was visibly ready to go home and get some sleep, and Teresa was unsatisfied and furious with herself—more furious still with the silent woman who looked back at her from behind the red cigarette-ember in the car window: a luminous dot like those on the fishing boats that worked all night, and on the boats in her memory. So she pulled on her jeans again, got out of the car, said, So long, nice knowing you. She hadn't even caught the kid's name, and if it mattered to him, then *que chingue a su madre.*

That same night, when she got to her room, Teresa took a long, hot shower, and then she got drunk and lay naked on her bed, facedown—so drunk that she vomited, long arcs of bile—and fell asleep at last with one hand between her thighs, her fingers inside her sex. She could hear the distant sound of Cessnas and speedboat engines, and the voice of Luis Miguel singing from the cassette player on the night table. *If they let us, if they let us, we will love each other all our lives.*

She woke up that same night, shivering in the darkness, because she had finally discovered, in a dream, what was going on in that little Mexican novel by Juan Rulfo. It was the one she'd never quite understood before, no matter how hard she'd tried. *I came to Comala because I was told that my father, a certain Pedro Páramo, was living there. . . .*

¡Híjole! The characters in that story were all dead, but they just didn't know it.

You've got a phone call," Tony said.
Teresa put the dirty glasses in the sink, set the tray on the counter, and went down to the end of the bar. It was the butt-end of a

long, hot, hard day: thirsty men, women in dark sunglasses with their pussies in the sun—some of them had no shame—ordering beers and drinks all day; and her head was splitting and her feet burned from walking back and forth from the bar to the lounge chairs over the hot coals of the sand, waiting on table after table, and sweating like crazy in the blinding glare of that blast oven. It was late afternoon, and some of the bathers were beginning to leave the beach, but she still had a couple of hours of work ahead of her.

She dried her hands on her apron and picked up the telephone. Nobody had called her since she'd gotten out of El Puerto, either at the kiosk or anywhere else, nor could she imagine why anybody would do so now. Tony must have been thinking the same thing, because he watched her out of the corner of his eye as he dried glasses and lined them up on top of the bar.

"Hello," she said warily.

She recognized the voice at the first word, with no need for the person to say, It's me. A year and a half hearing that voice day and night had engraved it in her memory. So she smiled and then laughed out loud, almost joyously. *¡Órale, mi teniente!* How great to hear your voice. How's life treating you? She was truly happy to hear that self-assured, composed tone of voice, that person who took things as they came. That person who knew herself and other people as well, because she knew how to look at them, and she had learned even more from people's silences than from their words. At the same time, in one part of her mind, Teresa thought, *Chale,* I wish I could talk like that, dial a telephone number after all this time and say, *How's it hanging, Mexicanita, you silly bitch you, I hope you've missed me while you were screwing half of Marbella, now that nobody's watching you. We going to see each other, or have you moved on?*

Teresa asked whether she was really out, and Patty O'Farrell laughed and said, "Of course I'm out, silly, out three days ago, and going from one homecoming to another—I don't sleep, and then they wake me up again! And every time I catch my breath or regain consciousness I've tried to find your telephone number—and I finally found it, about time, huh?—so I could tell you that those fucking dyke guards could not keep the old Abbé down, and that they can finally shove the Château d'If up their asses, and that it's about time for Edmond Dantès and his friend Faria to have a long, civilized conversation somewhere where the sun doesn't come in through bars. So I thought you could take a bus, or a taxi if you've got some money, or whatever, and come to Jerez, because tomorrow they're throwing me a little party and the truth is, without you, parties are weird. How about that, puss? Jail-house habits are hard to break, huh? So, you coming or not?"

It was quite a party. A party at a country house in Jerez, what the Spaniards called a *cortijo*, one of those places where it took you for-ever to get from the archway at the entrance of the grounds to the house itself, at the end of a long gravel driveway, with expensive cars parked at the door and walls of red-ocher plaster and windows with wrought-iron grilles that reminded Teresa—this is where they come from, she realized—of old Mexican haciendas. The place was like one of those houses in the magazines: rustic furniture ennobled by antiq-uity, dark paintings on the walls, terra-cotta floors, beamed ceilings. And a hundred or so guests drinking and talking in two large rooms and out on the terrace with its grape arbor extending toward the rear, a roofed bar to one side, an enormous wood-fired grill, and a pool. The sun was just setting, and the dusty dull gold light gave an almost ma-terial consistency to the warm air, out on the horizon of green vine-yards softly rising and falling into the distance.

"I like your house," Teresa said.

"I wish it was mine."

"But it belongs to your family."

"There's a big difference between my family and me."

They were sitting under the grape arbor, in wooden chairs with linen-upholstered cushions, each with a glass in hand, looking at the people milling about nearby. Everything in keeping, Teresa decided, with the place and the cars at the door. At first she'd been ill at ease in her jeans and high heels and simple blouse, especially when some people looked at her strangely when she arrived, but Patty O'Farrell—in a mauve cotton dress, pretty embossed sandals, her blond hair cut short as she always wore it—reassured her. "Here," she said, "everybody dresses the way they want to. And you look terrific. That hair pulled back so tight, with the part down the middle, looks wonderful on you. Very native. You never wore it like that in lockup."

"In lockup I didn't go to any parties."

"Oh, yes you did!"

And the two of them laughed, remembering. There was tequila, Teresa discovered, and alcohol of all kinds, and uniformed servants moving about with trays of hors d'oeuvres. Perfect. Two flamenco gui-tarists were playing at the center of a group of guests. The music, happy and melancholy at the same time, rising and falling in gusts of sound, fit the place and the landscape in the background. Sometimes the people listening clapped, and some of the young women danced, arms high, fingers snapping, heels tapping, pretending to be Gypsies, and then conversed with their companions. Teresa envied the self-possession that allowed them to move about like that, greet people, talk, smoke in that distinguished way that Patty also had, one arm across their lap, one hand holding the other elbow, the arm vertical, the smoking cigarette between their fingers. This may not have been the highest of high society, she concluded, but it was fascinating to watch them—they were so different from the people she'd met in Culiacán with Güero Dávila, thousands of years and miles from her most recent past and from what she was, or ever would be. Even Patty seemed an unreal link between those different worlds. That's the way you're supposed to act, she decided, and I wish I could learn how. And how nice to be able to observe it all, so unimportant and invisible that nobody even noticed you.

Most of the male guests were over forty, with dark jackets, good shoes and watches, and informal touches—open shirts, no tie. Their skin was tanned, and not exactly from working in the fields. As for the women, there were two definite types: good-looking girls with long legs, some a little ostentatious in their clothing and jewelry, and others that were better dressed, more sober, with fewer adornments and makeup, on whom plastic surgery and money—one permitted by the other—sat very naturally. Patty's sisters belonged to that second group: nose jobs, facelifts, blond hair with tips and streaks, that marked Andalucían accent that betokened good breeding, elegant hands that had never washed a dish, designer clothes. Around fifty the older one, forty-something the other, Teresa figured. They resembled Patty from the front—the oval faces, the way they twisted their mouths when they talked or smiled. They'd looked Teresa up and down with that same arching of the eyebrows—two circumflexes that took her in and put her down in mere seconds—before returning to their social obligations and their guests.

"Pigs," Patty muttered when they'd turned their backs, just as Teresa was thinking, *Órale*, what was I thinking, wearing this smuggler outfit. I should have worn something else, the silver bracelets and a skirt instead of jeans and heels and this old blouse that they looked at like it was a dishrag.

"The older one," Patty said, "is married to a lazy idiotic bum, that potbellied bald guy laughing like a hyena in that group over there, and the other one kisses up to my father the way he likes it. Although the truth is, they both kiss his ass."

"Is your father here?"

"Good god, of course not." Patty crinkled her nose elegantly, her whisky on the rocks halfway to her mouth. "That old *cabrón* lives under glass in his apartment in Jerez. . . . He's allergic to the country." She laughed maliciously. "Pollen and all that."

"Why did you invite me?"

Without looking at her, Patty finished raising her glass to her lips. "I thought," she said, her lips moist, "that you'd like to have a drink with me."

"There are bars to have drinks in. And this is not my scene."

Patty set her glass down on the table and lit a cigarette, although the previous one was still burning in the ashtray.

"Mine, either. Or at least not entirely." She looked around contemptuously. "My sisters are absolute imbeciles—throwing a party to welcome me back into society. Instead of hiding me, they show me off, get it? That way they can act like they're not ashamed of the lost sheep. . . . Tonight they'll go to bed with their cunts cold and their consciences easy, like they always do."

"Maybe you're being unfair to them. Maybe they're really glad."

"Unfair? . . . Here?" She bit her lower lip with an unpleasant smile. "Would you believe it if I told you that nobody has yet to ask me how it was for me in prison? . . . Taboo subject. Just, Hey, sweetheart. *Kiss, kiss.* Like I'd been on vacation in the Caribbean."

Her tone was lighter than in El Puerto, Teresa thought. More flighty, frivolous; more talkative. She says the same things and in the same way, but there's something different, as though here she feels the need to give me explanations that in our former life were unnecessary. Teresa had been watching her from the first moment, when Patty stepped away from some people to greet her, and then when she left her alone a couple of times, going and coming among the guests. It took a minute to recognize her, to really believe it was her behind those smiles, the gestures of complicity with people who were strangers to Teresa, to really believe it was Patty accepting cigarettes, inclining her head while someone lit them for her.

When Patty returned and they went out to sit on the terrace, Teresa finally began to recognize her. And it was true that now she explained things more, justified them, as if unsure that Teresa would understand, or—the thought now struck Teresa—approve.

That possibility gave her something to think about. Maybe, she ventured after some reflection, the personal legends that work behind bars don't work on the outside, and once you're out you have to establish who you are all over again. Confirm it in the light of the street. Maybe Lieutenant O'Farrell is nobody here, or not what she really wants to be.

And maybe, also, she's afraid that I'll realize that. My advantage is that I never knew what or who I was while I was on the inside, and so maybe that's why I'm not worried about what or who I am outside. I've got nothing to explain to anybody. Nothing to convince anybody about. Nothing to prove.

"You still haven't told me what I'm doing here," Teresa said.

Patty shrugged. The sun was lower now on the horizon, turning the air scarlet. Her short blond hair was set on fire in that light.

"I will—in due time." She half closed her eyes, looking into the distance. "For now, just enjoy this."

Maybe the change in Patty had some simple explanation, thought Teresa. A lieutenant without any troops, a retired general whose prestige goes unrecognized in the civilian world. Maybe she's invited me here because she needs me. Because I respect her and I know that period in her life, and these people don't. As far as they're concerned, she's just a society girl with a drug problem, a black sheep that these people—this family, this class—take in and tolerate because they never renounce their own in public, even if they hate them or hold them in contempt. Maybe that's why she needs company so much. She needs a witness. Somebody that knows, and that sees all this, and that can keep her mouth shut. Down deep, life is very fucking simple: You can divide people into those you're obliged to make conversation with while you have a drink, and those you can drink with for hours without saying a word, like Güero Dávila did in that cantina in Culiacán. People who know, or intuit, enough for there to be no need for words, and who're behind you even if they're not totally with you. They're just there. And maybe this is that case, although I have no idea where that takes us. To what new variant on the word "solitude."

"To your health, Lieutenant."

"And to yours, Mexicana."

They clinked glasses. Teresa looked around, enjoying the fragrance of the tequila. In a group of guests near the pool she saw a tall young man—so tall he stood out from everyone around him. He was thin, with very black hair, slicked back and glistening, long and curly at the neck. He was wearing a dark suit, white shirt with no tie, shiny black shoes. The pronounced jaw and big curved nose gave him an interesting profile, like a skinny eagle. A guy with class, she thought. Like those super-Spaniard types one imagines from days gone by, aristocrats and hidalgos and all that—Malinche must have gone over to the other side for *some* reason—who probably never actually existed.

"Nice people here," Teresa said.

Patty turned to follow her eyes. "Oh god," she groaned. "Boring and more boring."

"They're your friends."

"I don't have any friends, my dear." Her voice had hardened a notch, more like in the old days.

"*Chíngale*"—Teresa pulled her head back as though dodging a blow—"I thought you and I were."

Patty looked at her wordlessly and took a sip of her drink. Her eyes seemed to be laughing; there were wrinkles all around them. She finished her whisky, put the glass down on the table, and brought her cigarette to her lips without saying anything.

"Anyway," said Teresa after a moment, "the music is nice and the house is beautiful. They were worth the trip." She looked distractedly at the eagle-faced man, and once again Patty followed her gaze.

"Yeah? . . . Well, I hope you don't resign yourself to so little. Because this is nothing in comparison to what you could have."

Hundreds of crickets were chirping in the darkness. A lovely moon was rising, illuminating the grapevines, silvering every leaf; the walk lay white and curving before them. Behind them the lights of the enormous country house glimmered. The remains of the party had been cleared and the downstairs put in order for some time already, and now the mansion was silent. The last guests had said their good nights and Patty's sisters and brother-in-law were on their way back to Jerez after a nice heart-to-heart talk with Patty on the terrace, discussing her plans for the future, everyone uncomfortable and wanting the conversation over with. And the Lieutenant was right to the end— no one mentioned, even in passing, Patty's years in El Puerto de Santa María. Teresa, whom Patty had insisted stay over, wondered what in the world her former rackmate had on her mind that night.

Both of them had drunk quite a bit that evening, but not enough. So as silent servants had gone about magically eliminating all traces of the party, Patty had disappeared, then reappeared, surprise, surprise, with a gram of white powder that made their minds very clear and sharp indeed after it was razor-bladed into lines on the glass top of the table. Unbelievable stuff—stuff Teresa knew how to appreciate. Then, as clear-sighted and alert as though the day had just begun, they walked unhurriedly off toward the dark vineyards beyond the terrace. With no particular destination.

"I want you real awake for what I'm going to tell you," said Patty, recognizable again.

"I am very fucking awake," said Teresa. And she was prepared to listen. She had emptied another glass of tequila as they walked, and then had set the glass down at some point on the path. And being awake—she thought, without knowing what made her think it—was very much like being all right again. Like finding yourself unexpectedly at home in your own skin. Without thoughts, without memories. Just the immense night and the familiar voice speaking in a secretive whisper, as if someone might be crouching in the shadows, spying on them in that strange light silvering the broad vineyards. And she could also hear the chirping of the crickets, the sound of her friend's footsteps, and the swishing of her own bare feet—she had left her heels on the terrace—on the loose soil of the path.

". . . And that's the story," Patty concluded.

Well, I have no intention of thinking about your story now, Teresa told herself. I don't plan to consider or analyze anything tonight as long as the darkness lasts and there are stars up there, and the tequila and coke have got me feeling like this for the first time in so long. I don't know why you waited until today to tell me all this, or what you intend to do about it. I listened to that story of yours like I'd listen to a novel. And I prefer it that way, because otherwise I'd be forced to acknowledge the existence of the future. So let's agree that you told me a nice story, or rather finished telling me what you started whispering about when we were rackmates. Then I'll go back and sleep, and tomorrow, in the daylight, I'll start a new day.

And yet, Teresa admitted to herself, it was a good story. The boyfriend shot dead, the half-ton of coca that nobody ever found. Now, after the party, Teresa could picture the boyfriend, a guy like the ones she'd seen in the house, with a dark jacket and a shirt with no tie and all very elegant. Like the second or third generation of Colonia Chapultepec but better, spoiled like those society kids in Culiacán that drove to high school in their 4x4s escorted by bodyguards. A boyfriend who was lowlife and society at the same time—white powder dusting his nose a gram at a time, fucking other girls and letting her fuck other guys and other girls, too, and playing with fire until he got burned, getting mixed up in a world where fuck-ups—not to mention amateurism, with a little bit of spoiled machismo stirred in—exacted a high price.

They killed him and two others, Patty had said, and Teresa knew better than many people what kind of fucked-up thing her friend was talking about. They killed him for lying to them and double-crossing them and not doing what he said he'd do, and it was bad luck, the worst, because the next day the Narcotics Division moved in, because the other half-ton of coca, they were following it real close, and they had bugged everything, down to the glass of water he gargled with after he brushed his teeth. The hit was done by the Russian mafia, who got kind of drastic when some bullnecked Boris wasn't happy with the boyfriend's explanations of the suspicious loss of half a shipment that had come into the port of Málaga in a single container. And those Communists recycled into gangsters tended to wipe the slate clean— after many fruitless attempts to recover the cargo, when their patience ran out, one of the boyfriend's partners had been found dead in his house in front of the TV, and the other was discovered out on the Cádiz–Seville highway. Patty's boyfriend got it as he was leaving a Chinese restaurant in Fuengirola, three in the head as he opened the car door, two by accident for her, since they thought she wasn't in the loop. But fuck being out of the loop—she was definitely in it. Because the boyfriend was one of those bigmouths that spill things before and after they come, or when they've got their nose in the powder. Which meant that at some point, in bed or after a few lines, he had told Patty that the stash of coke, the half a shipment, half a ton that everybody thought was lost and sold off on the black market, was still all packed up nice and neat and stashed in a cave on the coast near Cape Trafalgar, waiting for somebody to come and give it a lift home. And after the murder of her boyfriend and the others, the only person that knew the location was Patty. So when she got out of the hospital and the Narcotics Division guys were waiting for her in the parking lot, all that happened when they asked her about the famous half a ton was that her eyebrows went up practically to her hairline. *What!* I have no fucking idea what you're talking about, she said, looking them dead in the eye, one by one. And after a lot of subsequent huffing and puffing on their part, they believed her.

So what do you think, Mexicana?"
    "I don't think."
    She had stopped, and Patty was looking at her. The light of the moon behind Patty fell on her shoulders and the crown of her head, whitening her short hair as though she'd suddenly gone gray.
    "Make an effort."
    "I don't want to. Not tonight."
    A glow. A match and then a cigarette illuminating Lieutenant O'Farrell's chin and eyes. It's her again, thought Teresa. The old one.
    "You really don't want to know why I've told you all this?"

"I know why. You want to recover that stash of coke. And you want me to help you."

The ember glowed twice in silence. They began walking again.

"You've done things like this," Patty insisted. "Incredible things. You know the places. You know how to get there and get back."

"What about you?"

"I've got contacts. I know what to do afterward."

Teresa continued to refuse to think. It's important, she told herself. She was afraid that if she thought too much, she'd see the dark water, the lighthouse flashing in the distance again, or the black rock where Santiago was killed.

"It's dangerous to go there." Teresa surprised even herself, saying that. "Plus, if the owners find out . . ."

"There are no owners anymore. A lot of time has gone by. Nobody remembers."

"People remember things like that forever."

"Well, then," Patty said, and walked a few steps in silence, "we'll negotiate with whoever we need to."

Incredible things, she'd said. It was the first time Teresa had heard her say anything that sounded so much like respect. And she's not trying to do a snow job on me, Teresa told herself. She's capable of trying to manipulate me, but not this time. I know her, and I'm sure she was sincere.

"And what do I get out of it?"

"Half. Unless you prefer to go on being a waitress selling beer to tourists."

That nasty slash reawakened the heat, the T-shirt soaked with sweat, the suspicious look from Tony on the other side of the bar, her own animal exhaustion. The voices of the swimmers, the smell of bodies smeared with oils and creams. All that lay a four-hour bus ride from this stroll under the stars. A soft sound among the nearby branches interrupted her thoughts. A whir of wings, startling her.

"It's an owl," said Patty. "There are a lot of owls here. They hunt at night."

"What if the stash is not still there?" said Teresa.

And yet . . . she thought finally. And yet . . .

9. Women can, too

It had rained all morning, heavy sheets that raised foggy spatters in the surf, with gusts of wind that drove the rain and blotted out the gray silhouette of Cape Trafalgar. With the rubber dinghy and outboard motor sitting useless on the trailer, they smoked on the beach, inside the Land Rover, listening to music, watching the water run down the windshield and the hours pass on the dashboard clock. Patricia O'Farrell was in the driver's seat, Teresa in the other, with a thermos of coffee, bottles of water, packets of tobacco, thick ham and white cheese on good dense rolls with thick golden crust, notebooks with hand-drawn maps, and a nautical chart of the area, the most detailed one Teresa could find. The sky was still dingy gray—the tail end of a spring that was resisting the coming of summer—and the low clouds were scudding toward the east, but the ocean, an undulating, leaden surface, was calmer, and the only whitecaps were breakers on the rocks, farther down the coast.

"We can go now," said Teresa.

They got out of the Land Rover, stretching their stiff muscles as they walked along the wet sand, and then they opened the tailgate and took out the wetsuits. There was still a light, intermittent drizzle, and Teresa got goosebumps when she took off her clothes. It's cold as hell, she thought. She pulled the tight neoprene pants on over her bathing suit, and zipped up the vest without pulling the hood up over her hair, which was gathered into a ponytail. Two girls going scuba diving in this weather, she said to herself. Gimme a break. Although if somebody is stupid enough to be out in this weather, I guess they'll buy it.

"Ready?"

She saw her friend nod without taking her eyes off the enormous gray expanse that undulated out there in front of them. Patty was not used to this kind of situation, but she took it all with reasonable aplomb—not too much chatter, or nerves, at least that you could see. She just looked preoccupied, although Teresa had noticed how many cigarettes she'd smoked while they were waiting, one after another. She had one in her mouth now, wet with mist, and she squinted as she pulled the wetsuit up onto her legs. And she'd had a snort just before they got out of the car, a precise ritual, a new bill rolled up, two lines on the plastic sleeve that held the automobile registration.

But Teresa wouldn't join her this time. It was another kind of alertness she needed, she thought as she finished gathering up her equipment, mentally reviewing the chart that she had studied for so long it was engraved on her memory: the line of the coast; the curve toward the south, toward Barbate; the steep, rocky cliff at the end of the clean beach. And there, not on the chart but pointed out very carefully by Patty, the two large caves and one small one hidden between them, inaccessible from land and hardly visible from the sea—the Marrajos Caves.

"Let's go," Teresa said. "We've only got four hours of daylight."

They put their backpacks—zip-lock bags, knives, lengths of nylon rope, waterproof flashlights—and their harpoons in the rubber boat, for appearance' sake, and after unbuckling the belts on the trailer, dragged the boat down to the shore. It was a nine-foot gray rubber Zodiac. The gas tank was full, and the fifteen-horsepower Mercury, checked by Teresa the previous day, like back in the old days, was ready. They fitted it onto the motor brackets and tightened the wing nuts. Everything in order, the motor horizontal and the propeller up. Then, one on each side, pulling on the safety lines, they dragged it into the water.

In cold water up to her waist, pushing the inflatable raft outside the breakers, Teresa made an effort not to think about the past. She wanted her memories to bring her nothing but useful experience, essential technical knowledge, not to burden her with dead weight.

Patty helped her climb aboard as she scaled the slippery rubber. The sea was pushing them toward the beach. Teresa started the engine on the first try, a quick, sharp tug on the rope. The noise cheered her heart. Here we are again, she thought. For good or ill. She told Patty to go forward to balance the weight, and she herself settled down beside the motor, steering the boat away from shore and then toward the black rock down at the end of the sandy beach, which shone silvery-white in the gray light. The Zodiac handled well. Teresa steered it the way Santiago had taught her, dodging the crests, bow into the sea and then sliding down the other face of the waves. Enjoying it. *Chale*, even like this, nasty, choppy, gray, the ocean was beautiful. With delight she inhaled the wet air that brought memories of salt spray, scarlet sunsets, stars, night hunts, lights on the horizon, Santiago's impassive profile silhouetted in the helicopter's spotlight, the HJ's flashing blue eye, the bounces on the black water jolting her kidneys. How sad everything was, yet how beautiful. Now there was still a fine misty drizzle, and gusts of salt spray pelted her face. She looked at Patty, dressed in the blue neoprene that clung to her figure: she was gazing out at the water and the black rocks without entirely concealing her apprehension. If you only knew, *carnalita,* thought Teresa. If only you'd seen the things I've seen on these seas.

But Patty was a trouper. They'd talked a hundred times about the consequences if things went south, including the possibility that the half-ton of coke wasn't there at all. Lieutenant O'Farrell had her obsession, and she had balls. Maybe that was the least reassuring thing about her—too much balls and too big an obsession. That, Teresa thought, didn't always go hand in hand with the cool head this kind of business called for. On the beach, while they were waiting in the Land Rover, Teresa had realized something: Patty was a companion, even a partner, but not a solution. However this ended, there was a long stretch that Teresa would have to travel by herself; nobody was going to make the trip any easier.

Although she could never quite pin down how it happened, the dependency that Teresa had felt up to now, on everything and everybody—or rather, her stubborn belief in that dependency—began to change into a certainty that she really was an orphan in the world. The conviction had begun to form in prison, in those last months, and maybe the books she'd read had had something to do with it, the hours spent lying awake, waiting for the sun to come up, the reflections that the peace of that time brought to her head. Then she'd gotten out, and was once again alive and in the world. And the time that had passed working at the beach kiosk, in what turned out to be just another wait, only confirmed the truth.

But she'd been aware of none of this until the night of the party at the estate in Jerez. As they were walking through the dark vineyards and she heard Patty speak the word "future," Teresa saw in a kind of flash that Patty was perhaps not the stronger of the two. Just as hundreds of years earlier, in another life, Güero Dávila and Santiago Fisterra had not been, either. It might be that ambition, plans, dreams, even bravery, or faith—even faith in God, she decided, shivering—didn't give you strength, but took it away. Because hope, even the mere desire to survive, made a person vulnerable, bound to possible pain and defeat. Maybe that was the basic difference between some human beings and others, and that was the case with her. Maybe Edmond Dantès was wrong, and the only solution was *not* to trust, and *not* to hope.

The cave was hidden behind huge boulders that had fallen off the cliff face. Teresa and Patty had done reconnaissance four days earlier: from thirty feet up, standing on the cliff's edge, Teresa had studied and made a note of every rock, taking advantage of the clear day, the clean, calm water, to consider the bottom, its irregularities, and the way to approach the cave by sea without having a sharp edge underwater puncture the Zodiac.

And now they were there, swaying in the water while Teresa, with light touches on the gas and zigzagging adjustments of the tiller, tried to stay clear of the rocks and find a safer way in. Finally she realized that the Zodiac could make it into the cave only in calm water, so she steered toward the larger opening to the left. And there, beneath the overhang of the cave entrance, in a place where the ebb and flow wouldn't push them against the cliff face, she told Patty to drop the folding grapnel, which was tied to the end of a thirty-foot line. Then they both slid down the sides of the boat into the water and swam with another line to the rocks, which the swell covered and uncovered with each movement. They floated easily, thanks to their wetsuits.

When they reached the rocks, Teresa tied the line to one, warning Patty to be careful of the sea-urchin spines, and then they made their way slowly along the rocky coast, from the big cave to the smaller one, wading in water that rose and fell from their waists to their chests. Sometimes a breaking wave forced them to hold on to something so as not to lose their footing, and then their hands were cut and scratched by the sharp rocks, or they could feel the tugging at the neoprene around their elbows and knees. It was Teresa who, after looking down from the top, had insisted on the suits. "They'll keep us warmer," she said, "and without them we'll get cut to ribbons."

"Here it is." Patty pointed. "Just the way Jimmy described it . . . The arch up above, the three big rocks, and that little one. See? . . . We've got to swim in to where it gets shallow, and then we can stand."

Her voice echoed in the large opening. There was a strong smell of rotting seaweed, the mossy rocks that the swells constantly covered and uncovered. The two turned away from the light and pushed forward into the semidarkness. Inside, the water was calmer; they could still see the bottom clearly when it fell away and they had to swim a few yards. Almost at the end of the cave they found some sand, scattered pebbles, and shreds of dead seaweed. That far in, it was dark.

"I need a goddamn cigarette," Patty muttered.

They waded out of the water and fished cigarettes out of the waterproof pockets of their packs. They smoked for a while, looking at one another. The arc of light at the entrance was reflected in the water until about halfway in, and it cast a grayish light over them. Wet, their hair stringy, fatigue on their faces. Now what? they seemed to ask each other silently.

"I hope it's still there," Patty whispered.

They stayed where they were long enough to finish their cigarettes. If a half-ton of cocaine was really just steps away, nothing in their lives would ever be the same once they'd covered that distance. And both of them knew it.

"*Órale,* there's still time, *carnalita.*"

"Time for what?"

Teresa smiled, turning her thought into a joke. "Well, I'm not sure. Maybe to not find out."

Patty smiled, too, distantly. Her mind was already a few steps farther ahead. "Don't be stupid," she said.

Teresa squatted down to look for something in the backpack at her feet. She had loosened her hair, and the ends were dripping water inside the pack. She took out her flashlight.

"You know something?" she said, testing it.

"No. But you'll tell me."

"I think there are dreams that can kill you." The walls, now lighted by the flashlight, were of black rock, and stalactites could be seen hanging from the ceiling. "More than people, or disease, or time."

"So?"

"So nothing. Just occurred to me, that's all. A minute ago."

Patty didn't look at her; she was hardly paying attention. She had picked up her own flashlight, and had turned toward the rocks at the rear of the cave, lost in thought.

"What the fuck are you talking about?"

A distracted question, not interested in a reply. Teresa didn't answer. She looked at her friend attentively, because her voice, even if you took into account the effect of the echo inside the cave, sounded strange. *I hope she hasn't decided to shoot me in the back, in this treasure cave, like pirates in some book,* Teresa said to herself, only half amused. Despite the absurdity of the idea, she caught herself looking down at the reassuring handle of the diving knife sticking up out of her open pack. Jesus, no need to creep yourself out. And she kept telling herself that as they collected their equipment, slung their packs over their backs, and walked carefully farther in, their flashlights illuminating the rocks and seaweed. The floor rose gently toward the rear. Two shafts of light revealed a dogleg to the left. Down it were more pebbles and rocks and dead seaweed—thick carpets of it washed up against a hole in the cave wall.

"It would have to be in there," said Patty.

Híjole, Teresa suddenly realized: *Lieutenant O'Farrell's voice is quivering.*

I gotta admit," said Nino Juárez, "that it was a very ballsy thing to do." There was nothing about the former head of the DOCS—the organized-crime unit for the Costa del Sol—that would have led one to take him for a cop. Or even an ex-cop. He was a small, thin man, almost fragile. He had a sparse blond beard and wore a gray suit, no doubt very expensive, with a silk tie-and-handkerchief combination, and a Patek Philippe on his left wrist, under the French cuff of his pink-and-white-striped shirt with its designer cuff link. He looked like he'd just stepped out of the pages of a men's fashion magazine, although he'd actually come straight from his office on Madrid's Gran Vía. "Saturnino G. Juárez," read the business card I'd put in my wallet. "Director of Internal Security." And in one corner was the logo of a chain of department stores with hundreds of millions of dollars in annual sales.

Life's little ironies, I thought. After the scandal a few years earlier that cost Juárez—then known simply as Nino Juárez, or Chief Juárez—his career, here he was again: impeccable, triumphant, with that interpolated G. that gave his name a new respectability and this new look of a man with money coming out his ears, not to mention new power, new influence, new influential friends, and more men and matériel under his command than ever before. You never ran into men like him in the unemployment lines; they knew too much about people, sometimes more than people knew about themselves. The articles in the press, the file at Internal Affairs, the decision from National Police Headquarters relieving him of service, the five months in jail in Alcalá-Meco—that was all old news. How lucky to have friends. Old comrades-in-arms who return favors, and who have money or good contacts for securing them. There's no better unemployment insurance than a list of the skeletons in people's closets. Especially if you'd helped people hide them there.

"Where should we begin?" he asked, trying his appetizer.

"At the beginning."

"Then it's going to be a long lunch."

We were in Casa Lucio, in the Cava Baja. Not only was I paying for his lunch—*huevos con patatas,* tenderloin of beef, a Viña Pedrosa '96— I had also, in a sense, bought his presence there. I did it my own way, using some of my old tactics. After his second refusal to talk about Teresa Mendoza, but before he'd had the chance to tell his secretary not to put through any more of my calls, I put it to him straight out. "With you or without you," I said, "the story is going to get told. So you can choose between being in the story—your role described in explicit detail, down to a photograph of your first communion—or staying out of it and wiping the sweat off your forehead with a great deal of relief."

"And what else?" he asked.

"Not a cent," I replied. "But I'd be delighted to buy you dinner—and dessert. You gain a friend, or almost a friend, and I owe you one. You never know. . . . So what do you think?" He was smart enough to think just what I thought, so we agreed on the terms: nothing compromising attributed to him, few dates or details that could be traced back to him.

And there we were. It's always easy to come to an agreement with a son of a bitch. What's hard is the other ones—but there aren't many of those.

"The half-ton part is true," Juárez confirmed. "High-quality stuff, hardly cut at all. Brought in by the Russian mafia, who at the time were beginning to get a foothold on the Costa del Sol and open up their first contacts with the South American narcos. That load had been the first big operation, and when it failed, it put a damper on the Colombian connection for a long time. . . . Everybody figured the half-ton was lost, and the guys from South America were laughing at the Russkis for whacking O'Farrell's boyfriend and his two partners without making them talk first. . . . 'I ain't doin' any more business with amateurs,' Pablo Escobar was reputed to have said when he heard what happened. And now all of a sudden the Mexicana and the O'Farrell chick show up with five hundred keys out of thin air."

"How did they get their hands on the cocaine?"

"That I don't know. Nobody found out, as far as I know. But whatever—it showed up on the Russian market, or rather started showing up. And it was Oleg Yasikov that brought it there."

I had that name in my notes: Oleg Yasikov, born in Solntsevo, a mafioso neighborhood in Moscow. Military service with what was still the Soviet army in Afghanistan. Owner of discotheques, hotels, and restaurants on the Costa del Sol. And Nino Juárez filled in the rest of the picture for me. Yasikov had washed up on the Málaga coast in the late eighties—thirty-something, polyglot, quick-witted, just stepped off an Aeroflot flight with $35 million to spend. He started by buying a disco in Marbella that he named Jadranka, which took off right away, and within a couple of years he was the boss of a solid money-laundering infrastructure based on hotels and real estate, apartments and big pieces of land near the coast. A second line of businesses, created around the disco, consisted of heavy investments in Marbella nightlife, with bars, restaurants, and luxury whorehouses staffed by Slavic women brought in directly from Eastern Europe. All very clean, or almost clean: low-profile money-laundering only. But the DOCS had confirmed his ties to the Babushka, a powerful Solntsevo organization made up of ex-cops and Afghanistan veterans who specialized in extortion, stolen cars, smuggling, and white slavery and who were very interested in branching out into the drug trade. The group already had one hook-up in northern Europe: a sea route that linked Buenaventura, in Colombia, with Saint Petersburg via Göteborg, in Sweden, and Kotka, in Finland. And Yasikov was given the assignment of, among other things, exploring an alternative route through the eastern Mediterranean, a hook-up that would be independent of the French and Italian mafias that the Russians had used up till then as intermediaries. That was the context.

The first contacts with the Colombian narcos—the Medellín cartel, specifically—consisted of simple trades of arms for cocaine, with very little money changing hands: shipments of Kalashnikovs and RPGs from Russian arms depots. But things never quite jelled. The lost drugs were just one of several fuck-ups that had made Yasikov and his Moscow associates . . . uncomfortable, shall we say. And all of a sudden, when Yasikov and his friends had almost forgotten about them, those five hundred keys fell out of the sky on them.

"I've been told that the Mexicana and the other girl went directly to Yasikov, to negotiate," Juárez explained. "In person, with a sample, a package still in the original wrapper . . . Apparently, the Russian took it hard at first and then *really* badly. But the O'Farrell chick stood up to him—she told him she'd paid her debt already, that the bullets that hit her when her boyfriend got whacked had reset the counter to zero. That they'd played the game straight, and now they wanted their reward."

"Why didn't O'Farrell and Teresa just distribute the drugs wholesale themselves?"

"There was too much of it for beginners to handle. And Yasikov would not have liked it."

"Was it that easy to tell where it came from?"

"Sure." With expert motions of his knife and fork, the ex-cop cut himself a bite of the tenderloin served on a pottery plate. "Everybody knew whose girlfriend O'Farrell had been."

"Tell me about the boyfriend."

"The boyfriend's name"—Juárez grinned contemptuously as he cut again—"was Jaime Arenas, Jimmy, to his friends. From a good family in Seville. Pansy-ass, if you'll pardon the French. High-dollar interests in Marbella and family business dealings in South America. He was ambitious and he thought very highly of himself—thought he was smarter than those stupid drug lords, you know. So when he got his hands on that cocaine, he decided to play a little game with the to-varich fellow. Hadn't dared try anything like that with Pablo Escobar, but the Russians didn't have the reputation back then that they have now. Thick-necked apes, I imagine he figured them for. So he put the snow in hiding while he negotiated an increase in his commission, despite the fact that Yasikov had already paid cash money to the Colombians for their part—this time there'd been more cash than weapons. Jimmy started making excuses, beating around the bush, not taking phone calls, until the Russian finally lost his patience. Lost it so bad that he whacked Jimmy and his two partners, all at the same time."

"The Russians were never very subtle." Juárez clucked his tongue critically. "And they're probably less so now."

"How did Yasikov and Jimmy Arenas ever get hooked up in the first place?"

Juárez pointed his fork at me, as though congratulating me on the question. Back then, he explained, the Russian gangsters had one major problem. Like now, but more so. Which is that they stuck out like sore thumbs. You could see them a mile away: big, gruff, blond, with those ham hands and those cars and those showy whores always on their arms. Not to mention how truly pitiful they were at languages. The minute they set foot in Miami or any other American airport, the DEA and the state and local police were on their ass like the spandex on those whores. So they needed intermediaries, fronts, that kind of thing.

Jimmy Arenas played the part pretty well at the beginning; he started out by getting them liquor from Jerez to smuggle into northern Europe. He also had good contacts in Latin America, and he muled for the hot discos in Marbella, Fuengirola, and Torremolinos. But the Russkis wanted their own networks: import-export. The Babushka, Yasikov's friends in Moscow, could already get blow wholesale by using Aeroflot flights from Montevideo, Lima, and Bahía, which weren't under the same kind of surveillance as the ones from Rio or Havana. So half-kilo shipments could be smuggled in via the airport at Cheremetievo on an individual basis, but the pipeline was too narrow. The Berlin Wall had just come down, the Soviet Union was crumbling, and coke was the hot thing in the new Russia of fast and easy money.

"And we now know that the Russians had not underestimated the market," Juárez went on. "Just to give you an idea of the demand, a gram sold today in a disco in Saint Petersburg or Moscow is worth thirty or forty percent more than in the U.S."

The ex-cop chewed his last mouthful of meat, then helped it down with a long sip of wine.

"Imagine," he went on, "Comrade Yasikov scratching his head trying to figure out a way to thread the needle big-time again. And all of a sudden a half-ton of coke appears that doesn't require setting up a whole operation from Colombia—it's right there, no risks, all pure profit, practically speaking.

"And as for the Mexicana and the O'Farrell girl, like I said, there was no way for them to do it on their own. . . . They didn't have the money or the connections or the infrastructure to put five hundred kilos on the street, and the first gram that showed up on a corner somewhere, the whole fucking sky would have fallen on them: the Russkis, the Guardia Civil, my people. . . . They were smart enough to see that. Only an idiot would have started by dealing a little here, a little there, and before the Guardia or my guys were able to cuff 'em, they'd have been stuffed in the trunk of a car, probably in several well-carved pieces. R.I.P."

"But how could they know they wouldn't wind up like that anyway? . . . That the Russians would keep their part of the deal?"

"They couldn't," Juárez said. "They just decided to risk it. And

Yasikov must've taken a shine to them. Especially to Teresa Mendoza, who even proposed a couple of variants on the deal."

Did I know about that Gallego that had been her boyfriend? Yeah? Well, that was where her experience in all this came from. The Mexicana had a past. And she had something else it took—she had a tremendous pair of balls. Juárez' outstretched fingers made a circle the size of a dinner plate.

"And another thing. You know how some girls have this calculator between their legs, *clickety-click,* and *ka-ching,* the bill comes out? Well, the Mexicana had a calculator here"—he tapped his temple—"in her head. There's one eternal truth about women—sometimes you hear the song of a siren, and what you end up with is a sea wolf."

Saturnino G. Juárez had to know that better than most. I silently remembered the size of his bank account in Gibraltar, which had been aired in the press during his trial. Back then, Juárez had a little more hair and wore just a moustache; that was his look in my favorite photograph, in which he posed between two uniformed colleagues at the door of a court in Madrid. And look at him now, after paying the modest price of five months in prison and expulsion from the National Police Corps—calling the waiter over to order a cognac and a Havana cigar, to aid digestion. Not a lot of evidence, bad jury instructions from the judge, very able lawyers. I wondered how many people owed him favors, including Teresa Mendoza.

"So, bottom line," Juárez concluded, "Yasikov made the deal. Besides, he was on the Costa del Sol to invest, and the Mexicana looked like an interesting investment. So he kept his word like a gentleman. . . . And that was the beginning of a beautiful friendship."

Oleg Yasikov looked at the package on the table: white powder in a double layer of plastic shrink-wrap sealed with wide, thick tape, still obviously intact. A thousand grams, vacuum-packed, just the way it was packaged in the underground laboratories in Yari, in the Amazon jungle.

"I admit," he said, "that you two are playing it pretty cool. Yes."

He spoke Spanish well, Teresa thought. Slowly, with many pauses, as though carefully setting one word after another. His accent was very soft, and in no way did he resemble the evil, terrorist, drug-smuggling Russians in movies, the kind who *keel Amehricahn enehmy.* Nor did he look like a mafioso or a gangster. His skin was light, his eyes big, bright, and childlike, with a curious mixture of blue and yellow in the iris, and his straw-colored hair was short, like a soldier's. He was wearing khaki

pants and a navy-blue shirt, the cuffs turned up to reveal a diver's Rolex
on the left wrist, powerful forearms with a dusting of blond hair. The
hands resting at each side of the package, not touching it, were big, like
the rest of his body, and on one finger was a heavy gold wedding ring.
He looked healthy, strong, and clean. Patty O'Farrell had said that he
was also—and especially—dangerous.

"Let me see if I understand. You—you two girls—offer to return a
shipment of goods that belongs to me, but only if I pay for it again.
How do you call that? . . ." He reflected a moment, almost amused,
seeking the word. "Extortion?"

"That," said Patty, "is taking things way too far."

She and Teresa had discussed this for hours, backward and forward,
front and back, since the trip to the Marrajos Caves and until just an
hour before coming to this meeting. All the pros and cons, over and
over. Teresa wasn't convinced that their arguments would be quite as
effective as Patty thought they would, but it was too late now to turn
back. Patty—tasteful makeup for the occasion, expensive dress, self-as-
surance in keeping with her role as a high-powered female executive—
started to explain again, although it was clear that Yasikov got it the
first time, the minute they put the brick on the table. This, of course,
came after the Russian—with an apology that sounded at best neutral—had ordered two bodyguards to pat them down for hidden mi-
crophones. "Technology," he said, shrugging.

After the gorillas closed the door, he'd offered them a drink; they
both declined, although Teresa's mouth was dry. Then he sat down behind the table, ready to listen. Everything was neat and tidy—not a
piece of paper in sight, not a file folder. Walls the same cream color as
the wall-to-wall carpet, paintings that looked expensive, a large Russian icon inlaid with a great deal of hammered silver, a fax in one corner, a multiline telephone and a cell phone on the table. An ashtray. An
enormous gold Dupont lighter. Chairs of white leather. Through the
large windows in the office—the top floor of a luxury apartment house
in Santa Margarita—you could see the curve of the coast and the line
of surf on the beach all the way down to the breakwaters, and the masts
of moored yachts, and the white houses of Puerto Banús.

"Tell me one thing," Yasikov suddenly interrupted Patty's clumsy explanation. "How did you do it? . . . Go to the place where it was hidden.
Bring it here without calling attention to yourselves. Yes. You have
taken risks. I think. You are still taking them."

"That doesn't matter," Patty told him.

The gangster smiled. Come on, that smile said, tell the truth. It'll be
all right. His was a smile that made you want to trust him, Teresa

thought as she watched him. Or distrust so many other things that you wind up trusting him.

"Of course it matters," Yasikov replied. "I looked for this merchandise. Yes. I didn't find it. I made an error. About Jimmy, I mean. I didn't know that you knew. . . . Things would be different, no? How time flies. I hope you've recovered. After the incident."

"Perfectly recovered, thank you."

"I should thank *you* for one thing. Yes. My lawyers said that you never mentioned my name in the investigations and interrogations. No."

Patty frowned sarcastically. In the tanned triangle of her cleavage one could see the scar from the exit wound.

"I was in the hospital," she said. "With holes in me."

"I mean later." The Russian's eyes were almost innocent. "The interrogations and the trial. That part."

"You see now that I had my reasons."

Yasikov reflected on her reasons.

"Yes. I see. But still, your silence saved me some trouble. The police thought you knew nothing. I thought you knew nothing. You have been patient. Yes. All these years . . . There had to be some motivation, yes?" He tapped his chest. "Inside."

Patty took out another cigarette, which the Russian, despite having the enormous Dupont on the table, made no move to light for her, even when it took several seconds for her to find her own lighter in her purse. *Stop shaking,* Teresa thought, looking at Patty's hands. Control that twitching in your fingers before the son of a bitch notices and this tough-girl façade starts cracking and this whole thing goes to *la chingada*.

"The packages are still hidden where they were. We only brought one."

The discussion in the cave, Teresa remembered. The two of them inside, counting packages in the beam from the flashlights, half euphoric and half scared shitless. One for now, while we think—and leave the rest, Teresa had insisted. Taking it all with us now is suicide, so let's not be stupid. I know they shot you and all, but I didn't come to your lovely country as a tourist, either, you blond bitch. Don't make me tell you the whole story, which I've never told you so far. A story that has no resemblance to yours—since you managed to get shot wearing Carolina Herrera. Don't fuck with me. In this kind of deal, when you're in a hurry, the best thing you can do is go slow.

"Has it occurred to you that I can have you followed?" said Yasikov. Patty rested the hand holding the cigarette in her lap. "Of course that's occurred to us." She inhaled and returned the hand to her lap. "But you can't follow us to where it's hidden. Not there."

"Oh, I see. Mysterious. You are mysterious ladies."

"We'd realize we were being followed and disappear. And find another buyer. Five hundred kilos is a lot."

Yasikov said nothing to that, although his silence indicated that five hundred kilos was, in fact, too much in every way. He kept looking at Patty, and once in a while he gave a brief glance in the direction of Teresa, not talking, not smoking, not moving; just watching and listening, almost holding her breath, her hands on the legs of her jeans to absorb the sweat. A light blue polo shirt, tennis shoes in case she had to make a quick getaway and slither between somebody's legs, her only jewelry the *semanario* of Mexican silver on her right wrist—in sharp contrast to Patty's elegant clothes and heels. They were there because Teresa had insisted on this solution. At first Patty had wanted to sell the drugs in small amounts, but Teresa had managed to convince her that sooner or later the real owners would figure it all out. It's better if we work straight, she counseled. A sure thing, even if we lose a little. All right, Patty had finally agreed. But I talk, because I know how that fucking Bolshevik's mind works. And there they were, while Teresa became more and more certain that they'd made a mistake.

She'd been around people like this since she was a girl. They might speak a different language, look different, wear different clothes, make different gestures, but underneath they were all the same. This was going nowhere, or rather somewhere they didn't want to go. When all was said and done—Teresa was realizing this too late—Patty was just a spoiled society chick, the girlfriend of a wet-behind-the-ears asshole who had been in the business not out of necessity, but because he was stupid. A guy who thought he was cool—like so many others. As for Patty, she had lived a life of appearances that had nothing to do with the real thing, and the time she'd spent in prison had done nothing but blind her even more. Here in this office she wasn't Lieutenant O'Farrell—she wasn't anybody. The blue eyes with flashes of yellow that were looking at them—*that* was where the power was here. And Patty was making an even bigger mistake than coming here in the first place. It was a mistake to put it to him this way. To refresh Oleg Yasikov's memory, after so much time had passed.

"That's just the problem," Patty was saying. "Five hundred kilos is too much. That's why we've come to you first."

"Whose idea was it?" Yasikov didn't seem flattered. "Me the first option? Yes."

Patty looked at Teresa.

"Hers. She's the deep thinker." She gave a quick, nervous smile between puffs on her cigarette. "She's better than I am at calculating the risks and probabilities."

Teresa felt the Russian's eyes studying her; he looked at her for a long time. He's wondering what it is that joins us, she decided. Prison, friendship, business. Whether men are my thing or we're a couple.

"I still don't know what," said Yasikov, asking Patty without taking his eyes off Teresa. "She's doing in this. Your friend."

"She's my partner."

"Ah. It's good to have partners." Yasikov turned his attention back to Patty. "It would also be good to talk. Yes. Risks and probabilities. You might not have time to disappear to find another buyer." He paused deliberately. "Time to disappear voluntarily. I think."

Teresa saw that Patty's hands were trembling again. And how I wish, she thought, I could get up right now and say, *Quihubo,* don Oleg, see ya around. Didn't even see that third strike coming. You keep that shipment, right, and forget this *chingada.*

"Maybe we should . . ." Teresa began.

Yasikov looked at her, almost surprised. But Patty was already at it again: You wouldn't gain anything by that. Not a thing, except the lives of two women. And you'd lose a lot. And the fact was, Teresa decided, that apart from the trembling hands that transmitted their shaking to the spirals of cigarette smoke, the Lieutenant was handling this very well. And she didn't give up easily. But both of them were dead women. She was about to say that aloud. We're dead, Lieutenant. Let's pack up and get out of here.

"It takes time to lose a life," the Russian was philosophizing, although as he continued, Teresa realized that there was nothing philosophical about it. "I think that during the process one winds up telling things . . . I do not like to pay twice. No. I can get it back. And without paying."

He looked at the brick of cocaine sitting on the table, between his two hamlike, immobile hands. Patty clumsily stubbed out her cigarette in the ashtray just inches away from those hands. And this is it, Teresa thought in desolation. She could smell the other woman's panic. Then, without thinking, she heard her own voice again:

"You might be able to get it back without paying," she said. "But you never know. It's a risk, a hassle. . . . You'd be depriving yourself of a sure profit."

The yellow-ringed irises fixed on her, interested.

"Your name?"

"Teresa Mendoza."

"Colombian?"

"Mexico."

She was about to add Culiacán, Sinaloa—which in this business was blowing your own horn—but she didn't. Fish get caught because they open their mouth one time too many. Yasikov had still not taken his eyes off her.

"Deprive myself. You say. Convince me of that."

Convince me of the utility of keeping you alive, read the subtitle. Patty had leaned back in her chair, like an exhausted fighting cock taking a breather against the pit wall. You're right, Mexicana. My breast is wounded and bleeding, and it's your turn now. Get us out of this. Teresa's tongue was stuck to the roof of her mouth. A glass of water—she'd give anything to have asked for a glass of water.

"With a kilo going for twelve thousand dollars," she said, "the half-ton probably cost you, at point of origin, about six million. . . . Right?"

"Right." Yasikov was looking at her inexpressively. Cautiously.

"I don't know how much the intermediaries got, but in the U.S. a kilo would sell for twenty thousand."

"Thirty thousand for us. This year. Here." Yasikov had still not moved a muscle, especially a muscle of his face. "More than for your neighbors. Yes. The Yankees."

Teresa did a quick calculation. She was chewing that nopal. Her hands—to her surprise—were not trembling. Not just then.

"In that case," she said, "and at current prices, a half-ton on the street in Europe would go for fifteen million dollars. And that, according to my partner, was much more than you and your associates paid four years ago for the original shipment. Which was, and you can correct me if I'm mistaken here, five million in cash and one million in . . . what would you call it?"

"Technology," Yasikov replied, amused. "Secondhand."

"Six million in all," nodded Teresa, "with one thing and another. Technology included. But what matters is that half a ton now, the half-ton we're offering, is only going to cost you another six. One payment of three million on delivery of the first third, another three as payment for the second third, and the rest of the goods once the second payment is confirmed. We're selling it at cost."

She saw that the Russian was considering this. Shit, she thought, you're slow, *cabrón*. You still don't see the profit, and as far as you're concerned we're still just two little dead girls.

"You want"—Yasikov was shaking his head slowly—"to make us pay twice. Yes. For that half-ton. Six and six."

Teresa leaned forward, placing her fingers on the edge of the table.

So why aren't my hands trembling, she wondered. Why aren't these seven bangles tinkling like a silver rattlesnake, when I'm about to stand up and take off running.

"In spite of that"—she was also surprised at how calm her voice sounded—"you will still be realizing a profit of three million dollars on a shipment that you thought was lost, and that I'll lay odds you've already worked into your overhead charges in one way or another. . . . But in addition, if we do the math, those five hundred kilos are worth sixty-five million dollars once it's cut and ready to distribute on the wholesale market in your country, or wherever you want. . . . Deducting the old and new expenses, your people would still see fifty-three million dollars in profits. Fifty, if you deduct the three for transportation, delays, and other minor inconveniences. And your market would be supplied for a long time to come."

She stopped talking, but remained fixed on Yasikov's eyes. The muscles in her back were tense and her stomach was in a knot that actually hurt, from the fear. But she had been able to put it to him in the driest, most straightforward way, as if instead of laying her and Patty's lives on the table she were proposing a routine commercial operation with no consequences to anybody. The gangster was studying Teresa, who could also feel Patty's eyes on her, but there was no way in the world she was going to return that second gaze. Don't look at me, she was mentally begging her friend. Don't even blink, *carnalita,* or we're done for.

"I am afraid . . ." Yasikov began.

This is it, Teresa told herself. All you had to do was look at the Russian's face to see that there was no way he was buying this deal. And that hit Teresa like a lightning bolt. We've been innocent schoolgirls, she thought. The fear wound itself about her intestines, strangling them. This looks like the fucking end of everything.

"There's something else," she improvised. "Hash."

"What about it?"

"I know that business. And I know you people don't have hash."

Yasikov looked a little disconcerted. "Of course we do."

Teresa shook her head confidently. Don't let Patty open her mouth and blow us away, she begged. Inside her, the road laid itself out with uncanny clarity. A door opened, and that silent woman, the one who sometimes resembled her, was watching her from the threshold.

"A year and a half ago," Teresa said, "you were dabbling in it here and there, and I doubt things are any different today. I'm sure you're still in the hands of Moroccan suppliers, Gibraltar transporters, and Spanish intermediaries. . . . Like everybody else."

The gangster raised his left hand, with the wedding ring, to touch his face. I've got thirty seconds to convince him, thought Teresa, before we have to stand up, walk out of here, and take off running—before they catch us again in a day or two. Fuck that. It'd be a real bitch to get the Sinaloa gang off your back and come all this way, just to get whacked by a fucking Russian.

"We want to propose something to you," she said. "A business deal. Of those six million dollars split up into two payments, the second would be retained by you as our associate, in exchange for something you need very much."

A long silence. The Russian did not take his eyes off her. And I'm a mask, she thought. I'm an expressionless mask, playing poker like Raúl Estrada Contreras, professional card player, respected by people because he played an honest game, or at least that's what the corrido says, and this motherfucker is not going to make me blink, because my life's on the fucking line here. So look me in the eye, asshole. Like you'd look at my tits.

"What is that? That we need very much?"

Gotcha, thought Teresa. Hook, line, and sinker.

"Well, I don't know right now. I mean I do, but not all the details. Let's say boats, for starters. Outboard motors. Pick-up points. Payment for the first contacts and intermediaries."

Yasikov was still touching his face. "You have experience with these things?"

"Jesus fucking Christ. I'm putting my life on the line here, and my friend's, too. . . . You think I came here to sing rancheras?"

And that, Saturnino G. Juárez confirmed, was how Teresa Mendoza and Patricia O'Farrell became associates of the Russian mafia on the Costa del Sol. The proposal that the Mexicana made Yasikov at that first meeting tipped the scales. And it was all true: Besides that half-ton of cocaine, the Solntsevo Babushka needed Moroccan hashish so they wouldn't have to depend exclusively on Turkish and Lebanese suppliers. Until Teresa came along they'd been forced to go to the traditional mafias along the Strait, which were badly organized, expensive, and unreliable. And the idea of a direct connection was seductive.

The half-ton changed hands in return for $3 million deposited in a bank in Gibraltar and another $3 million used to finance an infrastructure whose legal front was named Transer Naga, S.L., with corporate headquarters on the Rock and a quiet cover operation in Marbella. For that, Yasikov and his people obtained, according to the agreement he reached with the two women, fifty percent of the profits the first year and twenty-five percent the second. The third year, the debt would be considered amortized.

As for Transer Naga, it was nothing more than a service enterprise: clandestine transportation of other people's drugs. The company's responsibility began when the drug was loaded on the Moroccan coast, and ended when somebody took charge of it on a Spanish beach or loaded it onto a boat on the high seas.

In time, through phone taps and other intercepted information, it was learned that the rule of never taking any share of ownership of the drugs had been imposed by Teresa Mendoza. Previous experience told her, she said, that everything was cleaner if the transport agency didn't get involved; that guaranteed discretion, and also the absence of names and evidence that could interconnect producers, exporters, intermediaries, receivers, and owners. The method was simple: A customer made his needs known, and Transer Naga counseled him on the most efficient means of transport. Then it *provided* the means. From point A to point C, and we contribute B.

In time, Saturnino Juárez said as I paid the check, the only thing missing was an ad in the yellow pages. And that was the strategy Teresa Mendoza followed from then on, never falling into the temptation to take part of her payment in drugs, the way other transporters did. Not even when Transer Naga turned the Strait of Gibraltar into the largest cocaine entry point in southern Europe, and Colombian blow started pouring in by the ton.

10. I'm in the corner of a cantina

They'd been going through the racks for almost an hour. It was the fifth store they'd been in that morning. Outside, on Calle Larios, the sun shone brightly—sidewalk cafés, cars, pedestrians in light clothes. Málaga in winter. And today, Patty was carrying out Operation Clotheshorse.

"I'm sick of loaning you things to wear, or seeing you dressed like a secretary. So clean under those fingernails and fix yourself up, 'cause we're going out. On a hunt. To polish your image a little bit. You ready or not?"

So there they were. They had had an early breakfast before they left Marbella, and then another on the terrace of the Café Central, watching people pass by. Now they were dedicating themselves to spending money. Too much, in Teresa's opinion. The prices were outrageous.

"So?" was Patty's response. "You've got money, I've got money, and besides, it's an investment. Sure profits guaranteed, just the way you like it. You'll be filling that purse tomorrow all over again, with your boats and your logistics and that whole water park you've put together, Mexicana. Not everything in the world is outboard motors and counterclockwise-rotating propellers or whatever you call them. It's time you looked like the girl leading the life you're leading. Or are about to be leading."

Patty was moving self-assuredly around the shop, taking clothes off the racks and tossing them to a saleswoman who was following her solicitously. "What do you think about this one?" She held an outfit, still on the hanger, against Teresa, to see the effect. "A jacket and pants is never last year, my dear. And the guys like it, especially in your, in my, in our world. . . . Jeans are all very well—you don't have to stop wearing them—but combine them with dark jackets. Navy blue is perfect."

Teresa had other things on her mind, things more complex than what color jacket to wear with jeans. Too many people and too many interests. Hours sitting over a notebook filled with numbers, names, places, trying to put all the pieces together. Long conversations with strangers to whom she listened attentively, cautiously, trying to learn everything from everybody. A lot depended on her now, and she asked herself whether she was really ready to assume responsibilities that had never crossed her mind before. Patty knew all this, but she didn't care, or didn't seem to. "All things in due time," she had said. "Today, clothes. Today, a little vacation. Today, shopping. Besides, the business is your thing—you run the show, and I watch."

In the shop, they moved to accessories. "See? . . . With jeans, what goes best is a low heel, like a moccasin, and those purses—Ubrique, Valverde del Camino. Those leather ones from Andalucía are great for you. For everyday."

There were now three of those particular purses in shopping bags stowed in the trunk of the car parked in the underground lot at the Plaza de la Marina.

"Not another day will go by," Patty had insisted, "without you filling up your closet with everything you need. And you're going to take my advice. I give the orders and you follow them, all right? . . . Besides, dressing is less a question of fashion than of common sense. The idea is this: a few pieces, but good ones, is better than a lot of cheap shit. The trick is putting together a basic wardrobe. Then, building on that, you can go in lots of different directions. Got it?"

She was almost never this talkative, Lieutenant O'Farrell. Teresa did in fact get it, though, because she found herself intrigued by this new way of looking at clothes, and at herself. Until then, she had dressed one way or another in response to two clear objectives: pleasing men—

her men—or being comfortable. Viewing clothes as a tool one needed in order to do one's work better, as Patty had put it with a laugh—that was a new one. Getting dressed not just for comfort or seduction—or even elegance, or status. No, it was more subtle than that. . . . Clothes could express a mood, an attitude, a person's power. A woman could dress like what she was or what she wanted to be, and that could make all the difference. There were other things you could learn, of course— manners, how to carry on a conversation, how to eat—provided you kept your eyes open.

"And there's nobody, Mexicana," Patty had said, "whose eyes are more open than yours are. Fucking Indian bitch. You read people like a book."

. . . "And then, when you want to wear something dressier . . ." They were coming out of the dressing room, where Teresa had stood before the mirror in a cashmere turtleneck. ". . . nobody says you have to dress boring. The trick is that in order to wear certain things you have to know how to move. And stand. And be. Not everybody can wear every-thing. This, for example: Don't even *think* about Versace. You'd look like a whore in Versace."

"Which is no doubt why you wear it sometimes."

Patty laughed. She was holding a Marlboro despite the "No Smok-ing" sign and several censorious looks from the saleswoman. One hand in the pocket of her knit jacket, which she wore over a dark gray skirt. The cigarette in the other. I'll put it out right away, my dear, she'd said when she lit the first one. This was the third.

"I've had training, Mexicana. I know when to look like a whore and when not to. But you . . . Remember that the people we deal with are impressed by classy types. Ladies."

"Please. I'm no lady."

"What do *you* know? Being one, looking like one, and becoming one—or never being anything—there's a very fine line between all those things. . . . You'll want to wear Yves Saint Laurent, things from Chanel and Armani for the more serious occasions. Crazy stuff like Galliano, you can leave for somebody else."

Teresa looked around. "Putting things together is hard." She didn't mind showing her ignorance to the saleswoman. It was Patty who spoke in a near-whisper.

"Well, there's one rule that never fails: Half and half. If you're sexy from the waist down, from the waist up you've gotta be demure. And vice versa."

They left the shop with their bags and walked up Calle Larios. Patty made Teresa stop before every store window.

"For everyday," she went on, "the ideal thing is these transitional pieces. And if you stay with one label, make sure it has a little of everything." She pointed out a suit dress, with a light black jacket with a round collar that Teresa thought was very chic. "Like Calvin Klein, for example. See? He's got everything from sweaters to leather jackets to evening dresses."

They entered the store. It was elegant, and the sales staff wore uniforms—short navy-blue skirts and dark stockings. To Teresa they looked like executives in some gringo movie. All tall and svelte, with exquisite makeup—like models, or stewardesses. And very, very accommodating. I'd never be able to get a job here, she thought. *Chale,* what fucking money will do.

"The ideal thing," said Patty, "is to come to stores like this one, that have good clothes from several labels. Keep coming back, get some confidence. A relationship with a salesgirl is important—they know you, know your likes and dislikes, what looks good on you. They call you, tell you such-and-such just came in. They take care of you, my love—they spoil you."

Accessories were upstairs: Italian and Spanish leather, belts, bags, glorious shoes by famous designers. This place, thought Teresa, is better than Sercha's in Culiacán, where the narcos' wives and girlfriends went twice a year, at the end of each harvest up in the sierra—chattering like parrots, with their jewelry, their dyed hair, and their wads of U.S. dollars. She'd shopped there herself, back when she was with Güero Dávila. But the things she was buying now made her feel insecure. Maybe because she wasn't sure they were really *her*: she'd traveled a long way, a *really* long way, and it was another woman who now looked out at her from the mirrors in these expensive shops.

"And shoes are absolutely fundamental," Patty was saying. "More than purses. Remember that no matter how well dressed you are, bad shoes make you look like a bag lady. Men can get away with bad shoes—like those hideous loafers with no socks that everybody started copying from fucking Julio Iglesias. But for us girls, it's, like, shocking. Unpardonable."

They wandered through displays of perfumes and makeup, sniffing and trying everything on Teresa's skin before they went off for prawns and mussels at El Tintero, on the beach at El Palo.

"You Latin American girls," Patty said, "love strong perfumes. Try to tone it down, eh? Makeup, too. When you're young, makeup makes you look older. And when you're old, it makes you look like an undertaker's model. . . ." They both laughed uproariously at that. "You've got big, dark eyes, beautiful eyes, and when you wear your hair with that part down the middle and all pulled back tight, very picturesque, like a real Mexican peasant, you look dynamite."

She said this as she gazed deep into Teresa's eyes, while the waiters moved back and forth through the tables set out in the sun with plates of fried eggs, sardines, potatoes alioli, calamari fritti. There was nothing superior or patronizing in her tone, just as when Teresa had arrived at El Puerto de Santa María and Patty had guided her through prison customs. Do this, don't do that. But now Teresa sensed something different: an ironic twist to Patty's mouth, in the wrinkles around her eyes when she smiled. You know what I'm wondering, thought Teresa—you can almost hear my thoughts. Why me, when I don't give you what you'd really like to have? My position is simple: I allowed myself to be lured in by the money, and I'm loyal because I owe you a lot. But that wasn't what you were looking for. So the question is, Why don't you lie to me and betray me and forget me? Or why not *yet?*

"Clothes," Patty was going on, her expression unchanged, "have to fit the occasion. It's always unsettling when you're having lunch and a woman comes in with a shawl, or you're having dinner and she comes in wearing a miniskirt. That shows lack of judgment, or upbringing. She doesn't know what's right, what the rules are, so she wears what looks to her like the most elegant thing she has, or the most expensive. That's what tells you she's nouveau."

Patty's smart, Teresa told herself. Much smarter than I am, and she's had everything. She even had a dream; when she was behind bars, it kept her alive. But it'd be nice to know what keeps her alive now. Apart from drinking like she drinks, and those girlfriends of hers from time to time, and snorting like there's no tomorrow, and telling me all the things we're going to do when we're multimillionaires. I wonder. But I probably ought to stop wondering so much.

"I'm nouveau," Teresa said.

It sounded almost like a question. She'd never used that word, or heard it, or read it in books, but she intuited what it meant. Patty laughed out loud.

"Ha! Of course you are. In a way, sure. But you don't have to advertise it. Soon you won't be, don't worry."

There was something dark in Patty's gestures, Teresa decided. Something that seemed to pain her and amuse her at the same time. Maybe, Teresa suddenly thought, it's just life.

"Anyway," Patty added, "if you make a mistake, the last rule is to pull it off with as much dignity as you can. After all, everyone makes mistakes once in a while." She was still staring at Teresa. "With clothes, I mean."

More Teresas kept popping up during this time—strangers, unfamiliar women who had always been there, though she hadn't known it. And some new ones appeared in the gray dawns and silences. She discovered them with curiosity—sometimes, with surprise.

That Gibraltar attorney, Eddie Alvarez, the one who'd been managing Santiago Fisterra's money and then hardly showed up to defend Teresa, he'd met one of those women.

Eddie was not a brave man. His dealings with the rough part of the business were what one would call peripheral—he preferred not to see or know about certain things. Ignorance, he'd said during our conversation at the Rock Hotel, is the mother of great wisdom and no little health. Which is why when he came home and turned on the stairway light and found Teresa Mendoza sitting on the stairs he jumped so hard that he dropped all the papers he was carrying.

"Jesus fucking Christ," he said.

Then he stood there speechless, leaning against the wall with the papers all over the floor—no intention of picking them up, no intention of doing anything except letting his heart stop thumping like a jackhammer in his chest. Meanwhile, Teresa, still sitting on the stairs, informed him slowly and in detail of the reason for her visit. She did it in her soft Mexican accent and with that air of a shy girl who seemed to have stumbled into all this by accident. No reproaches, no questions about the investments in paintings or the vanished money. Not a word about the year and a half in prison, or how the lawyer had washed his hands of her defense.

"At night, things always seem more serious," was all she said at first. "Things leave an impression, I suppose. Which is why I'm here, Eddie. To leave an impression on you."

The light on the stairway was on a timer; every ninety seconds or so it turned off. Teresa, from her seat on the stairs, would reach up and turn it on again, and the lawyer's face would look yellow, his eyes behind his glasses would have a frightened intensity, and the glasses themselves would be sliding down his greasy, sweaty nose.

"I want to leave an impression on you," she repeated, sure that the lawyer had been pretty impressed for a week now, ever since the newspapers had published a story on the murder of Sergeant Iván Velasco, who had been stabbed six times in the parking lot of a disco as he headed, at four in the morning, drunk of course, for his brand-new

Mercedes. By a drug addict, or a mugger prowling the parking lot. A robbery, that was all—watch, wallet, etc. But what made an impression on Eddie Alvarez was that the death of Sergeant Velasco had occurred exactly six days after another close acquaintance of his, Antonio Martínez Romero, alias Antonio Cañabota, had been found strangled in a *pensión* in Torremolinos, facedown and naked except for his socks, hands tied behind his back, apparently by a gay hustler who had approached Cañabota in the street about an hour before his demise. And putting two and two together would, in this case, be enough to leave an impression on anyone, assuming that "anyone" had enough memory—which Eddie Alvarez certainly did—to recall the role those two individuals had played in the Punta Castor affair.

"I swear, Teresa, I had nothing to do with it."

"With what?"

"You know. With anything."

Teresa bowed her head—she was still sitting on the stairs—considering the matter. The fact was, she knew that very well. Which was why she was there, instead of getting a friend of a friend to send a friend, as she'd done in the cases of Sergeant Velasco of the Guardia Civil and the *hombre de confianza*. For some time now, she and Oleg Yasikov had been doing each other little favors—you scratch my back, I scratch yours—and the Russian had people, drug addicts and muggers included, with picturesque abilities.

Then, evidently having thought it over, Teresa lifted her head. "I need your services, Eddie."

The glasses slid down his nose again.

"My services?"

"Papers, banks, corporations. That sort of thing."

Then Teresa laid it out for him. And when she did—easiest thing in the world, Eddie, just a few corporations and bank accounts, and you as the front man—she thought how ironic it was, how Santiago would have laughed at all this. She also thought about herself as she talked, as though she were able to split into two separate women: one practical, telling Eddie Alvarez the reason for her visit—and also the reason he was still alive—and the other one weighing everything with a remarkable absence of passion, from outside or from a distance, through the strange gaze that she was casting on herself, feeling neither anger nor desire for revenge. The same woman who'd put out a contract on Velasco and Cañabota, not to settle scores, but rather—as Eddie Alvarez would have put it, and in fact later did—out of a sense of symmetry. Things should be what they were—accounts balanced and closets in order. And Patty was mistaken. It was not always the Yves Saint Laurent dresses that left the biggest impression on men.

You'll have to kill," Oleg Yasikov had said. "Sooner or later." He had said this to her one day when they were walking along the beach in Marbella, below the waterfront promenade, in front of one of Oleg's restaurants, the Tsarevich—deep down, Yasikov was a sentimental guy—near the kiosk where Teresa had worked when she got out of prison.

"Not at first, of course," the Russian said. "Or with your own hands. *Nyet.* Unless you're very passionate or very stupid. Not if you stay outside, just looking in. But you will have to do it if you go to the essence of things. If you are consistent and are lucky, and you last. Decisions. Little by little. You will be going into unknown territory, an obscure place. Yes." Yasikov said all this with his head down and his hands in his pockets, looking at the sand before his expensive shoes—Patty would have approved, Teresa imagined. Alongside his six feet, three inches and his broad shoulders in a silk shirt a bit less sober than his shoes, Teresa looked smaller and frailer than she was. She wore a short skirt over her dark legs and bare feet, and the wind blew her hair into her face as she listened attentively.

"Making your decisions," Yasikov was saying, pausing, placing his words carefully one after another. "Right ones. Wrong ones. Sooner or later the job will include taking a life. If you're smart, having someone else take it. In this business, Tesa"—he always called her that, as he seemed unable to pronounce her whole name—"you can't get along with everybody. Or make everybody happy. No. Friends are friends until they aren't anymore. And then you have to act quickly. But there is a problem. Discovering the right moment. Exactly when they stop being friends.

"There is one necessary skill. Yes. In this business." Yasikov pointed two fingers at his eyes. "Looking at a man and instantly knowing two things. First, how much he's going to sell himself for. And second, when you're going to have to kill him."

Early that year they outgrew Eddie Alvarez. Transer Naga and its front corporations—headquartered in the lawyer's office on Line Wall Road—were doing all too well, and the enterprise needed a larger, more complex infrastructure than the one created by Eddie. Four Phantoms based at Sheppard's marina and two under the cover of a sportfishing operation in Estepona, maintenance, payments to pilots and "collaborators"—including half a dozen police officers and Civil Guardsmen—were not terribly complicated, but the clientele was expanding, the money was flowing in, and there were frequent international payments, so Teresa realized that more complex investment and money-laundering techniques had to be used. They needed a specialist who knew how to navigate the legal loopholes with maximum profit and minimum risk. And I've got the man, said Patty. You know him.

She knew him by sight. The first formal meeting took place in an apartment in Sotogrande. Teresa, Patty, and Eddie went, and there they met with Teo Aljarafe—Spanish, thirty-five years old, an expert in tax law and financial planning. Teresa remembered him immediately when Patty introduced them in the bar at the Hotel Coral Beach. She'd noticed him at the party at the O'Farrell estate in Jerez: tall, dark, thin, handsome. The thick black hair combed back, a little long at the neck, framing a bony face with that large aquiline nose she had remarked on. A very classic look, Teresa decided. The way you always imagined Spaniards to be, before you met them—thin and elegant, with that air of nobility that they almost never actually had.

Now the four of them were sitting around a sequoia table with an antique coffee service, a trolley of liquor and glasses under the window that opened onto the terrace, offering a panoramic view of the harbor with its yachts and sailboats, the sea, and a long stretch of the coast, all the way down to the distant beaches of La Línea and the gray mass of Gibraltar. It was a small apartment with no telephone, no neighbors on either side, and one reached it directly from the garage by private elevator; Patty had bought it—from her own family—in the name of Transer Naga and furnished it as a place to hold meetings: good lighting, an expensive modern painting on one wall, a white plastic board with red, black, and blue erasable markers. Twice a week, and always immediately before any meeting held there, an electronic-security specialist recommended by Oleg Yasikov swept the room for bugs.

"The practical part is nothing," Teo was saying. "Justifying income and lifestyle: bars, discos, restaurants, laundries. What Yasikov does, what lots of people do, and what we'll be doing. Nobody keeps track of the number of drinks or paellas you serve. So it's time to open a serious line that goes in that direction. Interconnected or independent investments and corporations that justify every gallon of gas in your car. Lots of invoices, lots of paper. Treasury won't hassle us if we pay enough taxes and everything's straight on Spanish soil, unless there are judicial actions already under way."

"The old principle," said Patty. "Don't shit where you live."

Elegant, distracted, her blond hair cut almost to the scalp, she was smoking cigarette after cigarette; she would nod, look around as though she were no more than a visitor. She was acting as if this was just some entertaining adventure. Another in a series.

"Exactly." Teo nodded. "And if I have carte blanche, I'll design the structure and present it to you all laid out, and I'll fit in what you already have set up. Between Málaga and Gibraltar, there are plenty of places and opportunities. And the rest is easy: once the train is loaded with all the various corporations' assets, we'll create another holding company to pay out dividends and you two will remain insolvent. Easy."

He had hung his jacket over the back of his chair and unbuttoned his cuffs and rolled them up over his forearms, although the knot in his tie was still impeccably tight. He spoke slowly, clearly, with a sober voice that Teresa found soothing. Competent and smart, Patty had once summarized him: from a good Jerez family, married to a girl with money, two young daughters. "He travels a lot to London and New York and Panama and places like that. Financial consultant to very high-level firms. My dearly departed idiot ex had some sort of business with him, but Teo was always much the more intelligent of the two. He gives his advice, collects his fee, and stands back, far in the background. A top-drawer mercenary, if you know what I mean. And he never gets involved in the dirty work, as far as I can tell. I've known him since I was a girl. He fucked me once, too, when we were younger. No big deal in bed. Quick. Self-centered. But back then I was no big deal, either."

"As for the serious matters, things get a bit more complex," Teo continued. "I'm talking about real money, the kind that never passes through Spanish soil. And I'd suggest forgetting about Gibraltar. It's a water hole in the jungle. Everybody has an account there."

"But it works," said Eddie Alvarez.

He seemed uncomfortable. Jealousy, maybe, thought Teresa, who was observing the two men closely. Eddie had done good work for Transer Naga, but his skills were limited. Everyone knew that. The Gibraltar attorney considered the Jerez financial advisor a dangerous competitor. And he was right.

"It works now." Teo gave Eddie the kind of sympathetic look you'd give a handicapped person whose wheelchair you're about to push down the stairs. "I'm not talking about what's been done thus far. But Gibraltar's full of amateurs gossiping in the corner bar, and a secret stays secret for about twenty-four hours. . . . Plus, for every three good citizens, one is bribable. And that goes in both directions: we can bribe them, but so can the police. . . . It's okay if you're fooling around with a few kilos, or tobacco, but we're talking about large quantities of important material. So Gibraltar's not the place."

Eddie pushed up his glasses. "I don't agree," he protested.

"I don't care." Teo's voice turned harder. "I'm not here to discuss smuggling cigarettes."

"I'm—" Eddie began. He placed his hands on the table, turning first to Teresa and then to Patty, seeking their support.

"A small-time shyster," Teo interrupted, finishing his sentence for him. He spoke the words softly, his face expressionless. Dispassionate. A doctor telling a patient there's a shadow on his X ray.

"I won't allow you—"

"Shut up, Eddie," said Teresa.

Eddie Alvarez' mouth froze. A kicked dog looking around disconcertedly. The loose tie and wrinkled jacket accentuated his slovenliness. I've got to watch that flank, Teresa told herself, glancing at him again while she heard Patty laugh. A kicked dog can be dangerous. She made a note in the little book she carried in her head. Eddie Alvarez: Consider situation later. There were ways to ensure loyalty despite a grudge. There was always a way to win a person over.

"Go on, Teo."

And Teo went on.

"The best thing is to set up corporations and do your financial business with foreign banks that are outside the oversight and control of the European Union: the Channel Islands, Asia, the Caribbean. The problem is that a lot of money comes from suspicious or criminal activities, and you have to allay official suspicion through a series of legal covers that no one will ask questions about.

"Otherwise the procedure is simple: delivery of merchandise is timed to coincide exactly with the transfer of the fee, by what's called a SWIFT transfer, an irrevocable bank order issued by the sending bank."

Eddie Alvarez, still chewing his own bone, returned to the conversation: "I did what was asked of me."

"Of course, Eddie," said Teo. She liked that smile of his, Teresa discovered. A balanced, practical smile: When the opposition is down, you don't kick him. "Nobody is saying you didn't do your job well. But it's time for you to relax, take some time off. Without neglecting your commitments, of course."

He was looking at Eddie, not at Teresa or Patty, who was still more or less on the fringes, with an expression that said she was enjoying this show immensely. "Your commitments, Eddie." That was the second lesson. A warning. And that guy knows his stuff, thought Teresa. He knows about kicked dogs, because he's no doubt kicked his share of them. All with soft words, every hair in place. The attorney seemed to get the message, because he collapsed almost physically. Out of the corner of her eye, Teresa sensed the uneasy look he gave her. Scared shitless. Just like at the door of his apartment house, with the papers all over the floor.

"What do you recommend?" Teresa asked Teo.

He made a gesture that took in the entire table, as though it were all there, in plain sight, among the coffee cups or in the black leather portfolio he had open in front of him, its pages blank, a gold fountain pen on top. His hands were dark, well cared for, manicured, with black hairs peeking out from under the rolled-up cuffs. Teresa wondered how old he'd been when he and Patty slept together. Eighteen, twenty. Two daughters, her friend had said. A wife with money, and two daughters. No question he was still sleeping with other women, too.

"Switzerland is too serious," Teo said. "It requires too many bonds and guarantees and confirmations. The Channel Islands are all right, and there are subsidiaries of Spanish banks that are based in London rather than Madrid, and that therefore demand financial opacity. But they're too close, too obvious, and if the European Union decides to pressure them someday, and England decides to tighten the screws, Gibraltar and the Channels will be vulnerable."

Despite everything, Eddie had not given up. Maybe it was patriotism. "That's what you say," he put in, and then muttered something unintelligible.

This time Teresa didn't say anything. She just kept looking at Teo, waiting for his reaction. He touched his chin, pensive. He sat like that for a second, his eyes down, and then looked up, straight at Eddie.

"Don't fuck with me, Eddie. Okay?" He had picked up the fountain pen, and after taking off the cap he drew a line of blue ink across the white page of his notebook, a line so perfectly straight and horizontal that he might have been using a ruler. "This is serious business, not running Winstons across the line." He looked at Patty and then at Teresa, the pen suspended over the paper, and at the end of the line he drew an arrow pointing to Eddie's heart. "Does he really have to be here for this conversation?"

Patty looked at Teresa, her eyebrows arched exaggeratedly. Teresa was looking at Teo. No one was looking at Eddie.

"No," Teresa said. "He doesn't."

"Ah. Good. Because we need to discuss some technical details."

Teresa turned to Eddie. He was taking off his glasses to wipe the nosepieces with a Kleenex, as though in the last few minutes they had been slipping more often than usual. He also wiped the bridge of his nose. His nearsightedness accentuated the bewilderment and fear in his eyes. He looked as pathetic and helpless as a duck soaked in crude oil on the ocean shore.

"Go downstairs and have a beer, Eddie. We'll see you later," said Teresa.

He hesitated, then put on his glasses as he clumsily got up. The sad imitation of a humiliated man. It was obvious that he was trying to think of something to say before he left, and that nothing occurred to him. He opened his mouth, closed it. Finally he left, in silence: a duck leaving black footprints, *chuff chuff chuff,* with a face that looked like he was going to throw up before he made it outside.

Teo drew a second blue line in his notebook, under the first, and just as straight.

"I would go to Hong Kong, the Philippines, Singapore, the Caribbean, or Panama," he said. "Several of my representatives operate with Grand Cayman, and they're very satisfied: six hundred and eighty banks on a tiny island two hours by plane from Miami. No tellers, virtual money, no taxes, confidentiality a sacred trust. They're only obliged to report transactions when there's proof of direct links to known criminal activity. . . . But since they have no legal requirements for a customer's identification, establishing those links is not possible."

Now he was looking at the two women, and three out of four times it was at Teresa. I wonder, she thought, what the Lieutenant's told him about me. Where everybody stands. She also wondered whether she was dressed appropriately: a loose ribbed sweater, jeans, sandals. For a moment she envied the mauve and gray Valentino outfit that Patty was wearing as naturally as a second skin. Elegant bitch.

Teo went on explaining his plan: A couple of nonresident corporations located abroad, covered by law firms with adequate bank accounts, to start with. And so as not to put all their eggs in one basket, transfer select amounts of money, laundered through a series of secure circuits, to fiduciary deposits and serious bank accounts in Luxembourg, Liechtenstein, and Switzerland. Dormant accounts, he insisted, that were not to be touched, as insurance for the long term. They could also invest their money in corporations that dealt in trusts, real estate, titles, things like that. Clean money—spotless, in fact—in case someday the Caribbean infrastructure had to be dynamited or everything else had to be blown to bits.

"Do you agree with all this?"

"It sounds like the right thing," Teresa replied.

"It is. The advantage is that now there's a lot of movement between Spanish banks and the Caymans, and we can get lost in all the wire traffic for the first deposits. I have a good contact in George Town: Mansue Johnson and Sons. Banking consultants, financial advisors, and attorneys. They do complete tailor-made packages."

"Isn't that going a little far, making everything way too complicated?" asked Patty. She had been smoking one cigarette after another, the butts accumulating in the saucer of her coffee cup.

Teo put the pen down on the notebook page. He shrugged. "That depends on your plans for the future. What Eddie did for you works for the current state of your business: it's that simple. But if things start picking up, you really need to prepare a structure that can handle any expansion, without rushing it and without improvisation."

"How long would it take you to have everything ready to go?" Teresa asked.

Teo smiled the same smile as before: restrained, a bit vague, very different from the smiles of other men she remembered. And she still liked it, or maybe it was that now she liked that kind of smile because it didn't mean anything. Simple, clean, automatic. More a polite gesture than anything else, like the gleam on a polished table or the shine on a new car. There was nothing compromising behind it: not sympathy, or dreams, or weakness, or obsessions. There was no intention to deceive, no attempt to convince or seduce; it was there only because it was linked to the character, inculcated in him through upbringing, the way his manners and the well-tied knot in his tie had been. He smiled the way he drew those ruler-straight lines on the blank pages of his notebook, and that was reassuring to Teresa. By this time she had read, and remembered, and she could look at a person and see many things. This man's smile was one of those that put everything in its proper place. I don't know whether it'll happen with him, she told herself—I really don't know if I'll ever screw another man. But if I do, it'll be a man who smiles like that.

"How soon can you give me the money to start? After that, a month, maximum, and the papers will be ready for you to sign. We can have the right people come here, or we can all go to a neutral site. An hour of signatures and paperwork, and it'll be done. . . . I also have to know who's in charge of everything."

He waited for a reply. He had said this in a light, offhanded way. A detail of no great importance. But he was still waiting, and he was looking at each of them in turn.

"Both of us," said Teresa. "We're in this together."

Teo took a second or two to answer. "I understand. But we need a single signature. The one who'll be sending the faxes or making the telephone calls. There are things that I can do, of course. That I'll *have* to do, if you give me a limited power of attorney. But one of you has to make the fast decisions."

Lieutenant O'Farrell's cynical laughter broke the silence. The fucking laugh of an ex-combatant who wipes her ass with the flag.

"That's her." She pointed at Teresa with her cigarette. "Somebody'll have to get up early every morning, and I don't get up till noon."

Miss American Express. Teresa asked herself why Patty decided to play it this way, and since when. Where she was pushing her, and why. Teo sat back in his chair. Now his eyes moved back and forth between the two women.

"It is my responsibility to tell you that you'll be leaving everything in her hands," he finally said to Patty.

"Sure."

"All right." Teo studied Teresa. "That's it, then."

He was no longer smiling, and his expression seemed to indicate he was appraising the situation. He's asking himself the same questions about Patty, Teresa told herself. About our relationship. Calculating the pros and cons. To what degree I represent profits. Or problems. To what degree she does.

At that, she began to sense many of the things that were going to happen.

Patty gave them a good, long look when they left the meeting, and the look continued as the three of them went downstairs in the elevator and then strolled along the docks of the harbor, tidying up the last details. They picked Eddie Alvarez up at the door of the Ke bar, where he resembled someone who'd just been the victim of a mugging and was expecting another, the ghost of Punta Castor and perhaps the memory of Sergeant Velasco and Cañabota making his throat tight. Patty seemed pensive, her eyes squinting, marked with wrinkles, with a touch of interest or amusement, or both—amused interest, interested amusement—bubbling inside her, somewhere in that strange head. It was as though she were smiling without smiling, mocking Teresa, and perhaps herself, a little, laughing at everything and everybody. She had been watching them with that strange expression when they left the apartment in Sotogrande, as if she had just planted pot up in the sierra and were waiting for the perfect moment to harvest it—and she continued watching them during the conversation with Teo along the docks, and then for weeks and months afterward, when Teresa and Teo Aljarafe began to grow close. And once in a while Teresa got a whiff of

that and was about to confront Patty, say, *Quihubo aquí, carnalita,*
what's up, *cabrona,* spit it out.

But then Patty would smile in a different way, more open, like, *Who,
me?* and light a cigarette, sip at her drink, pick at her food, do a line of
coke. Or she'd start talking about something with that frivolousness
she wielded so perfectly—frivolousness that Teresa had figured out
wasn't frivolousness at all—or anything like sincerity, either. Or Patty
might go back, for a time, to being what she'd been in the beginning:
the distinguished, cruel, cutting, quick Lieutenant O'Farrell, the comrade from back when, whose dark side you might occasionally glimpse.

Afterward, Teresa even came to wonder to what extent Patty had
sacrificed herself to fate, like a woman accepting the tarot cards that she
herself turns up. To what degree had Patty foreseen, or even fostered,
many of the things that eventually occurred between the two of them,
Teresa and Teo Aljarafe? And thus, in a way, among the three of them.

Teresa often saw Oleg Yasikov. There was good chemistry between
her and the big, quiet Russian, who looked at work, money, life,
and death with a dispassionate Slavic fatality that reminded her of certain men from northern Mexico. The two of them would sit drinking
coffee or take a walk after a work-related meeting, or go out to dinner
at Casa Santiago, on the sea walk in Marbella—Yasikov liked crayfish
in white wine sauce—with the bodyguards strolling along the sidewalk
across the street, along the beachfront. He was not a man of many
words, but when they were alone, talking, Teresa heard him say things,
almost offhandedly, that later she would spend hours turning over in
her head. He never tried to convince anyone of anything, or counter
one argument with another. I tend not to argue, he had once remarked.
They tell me it'll be less and I say, Ah, well, maybe it will be. Then I do
what I think is right. This guy, Teresa soon realized, had a point of view,
a very clear way of looking at the world and the beings who inhabited
it: he didn't kid himself that it was reasonable, or fair, or nice. Just useful. His behavior, his objective cruelty, suited her somehow.

"There are animals," he said, "that live on the bottom of the ocean
in a shell. Others go out and expose their bare skin—they risk it. Some
reach the shore. They stand up. They walk. The question is, How far do
they get before their time is up? Yes. How long do you last and what do
you achieve while you last? Which is why everything that helps you
survive is essential. The rest is superfluous. Disposable, Tesa. In my
work, as in yours, you have to move within the simple margins of those
two words. Essential. Superfluous. Understand? . . . And the second of

those words includes the lives of other people. Or sometimes excludes them."

So Yasikov wasn't so hermetic after all. No man was. Teresa had learned that it was silences, skillfully administered, that made other people talk. And it was in that way, little by little, that she approached the Russian gangster. One of Yasikov's grandfathers had been a czarist cadet in the days of the Bolshevik Revolution, and during the hard years that followed, the family preserved the memory of that young officer. Like many men of his class, Oleg Yasikov admired bravery—that, he would eventually confess, was what had made him admire Teresa. It was during a night of vodka and conversation on the terrace of the Salduba bar in Puerto Banús; she caught a sentimental, almost nostalgic, vibration in his voice when in a very few words he told the story of the cadet and later lieutenant in the Nikolaiev Cavalry Regiment, who had time to father a son before being shot by a firing squad, alongside Baron von Ungern Sternberg, in Mongolia, or Siberia, in 1922.

"Today is the birthday of Czar Nicholas," Yasikov said abruptly, the bottle of Smirnoff two-thirds empty, turning his head as though the specter of the young White Army officer were about to appear down at the end of the sea walk, among the Rolls-Royces and Jaguars and enormous yachts. Then he pensively raised his glass of vodka, holding it up to the light, and he held it aloft until Teresa clinked her glass against it, and then they both drank, looking into each other's eyes. And although Yasikov smiled self-mockingly, Teresa, who knew almost nothing about the czar, much less about the officer grandfather shot by a firing squad in Manchuria, realized that despite the Russian's grimace, he had just performed a serious and deeply felt ritual that she had been privileged to witness, and that her instinct to clink her glass against his had been right, because it brought her closer to the heart of a dangerous and necessary man.

Yasikov filled the glasses again. "The czar's birthday," he repeated. "Yes. And for almost a hundred years, even when that date was forgotten and that word was forbidden in the Union of Soviet Socialist Republics, the paradise of the proletariat, my grandmother and my parents and later I myself would drink a toast to him at home. Yes. To his memory and the memory of Lieutenant Yasikov of the Nikolaiev Cavalry Regiment. I still do. Yes. As you see. Wherever I am. Without opening my mouth. Even once during the eleven months that I spent rotting as a soldier. In Afghanistan." Then he poured more vodka, until the bottle was empty, and it occurred to Teresa that every human being has a hidden story, and that if you were quiet enough and patient enough you could finally hear it. And that that was good, a lesson that was important to learn. A lesson that was useful, above all.

The Italians, Yasikov had said. Teresa discussed it the following day with Patty. "He says the Italians want a meeting. They need reliable transportation for their coke, and he thinks our infrastructure can help them. They're happy with the hashish shipments and want to raise the stakes. It's too far a reach for the old Gallego *amos do fume.* They've got other connections, plus they're under surveillance by the police. So they've sounded out Oleg to see if we're willing to take it on. To open a big route for them through the south, that'll cover the Mediterranean."

"So what's the problem?"

"There'll be no turning back. If we take on this job, we're committed, we have to stay with it. And that means more investment. It makes things more complicated. And more risky."

They were in Jerez, having tapas—shrimp and *tortilla española*— and drinking Tío Pepe at the Carmela bar, at a table under the old arch. It was a Saturday morning, and the glaring sun illuminated the people strolling through the Plaza del Arenal—older couples dressed for the *aperitivo* hour, younger couples with children, groups around the doors of taverns or sitting around wine barrels set out in the plaza as tables. The two women had come to visit a winery that was up for sale by the Fernández de Sotos—a large building with walls painted red ocher and white, spacious patios surrounded by arches and grilled windows, and vast cool wine cellars full of oak barrels with their contents identified in chalk. The winery was in bankruptcy; it belonged to a family Patty had known all her life, ruined like others of Patty's class by expensive tastes, purebred horses, and a generation absolutely allergic to business: two sons who were playboys and partiers and who appeared from time to time in the police blotter of the newspapers, for corruption of minors.

The investment was recommended by Teo Aljarafe: "We'll keep the land with the limestone soil over by Sanlúcar and the old building in Jerez, and on the lot in the city we'll build apartments. The more respectable businesses we have, the better, and a *bodega* with a name and pedigree has real cachet." Patty had laughed about that "cachet" they were buying. "My family's name and pedigree never made me the slightest bit respectable," she said. But she did think the purchase was a good idea.

So the two of them went to Jerez, Teresa dressed elegantly for the occasion, jacket and gray skirt with black heels, her hair parted down the middle and pulled back in a chignon, two silver hoops at her ears. She should always wear as little jewelry as possible, Patty had suggested, and no costume jewelry, only the real thing. A simple bracelet once in a while, or that *semanario* of hers. A good chain around her neck—a chain was better than a necklace, but if she had to wear a necklace it should be good: coral, amber, pearls. . . . It's like art on your walls; better to have a good lithograph or antique print than a bad oil.

Patty and Teresa were accompanied by an obsequious administrator decked out at eleven in the morning as though he'd just come from high mass during Holy Week in Seville. They visited the *bodega,* noted the high ceilings, stylized columns, shadowy interiors; the silence reminded Teresa of Mexican churches built by the conquistadors. It was strange, she thought, how some old places in Spain gave her the sense that she was coming face to face with something already familiar to her. As though the architecture, the customs, the feeling of place were the echoes of things she thought belonged only to her own land. I've been here before, she would think as she turned a corner, or walked down a street, or stood before the portico of a mansion or a church. *Híjole.* Something in me has been this way before, and it explains part of what I am.

"If we just do transportation for the Italians, nothing will change," Patty said. "The guy that gets caught does the time. And that guy doesn't know anything. The chain stops there—no owners, no names. I don't see the risk."

She was finishing the last bites of tortilla, sitting silhouetted against the illuminated end of the arch; the light gilded her hair, and she had lowered her voice as she spoke.

Teresa lit a Bisonte. "I'm not talking about that kind of risk," she replied.

Yasikov had been very clear: "I don't want to deceive you, Tesa," he had said in Puerto Banús. "The Camorra, the Mafia, and the 'Ndrangheta can be bad people. There's a lot to win with them. If everything goes well. But if something goes wrong, there's a lot to lose. And on the other side, you've got the Colombians. Yes. Who are no nuns, either. The positive part is that the Italians work with the boys from Cali, who are not as violent as those lunatics in Medellín, Pablo Escobar and that gang of psychopaths of his. But if you go into this, it'll be forever. You cannot get off a moving train. No. Trains are good if there are customers in them. Bad if there are enemies. Have you ever seen *From Russia with Love*? . . . The bad guy that confronted James Bond on the train was Russian. And that is not a warning. No. Just advice. Yes. Friends are friends until . . ." He was about to finish the sentence, when Teresa finished it for him. "Until they aren't anymore," she said. And smiled. Yasikov looked at her, suddenly serious.

"You are a very clever woman, Tesa," he then said, after not speaking for several seconds. "You learn quickly, about everything and everybody. You will survive."

"What about Yasikov?" Patty asked now. "He's not in?"

"He's smart, and prudent." Teresa was watching people pass in front of the archway. "As we say in Sinaloa, he's got a plan, but he needs to fill that straight flush. He wants in, but he doesn't want to be the first one in. If we're in, he'll hitch a ride. With us taking care of the transportation, he can guarantee himself a reliable supply for his people, and one that's super-controlled. But first he wants to check out the system. The Italians give him the chance to test the waters with minimum risk. If everything works out, he'll come in. And if not, he'll just go on with what he's got now. He doesn't want to compromise his position here."

"Is it worth it?"

"Depends. If we do it right, it's a shitload of money."

Patty's legs were crossed: Chanel skirt, beige heels. She was swinging one foot as though following the rhythm of a song, one Teresa couldn't hear.

"All right, then. You're the business brains." Patty tilted her head to one side—all those wrinkles around her eyes. "Which is why it's so comfortable to work with you."

"I told you there are risks. We can lose everything—including our lives. Both of us."

Patty's laughter made the waitress turn to look at them.

"I've lost everything before. So you decide. You're my girl."

She was still looking at her in that way. Teresa said nothing. She picked up her glass of sherry and brought it to her lips. With the taste of the tobacco in her mouth, the wine was bitter.

"Have you told Teo?" Patty asked.

"Not yet. But he's coming to Jerez this afternoon. He'll have to be told, of course."

Patty opened her purse to pay the check. She pulled out a thick wad of bills—very indiscreetly—and some fell to the ground. She leaned over to pick them up.

"Of course," she said.

There was something in what she and Yasikov had talked about in Puerto Banús that Teresa didn't tell Patty. Something that forced her to look around with concealed suspiciousness. That kept her lucid and alert, that complicated her thoughts on those gray dawns that still found her lying wide awake. "There are rumors," the Russian had said.

"Yes. Things. Someone told me that there is interest in you in Mexico. For some reason"—he studied her as he said this—"you have aroused the attention of your countrymen. Or their memory. They ask whether you are the same Teresa Mendoza that left Culiacán four or five years ago. . . . Are you?"

"Keep talking," Teresa said.

Yasikov shrugged. "I know very little more. Just that they're asking questions about you. A friend of a friend. Yes. They sent someone to find out what you're up to these days, and whether it's true that you're moving up in the business. That in addition to hashish you may be involved in cocaine. Apparently in your country there are people who are worried that the Colombians, since your countrymen have closed the door to the United States to them, may turn up here. Yes. And they cannot like the fact that a Mexican girl, which is also quite a coincidence, may be in the middle. No. Especially if they know this girl. From before. So be careful, Tesa. In this business, having a past is neither good nor bad, so long as you don't attract attention. And things are going too well for you for you not to attract attention. Your past, that past you never talk to me about, is none of my affair. *Nyet.* But if you left unpaid bills, there's always the possibility that somebody may want to collect."

L ong before, in Sinaloa, Güero Dávila had taken her flying. It was the first time for her. Güero parked the Bronco so that its headlights lit the yellow-roofed airport building, and after greeting the soldiers standing guard along the runway covered with small planes, they took off just at dawn, to see the sun come up over the mountains. Teresa remembered Güero beside her in the cabin of the Cessna, the sunlight reflecting off the green lenses of his Ray-Bans, his hands on the controls, the purring of the engine, the image of St. Malverde hanging from the dashboard—*God bless my journy and allow my return*—and the Sierra Madre shimmering like mother-of-pearl, with golden glints off the water in the rivers and lakes, the fields with their green smears of marijuana, the fertile plains, and off in the distance, the ocean. That early morning, seen from up in the sky, her eyes wide open in surprise, the world seemed clean and beautiful to Teresa.

She thought about that now, in a room in the Hotel Jerez, in the dark, with only the glow from the gardens and the pool backlighting the curtains at the window. Teo Aljarafe had gone, and the voice of José Alfredo was emerging from the stereo perched next to the television set and VCR. *I'm in the corner of a cantina,* he was singing. *Listening to a song that I requested.* Güero had told her that José Alfredo Jiménez had died drunk, composing his last songs in cantinas, the lyrics written down by friends because José Alfredo couldn't even hold a pencil anymore. "Your Memory and I," this one was called. And it certainly sounded like it was one of the last.

What had been bound to happen happened. Teo arrived at midafternoon for the closing on the Fernández de Soto *bodega.* Then they had a drink to celebrate. One, and then several. Then the three of them, Teresa, Patty, and Teo, walked through the old part of Jerez with its ancient palaces and churches, its streets filled with *tascas* and bars. And as they sat at a bar, when Teo leaned over to light the cigarette she had just put to her lips, Teresa felt his eyes on her. How long has it been, she asked herself. How long since . . . She liked his Spanish aquiline profile, the dark, secure hands, that smile stripped of all meaning and commitment. Patty smiled, too, but differently, as though from a distance. Resigned. Fatalistic. And just as Teresa was bringing her face down to the man's hands, which were cradling the flame in the hollow of his palm, she heard Patty say: I've gotta go, oh gosh, I just remembered something. See you guys later.

Teresa had turned to say, No, wait, I'm going with you, don't leave me here, but Patty was already gone, without looking back, her purse slung over her shoulder. So Teresa sat there watching her go while she felt Teo's eyes on her again. And at that, she wondered whether Patty and he had talked this over. What might they have said? What would they say afterward? But no—the thought stung like a whip. No way—no mixing business with pleasure. I can't afford that kind of luxury. I'm leaving, too. Yet something in the middle of her body, in her womb, forced her to stay: a strong, dense impulse composed of weariness, loneliness, expectation, lack of will. She wanted to rest. Feel a man's skin, his fingers on her body, his mouth against her own. Put aside all this initiative for a while and entrust herself to someone who would act for her. Think for her. Then she recalled the torn photograph she always carried in her wallet, in her purse. The wet-behind-the-ears girl with the big eyes, with a male arm over her shoulders—ignorant of almost everything, looking out at a world that resembled the one she'd seen from the cabin of a Cessna on a pearl-colored morning. She turned, finally, slowly, deliberately. And as she did so, she thought, *Pinches hombres cabrones,* always so fucking smart, but they almost never think. She was absolutely certain that sooner or later, one of them, or both, would pay for what was about to happen.

There she was now, alone. Listening to José Alfredo. It had all happened very predictably and quietly, without too many words or unnecessary gestures. As antiseptic as the smile on the face of this experienced, skilled, and attentive Teo. Satisfactory in many ways. And suddenly, almost at the end of the several endings that he brought her to, Teresa's calm mind found itself once again looking at itself—looking at her—like so many other times before: naked, sated at last, her tousled hair in her face, serene after the excitement, desire, and pleasure, knowing that being possessed by others, or abandoning herself to them, had all ended at the León Rock. And she saw herself thinking about Patty, the way she'd shivered when Teresa kissed her on the mouth in their cell in prison, the way she'd watched Teresa while Teo lit her cigarette in the bar. And she told herself that maybe what Patty wanted was precisely that: to push her toward herself. Toward that image in the mirrors with its lucid gaze—the image that never allowed itself to be deceived.

After Teo left, she'd gone into the shower, the water very, very hot, the steam fogging up the mirror, and she'd scrubbed her skin with soap—slowly, carefully—before dressing and going out for a walk, alone. She wandered through the city until in a narrow street with grilled windows she heard, in surprise and wonder, a song from Mexico. *I want my life to end as I sit over a glass of wine.* That's impossible, she said to herself. That can't be happening here, now. So she raised her eyes and saw the sign above the door: "El Mariachi—Cantina Mexicana." And at that she laughed almost out loud, because she realized that life and fate play subtle games that sometimes turn out to be obvious. *Chale.* She pushed the swinging door open and entered an authentic cantina—bottles of tequila behind the bar, a pudgy young waiter serving Corona and Pacífico beers to the people at the tables, and a CD by José Alfredo on the stereo. She ordered a Pacífico just so she could touch its yellow label, and she raised the bottle to her lips, sipped just enough to savor the taste that brought back so many memories, and then ordered a Herradura Reposado, which was served to her in the authentic *caballito.*

Now José Alfredo was saying, *Why did you come to me seeking compassion, when you know that I'm writing my last song.* Teresa felt an intense wave of happiness wash over her, a feeling so fierce that she thought she might almost faint. And she ordered another tequila, and then another—the waiter had recognized her accent and smiled pleasantly. *When he was in cantinas,* another song began, *he felt no pain or grief.* She pulled a wad of bills out of her purse and told the waiter to bring her an unopened bottle of tequila, and that she'd also buy that CD that was playing. "I can't sell it," the young man said, surprised. So she pulled out more money, and then more, covering the bar as the astonished waiter looked on. Finally he brought her the bottle and the two double CDs by José Alfredo, four CDs with a hundred songs. I can buy anything, she thought absurdly—or not so absurdly, after all— when she left the cantina with her treasures, not caring that people might see her carrying the bottle. She walked to the taxi stand—she could feel the street moving strangely under her feet—and returned to her hotel.

And there she still was, with the bottle almost half empty, accompanying the recorded lyrics with words of her own. *Listening to a song that I requested. They're serving me my tequila now. And my thoughts journey to you.* The room was in dusky light from the lamps in the garden and around the pool: rumpled sheets; Teresa's hands as she smoked *basucos,* picked up the glass and the bottle on the night table. *Who hasn't known the betrayal of a love affair gone wrong? Who hasn't gone into a cantina for a tequila and a song? And I wonder just who I am now,* José Alfredo was singing, as Teresa silently moved her lips.

Quihubo, carnala. I ask myself how other people see me, and I hope they see me from way far away.

What was that? The need for a man? *Órale.* Falling in love. *No, gracias,* not anymore.

"Free" was perhaps the word, despite its grandiloquence, its poetry. She didn't even go to mass anymore. She looked up, at the dark ceiling, and saw nothing. *They're pouring me one for the road,* José Alfredo was singing just then, and she sang along. No, I won't be going just yet— right now all I want is to hear "The Woman Who Left" one more time.

She shivered. On the sheet, beside her, was the torn photograph. Being free made you very cold.

11. I don't know how to kill, but I'm going to learn

The installations of the Guardia Civil in Galapagar are on the outskirts of the village, which is near El Escorial: smaller houses for the guardsmen's families and a larger building for the headquarters offices, with the snowy gray landscape of the mountains in the background. Directly behind—one of life's little paradoxes—some nice-looking prefabs where a community of Gypsies live. The two populations inhabit the place in a live-and-let-live proximity that gives the lie to so many of García Lorca's clichés about the Heredias, Camborios, and tricorne-wearing soldiers.

After identifying myself at the gate, I left my car in the parking lot, under the eye of the soldier at the entrance. A tall, blond guard—in his uniform he was green down to the ribbon tying the ponytail that emerged from under his beret—led me to Captain Víctor Castro's office: a small room with a computer on the desk and a Spanish flag on the wall, next to which were hanging, whether as decoration or trophies I never learned, a Mauser Coruña from 1945 and a Kalashnikov AKM assault rifle.

"All I can offer you is a cup of really terrible coffee," he said.

I accepted his offer, and he himself brought me a cup from the machine in the hallway, stirring the tarry black liquid with a plastic spoon. It was, indeed, unspeakably bad. As for Captain Castro, he was one of those men one likes at first sight: serious, with efficient manners, impeccably turned out in his olive-green fatigues and buzz-cut gray hair, a moustache that was turning gray, and a gaze as direct and open as the handshake he'd given me when we met. He had the face of an honest man, and it may have been that, among other things, that had led his superiors, some time back, to put him in charge of the Delta Four group, on the Costa del Sol, for five years. But according to my sources, Captain Castro's honesty proved to be something of an inconvenience even to his superiors. That, perhaps, explained why I was visiting him in an out-of-the-way village up in the Sierra de Madrid, in a command post with thirty guardsmen the rank of whose commanding officer should not have been as high as that of Captain Castro, and why it had taken me a good bit of work—calling in favors, twisting a few arms— to persuade Guardia Civil national headquarters to authorize this interview. As Captain Castro himself noted that afternoon, philosophically, when he politely accompanied me to my car, Boy Scouts never have much of a career in this line of work.

Now we were talking about specifically *his* career. He was sitting at the desk in his little office, with his eight multicolored ribbons sewn on the left side of his jacket, across from me with my coffee. Or to be more precise, we were talking about the day Teresa Mendoza first came to his attention, back when he was investigating the murder of a Civil Guardsman in the Manilva detachment, one Sergeant Iván Velasco, whom Castro described—he was very careful in his choice of words— as an agent of questionable honesty. Others whom I'd consulted about this individual—among them the ex-cop Nino Juárez—had not been quite so circumspect, defining him instead as a thoroughgoing asshole son of a bitch.

"Velasco was murdered in a very suspicious way," Castro explained. "So we worked on that for a while. Certain overlaps with episodes of smuggling, among them the matter of Punta Castor and the death of Santiago Fisterra, led us to link Velasco's murder to Teresa Mendoza's release from prison. Although nothing could ever be proved, that was what led me to her, and in time I became a specialist in the Mexicana: surveillance, videotapes, telephone taps—with a court order, of course. . . . You know the drill." He looked at me, taking for granted that I did in fact know the drill. "It wasn't my job to pursue drug trafficking, just investigate that world. The people the Mexicana bought and corrupted, including bankers, judges, and politicians. And people in my line of work, too: Customs officers, Civil Guardsmen, cops."

The word "cops" made me nod, interested. Surveillance on the guys doing surveillance. Enforcement on the enforcers.

"What was Teresa Mendoza's relationship to Commissioner Nino Juárez?"

He hesitated, and he seemed to be calculating the worth, or currency, of each detail he was going to give. Then he made an ambiguous gesture.

"There isn't a lot I can tell you that the newspapers didn't publish at the time. . . . The Mexicana managed to infiltrate even the DOCS. Juárez, like so many others, wound up working for her."

I set my styrofoam cup on the desk and leaned forward.

"She never tried to buy you off?"

Captain Castro's silence became uncomfortable. He looked at the cup inexpressively. For a moment I feared the interview was over. It's been a pleasure, sir. *Adiós* and *hasta la vista*.

"I understand many things, right?" he said at last. ". . . I understand, although I can't condone, the fact that somebody earning a very low salary might see the opportunity if someone says to him, Listen, tomorrow when you're at such and such a place, instead of looking this way look that way. And in exchange, that person sticks out his hand and gets a wad of bills. That's only human. Everybody has his own way of looking at things. And we all want to live better than we live now. . . . The thing is, some people have limits and others don't."

He fell silent again and raised his eyes. I tend to doubt people's innocence, but that look I didn't doubt. Although one never knew . . . Anyway, people had talked to me about Captain Víctor Castro, number three in his class, seven years in Intxaurrondo, one as a volunteer in Bosnia, distinguished service medal with red ribbon.

"Of course they tried to buy me," he said. "It wasn't the first time, or the last." Now he allowed himself a gentle, almost tolerant smile. "Even here in this village people try from time to time, on a different scale. A ham at Christmas from a builder, an invitation to dinner from a city councilman . . . I'm convinced that every man and every woman has a price. Maybe mine was too high. I don't know. But whatever the case, me they didn't buy."

"Which is why you're here?"

"This is a good posting," he said as he looked at me impassively. "Quiet. I've got no complaints."

"Is it true, as people say, that Teresa Mendoza at one point had contacts in the Guardia Civil high command?"

"You should ask the high command about that."

"And that you worked with Judge Martínez Pardo in an investigation that was halted by the minister of justice?"

"I'll tell you the same as before: Ask the Ministry of Justice."

I nodded, accepting his rules. For some reason, that terrible coffee in a styrofoam cup increased my liking for him. I remembered former Commissioner Nino Juárez at the table in Casa Lucio, savoring his Viña Pedrosa '96. How had my interlocutor put it a minute ago? Ah, yes. Everybody has his own way of looking at things.

"Talk to me about the Mexicana," I said.

At the same time I took a copy of the photograph shot from the Customs helicopter out of my pocket, and I laid it on the table: Teresa Mendoza spotlighted in the middle of the night with a cloud of spray sparkling around her, her face and hair wet, her hands on the shoulders of the man piloting the speedboat. Rushing at fifty knots toward the León Rock and his destiny. "I know that photo," said Captain Castro. But he sat there looking at it pensively for a long time before pushing it back toward me.

"She was very smart and very fast," he added a moment later. "Her rise in that very dangerous world was a surprise to everyone. She took big risks and was lucky. . . . From the woman riding with her boyfriend in that speedboat to the woman I knew, it's a big jump, I'll tell you. You've seen the press reports, I presume. The photos in ¡Hola! and all that. She got refinement, manners, a bit of culture. And she became powerful. A legend, they say. The Queen of the South. The reporters called her that. . . . To us, she was always just La Mexicana."

"Did she kill people?"

"Of course she killed people. Or had people killed. In that business, killing is part of a day's work. But she was clever. No one could ever prove anything. Not a killing, not a shipment of drugs, nada, zip, nothing. Even the tax guys in Treasury were after her, to see if they couldn't get at her that way, for tax evasion or some other offense. Nothing . . . I suspect she bought off the agents that were investigating her."

I thought I detected a hint of bitterness in his words. I gave him a querying look, but he leaned back in his chair—Let's not take that road, he seemed to be saying. It's a little off the subject, and not my area of expertise.

"How did she go so far so fast?"

"I told you—she was very intelligent. And lucky, of course. She came on the scene just when the Colombian cartels were looking for alternative routes in Europe. But besides that, she was an innovator. . . . If the Moroccans now have a monopoly on all the traffic on both sides of the Strait, it's thanks to her. She started depending more on those people than on the drug smugglers from Gibraltar or Spain, and she turned a disorganized, almost homegrown organization into an efficient business operation. She even changed the look of her employees. She made them dress right, none of those heavy gold chains and tacky silk shirts—simple suits, cars that didn't call attention to themselves, apartments instead of big houses, taxis to go to appointments. . . . And so, Moroccan hashish aside, she was the one who set up the cocaine networks that served the eastern Mediterranean, and she managed to elbow out the other mafias and Gallegos that wanted to work it. Nothing she moved was her own, as far as we could learn. But almost everybody depended on her."

The key, Captain Castro went on to tell me, was that the Mexicana used her technical experience with speedboats for large-scale operations. The traditional boats had been Phantoms with those stiff hulls that made them prone to break up on the open sea, and Teresa was the first to realize that a semi-rigid boat could tolerate bad weather and bad seas better because it got banged up less. So she put together a flotilla of Zodiacs, or "rubbers," as they were known in the Strait: inflatable boats that in the last few years had become available in lengths up to fifty feet, sometimes with three motors—the third not for extra speed, since the boat's limit was around fifty knots, but rather to maintain power. The larger size also allowed the boat to carry reserves of fuel. Greater range, more cargo aboard—it was the perfect solution. That way she could work in good or bad seas in places quite a distance from the Strait, such as the mouth of the Guadalquivir, Huelva, and the desert coastlines of Almería. Sometimes she would go as far as Murcia and Alicante, using fishing boats or private yachts, which could lay far offshore, on the high seas, as relay boats. She carried out operations with ships that came directly from South America, and she used the Moroccan connection, the entrance of cocaine through Agadir and Casablanca, to organize air transports from runways hidden in the mountains of the Rif to small Spanish landing sites that weren't even on the maps. What they called "bombings" were also in fashion: twenty-five-kilo packages of hashish or coke wrapped in fiberglass and strapped with flotation devices that they'd throw into the ocean to be recovered by fishing boats or speedboats. Nothing like that, Captain Castro said, had ever been done in Spain before.

Teresa Mendoza's pilots, recruited from among the daredevils that flew crop-spraying planes, could take off and land on dirt highways and two-hundred-yard runways. Using the moon, they would fly low between mountains or just skim the surface of the ocean, taking advantage of the fact that Moroccan radar was almost nonexistent and that the Spanish air-detection system had, or has—the captain made a huge circle with his hands—holes this big in it. Not to mention that there was always somebody who, palm duly greased, would close his eyes when a suspicious blip appeared on the screen.

"We confirmed all this later," Castro said, "when a Cessna Skymaster crashed near Tabernas, in Almería, loaded with two hundred kilos of cocaine. The pilot, a Polish guy, was killed. We knew it was one of the Mexicana's operations, but nobody could ever prove the connection. For that operation or any other."

She stopped in front of the window of the Alameda Bookstore. Recently she'd been buying a lot of books. There were more and more of them in her house, lined up neatly on shelves or laid randomly on the furniture. She would read until late at night, or sit during the day on the terrace facing the ocean. Some were about Mexico. In this Málaga bookstore she'd found several authors from her homeland: detective novels by Ricardo Garibay, a *True History of the Conquest of New Spain* by one Bernal Díaz del Castillo, who had been with Cortés and Malinche, and a three-volume collection of essays by Octavio Paz— she'd never heard of this Paz before, but he seemed to be a very important writer in Mexico. This volume was titled *El Peregrino en Su Patria—The Pilgrim in His Homeland.* She read the entire thing—slowly, with difficulty, sometimes skipping the many pages she couldn't understand. But some of it stuck: a trace of something new that made her think about the country she had been born in—that proud, violent land, so good and so miserable at the same time, always so far from God and so close to the fucking gringos—and about herself. They were books that made her think about things she had never thought about before.

She also read the newspapers and tried to watch the news on TV. That and the telenovelas, the soaps that ran in the evening, although now she spent more time reading than anything else. The advantage of books, as she discovered when she was in El Puerto de Santa María, was that you could appropriate the lives, stories, and thoughts they contained, and you were never the same person when you closed them as when you had opened them for the first time. Very intelligent people had written some of those pages, and if you were able to read with humility, patience, and the desire to learn, they never disappointed you.

Even the things you didn't understand stuck here, in a corner of your head, ready for the future to give them meaning, to turn them into beautiful or useful lessons. Thus *The Count of Monte Cristo* and *Pedro Páramo*, which for very different reasons remained her favorites—she had read them so many times she'd lost count—were now familiar journeys, which she had managed to almost completely master. Juan Rulfo's book was a challenge from the beginning, and now it gave her a sense of satisfaction to turn its pages and understand: *I wanted to go back, because I thought I might find the heat I'd just left, but I could tell the cold was coming from inside me, from my own blood.* Fascinated, shivering with pleasure and fear, she had discovered that all the books in the world were somehow about her.

And now she was studying the display in the store window, seeing whether there might be some title or cover that attracted her. With un-known books, she tended to let herself be guided by the covers and the titles. There was one by a woman named Nina Berberova that she'd read because of the portrait of a young woman playing the piano on the cover, and she had liked the story so much that she had sought out other titles by the same author. Since Berberova was Russian, Teresa gave the book—*The Accompanist,* it was called—to Oleg Yasikov, who read nothing but the sports page or things related to the times of the czar. Loony, that pianist, the gangster had said a few days later. Which showed that he had at least opened the book.

The morning was a sad one, a bit cool for Málaga. It had rained, and a misty haze hung over the city and port, turning the trees on the Alameda gray. Teresa had spotted a novel in the window called *The Master and Margarita.* The cover was not particularly attractive, but the author's name looked Russian, and Teresa smiled at the idea of Yasikov and the face he'd make when she gave him the book. She was about to go in and buy it when she saw her reflection in a mirror in the corner of the window: hair pulled back and falling over her shoulders, silver earrings, no makeup, an elegant three-quarter-length leather coat over blue jeans and brown leather boots. Behind her, the light traffic toward the Tetuán bridge, and only a few people out on the sidewalk. All at once everything inside her froze, as though her blood and heart and thoughts had turned to ice, or stone. She felt it before she could think about it. Even before she knew how to interpret it. But it was un-mistakable, familiar, and menacing: The Situation.

She'd seen something, she thought in a rush, not turning around, standing motionless before the mirror that allowed her to look behind her, over her shoulder. Frightened. Something that didn't go with the scene but that she couldn't identify. *One day*—she remembered Güero Dávila's words—*someone will come up to you. Someone you may know.* She carefully scanned the visual field the mirror gave her, and she became aware of the presence of two men crossing the street from the median strip of the Alameda, walking unhurriedly, dodging cars. There was something familiar about both of them, but she didn't realize that until a few seconds later. First, a detail caught her eye: despite the cold, both men were carrying their jackets folded over their right forearms. Then she felt the blind, irrational, ancient fear she'd thought she would never feel again. And only when she had hurried into the bookstore and was about to ask the clerk if there was a back way out, did she realize that she had recognized Gato Fierros and Potemkin Gálvez.

She ran again. Actually, she hadn't stopped running since the telephone rang in Culiacán. A flight with no direction, no destination, that had carried her to unforeseen people and places. Hardly had she hurried out the back door of the bookstore, her tense muscles awaiting a bullet, when she began to run down Calle Panaderos, not caring whether she attracted attention. She ran past the market—once more the memory of that first flight—and kept on straight until she reached Calle Nueva. Her heart was beating at sixty-eight hundred rpms, as though a souped-up V-8 were inside her chest. *Vroom, vroom.* She turned to look back from time to time, hoping against hope that the hit men were still waiting for her to come out of the bookstore. She slowed down when she almost slipped on the wet sidewalk. Calmer now, more rational. You're going to crack your skull, she told herself. So take it easy. Don't be stupid—think. Not about what those two assholes back there are doing, but about how to get rid of them. How to save yourself. You'll have time to think about the why of all this later, if you're still alive.

Impossible to go to the police, or back to the Cherokee with its leather seats—that ancestral Sinaloa taste for the all-terrain SUV—that was parked in the underground lot at the Plaza de la Marina. Think, she told herself again. Think, or you could die before the day's out. She looked around, confused and feeling helpless. She was in the Plaza de la Constitución, a few steps from the Hotel Larios. Sometimes she and Patty, when they were out shopping, would have a drink in the bar on the second floor, a pleasant place from which they could look out over—keep under surveillance, in this case—a good bit of the street. The hotel, of course. *Órale.* She took her cell phone out of her purse as she entered the hotel. *Beep, beep, beep.* This was a problem that only Oleg Yasikov could solve.

It was hard for her to get to sleep that night. She would jump awake, startled, and more than once she heard a voice moaning in the darkness, discovering when she came awake that it was her own. Images of the past and present mingled in her head: Gato Fierros' smile, the burning sensation between her thighs, the blasts of a Colt Double Eagle, the half-naked flight through the shrubbery that scratched her legs. Like yesterday, like right now, it seemed. At least three times she heard one of Yasikov's bodyguards knocking on her bedroom door. Tell me you're all right, *señora*. Do you need anything?

Before sunrise she got up and dressed and went out into the living room. One of the men was nodding on the couch and the other one raised his eyes from a magazine before rising to his feet, slowly. A cup of coffee, *señora*? A drink? Teresa shook her head and went to sit beside the window that overlooked the port of Estepona. Yasikov had put the apartment at her disposal. Stay as long as you want, he said. And avoid going home until everything blows over. The two bodyguards were middle-aged, heavyset, and quiet. One with a Russian accent and the other without any sort of accent at all, because he never opened his mouth. Both without identity. *Telki*, Yasikov called them. Soldiers. Taciturn men who moved slowly and whose professional eyes seemed to take in everything at once. They had not left her side since they walked into the hotel bar without attracting attention, one with a gym bag over his shoulder, and accompanied her—the one who talked asked her first, softly and politely, to describe the *pistoleros*—to a Mercedes with blacked-out windows that was waiting outside. Now the gym bag was open on the table, and inside it gleamed the bluing of a Skorpion machine pistol.

She saw Yasikov the next morning. "We're going to try to solve this problem," he told her. "Meanwhile, try not to show yourself in public. And now it would be useful if you would explain just exactly what's going on. Yes. What account these men are here to collect. I want to help you, but I can't make enemies for no reason, or interfere in the affairs of people I might be doing other business with. *Nyet.* If this is just Mexicans, I don't care, because I can't lose anything there. No. But if it's Colombians I need to stay on good terms. Yes."

"They're Mexicans," said Teresa. "From Culiacán, Sinaloa. My *pinche* hometown."

"Then I don't care," Yasikov replied. "I can help you."

So Teresa lit a cigarette, and then another and another, and for almost an hour told her interlocutor everything about the period of her life that for a while she had thought was over forever: Batman Güemes, don Epifanio Vargas, Güero Dávila's off-the-books shipments, his death, her flight from Culiacán, Melilla, Algeciras.

"That fits the rumors I'd heard," Oleg said when she had finished. "Except for you, we never see Mexicans here. No. Your success in business must have refreshed their memory."

They decided that Teresa would go on living a normal life—I can't be locked up, she had said; I spent enough time in a cell in El Puerto—but taking precautions, and with Yasikov's two *telki* beside her night and day. "You should also carry," the Russian suggested. But she refused: "No way. I'm clean and I want to stay clean. Illegal possession is all those assholes need to throw me in prison again." After thinking about it, Yasikov agreed. "Be careful, then," he said. "And I'll take care of the rest."

Teresa was careful. During the next week she lived with the bodyguards as virtually a second skin, avoided being seen in public too much, and stayed away from her home—a luxury apartment in Puerto Banús, which around this time she was considering replacing with a house on the seashore, in Guadalmina Baja—and it was Patty who went back and forth with clothes, books, and other necessities.

"Bodyguards, just like in the movies," Patty would say.

She spent a great deal of time with Teresa, talking or watching TV, the coffee table dusted with white powder, before the inexpressive eyes of Yasikov's two men. After a week, Patty turned to them and said, "Merry Christmas"—it was the middle of March—and put two thick wads of bills on the table, next to the bag with the Skorpion in it. "A little present. For you. To thank you for how well you're taking care of my friend."

"We're paid," said the one who spoke, after looking at the money and then at his comrade. And it occurred to Teresa that either Yasikov paid his people very well or they had a lot of respect for him. Maybe both. She never learned what their names were. Patty always called them Pixie and Dixie.

The two packages have been located," Yasikov reported. "A colleague who owes me some favors just called. I'll let you know what happens." He spoke to Teresa by phone the day before the meeting with the Italians, giving the news no apparent importance, in the course of a conversation about other matters.

Teresa was with her people, planning the purchase of eight thirty-foot rubbers that would be stored in a large warehouse in an industrial park in Estepona until they were to be launched. When she got off the phone she lit a cigarette to give herself some time, wondering how her friend the Russian was going to solve this problem. Patty looked at her. Sometimes, Teresa decided irritatedly, it's like she can read my fucking mind.

Teo was in the Caribbean, and Eddie, relegated to an administrative role, was overseeing the bank paperwork in Gibraltar. So besides Patty, two new board members for Transer Naga were present: Farid Lataquia and Dr. Ramos. Lataquia was a Lebanese Maronite who owned an import firm, the front for his real activities, which amounted to getting his hands on things that people needed. Small, charming, nervous, his hair thinning at the crown of his head but compensated for by a bushy moustache, he had made some money in arms trafficking during the Lebanese war—he was married to a Gemayel daughter—and he now lived in Marbella. Given enough money, personnel, and equipment, he could find anything. Thanks to him, Transer Naga had reliable transport for cocaine: old fishing boats from Huelva, private yachts or over-the-hill low-tonnage merchant vessels that before loading salt in Torrevieja would pause on the high seas to take on drugs that had entered Morocco via the Atlantic, and in certain cases act as feeder ships to speedboats operating off the eastern coast of Andalucía.

As for Dr. Ramos, he had been a physician in the merchant marine, and he was Transer Naga's tactical officer: he planned operations, specified loading and drop-off points, designed diversionary tactics, camouflage. In his fifties, with gray hair, tall and very thin, careless in his dress and, apparently, his personal hygiene, he always wore old knit cardigans, flannel shirts, and wrinkled pants. He smoked old pipes with burned-out bowls, filling them slowly and deliberately—he was the calmest man in the world—with an English tobacco he carried in its original tin, which, with the keys, coins, lighters, tamps, and other unpredictable objects he always had about him, made his pockets lumpy and deformed. Once, when he pulled out a handkerchief—embroidered with his initials, as in the old days—Teresa saw a miniature flashlight on a Danone yogurt promotional keychain fall out. He sounded like a metal-recycling truck when he walked.

"A single ID," the doctor was saying. "All the Zodiacs with the same registration and name. Identical, for all practical purposes. And since we'll put them in the water one by one, there's not the slightest problem. On each trip, once they're loaded, you take the ID tag off and they're anonymous. To be even safer, we can abandon them afterward, or have somebody pick them up. Pay us for them, of course. So we can make back part of our investment."

"Isn't it risky, all with the same registration?"

"Like I say, they'll go in the water one by one. When A is on an operation, we'll put the number on B. That way, since they're all alike, we'll always have one tied up at the pier, clean. Officially, it won't ever have moved from there."

"What about port security?"

Dr. Ramos' face betrayed only the slightest smile, of sincere modesty. *That* was also his specialty: harbor police, mechanics, sailors. He haunted the docks, parking his old Citroën Deux Chevaux anywhere, chatting with anyone he ran into, his pipe between his teeth and that absentminded, respectable, avuncular appearance of his. He had a little motorboat in Cabopino that he went fishing in. He knew every spot along the coast and every soul between Málaga and the mouth of the Guadalquivir.

"That's under control. No one will give us any trouble. Of course, they might come in from outside to investigate, but I can't cover that flank. Outside security is not within my purview."

Teresa took care of that aspect herself, through Teo and some of Patty's contacts. One-third of Transer Naga's income went to "public relations" on both sides of the Strait; politicians, government personnel, state security agents. The key was in negotiating—depending on the situation—with either information or money. Teresa never forgot the lesson of Punta Castor, and she had let some sizable shipments be intercepted—overhead, she called it—in order to throw good publicity in the way of the director of the Costa del Sol organized-crime section, Commissioner Nino Juárez, an old friend of Teo Aljarafe's. The various regions of the Guardia Civil also benefited from privileged information and lowered operational security to make interceptions and boost their statistics. You scratch my back, I'll scratch yours—and suddenly, you owe me one. Or several.

There were a few lower-ranking officials, police officers, and Civil Guardsmen on whom this sort of delicacy was wasted; with them, a trusted contact would simply lay a sheaf of banknotes on the table, and that was that. Not everyone let themselves be bought, but even then, unit solidarity tended to kick in. It was rare for an officer to rat out a colleague, except in the most egregious cases. Besides, the line between drug running and fighting crime was sometimes not all that clear; many people worked both sides at once—paying informers with drugs, for instance—and money was the only rule that was never broken.

With regard to certain local politicians, not much tact was needed there, either. Teresa, Patty, and Teo had dinner several times with Tomás Pestaña, the mayor of Marbella, to talk about the rezoning of several pieces of land they were interested in building on. Teresa had quickly learned that the more profits you brought to those you deal with, the more support they gave you. In the end, it was in the interest of even the guy in the corner store that you run drugs. And on the Costa del Sol, like everywhere else, introducing yourself as a person with a large amount of money to invest opened many doors. After that, it was all a question of ability and patience. A question of compromising people step by step, without scaring them off, until finally their well-being depended on you. Letting it happen easy. Vaseline. Like with the courts: You started off with flowers and candy for the secretaries and you wound up taking the judge to bed. Or several judges. Teresa had managed to put three on the payroll so far, including the presiding judge of a regional court, for whom Teo Aljarafe had just purchased an apartment in Miami.

She now turned to Lataquia. "What about the motors?"

The Lebanese man made an ancient Mediterranean gesture, the fingers of one hand together, then turning and swiping upward.

"It hasn't been easy," he said. "We still lack six units. I'm making inquiries."

"And the accessories?"

"The Wiseco pistons came in three days ago, no problem. The ball bearings for the connecting rods, too . . . As for the motors, I can complete the order with different makes."

"I specified," Teresa said slowly, emphasizing every word, "two-hundred-twenty-five-horsepower *pinche* Yamahas. . . . That's what I specified."

Lataquia looked to Dr. Ramos for support, but the doctor's face remained inscrutable. He sucked at his pipe, lost in a cloud of smoke. Teresa smiled inside. They were all on their own in this game.

"I know," Lataquia said, still looking at the doctor, his tone somewhat resentful, "but finding sixteen motors all at once is not easy. Not even an official distributor can guarantee that many on such short notice."

"All the motors have to be identical," Dr. Ramos reminded him. "Or else *adiós,* cover."

On top of it, he's a collaborator, Lataquia's eyes said. *Ibn charmuta.* You people must think we Phoenicians can do miracles. "What a pity," he finally said. "All that expense for one trip."

"Look who's crying over the expenses," Patty chimed in, lighting a cigarette. "Mister Ten Percent." She expelled the smoke hard, pursing her lips. "The bottomless pit."

She laughed softly, out on the margin of the conversation as usual. Enjoying it.

Lataquia assumed his expression of a man misunderstood. "I'll do what I can."

"I'm sure you will." Teresa smiled.

Never show doubt in public, Yasikov had said. Surround yourself with advisors, listen carefully, take your time giving orders if necessary, but afterward, never hesitate in front of the people working for you, never let them debate your decisions once they're made. In theory, a boss is never wrong. Oh, no. Everything you say has been carefully considered beforehand. The most important thing is respect. "If you can, make them love you. Of course. That ensures loyalty, too. Yes. But if you have to choose, it's better to be respected than loved."

"I'm sure," she repeated.

Although even better than being respected is being feared, she thought. But fear can't be imposed all of a sudden; it has to come gradually. Any psychopath can scare people. What's hard is making people fear you little by little.

Lataquia was thinking, pulling at his moustache.

"If you authorize it," he said, "I can make inquiries elsewhere. I know people in Marseilles and Genoa. . . . It will take a bit longer. And there's the question of import permits and so on."

"Just do it. I want those motors." She paused, looking down at the table. "One more thing. We have to start thinking about a big boat." She raised her eyes. "Not too big. With all the legal cover in place."

"How much do you want to spend?"

"Seven hundred thousand. Seven-fifty, tops."

Patty wasn't following the conversation. She was just watching Teresa from a distance, smoking, saying nothing. Teresa avoided looking at her. Bottom line, she thought, you always say that I'm the one that runs the business. That you like it like that.

"For an Atlantic crossing?" Lataquia, who had caught the connotation of the extra fifty thousand, wanted to know.

"No. Just to be able to be more mobile, out there."

"Something up?"

Dr. Ramos allowed himself a frown of censure. Too many questions, said his phlegmatic silence. Look at me. Or at Señorita O'Farrell sitting over there, quiet as a mouse.

"Could be," Teresa replied. "How long do you need?"

She knew how long she had. And it was not much time. The Colom-

bians were on the verge of a quantum leap. A single shipment, everything at once, that would supply both the Italians and the Russians for
months. Yasikov had approached her about the possibility, and Teresa
had promised to think about it.

Lataquia pulled at his moustache again. "I don't know," he said. "A
trip to look around, the formalities, and the payment. Three weeks,
minimum."

"Less."

"Two weeks."

"One."

"I can try," Lataquia sighed. "But it'll cost more."

Teresa laughed out loud. She loved this *cabrón*'s act. One out of
every three words was money with him.

"*No me chingues*, Lataquia. Not a dollar more. And get a move on,
your beans are burning."

The meeting with the Italians was held the next afternoon, in the
apartment in Sotogrande. Maximum security. Besides the Italians—two men from the Calabrian 'Ndrangheta who'd arrived that
morning at the Málaga airport—only Teresa and Yasikov attended.
Italy had become the main European consumer of cocaine, and the
idea was to ensure a minimum of four shipments of seven hundred kilos a year.

One of the Italians, a mature man with gray sideburns and an impeccably tailored jacket that gave him the air of a sporty, fashionable,
prosperous businessman, spoke for the pair; the other man was silent
the entire time, except for when he leaned over once in a while to whisper a few words in his colleague's ear. The spokesman explained the
plan in detail, in acceptable Spanish. The time was ripe for establishing
this connection: Pablo Escobar was being hunted down in Medellín,
the Rodríguez Orejuela brothers had suffered reverses that severely
limited their ability to operate directly in the United States, and the
other Colombian clans needed to make up in Europe for the losses they
had suffered from being elbowed out of the U.S. by the Mexican
mafias. They, the 'Ndrangheta, but also the Sicilian Mafia and Neopoli-
tan Camorra—all on good terms, and all men of honor, he added very
seriously, after his companion whispered to him—needed to guarantee
themselves a constant supply of cocaine hydrochloride with a purity of
ninety to ninety-five percent. They'd be able to sell it for $60,000 a kilo,
three times as much as in Miami or San Francisco. They also needed
coca paste to be sent to local underground refineries. At this point, the

other man—thin, with a close-cropped beard, dark suit, and an old-fashioned look about him—whispered something else in his colleague's ear.

The first man raised an admonitory finger, furrowing his forehead the way Robert De Niro might in a gangster movie. "We keep our word to those who keep their words," he intoned.

It struck Teresa that in a world where gangsters went to the movies and watched television like everybody else, reality often imitated fiction.

"A broad-based, stable business," the man was now saying, "with a good outlook for the future, as long, of course, as the first operations meet everyone's expectations." Then he told Teresa something she'd come to the meeting knowing, thanks to Yasikov: The Colombians already had the first shipment prepared: a container ship, the *Derly*, was even now at the dock in La Guaira, Venezuela, ready to take aboard a roll-on, roll-off truck containing seven hundred five-gallon drums of automobile grease, each of which held a large package of coke. The rest of the operation was nonexistent, he said, shrugging and looking at Teresa and Yasikov as though it were all their fault.

To the surprise of the Italians and Yasikov himself, Teresa had come with a concrete proposal worked out almost to the last detail. She had spent all the previous night and this morning in a marathon strategy session with her people so she could lay out a plan to begin in La Guaira and end in the harbor of Gioia Tauro, in Calabria. She laid it out: dates, payments, guarantees, compensations in case of loss of the first shipment. She may have revealed more than necessary for the security of the operation, but in this phase, she knew that everything depended on impressing the customer. The support of Yasikov and the Babushka covered her only to a point.

So she filled in the gaps as the Italians asked questions, putting forward a perfectly calculated plan, no loose ends. She explained that she, or rather a small Moroccan corporation, Ouxda Imexport—a sister front company of Transer Naga's registered in Nador—would take charge of the merchandise in Casablanca. There it would be transferred to an old British minesweeper, the *Howard Morhaim,* sailing under the flag of Malta. Farid Lataquia had moved fast, reporting that very morning that the minesweeper was available.

The *Howard Morhaim* would then go on to Constanza, in Romania, where another shipment that was waiting in storage in Morocco would be delivered to Yasikov's people. The coordination of the two deliveries would make the transportation less expensive and also strengthen the security. Fewer trips, fewer risks. Russians and Italians sharing the expenses. A perfect example of international cooperation. Et cetera. The only condition was that Teresa would accept no payment in merchandise. All she did was furnish the transportation, and all she accepted in payment was dollars.

The Italians loved Teresa, and loved the deal. They had come just to feel out the possibilities, and they found an operation ready to go. When it came time to discuss the financial aspects—costs and percentages—the man in the elegant jacket took out his cell phone, excused himself, and spent twenty minutes in the other room talking. Teresa, Yasikov, and the bearded Italian waited around the table, which was covered with the papers on which Teresa had been jotting numbers, diagrams, and dates. They sat there in silence, looking at one another.

Finally the other Italian appeared in the doorway, smiling, and asked his colleague to join him for a moment. Yasikov lit a cigarette.

"They're yours," he said. "Yes."

Teresa collected the papers without a word. From time to time she looked over at Yasikov; the Russian was smiling encouragingly, but she was still serious. It ain't over, she thought, till it's over. When the Italians returned, the man in the elegant jacket did so cheerily, and his companion seemed more relaxed, less solemn. "*Cazzo,*" said the sunny-faced one, almost surprised. "We've never dealt with a woman." But he added that his superiors had given the green light. Transer Naga had just acquired the exclusive rights to the overseas transportation of cocaine into the eastern Mediterranean.

The Italians, Yasikov, and Teresa celebrated that night, first with dinner at Casa Santiago and then at Jadranka, where Patty joined them. Teresa learned later that cops from the organized-crime unit, under Nino Juárez, were photographing them from a Mercury parked across the street, in the course of a routine surveillance stakeout, but the photos had no consequences: the men from the 'Ndrangheta were never identified. Besides, when Nino Juárez was added to Teresa's payroll a few months later, that file, among many others, was misplaced forever.

At Jadranka, Patty was charming to the Italians. She spoke their language and was able to tell off-color jokes with an accent that the other two, amazed, identified as Tuscan. She asked no questions, nor did anyone allude to anything they had talked about in the meeting. Patty knew why these two were there, of course, but she played dumb. There'd be time later to find out the details. There was a great deal of laughter and drinking, which contributed to the general business climate. And naturally the evening included two tall, blond, beautiful Ukrainian girls, just arrived from Moscow, where they had made porno films and posed for magazines before joining the high-end prostitution ring controlled by Yasikov's organization. Nor did the evening lack several lines of cocaine, which the Italians, who turned out to be more extroverted than they had seemed at first, finished off in the Russian's office, from a silver salver. Patty joined right in. "Some noses on these guys," she remarked, rubbing her own powder-dusted nostrils. "These Mafia guys can snort from a yard away." She had drunk too much, but her intelligent eyes, fixed on Teresa, reassured her. Easy, Mexicana, I'll take care of these guys until the two Bolshevik whores can move in and relieve them of some fluid. You can tell me all about it tomorrow.

Once the party was rolling, Teresa began making motions to say good night. It had been a hard day; she was no night owl, and her Russian bodyguards were waiting for her, one down at the far end of the bar, the other in the parking lot. The music was thumping, and the revolving light on the dance floor illuminated her in flashes as she shook the hands of the men from the 'Ndrangheta. A pleasure, she said. It's been a pleasure. *Ci vediamo*, the men said, each with an arm around his blond. Teresa was buttoning her black leather Valentino jacket, about to leave, when she noticed a movement behind the bodyguard at the bar. She looked around for Yasikov, and she saw him coming toward her through the crowd. He had excused himself five minutes earlier, saying he had a phone call to make.

"Something wrong?" she asked when she saw his face.

"*Nyet*," he said. "Everything fine. I just thought that before you went home you might come with me a moment. A little ride," he added. "Not far." He was unusually serious, and Teresa's alarms went off.

"What's happening, Oleg?"

"It's a surprise."

Patty, sitting in conversation with the Italians and the two Ukrainian girls, was looking at Teresa inquisitively and was about to stand up, but Yasikov raised an eyebrow and Teresa shook her head. Then they left the bar, followed by the bodyguard. At the door the cars were waiting, Teresa's second bodyguard at the wheel of hers and Yasikov's armored Mercedes with his driver and a bodyguard in the front seats. A third car was waiting not far away, with two other men inside: the Russian's permanent escort, solid beef from Solntsevo, Dobermans as square as refrigerators. All the cars' engines were running.

"Let's go in mine," Yasikov said, ignoring Teresa's silent question.

What's he up to? she thought. This cagey *pinche* Russki *cabrón*. They drove in circles, in convoy, for some fifteen minutes, until they were certain they weren't being followed. Then they took the freeway to a housing development in Nueva Andalucía. The Mercedes drove up to a house with a small yard and high walls, still under construction. Yasikov, his expression unreadable, held the car door open for Teresa. She followed him up the front steps into an empty entry with bricks piled against a wall, where a muscular man in a polo shirt was sitting on the floor, leafing through a magazine in the light of a butane lamp. He got up when he saw them come in. Yasikov spoke a few words to him in Russian, and the other man nodded several times. They all went down into the basement, which was crisscrossed with beams and bare ceiling boards. It smelled of fresh concrete and humidity. In the half-darkness one could make out bricklayer's tools, buckets of dirty water, sacks of cement. The man in the polo shirt turned up the flame on a lamp hanging from a beam. And then Teresa saw Gato Fierros and Potemkin Gálvez. They were naked, their wrists and ankles tied with wire to white beach chairs. And they looked like they'd seen better nights.

That's all I know, I swear," Gato Fierros moaned.
  The Russians hadn't messed with them too much, Teresa saw, just enough to soften them up a little, almost informally, tenderize them while the muscle awaited more precise instructions. Then the Mexicans had been allowed to rest a couple of hours, to let their imaginations work—worrying less about what they'd been through than about what was to come. The razor cuts on their chests and arms were superficial, and they were barely bleeding now. Gato had a dry crust in his nostrils; his upper lip, split and swollen, reddened the saliva dribbling out of the corners of his mouth. The Russians had been a bit rougher when they used a piece of rebar on his belly and thighs: his scrotum was inflamed, and there were recent bruises on his swollen skin. He stank of urine and sweat and the kind of fear that loosens your bowels.
  While the man in the polo shirt asked question after question in a clumsy, heavily accented Spanish, punctuated with solid thwacks that buffeted the Mexican's face from one side to the other, Teresa's eyes, fascinated, were on the huge horizontal scar that deformed his right cheek: the mark of the .45-caliber bullet that she'd fired point-blank into his face in Culiacán, the day Gato Fierros decided it was a shame to kill her without enjoying her a little first—*She's going to die anyway, and it'd be a waste,* he had said. And then the sound of Potemkin

Gálvez' impotent, furious fist through the closet door—*Güero was one of us, man, remember, and this was his woman; we can kill her, man, but with a little respect.* The black barrel of the Python approaching her head, almost mercifully—*Stand back so you don't get spattered, carnal, and let's get out of here.*

Chale. The memory came in waves, increasingly intense, at last becoming physical, and Teresa felt the same burning in her womb as in her memory—pain and disgust, Gato Fierros' breathing in her face, the hit man's urgency within her, her resignation at the inevitable, the cold of the pistol in her bag on the floor, the blast. The blasts. The leap through the window, with the branches scraping her naked skin. The flight. Now she felt no hatred, she discovered. Just an intense cold satisfaction. A sensation of icy power, very calm and quiet.

"I swear that's all I know." The Russian's fists against the man's face echoed in the empty basement. "I swear on my mother. . . ."

The *hijo de la chingada* had a mother. Gato Fierros had a *pinche* mother like everybody else, over there in Culiacán, and every time he got paid for a hit or a rape or a beating he no doubt sent her money to make her old age a little easier. He knew more, of course. Although they'd just beaten him to guacamole, he knew more about a lot of things, but Teresa was sure that he'd told them everything about his trip to Spain and his intentions: The name of the Mexicana, the woman who had moved into the world of narcotics on the Andalucían coast, had reached all the way to Culiacán. So go take her out. Old scores to settle, uneasiness about the future, the competition, or who knew what. A desire to tie up loose ends. Batman Güemes was at the center of the spiderweb, naturally. These were his shooters, and they'd left the job half done. Now Gato Fierros, a lot less brave when he was tied up with wire to that stupid beach chair than he was back in that apartment in Culiacán, was singing to save himself some pain. That fucking butcher, such a macho pig with his pistol strapped to his belt back there in Sinaloa, fucking somebody's girl before he blew her away. It was all so neat and logical, and it gave Teresa a thrill.

"I tell you, I don't know anything," Gato was still moaning.

Potemkin Gálvez had more integrity. He squeezed his lips tight, stubbornly, so nothing could get out. And that was that. While Gato seemed to have taken singing lessons, this one shook his head at every question, although his body was as battered as his buddy's, with new bruises over the old ones that already covered his skin, cuts on his chest and thighs, which were unprecedentedly vulnerable, his fat, hairy nakedness spilling out over the chair, the wire that cut into his skin turning his swollen hands and feet a nasty purplish color. He was bleeding from penis, mouth, and nose, and drops of thick red blood dripped from his thick black moustache, to run in thin streams down his chest and belly. No way—it was clear that he wasn't the type to tell tales out of school, and even when the game was up, Teresa thought, there were classes, and types, and individuals who behaved one way or another. And although when the time came you might argue that it all amounted to the same thing, it actually didn't. Maybe he wasn't as imaginative as Gato, she reflected as she watched him—men with little imagination could more easily clam up, block out their minds under torture. The others, the ones that thought, gave it up quicker. They did half the job on themselves, thinking, anticipating, and by the time it was time to cook the meat, it was already tenderized. Fear is always more intense when you're capable of imagining what awaits you.

Yasikov looked on from a short distance away, his back against the wall, without uttering a word. It's your business, his silence seemed to say. Your decision. He was also no doubt wondering how it was possible for Teresa to take all this without the slightest tremor in the hand that held the cigarettes she was smoking, one after another—without blinking, without a single grimace of horror. Studying the tortured hit men with a dry, attentive curiosity that appeared to come not from her but rather from the other woman who was stalking around, looking at her the way Yasikov was, from the shadows of the basement. There were interesting mysteries here, she decided. Lessons about men and women. About life and pain and fate and death. And, like the books she read, all those lessons were about her, too.

The muscle in the polo shirt dried his bloody hands on his pants and, disciplined, turned to Teresa questioningly. His razor blade was on the floor, at Gato Fierros' feet. What's the point of more? she concluded. What's clear is super clear, and the rest I know firsthand. She looked over at Yasikov, who almost imperceptibly shrugged while casting his eyes meaningfully toward the sacks of cement piled in the corner. The fact that they were in the basement of this house under construction was no accident. It was all part of the plan.

I'll do it, she suddenly decided. She felt a strange desire to laugh. At herself. To laugh perversely. Bitterly. The truth, at least with regard to Gato Fierros, was that it was just a way to finish what she had started when she pulled the trigger of the Double Eagle so long before. *La vida te da sorpresas,* the song said—Life is full of surprises. *Sorpresas te da la vida. . . . ¡Híjole!* Sometimes it's full of surprises about yourself. Things that are there but that you didn't know were there. From the shadowy corners of the basement, the other Teresa Mendoza was still watching her intently. Maybe, Teresa reflected, she's the one who wants to laugh inside.

"I'll do it," she heard herself repeat, now aloud.

It was her responsibility. Her score to settle, her life. She couldn't let anybody else take that responsibility. The man in the polo shirt was looking at her curiously, as though his Spanish weren't good enough to understand what she'd just said; he turned to his boss and then looked at her again.

"No," Yasikov said softly.

He'd spoken and had moved at last. His back came up off the wall and he approached her. He was looking not at her but at the two Mexican hit men. Gato Fierros' head was bowed over his chest; Potemkin Gálvez was looking toward them as though they were invisible, his eyes fixed on the wall behind them. On nothing.

"This is my war," said Teresa.

"No," Yasikov repeated. He gently took her by the arm, as though inviting her to step outside with him. Now they stood face to face, studying each other.

"I don't give a fuck who does it," Potemkin Gálvez said abruptly. "Just stop fucking around and get it over with."

Teresa faced the *pistolero*. It was the first time she'd heard him open his mouth. His voice sounded hoarse, harsh, muffled. He was still looking right through Teresa, as though she were invisible. His naked corpulence, immobilized in the chair, gleamed with sweat and blood. Teresa walked over slowly until she stood very close, beside him. He smelled rank, of dirty flesh, battered and tortured.

"*Órale, Pinto*," she said to him. "What's the hurry? . . . You're gonna die in a minute, man."

He nodded slightly, his eyes still on that place where she had been standing before. And Teresa once more heard the sound of the splintering closet door in Culiacán and saw the barrel of the Python approaching her head; she once more heard the voice saying, *Güero was one of us, man, Gato, remember, and this was his woman, man. Get back so you don't get it all over you.* And maybe, she thought, she owed that same twisted consideration to him. Finish it quick, the way he'd wanted to with her. *Chale.* Those were the rules. She made a gesture toward Gato Fierros.

"You played it straight, Pinto. Not like this asshole."

It was not a statement directed at Pote Gálvez, exactly, or even a fully formed thought. It was just a fact that had entered her head at that moment. The hit man remained impassive, as though he hadn't heard. A new thread of blood fell from his nose, then hung in the dirty hairs of his moustache. She studied him a few seconds more, then stepped toward the door, pensively. Yasikov was waiting for her.

"Let Pinto go," she said.

It's not always right to wipe the whole slate clean, she thought. Because there are debts that must be paid. And strange moral codes that each person must understand in her own way. Things only she can decide on.

12. How 'bout if
I buy you?

In the light from the large skylights up in the vault of the huge dry-dock shed, the two gray floats on the inflatable Valiant looked like torpedoes. Teresa Mendoza was sitting on the floor, surrounded by tools, and her greasy hands were tightening down the new propellers on the two 250-horsepower outboards. She was wearing old jeans and a dirty shirt, and her hair, in two braids, hung at each side of her sweat-streaked face. Pepe Horcajuelo, her head mechanic, was beside her, watching the operation. From time to time, without her having to ask, he would pass Teresa some tool.

Pepe was small, almost tiny, and years before had been a rising star in the world of motorcycle racing. An oil slick on a curve had forced his retirement from the track, and after a year and a half of rehabilitation he had traded in his racing leather for mechanic's overalls. Dr. Ramos had discovered him when the head gasket on his Deux Chevaux burned out in Fuengirola and he went looking for a garage that was open on Sunday. The former racer had a good hand for engines, including marine engines, which he was able to get an extra five hundred rpms out of. He was one of those quiet, efficient types that like their work, and work hard, and never ask questions. And he was also—a basic requirement—discreet. The only visible sign of the money he'd earned in the last fourteen months was a Honda 1200 that was now parked near the big galvanized-iron hangar occupied by Samir Marina, a business backed by Moroccan capital, headquartered in Gibraltar— another of the sister front companies that Transer Naga owned down near the docks in Sotogrande. The rest, Pepe was diligently saving. For his old age. Because you never know, he would often say, what curve the next oil slick will be on.

"That's it," said Teresa.

She picked up the cigarette she'd left on the edge of one of the work stands and took a couple of puffs, staining the cigarette with grease. Pepe didn't like people smoking when they worked in the shop, and he didn't like other people fiddling with the engines whose maintenance was entrusted to him. But she was the boss, and the engines and boats and storeroom were hers. So neither Pepe nor anybody else could object. Besides, Teresa liked to do these things, keep her hand in, she called it, do a little mechanicking, move around the dock area, the dry docks. Sometimes she would take the engines or a new boat out for a test run. And once, piloting one of the new thirty-foot semi-rigids—it had been her idea to use the hollow fiberglass keels for fuel reserves— she was out all night, running at full throttle to see how the boat behaved in a choppy sea. But all that was a pretext to remember, and remind herself of, and maintain a link with, a part of herself she couldn't bear to let go. It may have had something to do with a lost innocence, with a state of emotion that now, looking back, she thought had been very close to happiness. *Chale,* she told herself, maybe I was happy back then. Maybe I really and truly was, though I never noticed.

"Hand me a five-millimeter socket. Hold that there . . . like that."

She stood back with a satisfied expression to look at the result. The stainless-steel propellers she'd just installed—one counterclockwise and one clockwise, to compensate for the pull created by the rotation—were of smaller diameter and greater screw pitch than the original aluminum ones, and that allowed the paired engines, attached to the rear deck of a semi-rigid, to develop a few more knots' speed on a calm sea. Teresa laid her cigarette on the stand again and inserted the last washers and bolts that Pepe handed her, and tightened them down. Then she took one last puff on the cigarette, put it out in the cut-down

Castro oil can she was using as an ashtray, and stood up, rubbing the small of her back.

"You'll let me know how they behave."

"I'll let you know."

Teresa wiped her hands off with a rag and went outside, squinting against the glare of the Andalucían sun. She stood there for several seconds, enjoying the place and the view: the dry dock's huge blue crane; the masts of the boats; the soft splashing of the water on the concrete launch ramp; the smell of ocean, rust, and fresh paint that the hulls out of water gave off; the clanking of the halyards in the breeze blowing in from the west, over the breakwater. She waved to the dry-dock operators—she knew every one of them by name—and skirting the sheds and sailboats up on braces she walked to the rear of the dry-dock area, where Pote Gálvez was waiting for her by the Cherokee. The SUV was parked under a stand of palm trees, with the gray-sand beach behind it, curving off toward Punta Cullera and the east. A good deal of time had passed—almost a year—since that night in the basement of the house under construction in Nueva Andalucía. That, and what had happened a few days later, when the hit man, with welts and bruises covering his body, had come in to see Teresa, escorted by two of Yasikov's men.

"I have something to discuss with *la doña*," he had told them. "Something urgent. And it has to be now."

Teresa gave him a cold, almost grim reception on the terrace of a suite in the Hotel Puente Romano, on the beach. The bodyguards watched them through two sliding-glass doors off the living room.

"You wanted to see me, Pinto? Maybe you'd like a drink?"

Pote Gálvez said *no, gracias,* and stood for several seconds gazing out at the ocean without really seeing it, scratching his head like a clumsy bear, his dark suit wrinkled, the double-breasted jacket looking like hell on him because it accentuated his girth. His Sinaloa-style iguana-skin boots were a discordant note in the business attire; Teresa felt a strange sympathy, almost a liking, for those boots. His shirt collar was buttoned for the occasion, and he wore a tie that was much too wide and colorful. She studied him with great attentiveness. *Pinche* rational human beings, leaking not just what they were saying but even, or especially, what they didn't say, or what they took their sweet time saying, like this fucking Mexican here now.

"You wanted to see me, Pinto?" she repeated, and Potemkin Gálvez turned slowly toward her, still in silence, then stood facing her. He stopped scratching his head to say softly, after glancing out of the corner of his eye at the men in the living room, "Well, *señora*—I came to thank you. Thank you for letting me live in spite of what I did, or what I was about to do."

"Surely you don't expect me to explain why," she replied flatly, harshly. And the hit man turned his eyes away again—

"No, of course not," and he repeated it twice, with that way of talking that brought back so many memories to Teresa, because it insinuated itself into her very heart. "That's all I wanted, to thank you, and to tell you thát Potemkin Gálvez owes you one, and he'll pay you back."

"And how does Potemkin Gálvez plan to pay me back?" Teresa asked.

"Well, *señora*, I already did, partway anyway," came the reply. "I talked to the people that sent me over here. On the telephone. I told them the truth: that these guys laid a trap for us and that Gato fell right in, and that there wasn't anything anybody could do, because they roughed us up pretty good."

"What people are we talking about?" asked Teresa, already knowing the answer.

"People," replied Pote, standing a little straighter, his proud eyes hardening a little. "*Quihubo, mi doña.* You know there are some things I don't talk about. Let's just say people. People from over there." And then, once again meek, pausing often, searching hard for the right words, he explained that those people, whoever they were, had taken it real hard that he was still breathing and that his buddy Gato had had his neck wrung that way, and that they'd explained real, real clear what his three options were: to finish the job, or to take the first plane back to Culiacán and face the consequences, or to hide out someplace where they couldn't ever find him.

"And which one have you decided on, Pinto?"

"Well . . . really . . . none of them look good to me, *señora*. Fortunately, I never had a family. So I don't have to worry about that part."

"So?"

"*Órale.* So here I am."

"And what am I supposed to do with you?"

"That's for you to decide, *mi señora*. I don't think that's my problem."

Teresa studied the *pistolero* again. You're right, she conceded after a second. She felt a smile about to emerge, but she suppressed it. Pote Gálvez' logic was elementary, yet perfectly accurate—she knew the rules. In a way it had been and still was her own logic, the logic of the hard-boiled world they both came from. Güero Dávila, she suddenly thought, would have had a good laugh at this one. Pure Sinaloa. Life's little jokes.

"Are you asking me for a job?"

"One day they might send somebody else," the *pistolero* said, shrugging in resigned simplicity, "and then I could pay back what I owe you."

So there stood Pote Gálvez beside the Cherokee now, waiting for her as he had every day since that morning on the hotel terrace: driver, bodyguard, messenger, whatever she needed. It was easy to get him a residency permit, and even—though it cost her—a weapons license, which she obtained through a friendly security company. That allowed him to carry, legally, in a holster under his arm or at his waist, a Colt Python identical to the one he had put to Teresa's head in another country and another life. The people from Sinaloa gave no more trouble: in the last few weeks, via Yasikov, Transer Naga had acted as intermediary, for free, in an operation that the Sinaloa cartel had about half worked out with the Russian mafias that were now entering Los Angeles and San Francisco. That smoothed out some of the tensions, or put to rest old ghosts, and Teresa received the unequivocal message that all was forgotten—live and let live, the counter set back to zero and enough *chingaderas*. Batman Güemes in person had cleared that up through reliable go-betweens, and although in this business any guarantee was only relative, the reassurance at least poured some oil on the troubled waters. There were not to be any more hit men—although Pote Gálvez, distrustful by nature and profession, never let down his guard. Especially given that as Teresa broadened her operations, relationships became more and more complex and enemies multiplied in direct proportion to her range and power.

"Home, Pinto."

"*Sí, patrona.*" In Pote Gálvez, what might have seemed officiousness, ass-kissing, was simply his old-fashioned Mexican way of showing the respect due an employer and a woman who had spared his life. He was subservient, even meek, and he was grateful, but he was still a professional killer, and Teresa, in turn, respected him for all that.

Home was a luxurious two-story house with an immense lawn and pool; it was finished at last, in Guadalmina Baja, next to the sea. Teresa got into the passenger seat while Pote Gálvez took the wheel. The work on the engines had brought her a couple of hours' relief from the concerns in her head. This was the culmination of a good stretch: four shipments for the 'Ndrangheta had been delivered with no problems, and the Italians were asking for more. The people from Solntsevo were also asking for more. The new speedboats could easily manage the transport of hashish from the coast of Murcia to the Portuguese border, with a reasonable percentage—those losses were also foreseeable—of interception by the Guardia Civil and Customs. The Moroccan and

Colombian contacts were working perfectly, and the financial infrastructure updated and improved by Teo Aljarafe was able to absorb and funnel off vast amounts of money, of which only forty percent was reinvested in operational expenses and expansion. But as Teresa expanded her activities, friction with other organizations in the same line of business increased. It was impossible to grow without taking up space that other people thought belonged to them. And then there were the Galicians and the French.

No problems with the French. Or rather, few and short-lived. Some of the Marseilles mafia's hashish providers worked on the Costa del Sol; they were grouped around two main capos: a French-Algerian named Michel Salem, and the Marseilles mobster Nené Garou. Salem was a heavyset, sixtyish man with gray hair and pleasant manners with whom Teresa had had a few not altogether satisfactory experiences. Unlike Salem, who specialized in moving hashish in recreational boats and was a discreet family man who lived in a mansion in Fuengirola with two divorced daughters and four grandchildren, Nené Garou was a classic French ruffian: an arrogant, wise-mouthed, violent gangster given to leather jackets, expensive cars, and spectacular women. Garou ran hashish, but also dealt in prostitution, short arms, and a little heroin. All Teresa's attempts to negotiate reasonable agreements with him had failed, and during an informal meeting with Teresa and Teo Aljarafe in a private room in a Mijas restaurant, Garou lost it—making threats too loud, too gross, and too explicit not to take seriously. This happened more or less when Garou had proposed that Teresa transport a quarter-ton of Colombian black-tar heroin for him, and she said no—the way she saw it, hashish was more or less for everybody and coke a luxury item for assholes who could pay for it, but heroin was poison for the poor, and she wasn't into that shit. Garou took that the wrong way. "No Mexican bitch is gonna bust my balls," was how he put it, as a matter of fact, and the Marseilles accent made it sound all the worse. Teresa, not a muscle in her face moving, very slowly stubbed out her cigarette in the ashtray before calling for the check and leaving the restaurant.

"What are we going to do?" was Teo's worried question when they got outside. "That guy is dangerous."

But Teresa said nothing about the meeting for three days—not a word, not a remark. Nothing. Inside, serene and silent, she was planning moves, thinking out the pros and cons, as though she were in a complex game of chess. Over the years, she had discovered that those gray predawn hours led to interesting reflections, sometimes very different from those she arrived at in the light of day. And three predawns later, the decision made, she went to see Oleg Yasikov.

"I've come to ask your advice," she said, although both of them knew that wasn't true. And when she laid it all out, briefly, using the fewest words possible, Yasikov looked at her for a few seconds before shrugging.

"You've grown a lot, Tesa," he said. "Yes. And when you grow a lot, these inconveniences come with the territory. But I can't get involved in this. No. Can't give you advice, either, because it's your war, not mine. One day—life is full of surprises—we might find ourselves in the same situation, you and I. Yes. Who knows. Just remember that in this business, a problem that goes unsolved is like a cancer. Sooner or later, it kills."

Teresa decided to apply a Sinaloan solution. *Me los voy a chingar hasta la madre de esos cabrones*—nothing's more impressive than a disproportionate reaction, she told herself, especially when they're not expecting it. Güero Dávila, who was a big fan of the Culiacán Tomateros, and who was laughing out loud in that cantina in hell where he now had his own table, would no doubt have described this as hitting every ball that came over the plate, and stealing second base off the assholes to boot.

This time she found her resources in Morocco, where an old friend, Colonel Abdelkader Chaib, supplied the appropriate personnel: ex-cops and ex–military types who spoke Spanish, had their passports and tourist visas in order, and came and went on the Tangiers–Algeciras ferry line. Hard, tough guys: muscle who received only the necessary information and instructions and who, should they be captured by Spanish authorities, could not be tied to anybody. They caught Nené Garou coming out of a disco in Benalmádena at four in the morning. Two young North African–looking men—he told the police later, when he'd recovered his ability to speak—approached him like they were going to mug him, and after taking his wallet and watch they broke his spine with a baseball bat. *Clack, clack.* "Broken into so many pieces it was like a baby rattle," was the graphic expression used by the hospital spokesman, who was later reprimanded by his superiors.

The same morning this story appeared in the police-blotter notes in the Málaga newspaper *Sur,* a telephone call came for Michel Salem at his house in Fuengirola. After a pleasant *Buenos días,* the caller identified himself as a friend and in perfect Spanish offered his condolences for the regrettable accident that Garou had suffered and that Monsieur Salem, he imagined, had no doubt recently learned of.

Then the voice told Salem that at that moment, his grandchildren—
three sweet girls and a boy, five to twelve years old—were playing in the
yard of the Swiss school in Las Chapas. They'd spent the previous day
at a McDonald's, at a birthday party for the eldest, a cute tomboy
named Desirée. Her usual route to and from school, like that of her sib-
ling and her cousins, was given in minute detail to Salem.

That same afternoon Salem received, by messenger, a package of
telephoto pictures of his grandchildren—at McDonald's and at the
school playground.

I spoke with Cucho Malaspina—black leather pants, English tweed
jacket, Moroccan bag over his shoulder—as I was about to go to
Mexico for the last time, two weeks before my interview with Teresa
Mendoza. We ran into each other at the airport in Málaga, where we
were waiting for our respective delayed flights.

"*Hola, qué tal,* love," he said. "How are you?"

I got myself a cup of coffee and he had orange juice, which he sipped
through a straw as we caught up on each other's lives: I read your
things, I see you on TV, the usual. Then we sat down together on a
couch in a quiet corner. "I'm working on something about the Queen
of the South," I told him, and he broke out in wicked laughter. It was
he who'd given her that sobriquet. The cover of *¡Hola!* four years before. Six pages in color with the story of her life, or at least the part he'd
been able to find out about, centering mostly on her power, her luxurious life, and her mystery. Almost all the photographs taken with a
telephoto. Something along the lines of *This dangerous woman controls
this and that. Reclusive multimillionaire Mexican, shadowy past, shady
present.* "Beautiful and enigmatic," read the caption of the single photo
taken from closer range: Teresa in dark glasses, dressed austerely and
elegantly, getting out of a car surrounded by bodyguards in Málaga, on
her way to testify before a judicial commission on drug trafficking that
was able to prove absolutely nothing against her.

By then, her legal and financial front was perfect, and the queen of
drug trafficking on the Strait, the czarina of drugs—as Madrid's *El País*
described her—had bought so much political and police protection
that she was virtually invulnerable. So nearly invulnerable, in fact, that
the Ministry of the Interior leaked her dossier to the press in an attempt to make public through rumor and journalistic "background"
what it couldn't prove in court. But that strategy backfired; the newspaper stories written from that background material turned Teresa

Mendoza into a legend: a woman thriving in a world of dangerous men.

From that point on, the rare photos taken of her, her rare appearances in public were always news. Paparazzi hounded her as much as they did the princesses of Monaco or some name-over-the-title movie stars, and there were always dozens of police complaints and even lawsuits against Teresa's bodyguards for assault and battery against photographers. A stable of Transer Naga attorneys handled these distractions.

"So you're writing a book about that creature."

"I'm finishing it. Or almost."

"Quite a character, isn't she?" Cucho Malaspina—intelligent, bitchy—looked at me as he stroked his moustache. "I know her well."

Cucho was an old friend of mine, from the days when I was a journalist and he was just beginning to make a name for himself writing a gossip column, contributing to the society pages, and appearing on evening TV talk shows. We had a conspiratorial respect for one another. Now he was a star, able to ruin a famous marriage with a dropped remark, a headline, a caption. Clever, creative, and nasty. The Guru of Gossip and Glamour—poison in a martini glass. It wasn't true that he knew Teresa Mendoza, but he had moved in those circles—the Costa del Sol and Marbella were a profitable hunting ground for the pink press— and a few times he almost got close to her. But each time he'd been shown the door with a firmness that on one occasion, at least, led to a black eye. He'd filed a complaint with the San Pedro de Alcántara police when a bodyguard—whose description fit Pote Gálvez to a T— had smacked him when he tried to have a word with Teresa as she was leaving a restaurant in Puerto Banús. *Good evening, señora. If it's not too much trouble I'd like to ask you about . . .* bam!

Apparently, it *was* too much trouble. So there were no answers, or further questions, or anything except that moustached gorilla blacking Cucho's eye with professional expertise. Twittering birds, colored stars, the reporter on his ass on the sidewalk, car doors slamming, and the noise of expensive tires laying rubber. The Queen of the South glimpsed fleetingly as she made her stunning exit from a fashionable restaurant blah blah blah.

"A sure draw for the public's insatiable thirst for scandal, imagine. 'Inquiring minds want to know,' right? A girl who creates a whole little underground empire in a matter of two or three years. An adventuress with all the ingredients: drugs, money, mystery. . . Always at a distance, protected by her bodyguards and her legend. The police unable to touch her, and her buying off half of southern Spain and a good bit of

North Africa. The Koplowitz of drugs . . . Remember those millionaire sisters? . . . Well, the same thing, but gone over to the dark side. When that gorilla of hers, a fat guy with a face like Indio Fernández', hit me, I've gotta tell you I was delighted. I lived two months on that! Then, when my lawyer asked for this incredible amount of money, which we never even dreamed of collecting, they paid in cash, my dear, in cash! I swear. We never got anywhere near the courthouse doors."

"Is it true that she and the mayor were close?"

The malicious smile widened under the moustache.

"Tomás Pestaña? . . . Thick as thieves, those two," he said as he sipped his orange juice. "Literally. Teresa was the golden goose for Marbella—charities, donations, investments. They met when she bought the land to build a house in Guadalmina Baja—lawns, gardens, pool, fountains, ocean views, the whole thing. But she filled it with books, too, as a matter of fact, because it so happens that the girl is practically an intellectual, did you know that? So they say. She and the mayor had dinner together often, or saw each other at the houses of mutual friends. Private meetings, bankers, builders, politicians, people like that . . ."

"Did they do business together?"

"Well, of course, my dear. Pestaña handed over a good deal of local control to her, and she always had a way of not making herself too conspicuous. Every time there was an investigation, agents and judges suddenly became uninterested and incompetent. So the mayor could hang out with her without upsetting anybody. It was very discreet, and very astute on the part of both, but especially her. Little by little she infiltrated city halls, the courts. . . . Even Fernando Bouvier, the governor of Málaga, was eating out of her hand. Everybody was making so much money that no one could do without her. That was what protected her, and gave her power."

Power, he repeated. Then he smoothed out the wrinkles in his leather pants, lit a Dutch cigar, and crossed his legs. "The Queen," he added, blowing cigar smoke into the room, "didn't like parties. In all those years she'd gone to two or three, tops. She'd go late and leave early. She lived all shut up in her house, and sometimes she could be photographed from a distance, walking on the beach. She liked the ocean. People said that sometimes she went out with the crews that were running the drugs, like she used to do when she didn't have a pot to piss in, but that was probably just part of the legend. Although she did like the water. She bought a big yacht, the *Sinaloa,* and would spend a lot of time on it, alone with the bodyguards and the crew. She didn't travel much. She'd be spotted here and there occasionally. Mediterranean ports, Corsica, the Baleares, the Greek islands. That's about it.

"I once thought we had her. . . . A paparazzo managed to sneak in with some concrete-layers who were working in the garden, and he got a couple of rolls—her on the terrace, at a window, things like that. The magazine that bought the pictures called me to write the text. But the story never came out. Somebody paid a fortune to block it, and the photographs disappeared. Abracadabra—poof! It's magic! They say it was handled by Teo Aljarafe in person. The good-looking lawyer. And he paid ten times what they were worth."

"I remember that. . . . The photographer had some trouble."

Cucho leaned over to knock the ashes off his cigar into the ashtray. He stopped in mid-movement. The wicked smile had become muted, knowing laughter.

"Trouble? . . . Oh my dear, don't make me laugh. With Teresa Mendoza, that word is the world's biggest understatement. The boy was a professional, a veteran, an expert at sniffing underwear and tracking down *liaisons dangereuses*. . . . Two weeks after the photos vanished, somebody broke into his apartment in Torremolinos, coincidentally with him in it at the time. Imagine! . . . After breaking, one by one, the fingers of both his hands, they cut him with a razor four times, apparently with no intention of killing him. . . . The news spread. Of course nobody ever again approached the house in Guadalmina, or even tried to get within twenty yards of that bitch."

"Love affairs?" I asked, changing the subject.

He shook his head—absolutely none. *Now* we were back in his specialty.

"No love affairs, zip. At least so far as I could ever find out. And you know I have my sources. There was talk of a relationship with that lawyer, Teo Aljarafe. Classy, good-looking, and well enough off for most. Also a son of a bitch. They traveled together. But he wasn't really her type. They probably fucked, you understand, but he wasn't her type. Trust my bitch-on-a-hot-scent nose, my dear. I'd say her type was more like Patricia O'Farrell."

"The O'Farrell girl," Cucho went on, after getting himself another orange juice and saying hello to some friends on the way back, "was coke—I mean horse—of a different color. They were friends and partners, although they were as different as night and day. But they'd been together in prison. Quite a story, O'Farrell's, huh? So promiscuous and all that. So perverse. And she was *really* classy. But under the designer outfits, a lesbian slut. With all the vices, including this one—" Here, Cucho touched the side of his nose meaningfully. "Frivolous as hell, so it's not easy to understand how those two, Sappho and Captain Morgan, could be together. Although the Mexicana ran the show, of course. It's not possible to conceive of the O'Farrell clan's black sheep putting that empire together all by herself.

"She was a dyke, and as out as they come. A cokehead like you wouldn't believe. And that led to lots of gossip. . . . People say O'Farrell knocked the rough edges off the Mexicana, who practically didn't know how to read and write. Whether that's true or not, by the time I knew her she dressed and acted classy. She always wore good clothes: quiet, dark, simple—very elegant, very chic. You're going to laugh, but one year we even included her in the nominations for the best-dressed list in Spain. Half seriously, I swear to God. And she *made the list!* Eighteenth or so. She was cute—not beautiful, but she knew how to make herself look smart." He sat pensively, his smile distracted, and after a few seconds he shrugged. "There was clearly something between those two. I don't know what they were—friends, lovers, what, but they were something. Very strange. Maybe that explains why the Queen of the South didn't have many men in her life."

The loudspeaker called Cucho's flight. He looked at his watch and stood up, hanging his black bag over his shoulder. I got up, too, and we shook hands. Good to see you, I said. Have a good trip.

"I hope to read that book, if they don't cut your balls off first," said Cucho. He winked.

As he walked away, he added, "Then there's the mystery, right? . . . What happened at the end with O'Farrell, and with the lawyer." Cucho laughed. "What happened with all of them."

It was a mild autumn, with cool nights and good business. Teresa Mendoza took a sip of the champagne cocktail she was holding and looked around. She was being observed, too, directly or surreptitiously, and there were whispered comments, murmurs, smiles that were sometimes admiring, sometimes uneasy. Lately, the media had paid a great deal of attention to her. Going over the coordinates of a mental plan, she imagined herself at the center of a complex web of money and power, full of possibility and also of danger.

She took another sip. Soft music, fifty select people, eleven o'clock at night. Over a black sea hung a yellow moon that looked as though it had been sliced in half horizontally, and it was mirrored in the Marbella inlet out there beyond the immense landscape twinkling with millions of lights. The living room was open to the garden on the side of the mountain, next to the Ronda highway. Access was controlled by security guards and municipal police. Tomás Pestaña, the host, in a white dinner jacket and red cummerbund, was moving from group to group, chatting, smiling, an enormous Havana cigar between the ringed fingers of his left hand, his eyebrows, as thick as a bear's, arched in constant surprise and pleasure. He resembled nothing so much as the villain in a 1970s spy movie. A likable scoundrel. Thank you so much for coming, my dear. How nice. How very nice of you. Have you met so-and-so? . . . And what's-his-name? . . .

That was Tomás Pestaña. He loved it. Loved to show off. Even show off Teresa, as though she were another proof of his success. A rare and dangerous trophy. Whenever someone asked him about her, he would affect a mysterious smile and shake his head knowingly: *If I told you some of the things I've seen* . . . "Everything that gives a man glamour or money is useful to me," he had once said. And with Teresa, the one was intimately connected to the other. Because Teresa Mendoza didn't just give a touch of exotic mystery to local society; she was also a horn of plenty. The latest operation calculated to win the mayor's heart—recommended by Teo Aljarafe—included payment of a municipal debt that threatened Marbella with a scandalous embargo of its properties and untold political consequences. Not to mention that Pestaña—garrulous, ambitious, astute, voted into office more times than anyone since the days of Jesús Gil—loved to boast of his relationships at "special" moments, even if only for a select group of friends or associates, the way art collectors show off their private galleries, which hold masterpieces, acquired illicitly, that can't be shown in public.

"Imagine a raid on this place tonight," said Patty. She had a joint between her lips and was laughing, her third drink in hand. "Course, no cop would have the balls," she added. "This is one mouthful that'd get stuck in his throat."

"Well, there's one cop here," Teresa replied. "Nino Juárez."

"I saw that *cabrón*."

Teresa took another sip as she finished mentally counting. Three financiers. Four high-level developers. A couple of middle-aged English actors who lived in the Zone to avoid taxes back home. A movie producer with whom Teo Aljarafe had just entered a useful partnership, since the producer went bankrupt once a year and Teo was an expert in moving money through companies with losses—in this case, movies that flopped. The owner of six golf courses. Two governors. A Saudi millionaire down on his luck. A member of the Moroccan royal family whose luck was still running strong. The main stockholder in a large hotel chain. A famous fashion model. A singer who'd flown in from Miami in his own plane. A former minister of the treasury and his wife, who had once been married to a well-known actor. Three super-exclusive call girls, great beauties notorious for their very unprivate love affairs with prominent politicians and millionaires . . . Teresa had talked for a while with the governor of Málaga and his wife—the wife had looked at her, half suspicious and half fascinated, the whole time, not opening her mouth, while Teresa and the governor agreed on the financing for an auditorium for the city's cultural events and three shelters for drug addicts. She had chatted with two of the developers and then stepped aside for a brief, useful word with the member of the Moroccan royal family, a partner of mutual friends on both sides of the Strait; he gave her his card. *You must come to Marrakesh. I have heard a great deal about you.* Teresa nodded and smiled without making any promises. *Híjole*—she imagined what the guy had heard, and from whom. Then she and the golf-course owner, whom she knew slightly, exchanged a few pleasantries. "I have an interesting proposal," he said. "I'll call you."

The singer from Miami was laughing in a nearby group, throwing his head back to show the chin he'd just had done by a famous plastic surgeon. "When I was a girl I was crazy about him," Patty told her. "And look at him now. *Sic transit . . .*" Her eyes glittered, her pupils very dilated. "Want somebody to introduce us?" she suggested.

Teresa shook her head, her drink at her lips. "Spare me, Lieutenant. And watch it, you've had three already."

"No, *you* spare *me*," Patty retorted, not losing her good humor. "What a bore you are, nothing but work, your whole fucking *puta* life."

Teresa looked around absentmindedly. The truth was, this wasn't exactly a party, although the pretext was to celebrate the mayor's birthday. It was a pure social ritual, a high mass, and held for no reason but to do business. "You have to go," Teo Aljarafe had insisted; he was now talking to a group of financiers and their wives—ever polite, suave, attentive, a glass in his hand, his tall silhouette slightly stooped, his aquiline profile turned courteously toward the ladies. "Even if it's just fifteen minutes, you've got to stop in," he told her. "Pestaña looks at some things in a very elementary way—it's black and white—and you can't send regrets for an evening like this. Besides, it's not just the mayor. With half a dozen *Buenas noches* and How are yous you can take care of a shitload of commitments. Open doors and grease the skids. Get the idea?"

"I'll be back," Patty was saying.

She'd put her empty glass down on a table and was walking away, toward the bar: high heels, back bare to the waist, in contrast to the austere little black dress Teresa was wearing, her only adornment a pair of earrings—simple pearls—and the silver *semanario*. On the way, Patty deliberately brushed against the back of a young woman who was chatting with some people, and the girl half turned to look at her. That cunt, Patty had said, flicking her head when she'd first seen her.

Teresa, used to her friend's provocative tone—sometimes Patty went too far on purpose when Teresa was around—shrugged. Too young for you, Lieutenant, she'd said. Young or not, replied Patty, in El Puerto she wouldn't have gotten away from me if she'd sprouted wings. Of course, she added after looking at her thoughtfully, I was wrong about Edmond Dantès. She smiled too brightly when she said this.

And now Teresa, concerned, was watching Patty walk away through the guests: she was weaving a bit, although she might be able to hold one or two drinks more before the first visit to the bathroom to powder her nose. But it wasn't a problem of drinking or snorting. *Pinche* Patty. Things were going from bad to worse with her, and not just tonight. As for Teresa, she'd had enough of this mingling, and she wanted to start thinking about going.

"*Buenas noches.*"

She'd seen Nino Juárez circling close by, studying her. Small, with his blond beard. Expensive clothes, no way to pay for them on his cop's salary. They crossed paths from time to time, at a distance. It was Teo Aljarafe who took care of that one.

"I'm Nino Juárez."

"I know who you are."

From the other side of the room, Teo, who never missed anything, gave Teresa a look of warning. He may be ours, when he's paid off, but that guy is a minefield, his eyes said. And besides, there are people watching.

"I didn't know you came to this sort of affair," said the cop.

"I didn't know *you* did."

That was not true. Teresa knew everything about the commissioner of the organized-crime unit: He liked the Marbella life, rubbing elbows with the rich and famous, appearing on television announcing the successful conclusion of some important operation, the rendering of some important service to the community. He also liked money. Tomás Pestaña and he were friends, and they lent each other support in many ways.

"It's part of my work." Juárez paused and smiled. "As it is of yours."

I don't like him, Teresa decided.

"There's a problem," Juárez said suddenly. His tone was almost intimate. He, like her, was looking around, smiling vaguely.

"Problems," said Teresa, "are not my problem. I have people to deal with them."

"Well, this one can't be dealt with quite that easily. And I prefer to tell *you* what it is, not somebody else."

And then he did, in the same tone and a very few words. A new investigation had begun, set in motion by a judge in the National Tribunal who took his work very, very seriously: one Martínez Pardo. This time, the judge had decided to leave the organized-crime unit out of it and use the Guardia Civil. Juárez was out of the loop, and he couldn't do anything to stop or derail it. He just wanted to make that clear before things started rolling.

"Who in the Guardia Civil?"

"There's a group that's good. Delta Four. It's headed by a captain named Víctor Castro."

"I've heard of him."

"Well, he's been working in secret on this operation for some time. The judge has come down a couple of times. Apparently they're tracking the last departure of semi-rigids out there. They want to intercept a few and trace them up the food chain."

"And this is serious?"

"Depends on what they find. You should know."

"So what about Organized Crime? . . . What do you plan to do?"

"Nothing. All I can do is sit back and watch. I told you, we've been bumped. With what I've told you, I've done my duty."

Patty was back, with another glass in her hand. She was walking straight, and Teresa figured that she'd visited the ladies' room to perk herself up.

"Oh, wow," she said as she approached. "Look who we have here. Law and order. And my, Grandma, what a big Rolex you have tonight. New?"

Juárez turned grim, looking at Teresa. You all right with this? he said wordlessly. Your partner is not going to be much help when the shit hits the fan.

"Excuse me," he said. "*Buenas noches.*" And he wandered off among the guests.

Patricia laughed softly, watching him.

"What was that *hijo de puta* saying to you? . . . His check didn't come in the mail yet?"

"It's not a good idea to yank people's chain like that." Teresa, uneasy, had lowered her voice. She didn't want to lose her composure, not here and not now. "Especially when they're cops."

"Don't we pay him? . . . So fuck 'im."

Patty jerked the glass to her lips, almost violently. Teresa wasn't sure whether the anger in her words was aimed at Nino Juárez or at her.

"Listen, Lieutenant. Don't fuck with me. You're drinking too much. And the other, too."

"So what? . . . It's a party, and tonight I feel like partying."

"Who's talking about tonight?"

"Oh, I see. Now you're my babysitter."

Teresa said no more. She looked fixedly into her friend's eyes, and Patty looked away.

"After all," Patty growled, "fifty percent of the payoff to that asshole comes from me."

Teresa still didn't reply. She was thinking. From afar, she felt the questioning look of Teo Aljarafe. This was never going to end. You plug one hole, and another one opens. And not everything could be fixed with common sense or money.

"How's the queen of Marbella?"

Tomás Pestaña had just appeared by their side—charming, back-slapping, vulgar. He wore a white dinner jacket that gave him the look of a short, chubby waiter. The mayor liked to live dangerously, as long as there was money or influence in it for him, and he and Teresa had a relationship based on mutual interests. He had founded a local political party, and he sailed the murky waters of real estate; the legend that was beginning to grow around the Mexicana reinforced his sense of power, and his vanity. It also reinforced his checking account. Pestaña had made his first fortune as a right-hand man for an important Andalucían real estate developer, buying land for the business through his boss' contacts and with his money. Later, when a third of the Costa del Sol belonged to him, he visited his boss to tell him he was quitting. Really? Yes, really. Well, listen, how can I thank you for your services? You already did, was Pestaña's reply. I put it all in my name. For months after the boss got out of the hospital, after his heart attack, he was on the lookout for Pestaña, and he had a gun in his belt for when he found him.

"An interesting group of people, don't you think?" said Pestaña.

The mayor, who never missed a trick, had seen her talking to Nino Juárez, though he never would have said so explicitly. They exchanged compliments: Happy birthday, Mr. Mayor. Wonderful party. Teresa asked what time it was, and the mayor told her.

"We're still on for dinner Tuesday, of course," said Teresa. "Same place as always. Now Patty and I really have to go—have to get up early tomorrow morning."

"You'll have to go by yourself, sweetie," Patty said. "I'm having a wonderful time right here."

With the Galicians, things were a little more complicated than with the French. In fact, it was like threading a needle with a piece of hawser, because the gangs in northwest Spain had their own contacts in Colombia, and sometimes worked with the same people Teresa did. Plus, these were serious tough-guy gangster types, they had years of experience, and they were on home turf, after the *amos do fume,* who controlled the tobacco-smuggling rings, had retooled themselves for drugs and were now *amos da cocaína.* The Galician coves and inlets were their territory, but they had been extending it southward, toward the mouth of the Mediterranean and North Africa. So long as Transer Naga transported only hashish along the Andalucían coastline, relations with the northwestern Spaniards, though cool, were live-and-let-live. But cocaine was different. And recently, Teresa's organization had become a serious competitor. All this emerged in a meeting held on neutral ground, a large country house in Cáceres, near Arroyo de la Luz, between the Sierra de Santo Domingo and the N-521 highway—a place surrounded with pastures for the cattle and thick stands of oak. The huge white house was at the end of a road on which approaching cars raised clouds of dust, so an intruder could easily be seen from far away.

The meeting took place at mid-morning, and Teresa and Teo Aljarafe attended for Transer Naga, escorted by Pote Gálvez at the wheel of the Cherokee and, in a dark Passat behind them, two of their most trusted men—young Moroccans who had first proved themselves in the rubbers and later been recruited for security. She was wearing black, a well-cut designer pantsuit, and her hair, parted down the center, was gathered into a bun. The Galicians were already there: three of them, with three bodyguards at the door, next to the two BMW 732s they had arrived in. Everyone got right down to business, the gorillas looking warily at one another outside while the principals did the same inside, around a large rustic wood table in the center of a room with a beamed ceiling, stuffed deer and boar heads on the walls. There were sandwiches, soft drinks and coffee, boxes of cigars, and notepads, as for a typical business meeting—although this one got off on the wrong foot when Siso Pernas, of the Corbeira clan, the son of don Xaquin Pernas, *amo do fume* of the Ría de Arosa, began by laying out the situation, speaking entirely to Teo Aljarafe as though the lawyer were the interlocutor of choice and Teresa there just as decoration. The issue here,

Siso Pernas said, was that the Transer Naga people had their finger in
too many pies. No objection to expansion into the Mediterranean, the
hashish and all that. Or to them moving coke on a reasonable scale—
there was enough business to go around. But everybody in his own territory, and with respect for seniority, which in Spain—he continued to
look only at Teo Aljarafe, as though he were the Mexican—was always
rule number one. And as for territories, Siso Pernas and his father, don
Xaquin, covered the Atlantic operations, the big shipments by boat
from Latin American ports. They had always been the operators for the
Colombians, ever since don Xaquin and the Corbeira brothers and the
people of the old school, pressured by these new generations, had
started to move out of tobacco and into hashish and coke. So they had
come with a proposal: No objection to Transer Naga working the blow
that came in through Casablanca and Agadir, so long as they took it
into the eastern Mediterranean and it didn't stay in Spain. Because if
we were talking about direct shipments to the Peninsula and the rest of
Europe, then the Atlantic route, and all its branches to the north, belonged to the Gallegos.

"That's really what we're doing," said Teo Aljarafe. "Except with regard to the transportation."

"I know." Siso Pernas poured himself some coffee from the carafe in
front of him, after offering a cup to Teo, who shook his head; the Gallego's offer didn't include Teresa. "But our people are afraid that you
might be tempted to expand your business. Certain things are not
clear. Ships coming and going . . . We can't control that—and besides,
we expose ourselves to getting other people's operations blamed on
us." He looked at his two colleagues, as though they knew exactly what
he was talking about. "To having the Customs people and the Guardia
Civil on us like mosquitoes all the time."

"The sea is free territory," said Teresa.

It was the first she'd spoken, after the initial greetings. Siso Pernas
looked at Teo, as though the words had come from him. Friendly as a
razor blade, this guy. His colleagues did look at Teresa, out of the corners of their eyes. Curious, and apparently amused by the situation.

"Not for this," said the Galician. "We've been in the white-powder
business for a long time. We've got experience. We've made large investments." He was still addressing Teo. "And you people are beginning
to upset us. We might have to pay for your mistakes."

Teo glanced briefly at Teresa. The lawyer's dark, thin hands twirled
his pen. She sat impassively. Do your work, her silence said. All things
in due time.

"And what do the Colombians think?" asked Teo.

"They don't want to get involved," Siso Pernas sneered. Those *cabrón*
Judases, his smile implied. "They think it's our problem, and that we
ought to solve it here."

"What's the alternative?"

The Galician sipped at his coffee calmly and leaned back a bit in his
chair, giving all the appearances of a very self-satisfied man. He was
dirty blond, with a trimmed moustache. Good-looking, late twenties,
early thirties. Blue blazer over a white shirt. No tie. A second- or third-
generation junior narco, probably MBA, or maybe just B.A., in eco-
nomics and finance. In more of a rush than his elders, who kept their
money in a sock and always wore the same cheap suit. Less thoughtful.
Fewer rules and more push to make money, so he could buy high living and expensive women. More arrogant, too. Now we're getting
down to the nitty-gritty, his attitude seemed to say. He looked at the
colleague to his left, a blocky type with pale eyes. Job done. He turned
the details over to his assistant.

"From the Strait inside," the chunky man said, putting his elbows on
the table, "you people have absolute leave. We could load the merchandise in Morocco, if you want it there, but we alone bring it in from the
Latin American ports. . . . We're willing to offer certain special conditions, percentages, and guarantees. Including that we work together as
partners, but with us controlling the operations."

"How much simpler it can all be," Siso Pernas interjected, almost
from behind, "fewer risks."

Teo exchanged a look with Teresa. And if we don't go along? she said
with her eyes.

"And if we don't go along with that?" the lawyer repeated aloud.
"What happens if we don't accept those conditions?"

The heavyset man didn't reply, and Siso Pernas entertained himself
by examining his coffee cup thoughtfully, as though that eventuality
had never crossed his mind.

"Well, I don't know," he said at last. "We might have problems."

"Who?" Teo wanted to know. He leaned forward, calm, serious, the
pen between his fingers as though he were about to take notes. Secure
in his role, although Teresa knew that he desperately wanted to get up
and get out of that room. The problems the Gallego was hinting at
were not Teo's specialty. From time to time he turned toward her,
though without looking at her directly. I can only go so far, he implied.
What I can offer are peaceful negotiations, financial advice, and financial engineering, not hints and double meanings and threats floating
in the air. If this goes beyond a certain point, there's not much more I
can do.

"You . . . us . . ." Siso Pernas directed pleading looks at Teo's pen. "Nobody wants a disagreement."

His last words sounded like a splinter of glass. *Ding.* So this is that certain point, Teresa told herself, the place where push has come to shove. And I intend to shove. This is where the Sinaloa girl that knows what's at stake steps in. And she'd better be there, waiting for me to put her in the game. Because I need her *now.*

"*Híjole.* You planning to break our legs with baseball bats? . . . Like that French guy that was in the newspapers the other day?"

She was looking at Siso Pernas with a surprise that appeared authentic, although it didn't fool anyone—nor did it try to. The Galician turned toward her as though she had just materialized out of thin air, while his heavyset companion with the pale eyes looked at his fingernails, and the third man, a skinny guy with the hands of a farmworker, or a fisherman, picked his nose. Teresa waited for Siso Pernas to say something, but he remained silent, facing her with a mixture of irritation and confusion.

As for Teo, his worry had turned to manifest uneasiness. Careful, he mutely warned. Be very careful.

"Maybe," Teresa went on slowly, "it's that I'm not from here and I don't know the customs. . . . Señor Aljarafe is my attorney, and he has my entire trust, but when I do business I like people to address *me.* I'm the one who makes the decisions about my affairs. . . . Do you understand what I'm saying?"

Siso Pernas was still looking at her in silence, one hand on each side of his coffee cup. The air was thick enough to cut with a knife. You guys wanted to play, Teresa said. So you sing the song, and I'll supply the lyrics. And I do know something about *pinche* Gallegos.

"So now," she continued, "I'm going to tell you how I see this thing."

I hope I don't fuck this up, she thought. And she told him how she saw this thing. She did so very clearly, delivering each phrase separately and slowly, with pauses to let everyone catch the full meaning of what she had to say.

"I have the greatest respect for what you do in Galicia," she began. "You're tough, but I respect that. But that doesn't keep me from knowing that the police have you people under a microscope—most of you are under surveillance around the clock, and some of you are up for trial. There are rats everywhere, cops have infiltrated your whole operation, and once in a while one of you gets caught skimming. Just the way things ought to be, eh? But if there's one thing I base my business on, it's security, with a way of working that keeps leaks, as far as reasonably possible, from happening. Few workers, and most of them don't know each other. That prevents rats.

"It's taken me a long time to create that infrastructure, and I don't intend, one, to let it get rusty, and two, to endanger it with operations I have no control over. You want me to turn it over to you in exchange for a percentage, or something else, who knows what. That is, I sit back and give you the monopoly. I don't see what I get out of that, or why it makes good business sense for me. Except for the threats. But I don't think—you know?—that you're threatening me."

"What could we threaten you with?" asked Siso Pernas.

That accent. Teresa pushed away the ghost hovering nearby. She needed to stay calm, and to hit the right tone. The León Rock was a long way away, and she didn't want to crash into another one.

"Well, I'll tell you, two ways occur to me," she replied. "Either by leaking information that hurts me, or trying something directly. In both cases, you need to know that I'm just as bad-ass as anybody else. With one difference: I don't have a family that would make me vulnerable. I'm just one person, and I'm just passing through, and I could die tomorrow or disappear, or take off without packing my bags. I haven't even ordered a big fancy marble headstone for myself, despite the fact that I'm Mexican. You people, on the other hand, have possessions. *Pazos*, I think they call those big pretty houses in Galicia. Nice cars, friends . . . Families. You can send for Colombian hit men to come do your dirty work for you. But I can, too. You can even start a war, if it goes that far. All modesty aside, I can, too, because I've got so fucking much money you wouldn't believe it, and money buys a lot of army. But a war would attract the attention of the authorities. . . . I've noticed that the Ministry of the Interior doesn't like it when narcos start settling scores, especially if there are names attached, and property to confiscate, people to send to jail, trials under way. . . . You guys'll be in the newspaper every day."

"You will, too," Siso Pernas said with an irritated smile.

Teresa stared at him coldly for three seconds, very calm.

"Not every day, and not in the same pages. Nobody's ever proved anything against me."

The Gallego gave a crude, short laugh. "Well, you oughta tell me how you manage that."

"Maybe I'm just a little less stupid than you are."

What's said is said, she thought. Clear and straight out. And now let's see where these *cabrones* go. Teo was taking off and putting on the cap of his fountain pen. You're not enjoying this much, either, she thought. Which is why you get paid what you get paid. The difference is that you show it, and I don't.

"Everything can change," Siso Pernas said. "I mean for you."

Variant considered. Foreseen. Teresa took a Bisonte out of the pack in front of her, next to a glass of water and a leather portfolio. She did so as though she were thinking, and put the cigarette between her lips without lighting it. Her mouth was dry, but she decided not to touch the glass of water. The question is not how I feel, she told herself. It's how I look.

"Of course," she admitted. "And I have a feeling it will. But I'm still just one person. With my people, but otherwise just one. My business is intentionally limited. Everybody knows that the merchandise I transport is not mine. I just transport it. That reduces my possible losses. And my ambitions. You people, however, have a lot of doors and windows that somebody can get to you through. Lots of choices if somebody wanted to hurt you. People you love, interests you'd like to keep . . . There are plenty of places to hit you where it would hurt."

She looked into the man's eyes, cigarette in her mouth. Inexpressive. She sat like that, counting the seconds, until Siso Pernas, seeming to see the light, even if grudgingly, put his hand in his pocket, took out a gold lighter, and leaned over the table to offer her a light. Gotcha, she thought. You blinked. She thanked him with a nod.

"And you have no doors and windows?" the Gallego asked at last, putting away the lighter.

"You could try and see." Teresa exhaled as she spoke, her eyes squinting a bit. "It would surprise you to know how strong somebody can be who doesn't have anything to lose except herself. You have a very pretty wife, they say . . . A son."

Let's get this over with, she told herself. You don't have to frighten people all of a sudden. That can make them think there's no way out, and then they might do something crazy. The art is in scaring the shit out of them little by little—let the fear seep in, and last, and keep them awake at night—because then fear becomes respect. The line is subtle, and you have to keep a steady hand to find it without going over it.

"In Sinaloa we have a saying: I'm going to kill your whole family, and then dig up your grandparents and shoot *them*, and then bury them again. . . ."

While she was talking, without looking at anyone she opened the portfolio in front of her and took out a press clipping: a photograph of a soccer team. It was the team that Siso Pernas, a huge soccer fan, put generous amounts of money into. He was the president of the club, and in the photograph—Teresa had laid it very carefully and gently on the table, between them—he was posing before a game with the players, his wife, and his son, a nice-looking boy of ten wearing a team shirt.

"So don't fuck with me." Now she was looking the Galician straight in the eye. "Or as you say here in Spain, *hagan el favor de no tocarme los cojones.*"

The sound of water behind the shower curtain. Steam. He liked to shower in very hot water.

"They can kill us," Teo said.

Teresa was leaning on the door frame. Naked. She could feel the warm steam on her skin. "No," she replied. "First they'll try something less drastic, to test us. Then they'll try to reach the agreement."

"They've already tried what you call less drastic—the investigation of the rubbers that Juárez was telling you about, they leaked that to Judge Martínez Pardo. They've sicced the Guardia Civil on us."

"I know. That's why I played hardball. I wanted them to know we know."

"The Corbeira clan . . ."

"That's enough, Teo." Teresa shook her head. "I control what I do."

"That's true. You always control what you do. Or you sure make it look like you do."

Of the three sentences, Teresa reflected, you could have done without the third. But I guess here, you think you've got a right. The steam fogged up the mirror in the bathroom, making her a gray blur in it. Next to the washbasin, miniature bottles of shampoo and body lotion, a comb, soap in its wrapper. Parador Nacional de Cáceres. One of the national chain of inns. On the other side of the bed with its rumpled sheets, the window framed a medieval landscape: rocks outlined against the night, columns and porticos gilded by hidden spotlights. *Híjole,* she thought. Like in some gringo movie, but the real thing. *Vieja España*—old Spain.

"Hand me a towel, please," Teo asked.

He was almost obsessively clean. He always showered before and after, as though to add a nice hygienic touch to the act of screwing. Meticulous, neat, one of those men that never seem to sweat or have a single bacteria on their skin. The men that Teresa remembered naked were almost all clean, or at least looked like they were, but none of them as much as Teo. He had almost no odor of his own; his skin was soft, with only the slightest, most indefinable masculine smell, the smell of soap and aftershave, as unassuming as everything else about him. After making love he always smelled like her—her skin, her saliva, the strong, dense odor of her wet sex, as though she were taking possession of the man's body. Colonizing it. She handed him the towel, her eyes taking in his tall, thin frame, dripping in the shower stall. The black hair on his chest, legs, and sex. The calm, always welcome smile. The wedding ring on his left hand. She didn't care in the least about that ring, and apparently he didn't, either. Ours is a professional relationship—Teresa had said the only time, in the beginning, that he had tried to justify himself, or justify her, with a light, unnecessary remark—so cut the crap. Teo was smart enough to get it.

"What you said about Siso Pernas' son, was that for real?"

Teresa didn't answer. She had stepped toward the foggy mirror, wiping away some of the steam with her hand. And there she was, so blurred that it might not have been her at all, with the tousled hair, the big black eyes looking out at her like always.

"Nobody would think so, seeing you that way," he said.

He was beside her, looking at her in the open patch in the steam-frosted glass, drying his chest and back with the towel. Teresa shook her head slowly. What do you think, she said wordlessly. He gave her an absentminded kiss on the hair and went on drying himself as he walked into the bedroom, while she stood where she was, her hands on the washbasin, looking at her blurry reflection. I hope I never have to show you, she thought, speaking inwardly to the man shuffling around in the next room. I hope I don't.

"I'm concerned about Patricia," Teo said abruptly.

Teresa went just to the door, not entering the bedroom, and looked at him. He had taken a perfectly ironed shirt out of his suitcase—the *cabrón*'s clothes never got wrinkled when he packed—and was unbuttoning it to put it on. They had a table reserved for a half-hour later at the Torre de Sande. A truly great restaurant, he had said. In the old part of the city. Teo knew all the truly great restaurants, all the "in" bars, all the elegant shops. Places as custom-made for him as the shirt he was about to put on. Like Patty—they seemed to have been born into these places: two society types whom the world always somehow owed, although he wore it better than Patty did. All of this so terrific, and so far from Las Siete Gotas, Teresa thought, where her mother—who had never kissed her—washed dishes in a tub in the yard and slept with drunk neighbors. So far from the school where the runny-nosed boys would lift Teresa's skirt behind the schoolyard wall. Jack it off, bitch. For all of us. Give me and my boys a handjob or we'll break your face. So far from the wood-and-zinc roofs, the dirt under her bare feet, the *pinche* poverty.

"What's wrong with Patty?"

"You know what's wrong with her. And it's getting worse."

It was. Drinking and sniffing coke till you couldn't see straight was a bad combination, but there was more. The Lieutenant was coming apart, very quietly. The word might be "giving up," although Teresa couldn't quite decide what she was giving up on. Sometimes Patty seemed to be like one of those shipwrecked sailors that stop swimming for no apparent reason. *Glug, glug, glug.* Maybe because they don't think they'll ever be rescued or get to land, or maybe just because they're tired.

"It's her life—she's of legal age to do what she wants with it," she said.

"That's not the point. The point is whether that's good for you or not."

Just like Teo. He wasn't worried about O'Farrell, he was worried about the consequences of her behavior for Teresa. Is it good for you or not, boss.

The listlessness, the lack of spirit, the distance from which Patty dealt with the few responsibilities she still had at Transer Naga—this was the dark side of the problem. During business meetings—she went to fewer and fewer, delegating her power to Teresa—she always seemed absent, or she made jokes that were out of place, and everything was like a joke to her. She spent a lot of money, she didn't care, she turned serious things, which might mean a lot of money and resources and time invested, and not a few lives, into frivolities. A boat casting off and simply drifting away . . . Teresa wondered whether it was she herself who had relieved her friend of her obligations, or whether the distancing came from Patty, from the growing murkiness of her mind and her life. You're the boss, she would constantly say. And I applaud, drink, snort, and look on with pride. Maybe it was both, and Patty had simply drifted with the course of things—the natural, inevitable course that everything had followed since the beginning.

Maybe I was wrong about Edmond Dantès, Patty had remarked in Tomás Pestaña's house. He wasn't this, and you weren't him. I misjudged you, I got you wrong. Or maybe, as she said on another occasion—her nose covered with white dust and her eyes blank—the only thing that's happening is that sooner or later Abbé Faria always leaves the stage.

Fucked up, and dying a slow death. And not caring. Those were the words for it, and the first of them was the worst in this business, which was so sensitive to any sort of scandal. The latest episode was quite recent: a short, squat, lowlife teenage girl, who had bad friends and tougher sentiments, had been openly hustling Patty. Until one partic-

ularly sordid night of excesses—drugs, hemorrhaging, a visit to the
hospital at five in the morning—had threatened to wind up in the
newspaper. And it would have, had Teresa and Teo not moved all the
resources available to prevent it—money, favors, blackmail. They covered it up, deep.

Shit happens, Patty said when Teresa talked to her about it.

"It's all so simple for you, Mexicana. You've got it all, and somebody
to give you a cunt massage, to boot. So you live your life and let me live
mine, if you don't mind. Because I don't stick my nose in your business, or anybody else's. I don't ask questions, you hear? I'm your friend.
I paid for your friendship, and I'm still paying. I know the rules and I
keep 'em. And you, who buy everything so easy, just let me buy mine.
You always say it's half and half, not just in business or money. Well, I
agree. This is my free, deliberate, and *puta* half."

Even Oleg Yasikov had alerted Teresa about this. "Careful, Tesa. It's
not just money on the line, it's your freedom and your life. The decision is yours. Of course. But maybe you should ask yourself. Yes. Questions. For example, what part of all this is your fault. Or your responsibility. What part isn't. To what degree did you start all this, playing
her games. There are passive responsibilities that are just as bad as the
active ones. There are silences that we can't say we didn't hear absolutely clearly. Yes. From a certain point in a person's life on, they're
responsible for what they do—and what they don't do."

What would things have been like if . . . Teresa sometimes thought
about that. If I had . . . The key might lie there, but she couldn't see any
way to look over that increasingly clear and inevitable barrier. She felt
uncomfortable, or remorseful—it came over her in vague waves, as
though it filled her hands and she didn't know what to do with it. And
that irritated her. Why did she have to feel this? she asked herself. What
Patty had wanted never could be, and never was. Nobody deceived
anybody, and if Patty really *had* harbored hopes, or intentions, in the
past, she ought to have discarded them long ago. Maybe that was the
problem. Everything was finished, or almost finished, and Lieutenant
O'Farrell was left without even the goad of curiosity to make her live.
Teo Aljarafe might have been Patricia O'Farrell's last experiment with
Teresa. Or her revenge. From then on, everything was simultaneously
foreseeable and dark. And each of the two women would have to face
whatever it was alone.

13. I get planes off the ground in two and three hundred yards

There it is," said Dr. Ramos.

He had the hearing of a dog, Teresa decided. She herself couldn't hear a thing, except the swooshing of the light waves on the beach. It was a calm night, and the Mediterranean was a black expanse out beyond the inlet at Agua Amarga, on the coast of Almería. The moon made the sand on the shore look like snow, and flashes from the Punta Polacra lighthouse—three every twelve or fifteen seconds, her old professional instincts told her—shone at the foot of the Sierra de Gata, six miles to the southwest.

"All I can hear is the ocean," she replied.

"Listen."

She focused on the darkness, her ears straining. They were standing next to the Cherokee, with a thermos of coffee, plastic cups, and sandwiches, protected from the cold by sweaters and heavy slickers. The dark silhouette of Pote Gálvez paced back and forth a few yards away, guarding the dirt trail and the dry path that led down to the water.

"Now I hear it," she said.

It was nothing more than a distant droning barely distinguishable from the sound of waves against the shore, but it was growing louder and louder, and it seemed very low, as though it came from the sea and not the sky. It sounded like a speedboat approaching at high velocity.

"Good boys," Dr. Ramos remarked.

There was a touch of pride in his voice, like a man talking about his son or a talented student, but his tone was calm, as usual. This guy, thought Teresa, never loses his cool. She, however, was having a hard time controlling her uneasiness, making sure her voice came out with the serenity that the others expected. If they only knew, she said to herself. If they only knew. And even more so tonight, with what they had at stake. Three months in preparation for what would be decided in less than two hours, an hour and a half of which had already passed. The sound of engines was growing louder, and closer. The doctor brought his wristwatch up to his eyes before checking it with a quick flick of his lighter.

"Prussian punctuality," he said. "The right place and right on time."

The sound was coming closer and closer, and at very low altitude. Teresa peered into the darkness, and she thought she saw it—a small black dot, growing, just on the line between the shadowy water and the glimmering of the moon, still fairly far out.

"*Híjole,*" she whispered to herself.

It was almost beautiful. She had memories that allowed her to picture the sea viewed from the cabin, the muted lights on the instrument panel, the line of the shore silhouetted ahead, the two men at the controls, Almería VOR/DME at 114.1 on the dial to calculate ETA and distance above the water, dot-dash-dash-dash-dot-dash-dot, and then the coast sighted by moonlight, the search for landmarks in the flash from the lighthouse to the left, the lights of Carboneras to the right, the dark void of the inlet in the center. I wish I was up there, she thought. Flying by visuals like them, and with the balls to do it. Then the black dot got larger, still just above the water, while the sound of the engines became almost deafening—*rooooarrr,* as though the sound were coming straight at them—and Teresa made out a pair of wings materializing at the same altitude from which she and the doctor were looking at them. And then she saw the silhouette of the whole plane, flying very low, no more than fifteen feet above the water, the two propellers whirling like silver disks in the moonlight. Jesus shit. An instant later, buzzing them with a roar that left a cloud of sand and dry seaweed in its wake, the plane pulled up, its left wing dropped as it turned, and it disappeared into the darkness inland, between the Sierra de Gata and the Sierra Cabrera.

"There goes a ton and a half," the doctor said.

"It's not on the ground yet," Teresa replied.

"It will be in fifteen minutes."

There was no reason to remain in darkness anymore, so the doctor rummaged around in his pants pockets, pulled out his lighter once more, lit his pipe, and then lit the cigarette that Teresa had just put between her lips. Pote Gálvez walked over with a cup of coffee in each hand. A heavy shadow, anticipating her needs and desires. The white sand muffled his footsteps.

"¿Qué onda, patrona?"

"Everything fine, Pinto. Thank you."

She drank the bitter brew, no sugar but laced with brandy, enjoying her cigarette spiked with hashish. I hope everything continues to be fine, she thought. The cell phone in the pocket of her slicker would ring when the stuff was in the four trucks waiting beside the rudimentary runway: a tiny airport abandoned since the civil war, in the middle of the Almería desert near Tabernas, with the closest village a little over ten miles away. That would be the last stage in a complex operation that linked a shipment of fifteen hundred kilos of cocaine hydrochloride from the Medellín cartel to the Italian groups. Another pebble in the shoe of the Corbeira clan, which still believed it had a monopoly on the movements of the white lady on Spanish soil. Teresa smiled to herself. Pissed, those Gallegos are going to be if they find out. But the Colombians themselves had asked Teresa to study the possibility of moving, in one huge shipment, a large cargo that would be loaded in containers in the port of Valencia for delivery in Genoa, and all she did was solve the problem. The drug, vacuum-sealed in ten-kilo packages and stuffed into cans of automobile grease, had crossed the Atlantic after being taken from the original ship off the coast of Ecuador, around the Galápagos Islands, and put on an old merchant marine boat, the *Susana,* sailing under the Panamanian flag. The cargo was unloaded in Casablanca, and from there, under the protection of the Gendarmerie Royale—Colonel Abdelkader Chaib was still on the best of terms with Teresa—it was trucked to the Rif, to a warehouse used by Transer Naga for preparing hashish shipments.

"The Moroccans have played straight as arrows," remarked Dr. Ramos, his hands in his pockets. They were walking toward the car, with Pote Gálvez at the wheel. The SUV's headlights illuminated the

stretch of beach and rocks, with startled seagulls fluttering and twitching in the light.

"Yes, but the credit goes to you, Doctor."

"Not the idea."

"You made it possible."

Dr. Ramos sucked at his pipe wordlessly. It was hard for Transer
Naga's tactician to complain, or for that matter to show pleasure at a
word of praise, but Teresa sensed his satisfaction with the operation.
Because while the idea of the big plane—the air bridge, they called it—
was Teresa's, the mapping of the route and the operational details were
the doctor's. The innovation had consisted of using low-level flights
and secret runways for a larger and more profitable operation. Because
recently, there had been problems. Two Galician runs, financed by the
Corbeira clan, had been intercepted by Customs, one in the Caribbean
and the other off the coast of Portugal; a third operation, run entirely
by the Italians—a Turkish merchantman with half a ton on board, en
route from Buenaventura, in Colombia, to Genoa via Cádiz—had been
a complete failure, the cargo seized by the Guardia Civil, eight men in
prison. This was a difficult moment, all in all, and only after thinking
long and hard did Teresa decide to take the risk—but she used methods that had worked years before, back in Mexico, for Amado Carrillo,
the Lord of the Skies. Órale, she concluded. Why be creative, when
there are masters to follow.

She had put Farid Lataquia and Dr. Ramos to work on it. Lataquia
had protested, of course. Too little time, too little money, too little
profit. People think they can order up miracles, and so on. Meanwhile,
Dr. Ramos shut himself up with his maps and his diagrams, smoking
pipe after pipe, speaking only the absolute minimum necessary, calculating routes, fuel, sites. Holes in the radar that allowed a plane to reach
a certain spot between Melilla and Al Hoceima; the distance it would
be flying, mere feet over the water toward the north-northeast; areas
without surveillance where the Spanish coast could be penetrated;
landmarks for sight navigation without instruments; fuel consumption at low and high altitudes; zones where a medium-size plane
couldn't be detected as it flew over the ocean. He even felt out a couple
of air controllers that would be on duty on the right nights and in the
right places, to be sure that nobody sounded the alarm if some suspicious blip showed up on the screen. He had flown over the Almería
desert looking for a good place to land, and gone to the Rif mountains
to see the condition of the local airstrips for himself.

Lataquia found the plane in Africa: an old Aviocar C-212 that had
been used to carry passengers between Malabo and Bata—part of a

Spanish aid package to Equatorial Guinea. Built in 1978, but it still flew. A two-engine craft, with a cargo capacity of two tons. It could land at sixty knots on two hundred fifty yards of runway if the pilot backwashed the props and pushed the flaps to forty degrees. The purchase was made without any problems, through a contact at Equatorial Guinea's embassy in Madrid—the trade attaché's commission aside, the over-invoicing served to cover a couple of engines for the semi-rigids—and the Aviocar flew to Bangui, where the two Garret TPE engines were reworked and checked out by French mechanics. Then it was parked on a four-hundred-yard airstrip in the Rif mountains, waiting to take on the cocaine. Finding a crew hadn't been hard: $100,000 for the pilot—Jan Karasek, Polish, former crop sprayer, veteran of night flights running hashish for Transer Naga in his own Skymaster—and $75,000 for the copilot—Fernando de la Cueva, a former Spanish air force officer who had flown Aviocars when he was on active duty, before going over to civil aviation and then being laid off in a "job restructuring" by Iberia.

The Cherokee's headlights briefly swept the first few houses in Carboneras as Teresa consulted the clock on the dashboard. By now the two pilots, orienting themselves by the lights of the Almería–Murcia highway and then crossing it near Níjar, would have flown the plane up into the Sierra de Alhamilla. There, they'd turn slowly to the west, staying low but avoiding the network of high-tension electrical lines carefully drawn by Dr. Ramos on their flight maps. They'd soon be lowering the flaps for their landing on the clandestine runway illuminated only by the moon, one car's headlights at the beginning of the landing strip, and another's three hundred yards farther down: two quick flashes to signal the beginning and end of the strip.

In the plane's cargo hatch was merchandise valued at $45 million, of which Transer Naga would earn ten percent.

Before they got on the N-340, the three of them—Teresa, Dr. Ramos, and Pote Gálvez—stopped to eat something at a truck stop: truckers at tables in the back, hams and sausages hanging from the ceiling, wineskins, photographs of bullfighters on the walls, revolving racks with porno videos, and tapes and CDs of Los Chinguitos, El Fary, La Niña de los Peines. They stood at the bar for tapas: ham, fresh tuna with pimientos and tomato, sausage. Dr. Ramos ordered a brandy and Pote Gálvez, who was driving, coffee—a double. Teresa was looking for her cigarettes in her jacket pockets when a green and white Guardia Civil Nissan pulled up outside. Its occupants walked in, and Pote

Gálvez got very tense; he took his hands off the bar and with professional distrust half turned toward the newcomers, stepping out a bit to cover his employer's body with his own.

Easy, Pinto, she told him with her eyes. It's not today that we get fucked. Rural patrol. Routine. Two young agents in olive-drab uniforms, pistols in black holsters at their waists. They courteously said *Buenas noches* to all, put their caps down on a stool, and sat at the end of the bar. They seemed relaxed, and one of them looked at Teresa and her companions briefly, absentmindedly, while he poured sugar in his coffee with one hand and stirred it with the other. Dr. Ramos' eyes flashed as he and Teresa exchanged glances. If these rookies only knew, he wordlessly said, carefully stuffing tobacco into the bowl of his pipe. Oh, my. Then, as the officers were getting ready to leave, the doctor told the barman not to charge them, to put their coffee on his tab. One of them protested very politely, while the other gave them a smile. *Gracias.* No, the doctor said, thank *you,* for your service. *Gracias,* they said again.

"Good boys," the doctor said as the door closed behind them.

He'd said the same thing about the pilots, Teresa remembered, when the Aviocar's engines roared overhead on the beach. And that, among other things, was what she liked about the doctor. His perfect, unflappable equanimity. Anybody, seen from the right perspective, could be a good boy. Or girl. The world was a difficult place, with complicated rules, where each person played the role assigned by destiny. Everybody I know, she had heard the doctor remark, has reasons for doing what they do. Accepting that in the people around you, she concluded, made it easier to get along with them. The trick was to always look for the positive side. And smoking a pipe helped a lot. It gave you time—to think, to reflect, to wait. It gave you the chance to move slowly, and look into yourself, and look at others.

The doctor ordered a second brandy, and Teresa—there was no tequila here—a Galician aguardiente that brought tears to her eyes. The presence of the two guardsmen recalled to her a recent conversation, and old worries. Three weeks earlier, at Transer Naga's official headquarters, now in a five-story building on Avenida del Mar, in the center of Marbella, across the street from the park, she'd received a visit. An unannounced visit, which at first she'd refused to grant, until Eva, her secretary, showed her a court order that recommended that Teresa Mendoza Chávez, resident of blah blah blah, grant that interview, or be subject to certain subsequent unpleasantnesses. "Preliminary survey," the order said, though it didn't say preliminary to what. "And there are two of them," Eva added, with Pote Gálvez behind her at the door of Teresa's office, like a Doberman. "A man and a woman. Guardia Civil."

After thinking it over for a few seconds, Teresa had Eva call Teo Aljarafe, so that he would be ready should his services be required. She reassured Pote Gálvez with a gesture and told Eva to show the visitors into the conference room. They didn't shake hands. After a rudimentary greeting the three took seats at the large round table, from which all papers and files had first been removed. The man was thin, serious, not bad-looking, with prematurely gray hair in a brush cut, and a luxuriant moustache. He had a deep, pleasant voice, Teresa thought, as cultured as his manners. He was in street clothes, a worn corduroy jacket and khaki pants—civilian, but military at the same time.

"My name's Castro," he said, not mentioning his given name, although he seemed to have had second thoughts, and added, "Captain Castro. And this is Sergeant Moncada." While he made their brief introductions, the woman—redheaded, in a skirt and polo shirt, gold earrings, and with small, intelligent eyes—pulled a tape recorder out of the canvas bag on her lap and put it on the table.

"I hope you don't mind," she said. Then she blew her nose on a Kleenex—she looked like she had a cold, or an allergy—and left the tissue wadded up in the ashtray.

"Not at all," answered Teresa. "But in that case you'll have to wait while I call my attorney. And the same goes for taking notes."

After a look at her boss, Sergeant Moncada frowned, put the tape recorder back into her bag, and used another Kleenex. Captain Castro succinctly explained what had brought them there. In the course of a recent investigation, some reports had pointed toward businesses related to Transer Naga.

"There is proof of that, of course," said Teresa.

"Well, no. I'm sorry to say there's not."

"In that case, I don't understand why you're here."

"It's routine."

"Oh."

"We'd like you to cooperate with the Ministry of Justice."

"Oh."

Captain Castro told Teresa that an action by the Guardia Civil—the confiscation of inflatable boats presumably meant for use in drug trafficking—had been aborted because of an information leak and the unexpected intervention of the National Police. Agents from the Estepona division stepped in early, raiding a warehouse building in the industrial park, where, instead of the material the Guardia Civil was tracking, they found only two old motorboats, no longer being used. They found no proof, arrested nobody.

"I'm so sorry to hear that," Teresa said. "But I still don't understand what any of that has to do with me."

"Nothing, for the time being. The police blew it. Our investigation was ruined because somebody passed false information to the Estepona police. No judge would go forward with what we have now."

"*Híjole*. . . . And you've come to tell me this?" Her tone of voice made the officers exchange glances.

"In a way," Captain Castro said. "We thought your opinion might be helpful. At the moment we're working on half a dozen things related to that same area."

Sergeant Moncada leaned forward in her chair. No lipstick, no makeup. Her small eyes looked tired. The cold. The allergy. Maybe a long night last night—working, of course, Teresa ventured. Days without washing her hair. The gold earrings were incongruous.

"The captain means *your* area—in fact, you."

Teresa decided to ignore the hostility. She looked at the woman's wrinkled shirt.

"I don't know what you're talking about." She turned to the man again. "My affairs are all in public view."

"Not these affairs," Captain Castro said. "Have you ever heard of Chemical STM?"

"Never."

"Or of Konstantin Garofi, Limited?"

"Yes. I have shares in that company. A minority holding."

"How strange. According to our information, the Konstantin Garofi import-export company, with headquarters in Gibraltar, is owned entirely by you."

Maybe I should have waited for Teo, thought Teresa. But now was not the time to turn back. She raised an eyebrow.

"I imagine that if you claim that, you have proof of it."

Captain Castro stroked his moustache. He slowly, doubtfully shook his head, as though calculating exactly how much proof he had, or didn't have.

"Well, no," he said at last. "Unfortunately we don't, although in this case it doesn't matter much. Because we've received a report. A request for cooperation from the U.S. DEA and the Colombian government, regarding a shipment of fifteen tons of potassium permanganate seized in Cartagena."

"I didn't realize that shipping potassium permanganate was illegal."

She had leaned back and was looking at the officer with a surprise that to all appearances was authentic.

"In Europe it's not," was the reply. "But in Colombia it's a controlled substance. It's used in the processing of cocaine. And in the United States buying and selling more than a certain amount of potassium permanganate is restricted. It's one of the twelve precursors and thirty-three chemical substances on the list of controlled substances. As you may or may not know, potassium permanganate is one of those twelve products essential for making cocaine paste and cocaine hydrochloride. Combined with other chemicals, ten tons would be enough to refine eighty tons of cocaine. Which, if you'll forgive a well-used phrase, is nothing to sneeze at."

When he finished his speech, Captain Castro continued to look at Teresa inexpressively, as though that was all he had to say. She mentally counted to three. *Chale.* Her head was starting to hurt, but she couldn't allow herself to take out an aspirin in front of these two. She shrugged.

"And?"

"Well, the shipment went by sea from Algeciras. It had been bought by Konstantin Garofi from the Belgian company Chemical STM."

"I think it's odd that a company in Gibraltar would export directly to Colombia."

"We think it's odd, too." If there was sarcasm in his remark, it didn't show. "Actually, what happened is that the stuff was bought in Belgium, brought to Algeciras, and then signed over to another company registered on the island of Jersey, which put it in a container and shipped it first to Puerto Cabello, in Venezuela, and then to Cartagena. . . . And along the way it was repackaged—into barrels labeled magnesium dioxide."

It wasn't the Gallegos—Teresa knew that. This time it hadn't been them that had blown the whistle. The problem was in Colombia. Local problems, with the DEA behind them, probably. Nothing that would even remotely affect her.

"Where?"

"At sea. Because it left Algeciras labeled as what it was."

So that's the end of the line, sweetheart. Everybody off. Look at my hands on the table, taking a legal cigarette out of a legal package and lighting it with all the calm in the world. Hands as white and innocent as snow. So forget it. What's all this to me?

"Then you should ask that company headquartered in Jersey for an explanation," she said.

The sergeant made a gesture of impatience, but said nothing. Captain Castro bowed his head, as though grateful for a good piece of advice.

"It dissolved after the operation," he said. "It was just a name on Saint Helier Street."

"*Híjole*. And there's proof of all that?"

"Of that, yes indeed."

"Then the people at Konstantin Garofi got taken, eh?"

The sergeant opened her mouth to say something, but this time, too, she evidently thought better of it. She looked at her boss and then removed a notebook from her bag. You take out a pencil, thought Teresa, and you're on your ass on the street. Or maybe whether you take out a pencil or not.

"So," she went on, "if I understand this right, you're talking about the transportation of a legal chemical within the Schengen area. I don't see what's strange about that. I'm sure all the documents were in order, with bills of lading and destination documents and everything. I can't say I know all the details of Konstantin Garofi's operations, but as far as I know they're very careful to obey all the applicable laws. . . . And I'd never have stock in them if they weren't."

"Not to worry," said Captain Castro amiably.

"Do I seem worried?"

He looked at her without immediately answering.

"As far as you and Konstantin Garofi are concerned," he said at last, "everything seems legal."

"Unfortunately," added the sergeant. She licked her thumb to turn a page in the notebook.

Bullshit, thought Teresa. You want to make me think you've got the number of kilos of my last run written down in there?

"Would there be anything else?" she asked.

"There'll always be something else," replied the captain.

So let's move to second base, *cabrón*, thought Teresa as she stubbed out her cigarette in the ashtray. She did it with calculated violence, with a hard thumb. Just enough irritation, plus an ounce or two for good measure, despite the fact that her headache was making her feel increasingly uncomfortable. In Sinaloa, these two would already be bought off or dead. She had contempt for the way they showed up there, taking her for something she wasn't. So primitive. But she also knew that contempt led to arrogance, and that's where the mistakes started. Overconfidence kills more people than bullets.

"Let's make things clear," she said. "If you have something concrete that involves me, we can continue this conversation with my lawyers. If not, I'd appreciate it if you'd stop wasting my time."

Sergeant Moncada forgot about her notebook. She tapped the table, as though testing the quality of the wood. She seemed cranky. "We could continue this conversation down at headquarters. . . ."

There you go, thought Teresa. Straight where I was figuring we'd be going.

"Well, I don't think so, Sergeant," Teresa replied very serenely. "Because unless you had something concrete, which you don't, I'd be in your headquarters there just long enough for my attorneys to shove it up your ass. . . . With compensatory and punitive damages thrown in for good measure."

"There's no reason to be that way," said Captain Castro calmly. "No one's accusing you of anything."

"I'm sure of that. That nobody's accusing me of anything."

"Certainly not Sergeant Velasco."

This is a trap, Teresa thought. And she put on her Aztec mask.

"Sorry? . . . Sergeant who?"

The officer looked at her with cold curiosity. You're damn fine, Teresa thought, *bien padre.* With those good manners and that gray hair and that nice official, gentlemanly moustache. The bitch, however, ought to wash her hair more often.

"Iván Velasco," the captain said slowly. "Guardia Civil. Deceased."

Sergeant Moncada leaned forward again. Brusquely.

"A pig. You know anything about pigs, *señora?*" She said this with ill-repressed rage.

Maybe she's just in a shitty mood, thought Teresa. Or maybe it has something to do with being a redhead. Or maybe she's just over-worked, or unhappy with her husband—who the hell knows. Maybe she just needs a good screw. And it can't be easy being a woman in her line of work. Or maybe they take turns: good cop, bad cop. With a *cabrona* like they think I am, they decide the girl's going to be the bad cop. Logical. Like I give a fuck.

"Does this Velasco have something to do with the potassium permanganate?" asked Teresa.

"Be nice, now." The tone of voice did not sound friendly; the sergeant was digging something out from between her teeth with a finger-nail. "Don't go pulling our leg."

"Velasco kept bad company," Captain Castro explained, clearly, as he always did. "And he was killed some time ago, just about when you got out of prison. Remember? . . . Santiago Fisterra, Gibraltar, and all that? When you didn't even dream of being what you've become today."

Teresa's expression gave away nothing of what she might or might not remember. You've got squat, she thought. You just came to pull my chain.

"Well, you know, I don't think I do," she said. "I don't think I can place this Velasco."

"Can't place him," remarked the sergeant. She almost spat it out. She turned to her boss as if to say, What do you think, Captain? But Castro was looking out the window, as though thinking about something else.

"Actually, we can't connect you," Sergeant Moncada went on. "Besides, it's water under the bridge, right?" She licked her thumb again and consulted her notebook, although it was clear she wasn't reading anything there. "And that other guy, Cañabota, that got killed—that name's not familiar, either, I suppose? . . . The name Oleg Yasikov ring any bells? . . . And you never heard of hashish or cocaine or Colombians or Galicians?" She stopped herself, glumly, to let Teresa say something, but Teresa didn't open her mouth. ". . . Of course. You deal in real estate, the stock market, Jerez wineries, local politics, financial paradises, charity, and dinners with the governor of Málaga."

"And the movies," added the captain drily. He was still turned toward the window, with an expression as though he were thinking about almost anything else. An expression almost melancholy.

The sergeant raised a hand. "It's true. I'd forgotten that you were also into movies." Her tone was becoming more and more insulting— even vulgar, as though so far she had repressed it, or were now using it on purpose, as a provocation. "Between your multimillion-dollar businesses and your fancy lifestyle, with the paparazzi making you a star, you must feel like you're pretty much untouchable."

I've been provoked by better than you, Teresa said to herself. Either this bitch is incredibly naive, despite the venom, or they really have nothing to hang on to.

"Those paparazzi," she replied very calmly, "are now involved in court cases that won't soon be over for them. . . . And as for you, do you really think I'm going to play cops and robbers with you?"

It was the captain's turn. He had slowly turned back toward her, and was looking at her again.

"*Señora.* The sergeant and I have a job to do. That includes several ongoing investigations . . ." He cast a none-too-trusting glance at the sergeant's notebook. "The only purpose of this visit is to tell you that."

"How nice, how incredibly nice. Telling me like this, I mean."

"You see? We just wanted to talk for a while. Get to know you better."

"And," the sergeant put in, "maybe make you a little nervous."

Her boss shook his head.

"Señora Mendoza is not one to get nervous. She'd never have gotten where she is"—he smiled a little, the smile of an insurance salesman—"if she were. I hope our next conversation will take place under more favorable circumstances. For me, I mean."

Teresa looked at the ashtray, with her single cigarette butt among the wads of Kleenex. Who did these two take her for? Hers had been a long, hard road—too long and hard to put up with these stupid TV-detective antics. They were just a couple of snoops that picked their teeth and wadded up Kleenex and asked to go through your closets. Make her nervous? Don't make her laugh. Now she was pissed. She had things to do—take an aspirin, for example. The minute these jokers were out of there, she'd have Teo sue for harassment. And then she'd make a few telephone calls.

"I'm going to ask you to leave now," she said, standing up. And it turned out the sergeant knew how to laugh, Teresa discovered, although she didn't like the sound of it. The captain stood up at the same time as Teresa, but the sergeant remained seated, a little forward in the chair, her fingers gripping the edge of the table. With that dry, sneery smile.

"Just like that, ask us to leave? . . . Without threatening us, or trying to buy us off, like those shits in Organized Crime? . . . That would make us so happy . . . an attempt to bribe us."

Teresa opened the door. Pote Gálvez was there—thickset and vigilant, as though he hadn't moved an inch since they went in. And he probably hadn't. He held his hands slightly away from his body. Waiting. She calmed him with a look.

"You really are insane," Teresa said. "I don't bribe people, and I certainly don't threaten them."

The sergeant got up finally, almost grudgingly. She'd blown her nose again and was gripping the wad of Kleenex in one hand, her notebook in the other. She looked around—the expensive paintings on the walls, the view of the city and the sea. She was no longer reining in her anger and resentment. As she passed through the doorway behind her boss she stopped before Teresa, very close, and put the notebook in her bag.

"Of course. You have people who do it for you, don't you?" She brought her face closer, and her reddened eyes seemed to flame with rage. "Go ahead, try it. Try doing it in person just this once. You know what an agent in the Guardia Civil makes? . . . I'm sure you do. And also the people that die and rot because of all the shit you bring in . . . Why don't you try to bribe the captain and me? . . . I'd love to hear your offer, so I could drag you out of this office in handcuffs." She threw the wad of Kleenex on the floor. "You *hija de puta.*"

There was always logic to help keep things in perspective, after all. That was what Teresa was thinking as she crossed the almost dry bed of the river, with water gathered in small, shallow pools near the sea. A focus that was virtually mathematical, so unemotional it chilled the heart. A calm system of putting events in order, especially the circumstances at the beginning and end of the chain. It was what allowed you, in principle, to put aside guilt or remorse. That photograph torn down the middle—the girl with the trusting eyes, so far back there in Sinaloa—was her ticket of indulgences. And since it was all a question of logic, she could do nothing but move toward the place to which logic led her. Which was up toward the pinnacle of success in her business.

Yet there was always a paradox: What happens when life decides you've had enough success, and it hits you with the payback? The Real Situation. Once that thought occurs to you, you start lying awake, waiting for that moment to come. So you die little by little for hours, and days, and years. A long death, which you die pretty quietly on the outside, no screaming, no blood. But the more you think and the more you live, the more you die. She refused to die that way.

She stopped on some rocks, like stepping-stones on the beach, and looked out to sea. She wore a gray tracksuit and tennis shoes, and the wind blew her hair into her face. On the other side of the mouth of the Guadalmina, the surf broke against a sandbar, and in the background, in the bluish haze of the horizon, stretched the white silhouettes of Puerto Banús and Marbella. The golf courses were to the left, their fairways dipping down toward the shoreline and swirling around the ocher hotel building and the beach cabañas now closed for the winter. Teresa liked Guadalmina Baja at this time of the year, with its beaches deserted and only a few peaceful golfers moving in the distance. The luxury mansions silent, shuttered behind their high, bougainvillea-covered walls. One of these mansions, the one closest to the spit of land that ran out into the water, belonged to her. "Las Siete Gotas" was the name painted on a beautiful Spanish tile beside the entrance, a bit of irony that only she and Pote Gálvez understood. From the beach, all that could be seen was the high outer wall, the trees and shrubbery that peeked up over the top and camouflaged the security cameras, and the tiled roof and four chimneys: sixty-five hundred square feet of house on a lot that measured fifty-four thousand. The house was constructed on the model of an old Mexican hacienda, white with ocher details, a terrace off the second floor, a big porch open to the garden, the lawn, the tiled fountain, and the pool.

She could see a boat in the distance—a fishing boat working the waters close in to shore—and she stood there for a while watching it. She still felt a close link to the ocean, and every morning when she got up, the first thing she did was look out at the immense expanse of blue, gray, or violet—depending on the light and the day. She still instinctively calculated high and low tide, water depth, favorable or unfavorable winds, even when she didn't have anybody working out at sea. That coast, engraved in her memory with the precision of a nautical chart, was a familiar world to which she owed sadness and good fortune, and also images that she tried not to call up too often, for fear that her memory might change them. The house on the beach at Palmones. The nights on the Strait, flying along over the waves, the speedboat bumping under her. The adrenaline of the pursuit and the victory. The hard, tender body of Santiago Fisterra. At least I had him, she thought. I lost him, but first I had him. It was a very calculated, very intimate luxury to sit with a joint of hashish and a glass of tequila and remember those days, those moonless nights when the murmur of the surf on the beach came to them across the lawn. Sometimes she would hear the Customs helicopter fly over the beach, without lights, and she would think that it might be the man who'd jumped into the water to save her life when they crashed into the León Rock. Once, upset by the Customs pursuits, two of Teresa's men suggested they rough up the chopper pilot, that *hijo de puta,* break his fingers, beat the living shit out of him.

When she heard their plan, Teresa called in Dr. Ramos and ordered him to tell the two, repeating her words exactly, that that guy was just doing his job, exactly the same as we're just doing ours. Those are the rules, and if one day he crashes and burns during a pursuit or his chopper goes down on a beach somewhere, that's tough. Sometimes you win and sometimes you lose. But if anybody touches a hair on his head when he's not on duty, I'll have his skin peeled off him in strips. Is that clear? And apparently it had been.

Teresa still felt the personal tie to the ocean. And not just from the shore. The *Sinaloa,* a Fratelli Benetti 125 feet long and 21 feet wide, registered in Jersey, was tied up at the yacht club in Puerto Banús: a blindingly white, classically styled beauty with three decks, its interiors furnished with teak and iroko wood, marble bathrooms, four cabins for guests, and a thousand-square-foot salon presided over by a wonderful seascape by Montague Dawson—*Combat Between the Spartiate and the*

Antilla at Trafalgar—that Teo Aljarafe had bought for her at an auction at Claymore. Despite the fact that Transer Naga moved naval resources of all kinds, Teresa never used the *Sinaloa* for illicit activities. It was neutral territory, a world apart, which she wanted to keep separate from the rest of her life. Access restricted. A captain, two sailors, and a mechanic kept the yacht ready to sail at a moment's notice, and she went out on it often, sometimes for short sails of a couple of days, other times on cruises of two or three weeks. Books, music, a TV and video player. She never took guests, except sometimes Patty. The only person who always went with her, stoically suffering through his seasickness, was Pote Gálvez.

Teresa liked the long days in solitude, when the telephone didn't ring and there was no need to talk. She'd sit at night in the wheelhouse beside the captain—a taciturn merchant marine skipper hired by Dr. Ramos, whom Teresa had approved of precisely because of his economy of speech—and disconnect the autopilot, taking the wheel in a rough sea, bad weather. Or she'd spend calm, sunny days on a chaise on the aft deck with a book in her hands or watching the ocean. She also took a personal interest in maintaining the two 1,800-horsepower MTU turbodiesel engines that allowed the *Sinaloa* to cruise at thirty knots, leaving a straight, wide, powerful wake. She would often go down into the engine room, her hair pulled back into two braids, a kerchief across the top of her head, and spend hours there, whether in port or at sea. She knew the engines' every part. And once when they had a breakdown in a heavy sea and easterly wind to the windward side of Alborán, she worked four straight hours down there, covered with grease and grime, banging her head against the pipes and bulkheads while the captain tried to prevent the yacht from turning across the waves or drifting too far to leeward, until between her and the mechanic they solved the problem.

Once in a while, during a longer trip aboard the *Sinaloa*—through the Aegean to Turkey, the south coast of France, around the Lipari islands and through the Strait of Bonifacio—she would give orders to fix a course for the Balearic islands. She liked the calm anchorages north of Ibiza and Mallorca, almost deserted in the winter, liked to drop anchor off the sandbar between Formentera and the Es Freus passage. There, off the beach at Trocados, Pote Gálvez had recently had a run-in with some paparazzi. Two photographers from Marbella recognized the yacht and pedaled out on a tourist paddle boat to get the drop on Teresa, until Pote chased them off in the rubber dinghy. Result: A couple of broken ribs, another million-dollar payoff. Even so, the photograph was published on the front page of *Lecturas*: "The Queen of the South Relaxing in Formentera."

She walked back slowly. Every morning, even on the rare days of wind and rain, she walked down the beach to Linda Vista, alone. On the low rise next to the river she could see the solitary figure of Pote Gálvez, watching over her from a distance. She had forbidden him to accompany her on these walks, so he kept back, watching her go and come. A motionless sentinel, as loyal as a hunting dog uneasily awaiting the return of his owner. Teresa smiled inside. Between her and Pinto, time had forged a tacit complicity, made of past and present. Despite his years in Spain, Pote Gálvez looked like he'd just walked out of a Sinaloa cantina, and the *pistolero*'s strong Sinaloa accent, his clothes, his eternal iguana-skin boots, his Aztec-Mayan features and big black moustache, the way he acted, the way he moved his deceptive two-hundred-plus pounds meant more to Teresa than she was generally willing to admit. Batman Güemes' former hit man was actually her last link to Mexico. Shared nostalgia, which there was no real reason to talk about. Good memories, and bad. Evocative images that would rise up out of a phrase, a gesture, a look. Teresa lent her bodyguard cassettes and CDs of Mexican music: José Alfredo, Chavela, Vicente, Los Tucanes, Los Tigres, even a beautiful tape she had of Lupita D'Alessio—*I'll be your lover or whatever I have to be, I'll be whatever you ask of me*—and often, passing under the window of Pote's room at one end of the house, she would hear the songs, over and over again. Sometimes, when she was in the living room, reading or listening to music, he would pass by and stop a moment—respectful, distant, cocking an ear from the hall or the doorway, his expression unreadable, his eyes almost vacant, which in him was the sign of a smile. They never talked about Culiacán, or the events that had made their paths cross. Or about Gato Fierros, whose remains had been incorporated long before into the foundation of a nice cottage in Nueva Andalucía.

Only once had they spoken about all that, a Christmas Eve on which Teresa had given the staff the night off—a housekeeper, a cook, a gardener, and two Moroccan bodyguards that stood watch over the front entrance and the garden. She herself went into the kitchen and made tortillas, stuffed crab gratinée, and *chilorio*—pork with chiles—and then called Pote in and said, "Have a narco dinner with me, Pinto. *Órale*, it's gonna get cold."

They sat in the dining room, one at each end of the table, with candles lit in the silver candlesticks, and tequila and beer and red wine.

290 ■ Arturo Pérez-Reverte

They were both very quiet, listening to Teresa's music and the other music too, pure Culiacán and heavy shit, which Pote Gálvez got from over there once in a while: Pedro and Inés and their *pinche* gray pickup, El Borrego, El Centenario in the Ram, corridos about Gerardo, the Cessna, Twenty Women in Black. *They know I'm from Sinaloa*—the two of them singing along at this point—*which is why they mess with me.*

And when, to cap the evening, José Alfredo sang "El Caballo Blanco," the corrido about the White Horse (it was the bodyguard's favorite; he bowed his head and nodded to the music), she said, We're so far away from all that, Pinto, and he replied, That's the truth, *patrona,* but it's better to be too far away than too close.

He stared thoughtfully at his plate and then raised his head. "You ever thought about going back, *mi doña?*"

Teresa looked at him so fixedly that the *pistolero* squirmed in his seat and turned away. He opened his mouth, perhaps to apologize, when she smiled, distantly, and raised her glass of wine.

"You know we can't go back," she said.

Pote Gálvez scratched his temple.

"Well, I mean, I thought, I mean I can't, no . . . but you've got money, pull, connections now—you might could do it. . . . I mean, if you wanted to. You could do it."

"And you—what would you do if I went back?"

The bodyguard looked down at his plate again, wrinkling his brow, as though he had never considered that possibility. "Well, I don't know, *patrona,*" he finally said. "Sinaloa is so far away, and going back—that seems like it's even farther, you know? But you . . . you could . . ."

"Forget it." In a cloud of rising cigarette smoke, Teresa shook her head. "I don't want to spend the rest of my life in some fucking bunker in Colonia Chapultepec, looking over my shoulder and jumping every time I see a shadow."

"No . . . But it's a shame, you know. It's not a bad place."

"*Órale.*"

"It's the government, *patrona.* If there wasn't any government, or politicians, or gringos up there north of the Río Bravo, a man could live like a king there. . . . There wouldn't be any need for pot or any of that, no? . . . We'd live on pure tomatoes."

There were also the books. Teresa was still reading, and now even more. As time went on, she grew more convinced that the world and life were easier to understand through a book. Now she had a lot of them, and oak shelves on which she arranged them by size or collection, filling the walls of the library, which opened south, onto the garden. She'd furnished it with comfortable leather armchairs and good lighting, and she would sit there at night or on cold days to read. When it was sunny, she would go outside to one of the lounge chairs by the pool or in the shade of the cabaña—there was a barbecue grill nearby, where Pote Gálvez would cook meat to death on Sunday—and lie for hours, rapt in the pages of a book. She always read two or three at a time: something about history, she was fascinated by the history of Mexico at the time of the conquest, Cortés and all that; a sentimental or detective novel; and another novel, more complicated, one of those that took her a long time to finish and that she sometimes couldn't entirely understand but that always left her with the sensation that something had happened to her inside. She read almost randomly, mixing everything together. She found herself a little bored by a very famous novel somebody had recommended to her, *One Hundred Years of Solitude*—she liked *Pedro Páramo* better—but she found no more delight in the mysteries of Agatha Christie or Sherlock Holmes than in the tough books like *Crime and Punishment, The Red and the Black,* and *Buddenbrooks,* which was the story of a young society girl and her family in Germany at least a hundred years ago, maybe more. She'd also read an old, old book about the Trojan War and the voyages of the warrior Aeneas, where she came upon a phrase that made a great impression on her: *The only salvation of the conquered is to expect no salvation.*

Books. Every time she browsed the full shelves and touched the leatherbound spine of *The Count of Monte Cristo,* Teresa thought about Patty. They talked almost every day, although sometimes several days went by without their seeing each other. How are you, Lieutenant? How's tricks, Mexicana? By now Patty was refusing to take part in any activity directly related to the business. All she did was collect her paycheck and spend it: coke, liquor, girlfriends, trips, clothes. She would go to Paris or Miami or Milan and have a great time, do exactly what she wanted, not a worry in the world. Why should I, she'd say, if you drive this car like God himself. She continued to get into jams, conflicts it was easy enough to resolve with friendships, money, Teo's expertise. But her nose and her health continued to fall apart. More than a gram a day, tachycardia, dental problems. Dark circles around her eyes. She heard strange noises, she slept badly, she'd put on a CD and turn it off within seconds, get in the bathtub or the pool and get out again instantly, seized by an anxiety attack. She was loud, showy, and reckless. She talked too much. And to anybody. And when Teresa, choosing her words very carefully, confronted her with it, Patty would turn on her nastily: "My health and my cunt and my life and my part of the business are my business," she would say. "I don't ask what you do with Teo or how you handle the fucking money."

It had been a lost cause for some time, and Teresa was caught in a conflict that not even the sage advice of Oleg Yasikov—she continued to see her Russian friend occasionally—could find her a way out of. This is going to end badly, Yasikov had said. Yes. The only thing I hope you can do, Tesa, is stand back so you don't get splattered too much. When it happens. And I also hope that it's not you who has to make the decision.

Señor Aljarafe called, *mi señora*. He says the ham you ordered came in."

"Thank you, Pinto."

She walked across the lawn, followed at a distance by the bodyguard. The ham was the last payment made by the Italians—to an account on Grand Cayman via Liechtenstein, with fifteen percent laundered in a bank in Zurich. It was another piece of good news. The air bridge was working regularly, the bombings of bales of drugs with GPS devices— another of Dr. Ramos' technological innovations—were giving excellent results, and a new route opened by the Colombians through Haiti, the Dominican Republic, and Jamaica was making big profits for all concerned. The demand for cocaine base for clandestine laboratories in Europe continued to grow, and thanks to Teo, Transer Naga had just made a good connection for money laundering through the Puerto Rican lottery. Teresa asked herself how long this streak of good luck was going to last.

With Teo, professional relations were optimal, and the other kind— she'd never gone so far as to call them emotional—were perfectly adequate to her needs. He didn't come to her house in Guadalmina; they always met in hotels, almost always during business trips, or in an old house that he had had remodeled on Calle Ancha in Marbella. Neither put more into it than was necessary, neither risked much at all.

14. There's gonna be more hats than heads before I'm done

She'd been right—luck ran in cycles. After a good stretch, the year started off bad and by spring was worse. Bad luck combined with other problems. A Skymaster 337 with two hundred kilos of cocaine aboard went down near Tabernas during a night run, and Karasek, the Polish pilot, died in the crash. That alerted the Spanish authorities, who intensified aerial surveillance. Not long afterward, a general settling of internal scores between the Moroccan traffickers, the army, and the Gendarmerie Royale complicated relations with the people from the Rif. Several rubbers were intercepted in not altogether clear circumstances on one side and the other of the Strait, and Teresa had to go to Morocco to normalize the situation. Colonel Abdelkader Chaib had lost influence after the death of the old king, Hassan II, and establishing secure networks with the new strongmen in the hashish industry took time and a great deal of money.

In Spain, pressure from the courts, which had been inflamed by the press and public opinion, grew stronger: some legendary *amos da far-iña*—cocaine bosses—were taken down in Galicia, and even the powerful Corbeira clan had problems. And in the early spring, a Transer Naga operation ended in disaster when, halfway between the Azores and Cabo San Vicente, the merchantman *Aurelio Carmona* was boarded by Spanish Customs. The ship's hold was full of bobbins of industrial linen thread, in metal casings, but each huge bobbin was lined with sheets of lead and aluminum so that neither X rays nor lasers could detect the five tons of cocaine hidden inside.

"It can't be," said Teresa when she heard the news. "First, I can't believe that they got the information. Second, we've been watching the movements of the *Petrel* for weeks"—the Customs boarding vessel—"and it hasn't moved from its base. That's why we pay a guy inside there."

Dr. Ramos, smoking his pipe as calmly as though he had lost not five tons of cocaine but a tin of pipe tobacco, replied, "That's why the *Petrel* didn't leave port, boss. They left it tied up all quiet and peaceful to lull us, while they went out in secret with their boarding gear and their Zodiacs in a towboat that the merchant marine loaned them. They know we've got a man on the inside, and they're just playing it back on us."

Teresa was uneasy about the *Aurelio Carmona* interception. Not because of the interdiction of the cargo—profits and losses went into their respective columns as in any other business, and the losses were all figured into the overhead—but rather because of the evidence that somebody had fingered the shipment and that Customs had inside information. This is how they bust us wide open, she said to herself. Three possible sources for the tip-off occurred to her: the Galicians, the Colombians, and somebody in her own crew. The rivalry with the Corbeira clan continued, although without any spectacular faceoffs—some elbowing here and there, a foot stuck out to trip one another up, an "I'm keeping an eye on you, motherfucker, nothin' to bring you totally down, but you slip up and it's *adiós,* Mexicana, you know?" Through their suppliers in common, the Corbeiras could make trouble. If it was the Colombians, there wasn't much she could do—not much more than pass on the information and let them clean out their ranks for themselves. Then there was the third possibility, that the information came from within Transer Naga. If that was the case, they had to take some new precautions: box off access to plans—eyes only and need to know, just like the military—and lay a trap with marked information so they could follow the rat's trail, to see

where it led. But that took time. Discover the bird by its fucking drop-
pings.

H ave you thought about Patricia?" asked Teo.
    "Fuck that, *cabrón*. Don't go there."
    They were at La Almoraima, a short distance from Algeciras: a for-
mer monastery set in a forest of thick oak, now a small hotel with a
restaurant specializing in game. Sometimes they went for a couple of
days, taking one of the rustic, gloomy rooms opening onto the cloister.
They'd dined on venison and pears in red wine and were now having a
cigarette with their cognac and tequila. The night was pleasant for the
season, and through the open windows came the sound of crickets and
the murmur of the old fountain.
    "I don't mean she's passing information on to anybody," Teo said.
"Just that she talks too much. And that she's careless. And that she's
running around with people we can't control."
    Teresa looked out—the moonlight sifting down through the leaves
of the grapevines, the whitewashed walls, and the ancient stone arch-
ways: another place that reminded her of Mexico.
    "From that to revealing information about shipments," she replied,
"is a stretch. Besides, who's she going to tell?"
    Teo studied her awhile without speaking. "She doesn't have to tell
anybody in particular," he said finally. "You've seen how she is lately—
she rambles, she goes off on fantasies, she's paranoid and weird. And
she talks all the fucking time. All it takes is the wrong word dropped
here, some compromising information there, and anybody with an
ounce of brains can come to their own conclusions. We're having a
rash of 'coincidences' here, not to mention the judges on our case and
pressure from all over. Even Tomás Pestaña is keeping his distance
lately, just in case. That guy can see trouble coming a mile away, like
those people with arthritis that can tell you when it's going to rain. We
can still manage him, but if there's trouble, or too much pressure and
things go bad, he'll drop us in a heartbeat."
    "He'll hold. We know too much about his business."
    "Knowing isn't always enough." A shrewd, man-of-the-world ex-
pression came to his face. "In the best of cases, it can neutralize him,
but it can't make him stay on board. . . . He has his own problems. Too
many cops and too many judges can scare him. And nobody can buy
every cop and every judge in Spain." He looked at her hard. "Not even
you."

"So you're suggesting that we pick Patty up and beat the shit out of her until she tells us what we want to hear."

"God, no. All I'm saying is that maybe you should cut her out of the loop. She's got what she wants, and we don't have enough manpower to follow up on every skirt she chases."

"I think that was unnecessary."

"But true. There's that one girl that comes and goes like it was her own house. Patricia is out of control." Teo touched his nose meaningfully. "It's been going on for some time. And you've lost control, too. . . . Over her, I mean."

That tone, Teresa said to herself. I don't like that tone. My control is my business.

"She's still my partner," she replied, irritated. "Your boss."

An amused smile crossed the lawyer's face: Was she serious? But he said nothing. Your relationship is curious, he'd once told her. A friendship that no longer exists. And if you owe her, you've paid. . . .

"What she still is, is in love with you," Teo said after a pause, swirling the cognac in the snifter expertly. "That's the real problem."

The words came softly, almost in a whisper, and almost one by one. Don't go there, Teresa silently warned him again. That's none of your business. *Especially* not yours.

"It's strange to hear you say that," she answered. "She introduced you and me. She brought you to me."

Teo frowned. He looked away and then back. He seemed to be thinking, weighing, deciding between two loyalties, or maybe one of them. A loyalty that was now remote, faded. Maybe even expired.

"She and I know each other well," he said at last. "Or we did. Which is why I'm going to say this: From the beginning she knew what was going to happen between me and you. . . . I don't know what there was between you and Patty in El Puerto de Santa María, and I don't care. I've never asked. But whatever it was, she hasn't forgotten."

"And yet," Teresa insisted, "Patty brought you and me together."

Teo inhaled as though he were going to sigh, but he didn't. He looked at his wedding ring on his left hand, which was resting on the table.

"Maybe she knows you better than you think," he said. "Maybe she thought you needed somebody, in several ways. And with me, there were no risks."

"Risks like what?"

"Falling in love with you. Complicating your life." The lawyer's smile made his words seem trivial. "Maybe she saw me as a substitute, not as a rival or adversary. And depending on how you look at it, she was right. You've never let me go too far."

"I'm beginning not to like this conversation."

As though he had just overheard Teresa, Pote Gálvez appeared at the door. He was carrying a cell phone, and was more somber than usual. *Quihubo, Pinto*. The bodyguard looked hesitant, uncomfortable; he stood on first one foot, then the other, and he wouldn't step inside. Respectful. He was sorry to interrupt, *patrona*, he said at last. But it sounded important. Apparently *señora* Patricia was in trouble.

It was more than trouble, Teresa discovered in the emergency room of the Marbella hospital. It was a typical Saturday-night scene: ambulances outside, gurneys, voices, people in the hallways, doctors and nurses rushing about. She and Teo found Patty in the office of a solicitous chief of hospital services: her jacket was draped over her shoulders, her pants had dirt stains on the knees and the outside of the thighs, along her hip, and there was a bruise on her forehead, bloodstains on her hands and blouse. Somebody else's blood. A half-smoked cigarette lay in the ashtray, and another was between her fingers. There were also two uniformed police officers in the hall, the body of a dead young woman on a gurney, and out on the Ronda highway a car, Patty's new Jaguar convertible, wrapped around a tree on a curve with empty bottles on the floorboard and ten grams of cocaine like talcum powder on the seats.

"A party," Patty explained. "We were coming back from a fucking party."

Her tongue was thick and her expression confused, as though she couldn't quite understand what was going on. Teresa knew the dead girl, a young Gypsy-looking woman who had recently been with Patty constantly: eighteen, but with all the vices of an older woman, and as wiped out most of the time as a creature in her fifties—hot to trot and ready to screw anybody for what she wanted. She'd died instantly, when her face smashed into the windshield—her skirt had been up around her thighs and Patty had been fingering her at a hundred and ten miles an hour. One problem more, one problem less, Teo muttered coldly as he exchanged a look of relief with Teresa when they stood over the body, the sheet covering it stained with blood on one side of the head—half her brains, someone said, were on the hood, among the slivered glass.

"Let's look on the bright side, right? . . . We're rid of this little slut," Teo said. "Her snorting and her blackmailing. She was dangerous company, given the circumstances. And as for Patty, speaking of getting somebody out of the way, I wonder how things would have gone if . . ."

"Shut the fuck up," said Teresa, "or I swear you're a dead man."

She was shocked by her own words. She saw herself speaking them, without thinking, spitting them out as they came into her mind: softly, without any reflection or calculation whatsoever.

"I just . . ." Teo started to say.

His smile seemed frozen, and he was looking at Teresa as if seeing her for the first time. Then he looked around disconcertedly, fearing that someone had overheard. He was pale.

"I was just kidding," he finally said.

He was much less attractive like that—humiliated. Or scared. And Teresa didn't answer. He was the least of her concerns. She was concentrating on herself, digging deep, trying to bring up the face of the woman that had spoken in her place.

Fortunately, the police told Teo, Patty hadn't been at the wheel when the car went out of control on the curve, so that took care of the involuntary-homicide charge. The cocaine and the rest could be fixed with a little money, a great deal of tact, some timely telephone calls and visits, and the right judge, as long as the press didn't get wind of it. That last one was the vital detail. Because these things, the lawyer said— sometimes looking at Teresa out of the corner of his eye, pensively— begin with a story buried on page seventeen and wind up on page one. So be careful of that.

Later, when everything at the hospital and morgue had been seen to, Teo had stayed behind, making phone calls and taking care of the police—luckily, this was the municipal police, under Tomás Pestaña, not the Guardia Civil's traffic division—while Pote Gálvez brought the Cherokee around to the door, and Teresa took Patty out very quietly, before anyone could make a call and some reporter started sniffing around. And in the car, leaning on Teresa, the window open so the cool night air might wake her up, Patty started talking.

"I'm sorry," she kept repeating, almost in a whisper, the headlights of oncoming cars lighting her face in flashes. "I'm sorry for her," she said in a thick, muted voice, the words running together. "I'm sorry for that little girl. And I'm sorry for you, too, Mexicana," she added after a silence.

"Well, I don't give a fuck who or what you're sorry for," Teresa replied, fed up and ill humored, looking down the highway over Pote Gálvez' shoulder. "You should feel sorry for your fucking life."

Patty shifted position, leaning her head on the window behind her, and said nothing. Teresa squirmed uncomfortably. *Chale,* for the second time in an hour she'd said things she hadn't intended to say. Besides, she wasn't really irritated, not at Patty, anyway. In the end, it was she, Teresa, who was responsible for all this, or almost all of it. After a while, she took her friend's hand, which was as cold as the body they'd left in the hospital, under the blood-soaked sheet.

"How are you?" Teresa asked softly.

"I'm . . . all right." Patty didn't lift her head from the window. She leaned on Teresa again only when she got out of the SUV.

The minute they got her into bed, still dressed, she fell into an uneasy half-sleep, full of shivering and starts and moans. Teresa sat with her, in an armchair next to the bed, for a long time—the time it took to smoke three cigarettes and drink a big glass of tequila. Thinking. The room was almost dark, the curtains pulled back to reveal a starry sky and tiny, distant lights moving out at sea, beyond the shadows of the garden and the beach. Finally she stood up, to go to her own room, but at the door she thought better of it. She went and lay down on the edge of the bed, beside her friend, very quietly, trying not to wake her, and stayed there for hours. Listening to Patty's tormented breathing. And thinking.

A re you awake, Mexicana?"
"Yes."

After the whispered answer, Patty had moved closer. Their bodies touched.

"I'm sorry."

"It's all right. Go to sleep."

Another silence. It had been an eternity since the two of them had shared a moment like this, Teresa recalled. Almost since prison, in El Puerto de Santa María. Scratch the "almost." She lay motionless, her eyes open, listening to her friend's irregular breathing. Now she, too, couldn't sleep.

"Got a cigarette?" Patty asked after a while.

"Just mine."

"I'll take one."

Teresa got up, went over to the dresser, and took out two Bisontes laced with hashish from her purse. The flame from her lighter illuminated Patty's face, the purple bruise on her forehead. Her lips were dry and swollen, her eyes, with bags under them from fatigue, were fixed on Teresa.

"I thought we could do it, Mexicana."

Teresa lay faceup on the edge of the bed. She picked the ashtray up off the night table and put it on her stomach. Slowly, giving herself time.

"We did," she said at last. "We came a long way."

"That's not what I meant."

"Then I don't know what you're talking about."

Patty stirred beside her, changing positions. She's turned toward me, thought Teresa. She's looking at me in the darkness. Or remembering me.

"I thought I could take it," Patty said. "You and I this way. I thought it would work."

How strange everything was, Teresa meditated. Lieutenant O'Farrell. Herself. How strange and how far away, and how many bodies behind them, on the road. People we accidentally killed while we lived.

"Nobody deceived anybody. Nobody lied to anybody. Nobody twisted anybody's arm." As Teresa talked, she brought the cigarette to her mouth and saw the ember flare briefly between her fingers. "I'm where I always was." She exhaled the smoke after holding it in awhile. "I never tried—"

Patty interrupted. "Do you really think that? That you haven't changed?"

Teresa, irritated, shook her head. "And as for Teo . . ." she started to say.

"Good God!" Patty's laugh was scornful. Teresa felt her moving beside her as though she were shaking with laughter. "Fuck Teo."

There was another silence, this time very long. Then Patty began to talk again, very softly.

"He screws other women. . . . Did you know that?"

Teresa shrugged, inside and outside, knowing that her friend couldn't see or feel the gesture. She didn't know, she concluded. Maybe she'd suspected, but that wasn't the issue. It never had been.

"I never expected anything," Patty went on, her tone pensive, self-absorbed. "Just you and me. Like before."

Teresa suddenly had the urge to be cruel. Because of what Patty had said about Teo.

"The good times back in El Puerto de Santa María, right?" she sneered. "You and your dream. Abbé Faria's treasure."

She had never been sarcastic about that before. Never in this way. Patty didn't say anything.

"You were in that dream, Mexicana," she said at last.

It sounded like justification and reproach. But I'm not getting into that, Teresa told herself. It's not my game, and never was. So fuck it.

"Yeah, well, I didn't ask to be in it," she said. "It was your decision, not mine."

"That's true. And sometimes life comes around and bites you on the ass just by giving you what you want, you know?"

That doesn't apply to me, either, thought Teresa. I didn't want anything. And that's the biggest paradox of my whole *pinche* life. She stubbed out the cigarette and put the ashtray back on the night table.

"I never made the decision," she said aloud. "Never. It came and I stepped up. Period."

"So what happened with me?" asked Patty.

That was the question. Really, Teresa reflected, it all came down to that. "I don't know . . . At some point you dropped out, started drifting away."

"And at some point you turned into an *hija de puta.*"

There was a long pause. They were motionless. If I heard the sound of metal bars, thought Teresa, or the footsteps of a guard in the corridor, I'd think I was in El Puerto. The old nightly ritual of friendship. Edmond Dantès and Abbé Faria making plans for freedom and the future.

"I thought you had everything you needed," Teresa said. "I took care of your business, I made a lot of money for you. . . . I took the risks and did the work. Isn't that enough?"

Patty took a minute to answer. "I was your friend."

"You *are* my friend," Teresa corrected her.

"Was. You didn't stop to look back. And there are things that you never . . ."

"*¡Híjole!* Here's the wounded wife, complaining because her husband works all the time and doesn't think about her as much as he should. . . . Is that where this is going?"

"I never wanted . . ."

Teresa could feel her anger growing. Because it could only be that, she told herself. Patty was wrong, and she, Teresa, was getting pissed. *Pinche* Lieutenant, or whatever she was now, was going to wind up hanging the dead girl tonight around her neck, too. Even that, she had to sign the checks for. Pay the bills.

"God damn you, Patty. This is like some cheap fucking soap opera."

"Sure. I forgot I was talking to the Queen of the South."

She laughed quietly, choppily as she said this. That made it sound all the more cutting, and things were getting no better. Teresa raised up on one elbow. A mute rage was making her temples throb. Headache.

"What exactly the fuck is it that I owe you? . . . Just tell me, for Christ's sake, once and for all. Tell me and I'll pay you."

Patty was a motionless shadow haloed by moonlight shining in obliquely through the window.

"It's not that."

"No?" Teresa leaned closer. She could feel her breathing. "I know what it is. It's what makes you look at me strangely, because you think you gave up too much in exchange for too little. Abbé Faria confessed his secret to the wrong person . . . right?"

Patty's eyes gleamed in the darkness. A soft gleam, the reflection of the silver brightness outside.

"I never reproached you for anything, ever," she said very quietly.

The moonlight in her eyes made them look vulnerable. Or maybe it's not the moon, thought Teresa. Maybe we've both been fooling each other since the beginning. Lieutenant O'Farrell and her legend. She felt the urge to laugh, thinking, How young I was, and how stupid. Then came a wave of tenderness that shook her to the tips of her toes and shocked her—enough to make her half open her mouth. The rancor came next, almost as a relief, a solution, a comfort given her by the other Teresa, who was always around, in mirrors and shadows. She leapt at the support. She needed something to erase those three strange seconds, slay them with a cruelty as hard and definitive as an axe blow. She experienced the absurd impulse to turn toward Patty violently, straddle her, take her by the shoulders and shake her until her teeth rattled, pull off her clothes and say, Well, you're going to collect it all right now, once and for all, so we can finally put this to rest. But she knew not to do that. You couldn't pay back anything that way, and they were now too far apart—they'd followed paths that would never cross again. And in that double clarity, she saw that Patty knew this as well as she did.

"I don't know where I'm headed, either."

Teresa said that. And then she moved closer to the woman who had once been her friend, and embraced her in silence. She felt something shattered and irreparable within. An infinite despair, or grief. As though the girl in the torn photograph had returned and was crying deep down inside her.

"Well, be sure not to find out, Mexicana . . . because you might wind up getting there."

They lay like that, unmoving, in silence, the rest of the night.

Patricia O'Farrell committed suicide three days later, in her house in Marbella. A maid found her in the bathtub naked, up to her chin in the cold water. On the counter and the floor the police found several bottles of sleeping pills and a bottle of whisky. She had burned all her papers, photographs, and personal documents in the fireplace, and she left no note. For Teresa or anyone else. She just departed—like a woman walking quietly out of a room and closing the door behind her softly, so as not to make any noise.

Teresa didn't go to the funeral. She didn't even see the body. The same afternoon Teo Aljarafe called her to tell her what had happened, she went aboard the *Sinaloa,* alone except for the crew and Pote Gálvez, and spent two days at sea, lying on a chaise on the aft deck, staring at the boat's wake, never speaking a word. In all that time she never even read. She stared at the ocean and smoked. From time to time she drank some tequila. And from time to time Pote Gálvez' footsteps were heard on the deck; he prowled, as usual, but kept his distance. He approached her only when it was time for lunch or dinner, saying nothing, bringing a tray and waiting for his boss to shake her head before he disappeared again, or to bring her a jacket when clouds covered the sun, or when the sun set and the night turned cold.

The crew stayed even farther away. Pote had no doubt given instructions, and they were trying to avoid her. The skipper spoke to Teresa only twice: first when she came aboard and ordered him to sail, she didn't care where, until she said to stop, and next when, two days later, she came into the wheelhouse and said, "We're going back." For those forty-eight hours, Teresa didn't think for five minutes at a time about Patty O'Farrell or anything else. Whenever the image of her friend came to her, a wave, a seagull gliding in the distance, the reflection of sunlight off the water, the purring of the engines below, the wind that blew her hair into her face rushed to occupy all the useful space in her mind. The great advantage of the sea was that you could spend hours just looking at it, without thinking. Without remembering, either—or you could throw memories into the boat's wake as easily as they came, let them slide off you without consequences, let them pass like ship's lights in the night.

Teresa had learned that with Santiago Fisterra: it happened only at sea, because the sea was as cruel and selfish as human beings, and in its monstrous simplicity had no notion of complexities like pity, wounding, or remorse. Maybe that was why it was almost analgesic. You could see yourself in it, or justify yourself by it, while the wind, the light, the swaying, the sound of the water on the hull worked the miracle of distancing, calming you until you didn't hurt anymore, erasing any pity, any wound, and any remorse.

Finally the weather changed, the barometer fell five millibars in three hours, and a stiff gale began to blow. The skipper looked at Teresa, who was still sitting back on the aft deck, and then at Pote Gálvez. So Pote went back and said, The weather's turned bad, *mi doña*. You might want to give orders. Teresa looked at him without replying, and the bodyguard returned to the skipper, shrugging. That night, with easterly winds blowing between force 6 and 7, the *Sinaloa* sloshed about with engines at half-throttle, its bow into the wind and seas, spray leaping up over the wheelhouse in the darkness. Teresa stood at the wheel in the reddish light of the binnacle, one hand on the wheel and the other on the throttle lever, with the autopilot disconnected, while the skipper, the sailor on duty, and Pote Gálvez, who was buzzed on Dramamine, watched her from the aft cabin, clinging to their seats and the table, the coffee sloshing out of their cups each time the *Sinaloa* pitched and yawed. Three times Teresa went out and, buffeted by the wind, leaned over the leeward gunwale to throw up, then returned to the wheel without saying a word, her hair wet and tousled, dark circles around her eyes from sleepless nights, and calmly lit a cigarette. She'd never been seasick before. The weather grew calmer around dawn, with less wind and a grayish light that made the ocean look like a sheet of molten lead. It was only then that she gave the order to return to port.

Oleg Yasikov arrived at breakfast time. Blue jeans, dark blazer over a polo shirt, moccasins. Blond and stocky as always, although a little bigger around the waist lately. She greeted him on the rear terrace, beside the pool and the lawn that ran under the weeping willows down to the wall at the beach. It had been almost two months since they'd seen each other, at a dinner during which Teresa had warned him that the European Union was about to close its doors to a Russian bank in Antigua that Yasikov used for transferring funds to Latin America. It had saved him quite a few problems and a great deal of money.

"Long time, Tesa. Yes."

Now it was he who had wanted to see her. A telephone call the previous afternoon. "I don't need to be comforted," she had told him. "It's not that," the Russian answered. "*Nyet.* Just a little bit of business and a little bit of friendship. Yes. The usual."

"Want a drink, Oleg?" she asked him now.

The Russian, who was buttering a piece of toast, stared at the glass of tequila next to Teresa's coffee cup and the ashtray with four butts already in it. She was in a tracksuit, leaning back in a wicker chair, her bare feet on the rustic tile floor.

"Of course not," said Yasikov. "Not at this hour, for God's sake. I'm just a gangster from the extinct Union of Soviet Socialist Republics, not a Mexican with an iron stomach. Yes. Or asbestos, maybe. No. I'm not nearly as macho as you."

They laughed. "I see you can laugh," said Yasikov, surprised.

"And why not?" Teresa didn't flinch from the Russian's blue-eyed gaze. "Anyway, remember that we're not going to talk about Patty."

"I didn't come for that." Yasikov poured himself a cup of coffee, pensively chewed his toast. "There are things I have to tell you. Several."

"Breakfast first."

The day was gloriously sunny, and the water in the pool reflected it back in turquoise blue. It was nice out there on the terrace warmed by the early-morning sun, among the bougainvillea and other flowers, the birds singing. Teresa and Oleg unhurriedly ate their breakfast and chatted about this and that, reviving their old friendship as they always did when they met: small meaningful words and gestures, shared codes. They had come to know each other very well. They knew which words to speak and which not to.

"Let's start with the biggest thing first," Yasikov finally said when breakfast was obviously over. "There's a job for you. A big one. Yes. For my people."

"That means absolutely first priority."

"I like that word 'priority.'"

"You need smack?"

He shook his head.

"Hashish. My bosses have partnered up with the Romanians. They want to supply several markets there. Yes. Immediately. Show the Lebanese that there are alternative suppliers. They need twenty tons. Moroccan. Grade double-A. The best."

Teresa frowned. Twenty thousand kilos was a lot, she said. They would have to get it together first, and the time was not the best for that. With the political changes in Morocco, it still wasn't clear who you could trust and who you couldn't. She had even been keeping a shipment of coke in Agadir for a month and a half, afraid to move it until things got clearer. Yasikov listened attentively, and when she finished he nodded. "I understand. Yes. You decide. . . . But you'd be doing me a big favor. My people need that chocolate within a month. And I've gotten good pay for you. Very good pay."

"Pay is the least of it, Oleg. If the job's for you, the pay doesn't matter."

The Russian smiled and thanked her. Then they went into the house. On the other side of the library with its Oriental rugs and leather armchairs was Teresa's office. Pote Gálvez appeared in the hall, looked at Yasikov without a word, and disappeared again.

"How's your Rottweiler?" the Russian asked.

"He hasn't killed me yet."

Yasikov's laugh filled the room. "Who would ever have thought it," he said. "When I met him."

They went into her office. Every week, the house was swept by an expert in electronic counterespionage sent by Dr. Ramos. Even so, there was nothing compromising in the room: a desk, a personal computer with the hard drive as clean as a whistle, a map cabinet whose drawers held large nautical charts, maps, and other oversize papers, with the latest edition of *Ocean Passages for the World* on top.

"Maybe I can do it," Teresa said. "Twenty tons. Five hundred forty-kilo bundles. Trucks to transport it from the Rif to the coast, a big boat, a massive shipment in Moroccan waters, coordinating the places and times exactly—very exactly." She calculated quickly: twenty-five hundred miles between Alborán and Constanza, on the Black Sea, through the waters of six countries, including the passage through the Aegean, the Dardanelles, and the Bosporus. That would take incredible logistical and tactical precision. A lot of money in upfront expenses. Days and nights of work for Farid Lataquia and Dr. Ramos.

"But only," she concluded, "if you can assure me there'll be no problems unloading it in the Romanian port."

Yasikov nodded. You can count on that, he said. He was studying the Imray M20 chart, the eastern Mediterranean, which was laid out on the desk. He seemed distracted.

"You may want," he said after a minute, "to think hard about who you use to prepare this operation. Yes."

He said this without taking his eyes off the chart, his voice thoughtful-sounding, and then it took him a second or two to raise his eyes. "Yes," he repeated. Teresa got the message. She'd gotten it with his first words. *You may want to think hard* was the signal that something wasn't right. *Think hard . . . who you use to prepare this operation.*

"*Órale*," she said. "Talk to me."

A suspicious blip on the radar screen. The old hollow feeling in the pit of her stomach, that familiar friend, suddenly got hollower.

"There's a judge," said Yasikov. "Martínez Pardo, you know him all too well, I think. He's been on your tail for some time. And on mine. And other people's, too. But he has his preferences. You're one of them—the apple of his eye, you might say. He works with the police, the Guardia Civil, Customs. Yes. And he's beginning to pressure them."

"Tell me what you came to tell me," Teresa said impatiently.

Yasikov, hesitant, observed her. Then he turned his eyes toward the window. "I have people who tell me things," he went on. "I pay and they talk. And the other day I was in Madrid and someone talked to me about that last problem of yours. Yes. That ship they seized."

Yasikov stopped, took a few steps back and forth, tapped his fingers on the chart. He shook his head, as though indicating that what he was about to say had to be taken with a big grain of salt—he didn't know whether it was true or false.

"I feel like it was the Gallegos," Teresa said, to help him get it out.

"No. Or so people say. People say that the leak didn't come from there." He paused again, a long time. "They say it came from Transer Naga."

Teresa was going to open her mouth to say, "Impossible, I've checked it out." But she didn't. Oleg Yasikov would never have come like a kid in a schoolyard, to tell her something he'd heard third- or fourth-hand. So she started putting two and two together, formulating hypotheses, asking herself questions and answering them. Reconstructing chains of events. But the Russian was going for the shortcut.

"Martínez Pardo is pressuring somebody close to you," he said. "In exchange for immunity, money, who knows what. It could be true, or only part true. I don't know. But my source is grade A. Yes. He's never steered me wrong. And considering that Patricia—"

"It's Teo," she suddenly whispered.

Yasikov didn't finish his sentence.

"You knew," he said, surprised. But Teresa shook her head. She was filled with a strange iciness that had nothing to do with her bare feet. She turned away from Yasikov and looked toward the door, as though Teo himself were about to walk in.

"Tell me how the hell," the Russian, behind her, asked. "If you didn't know, why do you know now?"

Teresa still did not speak. She hadn't known, she thought, but it was true that now she did. That's the way this fucking life is, and its fucking little jokes. *Chale.* She concentrated, trying to put her thoughts in some reasonable order of priorities. And it wasn't easy.

"I'm pregnant," she said.

They went down to the beach for a walk, with Pote Gálvez and one of Yasikov's bodyguards following at a distance. Swells were breaking on the pebbles along the shore and wetting Teresa's bare feet. The

water was very cold, but she liked the way it felt on her skin. It made
her feel good—awake. They walked southwest, along the dirty sand
dotted with stretches of rocks and seaweed, toward Sotogrande,
Gibraltar, and the Strait. They would talk for a few steps and then fall
silent, thinking about what they had said or failed to say.

"What are you going to do?" Yasikov asked when he finished digest-
ing the news. "Yes. With both of them—the baby and the father."

"It's not a baby yet," Teresa replied. "It's not anything yet."

Yasikov shook his head as though she had confirmed his thoughts.
"But that's not the solution for Teo," he said. "Just for half the problem."

Teresa turned toward him, pulling her hair out of her eyes. "I didn't
say the first part was solved. I just said it wasn't anything yet. I haven't
made a decision about what it may be, or not."

The Russian studied her face, looking for changes, new signs, more
surprises, in her expression.

"I'm afraid, Tesa. That I can't. Offer you any help there. *Nyet.* It's not
my specialty."

"I'm not asking you for help, or advice, or anything, Oleg. Just that
you walk with me, like always."

"That I can do." Yasikov smiled, like the big blond Russian bear he
was. "Yes. I can do that."

A little fishing skiff was pulled up on the sand, one that Teresa always passed on her walks. Painted blue and white, very old and dilapi-
dated and uncared for. There was rainwater in the bottom, and pieces
of plastic and an empty soda bottle floated in it. A name, barely legible,
was painted on the bow: *Esperanza.*

"Don't you ever get tired, Oleg?"

"Sometimes," he replied. "But it's not easy. No. To say, This is it, this
is as far as I go, I want to get off. I have a wife," he added. "Beautiful.
Miss Saint Petersburg. A four-year-old son. Enough money to live the
rest of my life without a care. Yes. But there are partners. Responsibilities. Commitments. And not everyone would understand that I'm
really retiring. No. They're mistrustful by nature. If you go, you scare
them. You know too much about too many people. And they know too
much about you. You're a threat, and you're out there. Yes."

"What does the word 'vulnerable' make you think of?" Teresa asked.

Yasikov thought a second. "I'm not very good. At this language," he
said. "But I know what you mean. A son makes you vulnerable. . . .

"I swear to you, Tesa, that I've never been afraid. Of anything. Not
even in Afghanistan. No. Those fanatics, those crazy people and their
*Allah akbar*s that would turn your blood to ice. Well, no. I wasn't afraid

when I was starting, either. In the business. But since my son was born I know what it feels like. To be afraid. Yes. When something goes wrong, it's not possible anymore. No. To leave everything and just walk away. Run."

He had stopped and was gazing out at the ocean, the clouds gliding slowly toward the west. He sighed.

"It's good to run," he said. "When you have to. You know that better than anybody. Yes. That's all you've done your whole life. Run. Whether you wanted to or not."

He went on looking at the clouds. He raised his arms shoulder-high, as though to embrace the Mediterranean, and dropped them, impotently. Then he turned back to Teresa.

"Are you going to have it?"

She looked at him without responding. The sound of the water, the feel of the cold sea-froth on her feet. Yasikov looked at her fixedly, from his height. Teresa felt much smaller next to the huge Slav.

"What was your childhood like, Oleg?"

The Russian rubbed the back of his neck, surprised. Uncomfortable.

"I don't know," he said. "Like all childhoods in the Soviet Union. Neither bad nor good. The Pioneers, school. Yes. Karl Marx. The Soyuz. Fucking American imperialism. All that. Too much boiled cabbage, I think. And potatoes. Too many potatoes."

"I knew what it was to be hungry. All the time," said Teresa. "I had one pair of shoes, and my mother wouldn't let me put them on except to go to school, while I still went."

A wry smile came to her lips. "My mother," she repeated absent-mindedly. An old, mellow anger rose in her.

"She beat on me a lot when I was little. She was an alcoholic, and she turned into a kind of part-time whore when my father left her. She'd make me go out and get beers for her friends. She'd drag me around by my hair, and she'd kick me and hit me. She'd come in late at night with that nasty flock of crows of hers, laughing obscenely, or somebody would come to the door drunk looking for her. . . . I stopped being a virgin long before I lost my virginity to a bunch of boys, some of whom were younger than I was."

She fell silent, and remained quiet a good while, her hair blowing into her face. Slowly she felt the anger in her blood drain away. She took three or four deep breaths, to flush it out completely.

"I suppose Teo is the father," Yasikov said.

She held his gaze impassively. Wordlessly.

"That's the second part," the Russian whispered. "Of the problem."

He walked on without looking to see whether Teresa was following him. She stood, watching him move away, and then followed.

"I learned one thing in the army, Tesa," Yasikov said thoughtfully. "Enemy territory. Dangerous leaving pockets of the enemy behind you. Resistance. Hostile groups. Consolidating your gains requires that you eliminate points of potential attack. Yes. Points of potential attack. The phrase is used in all the books on warfare. My friend Sergeant Skobeltsin repeated it often. Yes. Every day. Before he got his throat cut in the Panshir Valley."

He had stopped walking and was regarding her again. This is as far as I can go, his eyes said. The rest is up to you.

"I'm beginning to be all alone, Oleg."

She stood quietly before him, and the fingers of surf pulled the sand out from under her feet each time they rolled up and pulled back. The Russian smiled a friendly, somewhat distant smile. Sad.

"How strange to hear you say that. I thought you'd always been alone."

15. Friends I have where I come from, people who say they love me

Judge Martínez Pardo was not a friendly sort of guy. I talked to him during the last days of my information gathering: twenty minutes of not particularly pleasant conversation in his office in the national court building. He only grudgingly agreed to see me, and only after I sent him a thick report on the state of my research thus far. His name was in it, naturally. Along with many other things. The usual choice was to take part comfortably, or stay out. He decided to take part, with his own version of the events. "Come and we'll talk," he said at last, when he came on the phone. So I went to the court building, he coolly shook my hand, and we sat down to talk, facing each other across his desk, with the flag and a portrait of the king on the wall.

Martínez Pardo was short, chunky, with a gray beard that didn't quite cover the scar on his left cheek. He was far from being one of those stars of the judiciary who appear on television and in the newspapers. Gray and efficient, people said. And bitter—an angry man. The scar dated back to a time when Colombian hit men hired by Gallego narcos had come after him. Maybe that was what had soured his temper.

We began by talking about the situation of Teresa Mendoza. What had taken her to where she was now, and the turn her life was going to take in the next few weeks, if she could manage to stay alive.

"I don't know anything about that," Martínez Pardo said. "I don't have a crystal ball for people's future, except when I'm given the opportunity to sentence them to thirty years. My job is to look into their past. Events. Crimes. And crimes, Teresa Mendoza has committed more than her share."

"You must feel frustrated, then," I ventured. "So much work for nothing."

It was my way of repaying the warmth of his manner with me, I suppose. He looked at me over the top of his glasses, as though deciding whether to hold me in contempt of court. Gray, efficient judges have sore spots, too, I told myself. Their personal vanity. Their frustrations. You've got her but you haven't got her. She slipped through your fingers, back to Sinaloa.

"How long were you after her?"

"Four years. A long time. It wasn't easy to gather the evidence we needed to prove that she was implicated in the drug traffic. Her infrastructure was very good. Very intelligent. It was full of security mechanisms, blind alleys. You'd take something apart and come to a dead end. Impossible to prove the connections up the ladder."

"But you did it."

"Only in part. We needed more time, more freedom to work. But we didn't have it. These people move in certain circles—including politics. Including my circle—judges. That allowed Teresa Mendoza to see things coming, and stop them cold. Or minimize the consequences. In this case in particular," he added, "it was all right. My assistants were all right. We were about to crown a long, patient effort with an important takedown. Four years getting the spiderweb all in place. And suddenly, it all went poof."

"Is it true that it was the Ministry of Justice itself that stopped the investigation?"

"No comment." He had leaned back in his chair and was staring at me with what seemed like annoyance.

"They say that it was under pressure from the Mexican embassy that the minister himself pressured you."

He raised a hand. An unpleasant gesture. An authoritarian hand, that of a judge who hasn't stopped being a judge just because his robes are off. "If you continue down that road," he said, "this conversation is over. Nobody has pressured me, ever."

"Explain to me, then, why in the end you didn't do anything to Teresa Mendoza."

He thought about my question a moment, perhaps to determine whether the form of the question—*Explain to me, then*—was enough to hold me in contempt. Finally he decided to let it go. *In dubio pro reo.* Or whatever.

"As I said, I didn't have enough time to put all the evidence together."

"Despite Teo Aljarafe?"

He looked at me again, like before. He didn't like me *or* my questions, and that one hadn't helped the situation. "Everything having to do with that name is confidential," he said.

I allowed myself a small smile. Come on, Judge. At this late date?

"Can't make much difference anymore," I said. "I'd imagine."

"It does to me."

I meditated on that a few seconds.

"I'll make you a deal," I said at last. "I'll leave the Ministry of Justice out of this, and you tell me about Aljarafe." I replaced the small smile with a gesture of friendly solicitude while he considered it.

"All right," he said. "But there are some details I can't reveal."

"Is it true that you offered him immunity in exchange for information?"

"No comment."

Bad start, I told myself. I nodded thoughtfully a couple of times before rejoining the fray:

"People assure me that you pursued Aljarafe relentlessly for a long time. That you had a hefty dossier on him and that you brought him in and showed it to him. And that there was no drug trafficking in it. That you got him from the money side. Taxes, money laundering, that sort of thing."

"That's possible."

He was regarding me impassively. You ask, I confirm. And don't ask for much more than that.

"Transer Naga."

"No."

"Be nice, Judge. I'm a good boy—answer a few of my questions, huh?"

Again he considered it for a few seconds. After all, he must have been thinking, I'm in this. This point is more or less common knowledge, and it's over.

"I admit," he said, "that the business dealings of Teresa Mendoza were always impervious to our efforts to penetrate them, despite the fact that we knew that more than seventy percent of the drug traffic in the Mediterranean came in through her. . . . Señor Aljarafe's weak spot was his private wealth. Irregular investments, movements of money. Personal accounts abroad. His name appeared on a couple of murky foreign transactions. There was material to work with there."

"They say he had properties in Miami."

"Yes. We learned there was a nine-thousand-square-foot house in Coral Gables, with coconut palms and its own dock, and a luxury apartment in Coco Plum, a neighborhood of lawyers, bankers, and stockbrokers. All, apparently, without the knowledge of Teresa Mendoza."

"A piggy bank. For a rainy day."

"You might say that."

"And you got him by the balls. And you scared him."

He leaned back in his chair again. *Dura lex, sed lex.* "I don't like that language," he told me.

I'm beginning not to like this whole interview, I thought. This holier-than-thou bullshit.

"Translate it as you see fit, then."

"He decided to collaborate with Justice. It was that simple."

"In exchange for . . . ?"

"In exchange for nothing."

I could only stare. Yeah, right. I believe that. Teo Aljarafe putting his neck in the noose for nothing. Yeah, right.

"And how did Teresa Mendoza react when she learned that her financial wizard was working for the enemy?"

"You know that as well as I do."

"Yes, I suppose I do. I know what everybody else knows, anyway. And also that she used him as a decoy in the Russian hashish operation. . . . But I wasn't referring to that."

My comment about the Russian hashish operation made things worse. Don't get smart with me, son, his expression said.

"Then," he suggested, "ask her, if you can."

"Maybe I can."

"I doubt that Teresa Mendoza gives interviews. Much less in her current situation."

I decided to make one last try.

"How do you see that situation?"

"I'm out of it," he replied, poker-faced. "I neither see nor don't see. Teresa Mendoza is no longer my concern."

Then he fell silent, distractedly leafing through some documents on his desk, and I thought that he'd ended our conversation. I know better ways to waste my time, I decided. I was getting to my feet, irritated, ready to take my leave of the judge. But not even a disciplined officer of the state like Judge Martínez Pardo could avoid the sting of certain wounds. Or avoid justifying himself. He remained seated, not raising his eyes from the documents. And then, suddenly, he repaid my time.

"It stopped being my concern after the visit of that American," he added bitterly. "The one from the DEA."

D r. Ramos, who had a peculiar sense of humor, had given the oper- ation to move twenty tons of hashish through the Mediterranean to the Black Sea the code name Tender Childhood. The few people who knew about it had spent two weeks planning with almost military precision, and that morning, they had learned from Farid Lataquia, who had closed up his cell phone with a satisfied smile after talking a few minutes in code, that he had found the perfect boat to serve as the shuttle for the merchandise. It was in the port of Al Hoceima, and it was an old, rundown ninety-foot fishing boat, renamed *Tarfaya,* that belonged to a Hispano-Moroccan fishing corporation.

Dr. Ramos, for his part, was coordinating the movements of the *Xoloitzcuintle,* a container ship sailing under the German flag with a crew of Poles and Filipinos; it made a regular run between the Atlantic coast of South America and the eastern Mediterranean, and at the moment was somewhere between Recife and Veracruz. Tender Childhood had a second front, or parallel track, in which a third boat, this time a cargo ship with a standard route—nonstop—between Cartagena and the Greek port of Piraeus, played a major role. This ship was the *Luz Angelita,* and although it was registered in the Colombian port of Tumaco, it sailed under the Cambodian flag for a Cypriot corporation. While the *Tarfaya* and the *Xoloitzcuintle* would handle the most delicate part of the operation, the role assigned the *Luz Angelita* was simple, profitable, and risk-free: It was going to be a decoy.

"Everything set to go, then"—Dr. Ramos nodded—"in ten days."

He took the pipe out of his mouth to stifle a yawn. It was almost eleven a.m., after a long night of work in the office in Sotogrande: a house, protected by the most modern security and electronic counter-surveillance equipment, that two years ago had replaced the apartment in the port area. Pote Gálvez stood guard in the vestibule while two other security men patrolled the lawn. In the living room were a television, a portable computer and printer, two cell phones with scramblers, a white board on an easel with erasable markers, and a large conference table, now littered with dirty coffee cups and full ashtrays. Teresa had just opened a window to air the place out. Her telecommunications expert was there, along with Farid Lataquia and Dr. Ramos. The young man was named Alberto Rizocarpaso, and he was from Gibraltar. This was what Dr. Ramos called the "crisis cabinet": the small group that constituted Transer Naga's general staff for operations.

"The *Tarfaya*," Lataquia was saying, "will wait in Al Hoceima, cleaning out its holds. Tune-up and gas. Harmless. Nice and quiet. We won't take her out until two days before the appointment."

"Good," said Teresa. "I don't want it out there for a week sailing in circles, calling attention to itself."

"Not to worry. I'll see to that myself."

"Crew?"

"All Moroccan. Skipper, Cherki. Ahmed Chakor's people, like always."

"Ahmed Chakor's not always to be trusted."

"Depends on what you pay him." Lataquia smiled. Depends on what you pay me, too, his smile said. "This time we're taking no chances."

Which means you're pocketing a little extra commission for yourself this time, too, Teresa said to herself. Fishing boat plus cargo ship plus Chakor's people equals a shitload of cash. She saw that Lataquia was smiling even more broadly, guessing what she was thinking. At least this *hijo de la chingada* doesn't hide it, she thought. It's all out in the open with him. And he always knows where the line is.

She turned to Dr. Ramos. "What about the rubbers? How many units for the transfer?"

The doctor had spread British Admiralty Chart 773 out on the table, the Moroccan coast from Ceuta to Melilla in precise detail. With the mouthpiece of his pipe he indicated a point three miles to the north, between the Vélez de la Goma rock and the Xauen bank.

"There are six available," he said. "For two runs of seventeen hundred kilos each, more or less. . . . With the fishing boat moving along this line, here, everything can be done in less than three hours. Five, if the seas are high. The cargo is ready in Bab Berret and Ketama. The loading points will be Rocas Negras, Cala Traidores, and the mouth of the Mestaxa."

"Why spread it out so much? . . . Isn't it better to do it all at once?"

Dr. Ramos looked at her, his expression grave. From another person the question would have offended him, but from Teresa it was normal. She was a micromanager, no doubt about that. Down to the last detail. It was good for her and good for everybody else, because the responsibility for the successes and failures was always shared, and no one had to give too many explanations later if something went wrong.

"Ball-bustingly meticulous," was how Lataquia put it, in his graphic Mediterranean style. Never to her face, of course. But Teresa knew. She knew everything about everybody on her team. Suddenly she found herself thinking about Teo Aljarafe. Pending, but to be solved in the next few days, too. She corrected herself: She knew *almost* everything about *almost* all of them.

"Twenty thousand kilos on one beach is a lot of kilos," the doctor explained, "even with the Moroccan cops in our pocket. . . . I prefer not to have that high a profile. So we've presented it to the Moroccans as three different operations. The idea is to load half the cargo at point one with the six rubbers at the same time, a quarter of it at point two with just three rubbers, and the other quarter at point three with the other three. . . . That way we cut the exposure, cut the risk, and nobody will have to go back to the same place for a refill."

"And what's the weather looking like?"

"At this time of year it can't be very bad. We have a three-day window, and the last night there's almost no moon. We might have some fog, and that could complicate the link-ups. But each rubber will carry a GPS, and the fishing boat will have one, too."

"Communications?"

"The usual: cloned cell phones or scramblers for the rubbers and the fishing boat, the Internet on the big boat . . . STU walkie-talkies for the transfer itself."

"I want Alberto out there, with all his equipment."

Rizocarpaso, the communications engineer, nodded. He was blond, with a baby face, almost no beard. Introverted. Very good at what he did. His shirts and pants were always wrinkled from the hours he spent with a radio receiver or at a computer keyboard. Teresa had hired him because he knew how to camouflage contacts and operations through the Internet, routing everything through the cover of countries that European and American police didn't have access to: Cuba, India, Libya, Iraq. In minutes he could open, use, and leave dormant several electronic addresses hidden behind local servers in those and other countries, using credit card numbers stolen or purchased through straw men. He was also an expert in steganography—the technique of hiding messages within apparently innocuous electronic documents—and the PGP encryption system.

"What boat?" the doctor asked.

"Any one—a sport boat. Discreet. The Fairline Squadron we have in Banús might work." Teresa pointed out a broad region on the nautical chart, east of Alborán, to the engineer. "You'll coordinate communications from here."

He gave a stoic smile. Lataquia and the doctor grinned at him mockingly; everyone knew he got deathly seasick on a boat, but Teresa no doubt had her reasons for ordering him to go.

"Where does the link-up with the *Xoloitzcuintle* take place?" Rizocarpaso wanted to know. "There are spots where there's almost no signal."

"You'll know in good time. And if there's no signal, we'll use the radio and cover ourselves with fishing channels. Change frequencies on code phrases, between a hundred and twenty and a hundred and forty megahertz. Make a list."

One of the telephones rang. The secretary in the office in Marbella had received a message from the Mexican embassy in Madrid. They were requesting that Señora Mendoza meet with a high-ranking official to discuss an urgent matter. "How urgent?" Teresa asked.

"They didn't say," the secretary replied. "But the official is already here. Middle-aged, well dressed. Very elegant. His card says Héctor Tapia, chargé d'affaires. He's been sitting in the waiting room for fifteen minutes. And another gentleman is with him."

Thank you for meeting with us, *señora.*"

She knew Héctor Tapia. She'd met him, superficially, several years earlier, during her dealings with the Mexican embassy when he helped cut through the paperwork for her dual nationality. A brief interview in an office in the Carrera Building, in San Jerónimo. A few more or less cordial words exchanged, some documents signed, a cigarette, a cup of coffee, a trivial conversation. She remembered him as extremely polite, quiet, businesslike. Despite knowing everything about her life—or perhaps because of it—he had been very helpful, keeping the red tape to a minimum. In some twelve years, he had been the only direct contact Teresa had had with official spheres in Mexico.

"Allow me to introduce Guillermo Rangel. He is from America."

Tapia seemed uncomfortable in the little conference room paneled in dark walnut, like a man not certain he's in the right place. The gringo, however, seemed right at home. He looked out the window at the magnolias on the lawn, inspected the antique English wall clock, the leather on the chairs, the valuable Diego Rivera drawing—*Notes for a Portrait of Emiliano Zapata*—on the wall.

"I'm actually of Mexican descent, like you," he said, still studying the portrait of the moustached Zapata. "Born in Austin, Texas. My mother was a Chicana."

His Spanish was perfect, with a slight norteño accent, Teresa noted. Many years of practice. Dark hair, brush-cut, the shoulders of a wrestler. White polo shirt under the light jacket. Dark, quick, intelligent eyes.

"Señor Rangel," said Héctor Tapia, "has certain information he would like to share with you."

Teresa motioned for them to take a seat in the armchairs arranged around a large hammered-copper Arabian tray table, and then sat down herself, placing a pack of Bisontes and her lighter on the table. She'd had time to fix herself up: hair pulled back into a ponytail with a silver clasp, dark silk blouse, black jeans, moccasins, suede jacket over the back of the chair.

"I'm not sure I'm interested in this information," she said.

The diplomat's silver hair, tie, and well-cut suit contrasted with the appearance of the gringo. Tapia had taken off his steel-framed glasses and was studying them, his brow furrowed in concentration, as though unhappy with the state of the lenses.

"I think in this particular information you will be," he said, putting on his glasses and looking at her persuasively. "Don Guillermo . . ."

The other man raised a large, meaty hand. "Willy. You can call me Willy. Everybody does."

"All right. Well, Willy here works for the government of the United States."

"For the DEA," the gringo said.

Teresa was taking a cigarette out of the pack. She continued to do so, showing no emotion.

"Sorry? . . . For who?"

She put the cigarette between her lips and reached for the lighter, but Tapia leaned over the table attentively—a click, and the flame was there.

"D-E-A," Willy Rangel repeated, pronouncing the letters slowly. "The Drug Enforcement Administration. My country's antidrug agency."

"*Híjole.* You don't say." Teresa exhaled the smoke, examined the gringo. ". . . This is kind of off the beaten track for you, isn't it? I didn't know your agency had interests in Marbella."

"You live here."

"And what do I have to do with anything?"

The two men contemplated her wordlessly, then looked at each other. Tapia raised one eyebrow. It's your case, friend, he seemed to be saying. I'm just here to watch.

"Let's understand one another, *señora*," said Willy Rangel. "I'm not here looking into anything that has to do with your current method of earning a living. Nor is don Héctor, who was kind enough to accompany me. My visit has to do with things that happened a long time ago. . . ."

"Twelve years ago," Héctor Tapia put in, as though from a distance. Or outside.

". . . And with other things that are about to happen. In Mexico."

"Mexico, you say."

"Mexico."

Teresa looked at the cigarette. I'm not going to finish it, the gesture said. Tapia understood perfectly; he gave the other man an uneasy look. *Órale,* we've lost her, he announced silently. Rangel seemed to be of the same opinion. So he went straight to the point.

"Does the name César Güemes mean anything to you—'Batman' Güemes?"

Three seconds of silence, two pairs of eyes waiting for her. She blew the cigarette smoke out as slowly as she could.

"Well, you know, I don't think it does."

The two pairs of eyes met. Then turned back to her.

"Nevertheless," said Rangel, "you knew him, several years ago."

"How strange. Then I should remember him, shouldn't I?" She looked at the wall clock, searching for a polite way to stand up and end this. "And now if you'll excuse me . . ."

The two men looked at each other again. Then Rangel smiled. He did it brazenly, almost a grin—he was a charmer, no doubt about it. In his business, Teresa thought, somebody who smiles that way has to reserve the effect for big occasions.

"Give me just five minutes more," he said. "To tell you a story."

"I only like stories with great endings."

"The end of this one depends on you."

And then Guillermo Rangel, whom everybody called Willy, started telling the story. The DEA, he explained, was not a special-operations unit. What they did, rather, was compile information, maintain a network of informers, pay them, produce detailed reports on activities related to the production, trafficking, and distribution of drugs, put names on all the players, and structure a case that could be taken to a judge. Which was why they used agents. Like him. People who infiltrated drug organizations and worked inside. Rangel himself had worked like that, first undercover in Chicano groups in California and then in Mexico, as a handler of undercover agents, for eight years, minus a period of fourteen months when he'd been sent to Medellín as the liaison between his agency and the local police search unit in charge of capturing and killing Pablo Escobar. And by the way, that famous photograph of the dead narco, surrounded by the men who'd killed him in Los Olivos, had been taken by Rangel. Now it was framed and hanging on the wall of his office, in Washington, D.C.

"I don't see how any of this can be of interest to me," said Teresa.

She put out her cigarette in the ashtray, unhurriedly, but determined to end this conversation. It wasn't the first time that cops, agents, or drug traffickers had come to her with stories. She didn't feel like wasting her time.

"I'm telling you all this," the gringo said simply, "as background, so you'll understand my work."

"I understand just fine. And now if you'll excuse me . . ."

She stood up. Héctor Tapia also stood up, reflexively, buttoning his jacket. He looked at Rangel, disconcerted and uneasy. But Rangel remained seated.

"Güero Dávila was a DEA agent," he said simply. "He worked for me, and that's why he was killed."

Teresa studied the gringo's intelligent eyes, which were waiting to see the effect his words made. So—you finally got to the punch line, she thought. Well, fuck you, unless you've got another bullet in that pistol. She felt like bursting out laughing. A peal of laughter stifled for almost twelve years, since Culiacán, Sinaloa. *Pinche* Güero's posthumous little joke. But all she did was shrug.

"Now," she said coolly, "tell me something I didn't know."

Don't even look at it," Güero Dávila had told her. "Don't even open it, *prietita*. Take it to don Epifanio Vargas and trade it for your life." But that afternoon in Culiacán, Teresa couldn't resist the temptation. Despite what Güero believed, she could think for herself—and feel. And she was curious—maybe the word was "dying"—to know what kind of hell she'd just been dropped into.

That was why, moments before Gato Fierros and Pote Gálvez appeared at the apartment near the Garmendia market, she broke the rules—turning the pages of the black leather notebook that held the keys to what had happened and what was about to happen. Names, addresses. Contacts on both sides of the border. She had time to grasp the reality before the shit hit the fan and she found herself running down the street holding the Double Eagle, alone and terrified, knowing exactly what she was trying to run away from. It was summed up very well that same night by don Epifanio Vargas himself. "Your man," he had said, "liked his little jokes too much. Liked to play around." The wagers he placed on his own cleverness had even included her.

Teresa knew all this when she went to the Malverde Chapel with the notebook she should never have read, cursing Güero for the way he'd put her in danger just to save her. A typical twisted fucking Güero way to deal with the situation. If they burn me, the *pinche* fucking *hijo de la pinche madre* had thought, there's no way out for Teresa. Innocent or not, those are the rules. But there was a remote possibility: show that she was really acting in good faith. Because Teresa would never have turned the notebook over to anybody if she'd known what was inside. Never, had she been aware of the dangerous game being played by the man who had filled those pages with deadly notes. By taking it to don Epifanio, godfather to her and to Güero himself, she showed her ignorance. Her innocence. She'd never have dared, otherwise.

And that afternoon, sitting on the bed in the apartment, turning the pages that were simultaneously her death sentence and her only possible salvation, Teresa cursed Güero because she finally understood it all. Taking off, just running, was condemning herself to death within a few miles. She had to take the notebook to don Epifanio, to show that she didn't know what was in it. She had to swallow the fear that was wringing her belly into knots, keep her head, give her voice just the right amount of anguish, just the right degree of pleading with the man Güero and she had trusted. The narco's *morra*, the scared little rabbit. *I don't know anything. You tell me, don Epifanio, why would I read that.* That was why she was still alive today. And why now, in the conference room of her office in Marbella, DEA agent Willy Rangel and chargé d'affaires Héctor Tapia were staring at her with their mouths open, one sitting, the other standing and with his fingers still at his jacket buttons.

"You've known all this time?" the gringo asked, incredulous.

"Twelve years."

Tapia dropped back into the chair. "*Cristo bendito,*" he murmured.

Twelve years, Teresa told herself. Surviving with and because of a secret about the people who killed Güero. Because that last night in Culiacán, in the Malverde Chapel, in the stifling atmosphere of heat and humidity and smoke from the altar candles, she had played the game laid out for her by her dead lover—she'd had almost no hope, and yet she'd won. Neither her voice nor her nerves nor her fear had betrayed her. Because he was a good man, don Epifanio. And he loved her. He loved both of them, despite realizing from the notebook—maybe he knew before, or maybe not—that Raimundo Dávila Parra, aka Güero, had been working for the American antidrug agency, and that that was almost certainly why Batman Güemes had dropped him. And so Teresa had been able to fool them all, gambling on this crazy game, walking the knife-edge, just as Güero had foreseen. She doesn't know anything. No way. How could she bring me the *pinche* notebook if she did? So let her go. *Órale.* It was one chance in a hundred, but it was enough to save her.

Willy Rangel was now observing Teresa very attentively, and with a respect that hadn't been there before.

"In that case," he said, "I'd ask you to take a seat again and listen to what I have to say, *señora.* Now you need to more than before."

Teresa hesitated, but the gringo's words had convinced her. She looked to one side and then the other, and then at the time, feigning impatience. "Ten minutes," she said. "And not one minute more."

She sat down again and lit another Bisonte. Tapia, now back in his chair, was still so stunned that it took him a moment before he even registered that a lady was lighting her own cigarette, so by the time he held out the lighter to her, murmuring apologies, it was too late.

Then the DEA man told the real story of Güero Dávila.

R aimundo Dávila Parra was from San Antonio, Texas. Chicano. After having worked from a very young age on the illegal side of the drug trade, bringing small amounts of marijuana over the border from Mexico, he was recruited by the DEA when he was arrested in San Diego with five keys of weed. He had talent, and he was an adrenaline junkie—he liked taking risks, feeling the rush. But he was cool, despite his outgoing appearance, and he was brave. After a period of training when he was supposedly in prison in northern California—part of the time he was, in order to make his cover look good—Güero was sent to Sinaloa, and his mission was to infiltrate the transportation networks of the Juárez cartel, where he had some old friends.

He liked the work. He also liked to fly, and he'd taken flying lessons as part of his training with the DEA, although as cover he took more lessons in Culiacán. For several years he infiltrated more and more deeply into the drug-trafficking world, using his job with Norteña de Aviación first as a right-hand man for Epifanio Vargas, with whom he worked in the big airbus operations led by the Lord of the Skies, and then as a pilot for Batman Güemes. Willy Rangel had been his handler. They never communicated by telephone except in cases of emergency.

They would meet once a month in discreet hotels in Mazatlán and Los Mochis. And all the valuable information that the DEA got on the Juárez cartel during that period, including descriptions of the fierce power struggles the Mexican narcos waged to gain independence from the Colombian cartels, came from the same source. Güero was worth his weight in coke.

Then his narco friends killed him. The formal pretext was true enough: Seeking that little extra thrill, Güero took advantage of his drug runs for the Sinaloans to transport his own stuff. He liked to live dangerously, and he brought his cousin Chino Parra into it. The DEA knew, more or less, what Güero was up to, but he was a valuable agent, so they looked the other way. The narcos, however, decided not to. For some time, Rangel had wondered whether it was because of Güero's back-door transports or because somebody broke his cover.

It took him three years to find out. A Cuban arrested in Miami who'd been working for people in Sinaloa turned state's evidence in exchange for a slot in the Witness Protection Program, and he filled eighteen hours of audiotape with his revelations. He told his interrogators that Güero Dávila had been murdered because somebody found out he was working for the feds. A stupid error: a U.S. Customs agent in El Paso somehow got access to a confidential report—no names, but the circumstances were pretty clear—and sold it to the narcos for $80,000. The narcos put two and two together, followed the trail, and at the end of it found Güero.

"The story about the drugs in the Cessna," Rangel concluded, "was a pretext. They were after *him*. What's strange is that the people that took him out didn't know he was working for us."

He fell silent.

"How can you be sure?"

The gringo nodded. Professional. "Ever since the murder of Agent Camarena, the narcos have known that we never forgive the murder of one of our men. That we don't give up until the people responsible die or are in prison. An eye for an eye. It's a rule, and if there's one thing they understand, it's rules."

There was a new coldness in his voice. We're bad to have as enemies, it said. We're nasty. And we've got all the money and all the persistence in the world.

"But they killed Güero as dead as you can get."

"Right." Rangel nodded again. "Which is why I say that whoever gave the direct order to lay the trap in the Espinazo del Diablo didn't know he was an agent. . . . You may have heard the name, although a few minutes ago you denied it: César 'Batman' Güemes."

"I don't recall it."

"No, of course not. Even so, I can assure you that he was just follow-ing orders. 'That dude is running his own stuff,' somebody told him. 'We need to take him out, make an example of him.' We know that Bat-man Güemes resisted—they had to beg him. Apparently, he liked Güero Dávila. . . . But in Sinaloa, commitments are commitments."

"And who, according to you, put the bug in Batman's ear and in-sisted that Güero get taken out?"

Rangel, smiling crookedly, rubbed his nose, turned to Tapia, and then back to Teresa. He was sitting on the edge of his chair, his hands on his knees. He didn't look like such a charmer anymore. Now he looked like a pissed-off hunting dog with a good memory.

"Another man I'm sure you've never heard of . . . Sinaloa's represen-tative to the House of Deputies, and future senator, Epifanio Vargas."

Teresa leaned against the wall and looked at the few customers that were in the Olde Rock at this hour. She could often think things through better when she was among strangers, watching, instead of be-ing alone with the other woman who was always hanging around, no matter where Teresa was. On the way back to Guadalmina she'd told Pote Gálvez to drive to Gibraltar, and after crossing the line she di-rected the bodyguard through the narrow streets until they came to the white façade of the English bar she used to go to—in another life—with Santiago Fisterra.

Pote Gálvez parked the Cherokee, and she went in. Everything was the same: the beams on the ceiling, the walls covered with historical en-gravings, naval souvenirs, and photographs of ships. At the bar, she or-dered a Foster's, the beer she'd always drunk with Santiago when they came here, and without tasting it she went to sit at the same table as al-ways, next to the door, under the engraving of the death of the English admiral—now she knew who this Nelson was and how he'd gotten his at Trafalgar. The other Teresa Mendoza was hanging back, studying her from a distance. Waiting for conclusions, for a reaction to everything she'd just been told, which had finally filled out the general picture the other woman had been explaining to her, and also cleared up the events back in Sinaloa that had led her to this place in her life. She now knew much more than she thought she knew, and she needed to sit and think.

It's been a pleasure, she'd said—*exactly* what she'd said when the man from the DEA and the man from the embassy finished telling her what they'd come to tell her and sat there watching her, waiting for a reaction. You two are crazy, it's been a pleasure, *adiós.* They left disappointed. Maybe they had expected comments, promises. Commitments. But her inexpressive face, her indifferent manner, left them little hope. No way. "She just told us to fuck ourselves," she heard Héctor Tapia say under his breath, so that she wouldn't hear, as they were leaving. Despite his perfect manners, the diplomat had that defeated look about him.

"Think about it carefully," the DEA man had said. His words of farewell.

"The problem," she said as she was closing the door behind them, "is that I don't see what there is to think about. Sinaloa is a long, long way away. *Adiós.*"

But she was sitting there now, in the bar in Gibraltar, thinking. Remembering point by point, putting everything Willy Rangel had told her in order in her head. The story of don Epifanio Vargas. The story of Güero Dávila. The story of Teresa Mendoza.

It was Güero's former boss, the gringo had said, don Epifanio himself, who'd found out about Güero and the DEA. During those early years as owner of Norteña de Aviación, Vargas had leased his planes to Southern Air Transport, a U.S. government cover company that flew the arms and cocaine that the CIA was using to finance the Contras in Nicaragua, and Güero Dávila, who back then was already a DEA agent, was one of the pilots who unloaded war matériel at the airport in Los Llanos, Costa Rica, and returned to Fort Lauderdale with drugs from the Medellín cartel. When that operation, and that period of history, was over, Epifanio Vargas had maintained his good connections on the other side, which was how he could later be informed of the leak from the Customs agent who'd ratted out Güero. Vargas had paid the rat, and for a good while had kept the information to himself, not making any final decision about what to do with it. The drug boss of the sierra, the former patient campesino, was one of those men that never rush into things. He was almost out of the business, he was taking another road now, the pharmaceuticals that he managed from a distance were doing well, and the state's privatizations in recent years had allowed him to launder huge amounts of money. He maintained his family comfortably, in an immense rancho near El Limón that replaced the Colonia Chapultepec house in Culiacán—and kept a lover, too, a former model and TV host, whom he set up in a luxurious place in Mazatlán. He saw no reason to complicate things with decisions that could come back to bite him and whose only benefit was revenge. Güero was working for Batman Güemes now, so he was no business of Epifanio Vargas'.

However—Willy Rangel had said—at some point things changed. Vargas made a lot of money in the ephedrine business: $50,000 a kilo in the United States, compared with $30,000 for cocaine and $8,000 for marijuana. He had good connections, which opened the doors of a political career; he was about to collect on the half a million a month he'd been investing in payoffs to public officials all these years. He saw a quiet, respectable future for himself, far from the potential problems of his old trade. After establishing ties with the principal families of the city and the state—money, corruption, complicity made very good relationships with these people—he had enough money to say *basta*, or to go on earning it by conventional means. So suddenly, suspiciously, people related to his past began to die: police officers, judges, lawyers. Eighteen in three months.

It was an epidemic. And in that scenario, the figure of Güero Dávila was also an obstacle: he knew too many things about the heroic times of Norteña de Aviación. The DEA agent was lurking in his past like a stick of dynamite that could go off at any time, and destroy Vargas' future.

But Vargas was smart, Rangel had said. Very smart, with that campesino shrewdness that had gotten him where he was today. He passed the job off to somebody else, without revealing why. Batman Güemes would never have taken out an agent of the DEA, but a pilot of two-engine Cessnas who was dealing behind his bosses' backs, fucking them over a little here and a little there—that was another thing. Vargas insisted to Batman: An object lesson, to teach the others that we can't let this happen, et cetera. Güero and his cousin. I've got a bone or two to pick with him, too, so consider this a personal favor you're doing me. Plus, you're his boss now—it's your responsibility to enforce discipline.

"How long have you known all this?" Teresa had asked Rangel.

"Part of it, for a long time. Almost when it happened." The DEA agent moved his hands to underscore the obvious. "The rest, about two years, when the witness I mentioned gave us the details . . . And he said something else." He paused, looking at her intently, as though expecting her to fill in the blanks. ". . . He said that later, when you started to grow over here on this side of the Atlantic, Vargas decided he'd made a mistake in letting you get out of Sinaloa alive. And he reminded Batman Güemes that he had unpaid bills over here . . . and Batman Güemes sent two hit men over here to finish the job."

That's your story, said Teresa's inscrutable expression. You think you know everything. "You don't say. And what happened?"

"You'd be the one to tell me that. Nothing more was ever heard of them."

Héctor Tapia gently interrupted. "Of one of them, Willy means. Apparently, the other one is still here. Retired. Or semi-retired."

"And why have you come to me with all this now?"

Rangel looked at the diplomat. Now it's your turn, his expression said. Tapia again took off his glasses and put them back on again. Then he studied his fingernails, as though he had notes written on them.

"Recently," he began, "Epifanio Vargas' political star has been rising. It has been, in fact, unstoppable. Too many people owe him too much. Many people love him or fear him, and almost everyone respects him. He was able to get out of the activities directly related to the Juárez cartel before it got into its serious trouble with Justice, when the struggle was carried on almost exclusively against its competitors in the Gulf. . . . In his career he has involved judges, businessmen, and politicians, *and* the highest authorities in the Mexican Church, police, and military—General Gutiérrez Rebollo, who was about to be appointed the republic's antidrug prosecutor before his links with the Juárez cartel were discovered and he wound up in the Almoloya prison, was a close friend of Vargas'. . . . And then there are the people themselves, the men and women in the street: since he was named state representative to the House of Deputies, Epifanio Vargas has done a lot for Sinaloa, invested money, created jobs, helped people—"

"That's not bad," Teresa interrupted. "Usually in Mexico, people steal from the state and keep it all for themselves. . . . The PRI did that for seventy years."

"Those are two different things," replied Tapia. "For the moment, the PRI is not in power. There's a new wind sweeping through the government, we all hope. Maybe in the end not much will have changed, but there is a will now to try. And all of a sudden, Epifanio Vargas appears on the scene, ready to become a senator."

"And somebody wants to screw him." Teresa saw it all now.

"That's one way of putting it. On the one hand, a very large sector of the political world, many linked to the current government, don't want to see a Sinaloan narco become a senator, even though he's officially retired and serving as a member of the House of Deputies. . . . There are also old accounts, which it would take too long to go into."

Teresa could imagine what those accounts might consist of. All of those *hijos de la pinche madre,* at war over power and money, the drug cartels and the friends of the respective cartels and the various political families, related to drugs or not. No matter who's in power in the "government." *México lindo,* as they say—beautiful Mexico.

"And for our part," Rangel added, "we haven't forgotten that he had a DEA agent killed."

"Exactly." That shared responsibility seemed to relieve Tapia. "Because the government of the United States, which as you know, *señora*, continues to follow our own country's politics very closely, would also not approve of Epifanio Vargas' becoming senator . . . So there has been an attempt to create a high-level commission to act in two phases—first, to open an investigation into Vargas' past, and second, if the necessary evidence can be gathered, to strip him of his government position and end his political career, perhaps even bring him to trial."

"At the end of which," Rangel added, "we do not exclude the possibility of requesting his extradition to the United States."

"And where do I fit into this happy plan?" Teresa asked. "What's the purpose of you flying all the way over here to tell me all this, like we were in the gang together back in the old days?"

Rangel and Tapia looked at each other. The diplomat cleared his throat, and while he was taking a cigarette from a silver case—offering one to Teresa, who shook her head—he said that the Mexican government had followed the, ahem, career of Señora Mendoza in recent years. They had nothing against her, since as far as they could tell, her activities took place outside the territorial limits of Mexico—she was an exemplary citizen, Rangel put in, so straight-faced that the sarcasm was almost lost. And in view of all that, the authorities were willing to come to an agreement. An agreement satisfactory to all concerned. Cooperation in exchange for immunity.

Teresa looked at them. Wary.

"What kind of cooperation?"

Tapia very carefully lit his cigarette. As carefully as he appeared to be meditating what he was about to say. Or the way to say it.

"You have personal scores there. You also know a great deal about the period when Güero Dávila was alive, and about Epifanio Vargas' activities," he finally said. "You were an eyewitness, and it almost cost you your life. . . . One might think that an arrangement would be of benefit to you. You have more than enough resources of all kinds to go into other activities, enjoying what you have with no worries for the future."

"You don't say."

"I do say."

"*Híjole.* To what do I owe this generosity?"

"You never take payment in drugs. Just money. You're a transporter, not an owner or distributor. The largest transporter in Europe at the moment, unquestionably. But that's it. . . . That leaves us a margin for reasonable maneuvering, in the face of public opinion. . . ."

"Public opinion? . . . What the fuck are you talking about?"

It took the diplomat some time to answer. Teresa could hear Rangel breathing; he was squirming in his seat uneasily, rubbing his hands together and interlacing his fingers.

"You are being given the opportunity to go back to Mexico, if you wish," Tapia went on, "or to move quietly to another country, wherever you like. . . . The Spanish authorities have even been sounded out in this regard: we have a commitment from the minister of justice to halt all proceedings and investigations currently under way . . . which, according to my information, are at a very advanced stage and could, in the short term, make things quite difficult for the, ahem, Queen of the South. . . . This would be a chance to start over—all debts forgiven."

"I didn't know the gringos' arm was so long."

"Depends on what we're talking about."

Teresa broke out laughing. "You're asking me," she said, still incredulous, "to tell you everything that you think I know about Epifanio Vargas. That I start ratting people out, at my age. And me from Sinaloa."

"Not just that you tell *us*," Rangel interrupted. "But that you tell it *there,* and to a judge."

"Where's 'there'?"

"In Mexico. Before the Justice Commission in the national prosecutor's office."

"You want me to go to Mexico?"

"As a protected witness. Absolute immunity. It would all happen in the Distrito Federal, under every kind of personal and judicial guarantee. With the thanks of the nation, and of the government of the United States."

Teresa suddenly stood up. Pure reflex, without thinking. This time, the two men also rose: Rangel disconcerted, Tapia uncomfortable. I told you so, said the last look Tapia gave the DEA agent. Teresa went to the door and yanked it open. Pote Gálvez was in the hallway, his arms held slightly away from his body, his stockiness falsely peaceful. If you have to, she told him with a glance, kick them out.

"You," she almost spat, "have gone crazy."

A nd there she was now, at her old table in the bar, reflecting about all that. With a tiny life in her belly, not knowing what she was going to do with it. The echo of that conversation in her head. Trying to think. Trying to feel. Turning over in her mind the last words of the conversation and many old memories. Pain and gratitude. The image of Güero Dávila—as motionless and silent as she was now, back in that cantina in Culiacán—and the memory of the other man sitting next to her late at night, in the Malverde Chapel. "That Güero of yours liked his little jokes, Teresita. You really didn't read any of it? Then get out of here, and try to bury yourself so deep that they can never find you."

Don Epifanio Vargas. Her godfather. The man who could have killed her, but who took pity on her. And who then thought better of it, but too late.

16. Unbalanced load

Teo Aljarafe returned two days later with a satisfactory report. Payments received promptly on Grand Cayman, efforts made to find a small bank of their own and a shipping company in Belize, good profits on the money—laundered of its powder and weed—deposited in three banks in Zurich and two in Liechtenstein. Teresa listened attentively to his report, looked over the documents, and signed a few papers after reading them carefully, and then they went to eat at Casa Santiago, on the boardwalk in Marbella, with Pote Gálvez sitting outside. Ham with fava beans and roasted crayfish, which was juicier and tastier than lobster. A Señorío de Lazán Reserva '96. Teo was talkative, charming, handsome. His jacket over the back of his chair, the sleeves of his white shirt rolled up twice over his tanned forearms, his firm wrists with a dusting of fine hair. His Patek Philippe, buffed fingernails, the wedding band gleaming on his left hand. Occasionally he turned his face away, looking out toward the street, wanting to see who came into the restaurant, his fork or wineglass in midair, and when he did he showed her that impeccable aquiline Spanish profile of his. A couple of times he rose to say hello to someone. Tomás Pestaña, who was having dinner in the rear with a group of German investors, had apparently not seen Teresa and Teo when he came in, but a few minutes later the waiter came over with a bottle of good wine. From the mayor, he said. With his compliments.

Teresa looked at the man sitting across from her, and she meditated. She wasn't going to tell him that day, or tomorrow or the next day, and maybe not ever, what she was carrying in her womb. And there was something else curious about that: At first she'd thought she would soon be able to feel something, have some physical awareness of the life that was beginning to develop inside her. But she felt nothing. Just the certainty of what was there, and her thoughts on it. Her breasts might have become fuller, and her headaches might have disappeared, but she felt pregnant only when she thought about it, reread the medical report, or looked at the calendar marked with two skipped periods. Still—it occurred to her just then, as she listened to Teo Aljarafe's banal conversation—here I am. Pregnant, like some stupid teenager without enough sense to take precautions. With something, or someone, on the way. Still undecided on what to do with my fucking life, with the life of this baby, or with Teo's life. She looked at him, as though searching for some sign.

"Is there anything under way?" Teo asked distractedly, sipping at the mayor's wine.

"Nothing for the moment. Routine stuff."

After dinner he suggested they go to the house on Calle Ancha or some good hotel on the Milla de Oro, where they could spend the rest of the evening, and the night. A bottle of wine, a plate of Iberian ham, he suggested. But Teresa shook her head. I'm tired, she said. I really don't feel like it tonight.

"It's been almost a month." Teo smiled.

That smile. Easy. He brushed her fingers, tenderly, and she sat looking at her motionless hand on the tablecloth, as though it weren't really hers. With that hand, she thought, she'd shot Gato Fierros in the face.

"How are your daughters?" she asked.

He looked at her, surprised. Teresa never asked about his family. It was a tacit pact with herself, which she had never broken. "They're fine," he said after a moment. "Fine."

"Good," she replied. "I'm glad. And their mother, I suppose. The three of them."

Teo put his dessert fork down and leaned over the table, looking at her quizzically.

"What's wrong?" he said. "Tell me what's happened today."

She looked around, the people at the tables, the traffic out on the avenue still lit by the sun setting on the ocean.

"There's nothing wrong." She lowered her voice. "But I lied to you. There's something under way. Something I haven't told you about."

"Why?"

"Because I don't always tell you everything."

He looked at her, worried. Impeccably open. Five seconds, almost exactly, and then he turned his eyes toward the street. When he turned them back, he was smiling slightly. Charming. He touched her hand again, and this time, too, she didn't pull it away.

"Is it big?"

Órale, Teresa said to herself. This is just the way things are, and in the end everybody makes their own destiny. The final push almost always comes from you and you alone. For good or ill.

"Yes," she answered. "There's a ship on the way. The *Luz Angelita.*"

It had grown dark. The crickets were chirping in the yard like they'd all gone crazy. When the lights were turned on, Teresa ordered them turned off again, and now she was sitting on the porch steps, her back against a column, gazing at the stars above the thick black tops of the weeping willows. She had a bottle of tequila, unopened, between her legs, and behind her, on a low table near the chaise longues, Mexican music was playing on the stereo. Sinaloan music that Pote Gálvez had lent her that afternoon—*Quihubo, patrona,* this is the latest by Los Broncos de Reynosa, tell me what you think:

My mule had started limping bad,
The load had all shifted to one side.
We were dodging pine cones on the path
Up in the sierra in Chihuahua.

Little by little, the former hit man was adding to his collection of corridos. He liked them tough, violent—mostly, he told her very soberly, to feed his nostalgia for all that. A man's from where a man's from, and you can't change that, he said. His personal jukebox included the entire norteño region, from Chalino—What lyrics, *doña*—to Exterminador, Los Invasores de Nuevo León, El As de la Sierra, El Moreño, Los Broncos, Los Huracanes, and other gangster groups from

Sinaloa and up that way, the ones that turned the police gazette into music, songs about mules and murders and lead and shipments of the good stuff, and Cessnas and new pickups, and Federales and cops, traffickers and funerals. As corridos had been to the Revolution in those bygone days, so the narcocorridos were the new epics, the modern legends of a Mexico that was there and had no intention of going anywhere, or changing—among other reasons because a not inconsiderable part of the national economy depended on the drugs. It was a marginal, hard world, of weapons, corruption, and drugs, in which the only law not broken was the law of supply and demand.

> *There Juan el Grande took one in the chest,*
> *But he died defending his people.*
> *He let my mule get past,*
> *And then he killed the lieutenant.*

"Unbalanced Load," the song was called. Kind of like mine, thought Teresa. On the cover of the CD, the Broncos de Reynosa were all shaking hands with each other, and under his coat, one of them had a huge pistol sticking out of his belt. Sometimes she would watch Pote Gálvez while she listened to these songs, fascinated by the expression on his face.

They would still have a drink together once in a while. Come on, Pinto, have a tequila. And they would sit, saying almost nothing, listening to the music, Pote respectful, keeping his distance. Teresa would hear him cluck his tongue and see him shake his head, *Órale*, feeling and remembering, mentally drinking at the Don Quijote and La Ballena and the Sinaloa dives that floated around in his memory, maybe missing his buddy Gato Fierros, who was no more than concrete-encased bones by now, nobody to take flowers to his grave and nobody to sing *pinche* corridos to his *pinche* memory—that *hijo de puta* Gato, whom Pote Gálvez and Teresa hadn't spoken another word about since then, ever.

> *Lamberto Quintero, our hero,*
> *Had a pickup truck tailing him.*
> *It was on the highway to Salado*
> *And they was just out for a spin.*

From the stereo now came the Lamberto Quintero corrido, which with José Alfredo's "El Caballo Blanco" was one of Pote's favorites. Teresa saw his shadowy silhouette come to the door, look out, and immediately move away again. She knew he was inside, always within range of her voice, listening. If you were in Mexico, you would already have so many corridos it wouldn't be funny, *patrona,* he'd said once. He didn't add, And maybe I would, too, but Teresa knew that he thought it.

Really, she decided as she stripped the band off the Herradura Reposado, every *pinche* man in Mexico aspires to that. Like fucking Güero Dávila. Like Pote. Like, in his own way, Santiago Fisterra. Have a corrido, real or imaginary, written about you, with your name on it—music, wine, women, money, adventure, even if it cost you your skin. And you never know, she thought, looking at the doorway where Pote had appeared. You never know, Pinto. After all, corridos are always written by other people.

> His buddy turns to him and says,
> That pickup's been tailing us some.
> Lamberto just grins and says,
> Why d'ya think I brought the machine guns?

She drank straight from the bottle. A swig that went down her throat with the force of a bullet. She stretched out her arm holding the bottle, held it up, offering it with a sarcastic grin to the woman looking down at her from the shadows of the lawn. *Cabrona,* why didn't you just stay in Culiacán? Sometimes I'm not sure whether it's you that's come over to this side or me that went over to the other side with you, or whether we've exchanged roles in this farce and maybe it's you that's sitting on the porch steps and me that's half hidden out there looking at you and what you're carrying inside you.

She'd talked about this once more—she had a feeling it was the last time—with Oleg Yasikov that same afternoon, when the Russian came by to see whether the hashish run was ready, after everything had been settled and they went out for a walk on the beach. Yasikov had looked at her out of the corner of his eye, studying her in the light of something new, which was neither better nor worse but simply sadder and colder.

"And I don't know," he'd said, "whether now that you've told me certain things I'm seeing you differently or whether it's you, Tesa, who is changing, somehow. Yes. Today, while we were talking, I was looking at you. Surprised. You had never given me as many details or talked in that tone of voice. *Nyet.* You were like a ship casting off. Forgive me if I don't express myself well. Yes. They're complicated things to explain. Even to think."

"I'm going to have it," she abruptly said. She spoke without thinking about it, point-blank, as though the decision had been forged at that instant inside her head, linked to other decisions that she had already made and was about to make. Yasikov had stood there, still, inexpressive, for a long time, and then he'd nodded—not to approve of anything, which wasn't his place, but rather to suggest that she was a person able to have or do whatever she wanted, and that he also thought her perfectly able to deal with the consequences. They took a few more steps and he looked out at the ocean, which was turning lead-gray in the dusk, and then, not facing her, said: "Nothing has ever scared you, Tesa. *Nyet.* Nothing. Since the day we met I have never seen you hesitate when it was a question of life and freedom. Never. That's why people respect you. Yes. That's why I admire you. And that's why," he concluded, "you are where you are. Yes. Now."

That was when she'd burst out laughing, a strange laugh that made Yasikov turn his head.

"Fucking *pinche* Russki," she said. "You don't have the slightest idea. I'm the other girl, the narco's *morra,* that you don't know. The one that looks at me, or the one I look at—I'm not sure which me is me. The only thing I'm sure of is that I'm a coward, with nothing I ought to have. I'll tell you—I'm so afraid, I feel so weak, so indecisive, that I burn up all my energy and my willpower, to the last ounce, in hiding the fact that I'm afraid. You can't imagine the effort. Because I never chose this, and the corrido, somebody else wrote the words to it. You. Patty. Them. What a *pendeja,* huh? I don't like life in general and mine in particular. I don't even like the parasitic fucking tiny life that's inside me. I'm sick with something that I refused to try to understand a long time ago, and I'm not even honest, because I won't talk about it. I've lived for twelve years like this. All the time pretending and not talking."

The two stood in silence, watching the ocean go dark. Finally, Yasikov nodded again, very slowly.

"Have you made a decision about Teo?" he asked softly.

"Don't worry about him."

"The operation . . ."

"Don't worry about the operation, either. Everything's in order. Including Teo."

She drank some more tequila. The words of the Lamberto Quintero corrido faded and she stood up and walked, bottle in hand, through the garden, beside the dark rectangle of the pool. *Watching the narco girls pass by, he let his guard down,* the song said. *When some well-aimed bullets took him down.* She walked among the trees; the branches of the weeping willows brushed her face. The last lines of the song faded away behind her. *You saw him go down, you bridge to Tierra Blanca. And you'll always be there to remind them that Lamberto can never be forgotten.* She came to the gate onto the beach, and just as she reached out to open it, she heard behind her, on the gravel, the footsteps of Pote Gálvez.

"No, Pinto. I want to be alone," she said without turning around.

The footsteps stopped. She kept walking, and took off her shoes when she felt the white sand under her feet. The stars made a vault of luminous pinpricks all the way down to the horizon, above a sea that whispered along the shoreline. She walked along the water's edge, letting the waves wet her feet. She saw two lights, motionless, wide apart: fishing boats working their nets near the coast. The distant brightness of the Hotel Guadalmina cast a wan light over her as she took off her jeans, T-shirt, and underwear and walked slowly into the water; it was cold now at night, it gave her goosebumps.

She was still carrying the bottle, and she took another swig to warm up, the rank fumes of the liquor rising through her nose and taking her breath away. The water reached her thighs, and soft waves rocked her back and forth as she found her footing on the sand. Then, not daring to look at the other woman, who was back on the beach beside the mound of clothes, watching her, she threw the bottle into the waves and let herself sink into the cold water, feeling its blackness close over her head. She swam a few yards along the bottom and emerged, shaking out her hair, brushing the water off her face. Then she began to swim farther and farther out on the dark, cold surface, propelling herself with strong, firm movements of her legs and arms, plunging her face in up to the eyes and lifting it out again to breathe, farther and farther out, so far from the beach that her feet no longer touched the bottom and everything disappeared except her and the sea. That sea as somber as the death that she felt like giving herself up to, so she could rest.

She swam back. And she was surprised to find herself doing that; her mind went around and around, asking why she hadn't kept swimming, right on into the heart of the night. By the time she touched the sandy bottom again, half relieved and half bewildered to feel terra firma once more, and came out of the water shivering with cold, she thought she had figured it out. The other woman was gone. She was no longer standing beside the clothes dropped on the beach. She's probably decided to go on ahead, thought Teresa, and she'll be waiting for me up ahead there, where I'm going.

The greenish glow of the radar screen illuminated the face of skipper Cherki from below, giving a silvery-green cast to the gray hairs of his unshaven chin.

"There she is." He pointed to a dark blip on the screen.

The vibration of the *Tarfaya*'s engines could be felt in the narrow wheelroom's walls. Teresa was leaning against the door, protected from the night's cold by a thick wool turtleneck sweater, her hands in the pockets of her slicker, right hand touching a pistol. The skipper turned to look at her.

"In twenty minutes," he said, "unless you give other orders."

"It's your ship, skipper."

Scratching his head under his wool cap, Cherki glanced down at the GPS screen. Teresa's presence made him uncomfortable, as it did the rest of the crew. It wasn't done, he'd protested at first. And it was dangerous. But nobody said he had a choice. After confirming their position, Cherki turned the wheel to starboard, keeping a close eye on the compass until it reached the point he wanted, and then switched on the autopilot. On the radar screen, the blip was directly ahead, twenty-five degrees west of the fleur-de-lys that marked north on this compass. Exactly ten miles. The other dark blips, the faint trails of two speedboats that had roared away after transferring their last bundles of hashish onto the fishing boat, had been out of radar range for thirty minutes. The Xauen banks lay far behind them.

"*Iallah bismillah,*" said Cherki.

We're going there, Allah willing, Teresa translated.

That made her smile in the darkness. Mexicans, Moroccans, or Spaniards, they all had their St. Malverde somewhere. She noticed that Cherki turned around from time to time, looking at her with curiosity and ill-concealed reproach. He was from Tangiers, a veteran fisherman. That night he would be earning more than his nets did in five years.

The swaying of the *Tarfaya* on the swells calmed a bit when the skipper pushed the throttle levers to accelerate along the new course; the sound of the engines grew louder. Teresa saw the needle on the gauge rise to six knots. She looked outside. Through the glass fogged by salt spray, the night flowed past as black as India ink. They were running with lights; on radar they could be seen as well without lights as with them, and a boat without lights raised suspicions. She lit a cigarette to counteract the smells—the gasoline that turned her stomach, the grease, the lines, the deck impregnated with the rank, sharp odor of old fish. She felt a knot of nausea in her throat. I hope I don't get seasick now, she thought. With these *cabrones* watching.

She left the wheelhouse, stepping into the night and onto the deck wet with spray. The wind made her feel better. Shadows huddled against the gunwale, among the forty-kilo bales wrapped in plastic, with rope handles to make them easier to handle: five well-paid Moroccans, trustworthy, who like Cherki had worked for Transer Naga several times before. She made out two more shadows, fore and aft, half silhouetted against the fishing boat's running lights: their escorts, Moroccans from Ceuta, young, taciturn, and in good shape, of proven loyalty, each with an Ingram MAC 11 submachine gun with fifty .380 caliber rounds under his life jacket and two MK2 grenades in the pockets. *Harkeños,* Dr. Ramos, who had a dozen men for situations like this, called them. "Take two *harkeños,* boss," he'd said. "So I won't have to worry while you're on board. Since you insist on going this time, which I think is an unnecessary and actually crazy risk to take, and you won't take Pote Gálvez, at least let me organize a little security detail. I know that everybody's paid and all that, but just in case."

She went aft and saw that the last rubber, a thirty-foot Valiant with two powerful outboard motors, was still there, towed on a heavy line, carrying thirty bales and its pilot, another Moroccan, under tarps. She stood at the wet gunwale and smoked, looking out at the phosphorescent spume raised by the fishing boat's bow. She didn't need to be there, and she knew it. Her queasiness worsened with the reproach. But that wasn't the point. She'd wanted to go, supervise it all in person, out of complex reasons that had much to do with the ideas she'd been turning over in her head over the last few days, with the inevitable course of things from which there was no going back. And she had felt fear—the familiar yet uncomfortable old physical fear, rooted in both her memory and the very muscles of her body—when a few hours earlier the *Tarfaya* had approached the Moroccan coast to supervise the loading of the bales from off the rubbers: low, flat shadows, dark figures, muted voices, no lights, not an unnecessary sound, no radio contact except anonymous squawks on the walkie-talkies on successive preestablished frequencies, a single cell-phone call by each boat to check that everything was all right on the land side, while skipper Cherki anxiously watched the radar screen for any blip, any sign of Customs, the chopper, the spotlight that would suddenly pick them out of the darkness and lead to disaster or hell—anything, in a word, unexpected.

Unexpected, but that could happen. Somewhere in the night, far out at sea, aboard the Fairline Squadron, struggling against seasickness with pills and resignation, Alberto Rizocarpaso sat at a portable computer connected to the Internet, his radio apparatus and his cables and his batteries all around, supervising everything like an air traffic controller following the movement of the planes he's responsible for. Farther north, in Sotogrande, Dr. Ramos would be smoking one pipe after another, alert to the radio and the cell phones that no one had used before and that were to be used once, and once only, that night. And in a hotel in Tenerife, hundreds of miles away, in the Atlantic, Farid Lataquia was playing out the risky bluff that would allow him, with luck, to bring Tender Childhood off according to plans.

It's true, thought Teresa—Dr. Ramos was right. I don't need to be here, yet here I am, leaning on the gunwales of this stinking fishing boat, risking my life and my freedom, playing this strange game that I can't even once avoid or delegate to someone else. Saying good-bye to so very many things that tomorrow, when the sun that's now shining in the Sinaloa sky comes up, will be gone forever. With a well-oiled Beretta and a full clip heavy in my pocket. I haven't carried a gun in twelve years, and the fact that I'm carrying it now has more to do with me, if something happens, than with the others. My guarantee that if something goes wrong I won't wind up in a *pinche* Moroccan prison, or a Spanish one, either. The certainty that at any moment I can go where I want to go.

She tossed her cigarette into the sea. It's like taking the last step, she reflected. The last test before you rest. Or the next-to-last.

Telephone, *señora.*"
She took the cell phone Cherki was holding out to her, went into the wheelhouse and closed the door. It was a Russian SAZ88, scrambled for use by the police and secret services, and Farid Lataquia had managed to find six of them—he'd paid a fortune on the black market. While she brought the phone to her ear she looked at the echo the skipper was pointing out on the radar screen. The dark blip of the *Xoloitzcuintle,* a mile away, appeared at every sweep of the antenna. There was light on the horizon, coming softly through the haze.

"Is that the Alborán lighthouse?" Teresa asked.

"No, Alborán is twenty-five miles away, and you can only see the lighthouse from ten. That's the boat."

She put the phone to her ear. "*Red and green at my one-ninety,*" said a male voice. Teresa looked at the GPS, then the radar screen, and repeated aloud what she'd heard; the skipper changed the range on the radar to calculate the distance. *"Everything okay by my green,"* said the voice on the phone, and before Teresa could repeat those words the person hung up.

"They've got us on visuals," said Teresa. "We'll board her on the starboard side."

They were outside Moroccan waters, but that didn't eliminate the danger. She peered out the windows at the sky, afraid she would see the dark cloud of the Customs helicopter. Maybe the same pilot, she thought, will be flying tonight. How much time between one thing and another. Between those two instants of my life.

She punched Rizocarpaso's number from memory. "Tell me from the top down," she said when she heard his laconic *"Zero zero."*

"In the nest and no news," was the reply. Rizocarpaso was in telephone contact with two men, one located on top of the Rock with powerful night-vision goggles and the other on the highway that ran beside the helicopter base at Algeciras. Each with a cell phone. Silent sentinels.

"The bird's still on the ground," she told Cherki as she hung up.

"Thank God."

She'd had to restrain herself from asking Rizocarpaso about the rest of the operation. The parallel phase. By now they ought to be getting word, and the lack of news was beginning to make her nervous. Or, looking at it another way, she said to herself with a bitter grin, beginning to reassure her. She looked at the brass clock on the wheelhouse bulkhead. No matter how things went, there was no need to torment herself anymore. Rizocarpaso would let her know as soon as he heard anything.

Now the ship's lights could be seen clearly, neatly, against the night. The *Tarfaya* would turn its lights off when it moved in close, so as to camouflage itself against the other boat's radar blip. She looked at the screen. Half a mile.

"You can prepare your men, skipper."

Cherki left the wheel room, and Teresa heard him giving orders. When she stepped to the door, the shadows were no longer huddled against the gunwale; they were moving around the deck laying out the lines and fenders they'd soon be needing, stacking bales on the port bow. They had hauled in the tow line, and the Valiant's outboard motor started up as its pilot began making his own approach. Dr. Ramos' *harkeños* still stood motionless, like statues, their Ingrams and grenades under their coats. The *Xoloitzcuintle* could be made out clearly now, with the containers aligned on the deck, and the mast and starboard lights, white and green, reflected on the crests of the waves.

Teresa saw the boat for the first time, and she approved of Lataquia's choice. A low draft, so the cargo was almost at water level. That would make the transfer easier.

Cherki reentered the wheelhouse, switched off the autopilot, and steered manually, approaching the container ship carefully, parallel to the starboard side and along the stabilizer fin. Teresa lifted the binoculars to study the boat: the *Xoloitzcuintle* had slowed but not stopped. She saw men moving around among the containers. Up top, on the bridge's starboard aileron, two other men were watching the *Tarfaya*: no doubt the captain and an officer.

"You can cut the engines, skipper."

The boats were near enough for their two radar blips to merge into one. The fishing boat was now dark, illuminated only by the lights of the other vessel, which had altered course slightly to protect the fin. The white mast light could no longer be seen, and the green light gleamed on the aileron like a blinding emerald. They were almost hull to hull, and on the sides of both the fishing boat and the container ship sailors were hanging out thick fenders. The *Tarfaya* adjusted speed, slow ahead, to match that of the *Xoloitzcuintle*. About three knots, Teresa calculated. A second later she heard what sounded like a muted gunshot: the report of the rope thrower. The men on the fishing boat picked up the hawser that ran to the back of the deck and secured it to the deck bits, without pulling too tight. The rope thrower fired again. One long line stern, one bow. Turning the wheel delicately, the skipper pulled alongside the container ship and left the engine running, but out of gear. The two boats were now moving at the same speed, the large one pulling the small one along. The Valiant, too, skillfully maneuvered by its pilot, was now linked up to the *Xoloitzcuintle*, on the fishing boat's bow, and Teresa watched the crew begin to lift bales. With luck, she thought, eyeing the radar and knocking on the wood of the wheel, it'll all be over in an hour.

Twenty tons headed for the Black Sea, with no intermediate ports. By the time the rubber set a course to the northwest, using the GPS connected to the Raytheon radar, the lights of the *Xoloitzcuintle* were disappearing over the dark horizon, far to the east. The *Tarfaya*, which had turned its lights back on, was a little closer, its mast light bobbing up and down as the boat moved through the waves, steaming unhurriedly southwest. Teresa gave an order, and the pilot of the speedboat pushed the throttle forward, accelerating, the hull of the semi-rigid skimming along, bouncing on the wave crests, with the two *harkeños* sitting in the bow to give it stability, the hoods of their windbreakers pulled up to protect them against the needle-like spray.

Teresa once again punched the memorized number, and when she heard Rizocarpaso's flat *"Zero zero,"* she said only, "The kids are in bed." Then she sat staring out into the darkness, toward the west, as though trying to see hundreds of miles out, before asking if there was any word yet. *"Negative,"* came the reply. She hung up and looked at the back of the pilot at the Valiant's control panel. She was worried.

The vibration of the powerful motors, the sound of the water, the bouncing against the waves, the night over them like a black sphere, all brought back memories, good and bad. But this wasn't the time. Too many things were in play, loose ends that needed tying up. And every mile the speedboat covered at thirty-five knots brought her closer to the unavoidable resolution of those matters. She felt like prolonging this race through a night without landmarks or references, with only tiny, very distant lights marking the land or the presence of other boats in the darkness to give any sense of space. Prolong it indefinitely, to hold off that ending; just sit suspended in the night and the sea, this limbo, this intermediate place without responsibilities, with nothing but waiting, with the roaring engines thrusting at her back, the rubber floats on each side tensing, elastic, with each leap of the hull, the wind and salt spray in her face, the dark back of the man leaning over the controls, reminding her so much of another man. Of other men.

It was, in sum, an hour as somber as herself. Or at least that was how the night felt, how she felt. The sky without even the thin crescent of moon, which had lasted only a while, no stars, a haze rolling in inexorably from the east, swallowing up the last gleam from the *Xoloitzcuintle*'s mast light. Teresa scrutinizing the dry heart, the calm mind that lined up every one of the remaining pieces like dollar bills in the packets of money she had held, hundreds of years before, on Calle Juárez in Culiacán—until that day the black Bronco pulled up beside her and Güero Dávila rolled down the window and she began, without realizing it, to walk the long road that had brought her here, now, in the Strait of Gibraltar, tangled in this absurd paradox. She'd come over a raging river, with the load all on one side. Or was about to.

"The *Sinaloa, señora.*"

The shout startled her out of her thoughts. *Híjole.* Sinaloa, eh? Tonight of all nights, and now of all times. The pilot pointed toward the lights rapidly approaching, out beyond the curtain of spray, the silhouettes of the bodyguards squatting at the bow. The yacht was running with all its lights on, white and sleek, its brightness slicing through the sea, toward the northeast. As innocent as a dove, Teresa thought, as the pilot turned the Valiant in a wide semicircle and approached the stern platform, where a crew member was waiting to help her aboard. Before the bodyguards coming over to boost her up could get to her, Teresa calculated the pitch and sway, put one foot on the float, and jumped across, taking advantage of the lift from the next wave crest. Without saying good-bye to the men in the speedboat or even looking back, she walked across the deck, her legs numb from the cold, while the crew member threw off the line and the speedboat raced away with its three occupants, mission accomplished, back to its base in Estepona.

Teresa went below to wash the salt off her face, lit a cigarette, and poured herself an inch of tequila. She drank it in one gulp, before the mirror in the bathroom. The violence of the drink brought tears to her eyes, and she stood there, cigarette in one hand and empty glass in the other, looking at the teardrops run slowly down her face. She didn't like her expression, or that of the woman who gazed out of the mirror back at her: dark circles under her eyes, her hair a mess, rigid with salt. And those tears. They met again, and she found her tireder, older. Teresa turned away abruptly and went into her cabin, opened the closet where she'd left her purse, pulled out the wallet with her initials, and sat for a long time, studying the wrinkled half-photograph.

The scrambled telephone in the pocket of her jeans rang. Rizo-carpaso's voice reported briefly, without unnecessary words or explanations: *"The kids' godfather has paid for the christening."* Teresa asked for confirmation, and the voice on the other end replied that there was no doubt: *"The whole family went to the party. They just reported in from Cádiz."*

Teresa hung up and stuck the phone back in her pocket. She felt the nausea returning. The liquor she'd drunk didn't go well with the humming of the engines and the swaying of the boat. With what she'd just heard and what was about to happen. She carefully returned the photo to her wallet, put her cigarette out in the ashtray, calculated the three steps that it would take her to reach the head, and after calmly covering that distance she knelt before the toilet and vomited up the tequila and the rest of her tears.

W hen she came out on deck, her face washed again, she was still wearing the slicker over the wool turtleneck. Pote Gálvez was waiting for her, motionless, a black shape on the gunwale.

"Where is he?" Teresa asked.

The bodyguard didn't answer right away. Perhaps thinking about it. Or giving her the chance to think.

"Below," he said at last. "In cabin four."

Teresa went down, holding on to the teak handrail. Pote Gálvez murmured, *"Con permiso, patrona,"* and stepped ahead of her to open the locked door. He gave a professional look inside and then stood aside to let her pass. Teresa entered, followed by the bodyguard, who locked the door again behind him.

"Customs," Teresa said, "boarded the *Luz Angelita* tonight."

Teo Aljarafe looked at her expressionlessly, as though he were far away and none of that had anything to do with him. His day's growth of beard gave his chin a bluish cast. He was lying on the bunk, dressed in wrinkled chinos and a black sweater, socks. His shoes were on the floor.

"They intercepted the boat three hundred miles west of Gibraltar," Teresa continued. "A couple of hours ago. They're towing it to Cádiz now. . . . They'd been following it since it set sail from Cartagena. . . . Do you know which boat I'm talking about, Teo?"

"Of course I do."

He's had time, she told herself. Here inside. Time to think. But he doesn't know where this is going.

"There's something you don't know," she said. "The *Luz Angelita* is clean. The most illegal thing they're going to find on her, when they empty her, will be a couple of bottles of whisky that the crew didn't pay tax on. . . . Do you know what that means?"

Teo, processing that, his mouth half open, didn't move.

"A decoy," he said at last.

"A decoy. And you know why I didn't tell you before that that boat was going to be used as a decoy? . . . Because when you passed the information on to the people you've been talking to, I needed everybody to believe it was a real run as much as you did."

"You ran another operation tonight."

You're still one smart *hijo de puta,* she thought, and I'm glad. I want you to understand why. All my men have died knowing why.

"Yes. Another operation that you didn't know anything about. While those bastards from Customs were rubbing their hands together and boarding the *Luz Angelita,* looking for a ton of coke that never got loaded on, our people were doing business someplace else."

"Very well planned . . . How long have you known?"

He could deny it, she suddenly thought. He could deny everything, protest, get all indignant, tell me I've gone crazy. But he's thought about it enough since Pote locked him in here. He knows me. Why waste time, he's probably thinking. What's the point?

"For a long time. That judge in Madrid . . . I hope you've made a lot of money on this. Although I'd like to think you didn't do it for money."

Teo grimaced, and she liked that. The *hijo de puta* almost managed to smile. In spite of everything. He was just blinking too much. She'd never seen him blink that much.

"I didn't do it for money."

"They squeezed you?"

Again, almost a smile. But it was only a sarcastic smirk. With little hope.

"Imagine."

"I understand," Teresa said.

"Do you really?" Teo was analyzing that word, his brow furrowed, in search of some sign of his future. "Yes, maybe . . . It was you or me."

You or me, Teresa repeated inwardly. But forget the others: Dr. Ramos, Farid Lataquia, Rizocarpaso, all the people that trusted in him and in me. People we're responsible for. Dozens of loyal people. And one Judas.

"You or me," she said aloud.

"Exactly."

Pote Gálvez had melted into the shadows of the bulkhead, and Teo and Teresa looked into each other's eyes calmly. A conversation like so many before. At night. All that they needed was music, a drink. A night like so many others.

"Why didn't you come and tell me? . . . We could have done something. We could have come up with a solution."

Teo shook his head. He'd sat up on the edge of the bunk, his feet on the floor.

"Sometimes everything gets so complicated," he said simply. "You get all tangled up, you surround yourself with things that become necessary. They gave me the chance to get out, and still keep what I have . . . start over from scratch."

"Yes. I think I can understand that, too."

That word again, "understand," and it seemed to illuminate Teo's head like a hope. He looked at her very attentively.

"I can tell you what you want to know," he said. "There won't be any need to . . ."

"Interrogate you."

"Right."

"Nobody's going to interrogate you, Teo."

He was still watching her expectantly, weighing her every word. More blinking. A quick glance at Pote Gálvez, then back to her.

"Very clever, the operation tonight," he said at last, tentatively. "Using me to put out the decoy . . . It never occurred to me. . . . Was it coke?"

He's probing, she told herself. He still hasn't given up on living.

"Hashish," she replied. "Twenty tons."

Teo thought about that. Again the attempt at a smile that never quite jelled.

"I guess it's not a good sign that you're telling me," he concluded.

"No. It's really not."

Teo wasn't blinking anymore. He was alert, searching for signs, but he alone knew what they were. Somber. And if you can't read it in my face, she told herself, or in the way I'm measuring my words with you, or the way I'm listening to what you still have to say, then all this time with me was wasted on you. The nights and the days and the conversation and the silences. Tell me, then, where you were looking when you embraced me, *pinche pendejo*. Although you may have more class than I thought. If you do, I swear, that reassures me. And makes me happy. The bigger a man you are, and all of them, the more it reassures me and makes me happy.

"My daughters," Teo whispered suddenly.

He seemed to finally understand, as though until now he'd been considering other possibilities.

"I have two daughters," he murmured, lost in his own thoughts, looking at Teresa without seeing her. The low light of the cabin made his cheeks look sunken, two dark hollows down to his jaw. He no longer looked like an arrogant Spanish eagle. Teresa observed Pote Gálvez' impassive face. Some time before, she had read a story of samurai: When they performed hara-kiri, another warrior would cut off their head so that they could die without losing their composure. The trigger man's narrowed eyes, alert to his employer's sign, reinforced the association. And it's a pity, Teresa told herself. The composure. Teo was holding up well, and I'd have liked to see him hold up until the end. Remember him that way when I don't have anything else to remember—if I manage to stay alive.

"My daughters," she heard him repeat.

It sounded muffled, with a slight tremor. All at once his voice had felt the cold. His eyes were vacant, staring into space, the eyes of a man who was already far away, dead. Dead meat. She'd known that meat when it was tense, hard. She'd taken pleasure from it. And now it was just dead meat.

"Come on, Teo, get real."

"My daughters."

It was all so very strange, reflected Teresa. Your daughters are my

child's sisters, or they will be, maybe, if seven months from now I'm
still breathing. And what the fuck does mine mean to me. What do I
care about that thing that's yours, too, and that you're leaving without
even knowing about, and what do you care whether you know or not.
She experienced no pity or sadness or fear. Just the same indifference
she felt toward what she was carrying in her belly, the desire to be done
with this scene the way a person would want to get through any hassle.

Casting off, Oleg Yasikov had said. And not looking back.

Then she nodded slowly, almost imperceptibly. Pote Gálvez took his
revolver out of his waistband and reached down for the pillow on the
bed. Teo said something about his daughters again, but whatever it was
became a long moan, or wail, or reproach, or sob. All four at once,
maybe. And as Teresa turned toward the door, she saw that his eyes
were still vacant, looking at the same spot, seeing nothing but the well
of shadows toward which he was being dragged. Teresa went out into
the corridor.

I wish he had put on his shoes, she thought. That was no way for a
man to die—in his socks. She heard the muffled shot just as she put her
hand on the rail to go up on deck.

She heard the *pistolero*'s footsteps behind her. She did not turn
around, but waited for him to catch up to her, on the wet gunwale.
There was a line of pale light in the east, and the lights of the coast glittered closer and closer, with the flashes of the Estepona lighthouse directly north. Teresa lifted the hood of her slicker. It was cold.

"I'm going back, Pinto."

She didn't say where; there was no need to. Pote Gálvez' heavy hu-
manity leaned farther out over the gunwale. Thoughtful and quiet.
Teresa could hear his breathing.

"It's time to settle some old debts."

Another silence. Above them, against the light of the bridge, she saw
the silhouettes of the captain and the crew member on watch. Deaf,
blind, and mute. Hearing and seeing nothing but their instruments.
They earned enough so that nothing that happened back on the stern
had anything to do with them. Pote Gálvez was still leaning out, looking down at the black water murmuring past below.

"You, *patrona*, always know what you're doing. . . . But I've got a
feeling this could be *cabrón*."

"I'll be sure you're okay, Pinto. You'll be taken care of."

He ran a hand through his hair. Perplexed.

"*Quihubo, mi doña.* . . . You think you're going to do this alone? . . . Don't insult me. . . ." He seemed truly hurt. Stubborn.

They stood watching the flashes from the lighthouse in the distance.

"They can take us both out," Teresa said softly. "Nasty."

Pote Gálvez said nothing for a while. One of those silences, she sensed, with life in the balance. She turned to look at him, and she saw him run his hand through his hair again and then drop his head between his shoulders. A big, loyal bear, she thought. Straight as an arrow. With that resigned air, determined to pay whatever it cost without another word. Like the rules said.

"Well, it's a pretty clear decision, *patrona.* . . . You might as well die in one place as another."

The bodyguard looked back, toward the wake of the *Sinaloa,* where the body of Teo Aljarafe, wired to a hundred pounds of lead, had sunk into the sea.

"And sometimes," he added, "it's better to choose how you die, if you can."

17. Half my drink,
I left on the table

It was raining in Culiacán, Sinaloa, and the house in Colonia Chapultepec was enclosed in a bubble of gray gloom. There was a definite line between the colors in the garden and the leaden tones outside it. On the window, the largest drops of rain melted into long streams that made the landscape look wavy, watery, and mixed the green of the grass and the leaves of the Indian laurel with the orange of the poinciana flowers, the white of the gardenias, the lilac and red of the bougainvillea and hibiscus. But the colors died away at the high walls that surrounded the garden. Beyond them, there was only a blurry, formless gray, in which one could barely distinguish, behind the unseen riverbed of the Tamazula, the two spires and white cupola of the cathedral and, farther on, to the right, the yellow-tiled bell towers of the Iglesia del Santuario.

Teresa was standing next to the window of a den on the second floor, gazing at the landscape, although Colonel Edgar Ledesma, assistant commander of the Ninth Military District, had advised her not to. "Every window," he had said, looking at her with the eyes of a cold, efficient warrior, "is an opportunity for a sniper. And you, *señora,* aren't here to give them opportunities."

Colonel Ledesma was a pleasant sort of man, very correct in his bearing, who wore his fifty years as lightly as he did his uniform and his close-cropped hair. But she was sick and tired of the limited view from the downstairs windows, sick of the large living room with fake French provincial sofas mixed with acrylic tables, horrendous pictures on the walls—the house had been seized by the government from a narco now in prison in Puente Grande. From the windows and the porch you could see only a slice of the lawn and the empty swimming pool. From upstairs you could see in the distance, at least if you were aided by memory, the city of Culiacán. You could also see one of the Federales who were assigned as her escort inside the walls: a man in a plastic poncho whose girth was expanded by a bulletproof vest. He was wearing a beret and carrying an AR-15, and he stood smoking under a mango tree that sheltered him from the drizzle.

Quite a bit farther away, behind a wrought-iron gate that opened onto Calle General Anaya, Teresa could see a military pickup and the green forms of two soldiers—*guachos,* everyone in Sinaloa called them—standing guard in combat attire. That was the agreement, she'd been informed by Colonel Ledesma four days earlier, when the chartered Learjet that was bringing her down from Miami—the only stop from Madrid, since the DEA discouraged the idea of any intermediate stop on Mexican soil—landed at the Culiacán airport. The Ninth District was in charge of general security, and the Federales took over on the inside. Transit police and the Judiciales, the special investigative police attached to the courts, had been excluded from the operation because they were considered easier to infiltrate, and because it was common knowledge that some of them moonlighted as hit men for narcotics gangs and cartels. The Federales might also be persuaded by greenbacks, but the elite group assigned to this mission, brought in from the Distrito Federal—no agent with any Sinaloan connections allowed—was supposedly unbuyable. As for the military, they weren't incorruptible but their discipline and organization made buying them very expensive. Harder to buy, then, and also more respected. Even when they were detailed up into the sierra, the campesinos always said they did their job without looking for angles or "considerations." And Colonel Ledesma had a reputation for being a tough, straight-shooting man, of absolute integrity. The narcos had murdered a nephew of his, a lieutenant. That helped.

"You should move away from that window, *patrona*. The wind . . ."

"*Chale*, Pinto"—she smiled at the bodyguard—"give me a break."

It had been like a weird dream, like witnessing a chain of events that weren't happening to her. The last two weeks lined up in her memory, a succession of intense and perfectly defined chapters. The night of the last operation. Teo Aljarafe reading his absence of future in the shadows of the cabin. Héctor Tapia and Willy Rangel looking at her in amazement in a suite of the Hotel Puente Romano when she presented her decision and her demands: Culiacán rather than the Distrito Federal—We do things right, she said, or not at all. The signing of confidential documents with guarantees for both parties, in the presence of the U.S. ambassador in Madrid, a high official of the Spanish Ministry of Justice, and an officer from Foreign Affairs. And then, once her bridges had been burned, the long trip across the Atlantic, the technical stopover on the Miami runway with the Learjet surrounded by police, the face of Pote Gálvez inscrutable each time they exchanged glances.

"They're going to want to kill you every minute," Willy Rangel had warned her. "You, your bodyguards, and anybody breathing anywhere near you. So you need to be very, very careful."

Rangel had accompanied her to Miami, briefing her on everything she needed to know and do. Instructing her in what was expected of her and what she, in turn, could expect. Afterward, if there was an afterward, there would be help for the next five years in setting her up wherever she wanted—the United States, Latin America, Europe—a new identity including American passport, official protection. Or nothing, if that's what she wanted. And when she replied that what came afterward was her business, and hers alone, thank you, Rangel rubbed his nose and nodded, as though he'd seen that coming. After all, the DEA figured that Teresa Mendoza had stashed away, in Swiss and Caribbean banks, between fifty and a hundred million dollars.

She continued to watch the rain fall outside. Culiacán. The night of her arrival, when at the foot of the Learjet's steps she boarded the convoy of military and Federales vehicles waiting on the runway, Teresa had seen off to the right the airport's old yellow control tower, with dozens of Cessnas and Pipers parked around it, and to the left the new facilities under construction. The Suburban she got into with Pote Gálvez was armored, with dark tinted glass. Just she, Pote, and the driver rode in it, and the driver had a police-frequency radio turned on. There were blue and red lights, *guachos* in combat helmets, Federales in street clothes or dark gray uniforms, armed to the teeth, sitting in the rear of the trucks or the open doors of Suburbans, their baseball caps and ponchos glistening with raindrops. Machine guns mounted on jeeps and pickups were aimed in every direction, and radio antennas whipped in the air as the vehicles took curves at top speed and the convoy moved through the city, to the deafening ululation of sirens. *Chale.* Who'd have thought, said Pote Gálvez' face, that we'd be coming back this way.

They drove at high speed down Zapata, turning at the A-l Valle gas station onto the north beltway. Then came the shore drive with the poplars and the big weeping willows whose graceful branches drooped to the ground, the lights of the city, the familiar places, the bridge, the dark waters of the Tamazula, Colonia Chapultepec. Teresa had thought she would feel something special in her heart when she was back here, but the truth was, she discovered, one place was not very different from another. She felt neither elation nor fear.

During the drive, she and Pote Gálvez had looked at each other many times. Finally Teresa asked him, "What's in your head, Pinto?" He took a moment to answer, staring out the window, his moustache a dark brushstroke, the spatters of water on the window speckling his face when they passed streetlights.

"Well, you know, nothing special, *patrona,*" he replied at last. "Just that it's strange." He said this without emotion, his norteño, Mayan face inexpressive. Sitting very straight and formal beside her on the leather seat, his hands crossed over his belly. And for the first time since that night in the basement in far-off Nueva Andalucía, he looked defenseless to Teresa. They hadn't let him carry a gun, although they told him there would be guns in the house, for personal protection, even with the Federales in the garden and the *guachos* on the perimeter, in the street.

From time to time the bodyguard turned to look out the window, recognizing this or that spot as they flew past. Not opening his mouth. As silent as when, before they left Marbella, she made him sit down with her and explained to him what was coming. For both of them. She was not fingering anybody, just collecting a big debt from *un hijo de su pinche madre.* Him and nobody else. Pote sat awhile thinking that over. "Talk to me," she'd finally said. "I need to know how you're looking at this before I let you go back over there with me."

"Well, I don't know how I'm looking at this," was his response. "And I tell you that—or rather don't tell you anything—with all respect. Maybe I even do have my opinion, *patrona.* Why say no if the answer's yes? But the opinion I have or don't have is my business. You think it's right to do something, you do it, and that's that. You decide to go, and I, well, I go with you."

She stepped away from the window and went to the table for a cigarette. The pack of Faros was beside the SIG-Sauer and the three full clips. At first Teresa wasn't familiar with that pistol, and Pote Gálvez spent one morning teaching her to take it apart and put it back together again, over and over until she could do it with her eyes closed. "If they come at night and it jams, you'd better know how to fix it without turning on the light." Now Pote Gálvez stepped over with a lit match, bowed his head briefly when she thanked him, and replaced Teresa at the window, to give a look outside.

"Everything's in order," she exhaled. It was a pleasure to smoke Faros after so many years.

The bodyguard shrugged, the gesture implying that in Culiacán, "order" was a relative term. Then he went out into the hall and Teresa heard him talking to one of the Federales stationed in the house. Three inside, six in the garden, twenty *guachos* on the outer perimeter—reliefs every twelve hours—keeping back the curious. The journalists, and the hired squad of executioners who by now were on the prowl, were waiting for their chance. I wonder, Teresa said to herself, how big a price the representative to the House of Deputies and future senator from Sinaloa, don Epifanio Vargas, has put on my head.

"What do you think we're worth, Pinto?"

He had come to the door again, with that look of a big clumsy bear he had when he wanted to be inconspicuous. Apparently quiet and slow-moving, as always. But she could see that behind the narrowed lids, his dark, suspicious eyes never lowered their guard, never stopped seeing everything around them.

"They'll take me out for free, *patrona*. . . . But you're a big fish to catch, now. Nobody would take it on for less than full retirement pay for life."

"You think it'll be the escorts, or that they'll come from outside?"

The bodyguard pursed his lips, thinking.

"I think from outside. The narcos and the police are the same thing, but not always. . . . Understand?"

"More or less."

"That's the truth. And the *guachos*—the colonel looks to me like the real thing, stand-up, you know? . . . He'll keep his men in line."

"That, we'll see about, no?"

"It'll be something to see, all right, *patrona*—see it once and for all, and get our asses out of here."

Teresa smiled when she heard that. She understood what he was saying. The waiting was always worse than the fight, no matter how bad the fight was. Anyway, she'd taken additional measures. Preventive measures. She wasn't born yesterday—she had money and she'd read her classics. The trip to Culiacán had been preceded by a campaign of information in the right places, including the local press. Just Vargas, was the motto. No squealing, no squawking, no ratting, no fingerpointing, no blowing the whistle on anybody but Epifanio Vargas: a personal matter, a mano a mano, a duel in the dust. Admission free, and everybody welcome to watch the show. But not another name or date. Nothing. Just don Epifanio, Teresa, and the ghost of Güero Dávila, burned to death on the Espinazo del Diablo twelve years ago. This was not a betrayal, this was a limited, personal payback, the kind of thing that could be understood very well in Sinaloa, where double-crossing was frowned on—you die, *cabrón*—but revenge was what filled the cemeteries. That had been the deal struck in the Hotel Puente Romano, and the Mexican government had signed on the dotted line.

Even the gringos had signed, although grudgingly. Concrete testimony, a concrete name.

The other drug bosses who used to be close to Epifanio Vargas, even Batman Güemes, had no reason to feel threatened. That, as one could well imagine, had reassured Batman and the others considerably. It also increased Teresa's chances of survival and reduced the fronts that had to be covered. After all, in the shark-feeding ground of Sinaloan drug money and narcopolitics, don Epifanio had been or was an ally, a pillar of the community, but also a competitor and, sooner or later, an enemy. A lot of people would be very happy if he could be taken out of action for such a low price.

T he telephone rang. It was Pote Gálvez who answered it, and he looked at Teresa as though the voice on the other end had just spoken the name of a ghost. But she wasn't the least bit surprised. She'd been expecting this call for four days. And the time was getting short.

T his is very irregular, *señora*. I can't authorize this."
Colonel Ledesma was standing on the living room rug, his hands behind his back, his uniform perfectly ironed, his boots, spotted with raindrops, gleaming. That short hair looks good on him, Teresa thought, even with all the gray. So polite and so clean. He reminded her of that captain in the Guardia Civil in Marbella, a long time ago, whose name she'd forgotten.

"It's less than twenty-four hours before your testimony."
Teresa remained seated, smoking, her legs in black silk pants

crossed. Looking up at him. Comfortable. Very careful to make things very clear.

"Let me tell you again, Colonel. I am not here as a prisoner."

"No, of course not."

"If I accept your protection it's because I want to accept it. But no one can keep me from going wherever I want to go. . . . That was the agreement."

Ledesma shifted his weight from one leg to the other. Now he was looking at Gaviria, the lawyer from the Mexican national prosecutor's office, his liaison with the civil authorities handling the case. Gaviria was also standing, although farther back, with Pote Gálvez behind him, leaning on the door frame, and the colonel's aide, a young lieutenant, looking over Pote's shoulder from the hall.

"Tell Señora Mendoza," the colonel pleaded with the lawyer, "that what she's asking is impossible."

Ledesma was right, Gaviria said. He was a rail-thin, pleasant man, shaved and dressed very correctly. Teresa glanced at him for no more than a second, her eyes taking him in and spitting him out as though he didn't exist.

"I'm not asking, Colonel," she said, "I'm telling. I intend to leave here this afternoon for an hour and a half. I have an appointment in the city. . . . You can take security measures, or not."

Ledesma, powerless, shook his head.

"Federal law forbids me from moving troops through the city. I'm already stretching it with those men I've got posted outside there."

"And the civil authorities . . ." Gaviria began.

Teresa stubbed out her cigarette with such force that the fire burned her fingertips.

"You and the civil authorities, let me tell you—don't worry your little head about me. Not a bit. I'll be there tomorrow, on the dot, to do what I said I'd do for the civil authorities."

"You have to consider that in legal terms. . . ."

"Listen. I've got the Hotel San Marcos full of very expensive lawyers." She motioned toward the telephone. "How many do you want me to call?"

"It could be a trap," the colonel argued.

"*Híjole,* no kidding!"

Ledesma ran a hand across the top of his head. He took a few steps around the room, Gaviria watching him anxiously.

"I'll have to consult with my superiors," the colonel said.

"Consult with whoever you want to," Teresa told him. "But get one thing straight: If I'm not allowed to keep that appointment, I'll interpret it as being held here against my will, in spite of the government's commitment. And that violates the agreement. . . . Plus, I remind you, in Mexico there are no charges against me."

The colonel looked at her fixedly. He bit at his lower lip as though a piece of loose skin were bothering him. He turned and started toward the door, but then stopped halfway.

"What do you gain by putting yourself at risk this way?"

It was clear that he really wanted to understand this. Teresa uncrossed her legs, brushing out the wrinkles in the silk.

"What I gain or lose," she replied, "is my business, and no fucking concern of yours."

She said it and then fell silent, and in a few moments she heard the colonel's deep, resigned sigh.

"I'll ask for instructions."

"So will I," the lawyer from the prosecutor's office added.

"*Órale.* Ask for all the instructions you want. Meanwhile, I want a car at the door at seven o'clock sharp. With him"—she pointed at Pote Gálvez—"inside and armed to the teeth. What you've got around us or on top of us, Colonel, is up to you."

She said this looking the whole time at Ledesma. And this time, she calculated, I can allow myself a smile. It makes quite an impression on them when a woman smiles as she twists their balls. What, Colonel? You thought you were the Marlboro man?

W*hhhp-whhhp. Whhhp-whhhp.* The monotonous sound of the windshield wipers, big drops of rain drumming like hail on the roof of the Suburban. The Federale who was driving turned the wheel to the left and started down Avenida Insurgentes, and Pote Gálvez, beside him in the passenger seat, looked to one side and the other and put both hands on the AK-47 in his lap. In his jacket pocket he was carrying a walkie-talkie tuned to the same frequency as the radio in the Suburban, and from the back seat Teresa could hear the voices of agents and soldiers taking part in the operation. Objective One and Objective Two, they were saying. Objective One was her. And they were going to meet Objective Two in just seconds.

Whhhp-whhhp. Whhhp-whhhp. It was still daylight, but the gray sky made the streets dark, and some businesses had turned their outside lights on. The rain multiplied the lights of the small convoy. The Suburban and its escort—two Rams belonging to the Federales and three Lobo pickups with soldiers manning machine guns in the back—raised fans of water from the brown torrent that overran gutters and drains and filled the streets on its way toward the Tamazula. A band of black crossed the sky, silhouetting the tallest buildings along the avenue, and a reddish band below it seemed beaten down by the weight of the black.

"A checkpoint, *patrona*," said Pote Gálvez.

There was the noise of a round being chambered in Pote's AK-47, and that earned the bodyguard a look out of the corner of the driver's eye. When they passed the checkpoint without slowing, Teresa saw that it was a military patrol and that the soldiers, in combat helmets, had pulled over two police cars and were holding the Judiciales at gunpoint with their AR-15s and M16s.

Clearly, Colonel Ledesma trusted the police just so far. Clearly, also, after searching for a loophole in the law that kept him from moving troops through the city, the assistant commander of the Ninth District had found one in the small print—after all, the natural state of a soldier was always very close to a state of siege. Teresa saw more Federales and *guachos* posted under the trees along the median, with transit police blocking the intersections and detouring traffic down other routes. And right there, between the railroad tracks and the large concrete block of the administration building, the Malverde Chapel seemed much smaller than she remembered it, twelve years before.

Memories. She realized that for that entire long round-trip journey, she had acquired only three certainties about human beings: that they kill, that they remember, and that they die. Because there comes a moment, she told herself, when you look ahead and see only what you've left behind—dead bodies all along the road you're walking down. Among them, your own, although you don't know it. Until you come upon it, and then you know.

She looked for herself in the chapel's shadows, in the peace of the pew set to the right of the saint's image, in the reddish half-light of the candles that sputtered among the flowers and offerings hung on the wall. The light outside was fading quickly, and as the dirty gray of the evening deepened, the flashing lights of one of the Federales' cars illuminated the entrance with intermittent red and blue. As she stood before St. Malverde, his hair as black as beauty-parlor dye, his white jacket and the kerchief at his neck, his Mayan-Aztec eyes, and his *charro* moustache, Teresa moved her lips to pray, as she'd done so many years before—*God bless my journy and allow my return.* But no prayer would come. Maybe it would be sacrilege, she thought. Maybe I shouldn't have wanted to have the meeting here. Maybe with the years I've become stupid and arrogant, and now I pay.

The last time she'd been here, there had been another woman gazing out at her from the shadows. Now Teresa looked for her, but didn't find her. Unless, she decided, I'm the other woman, or have her inside me, and the narco's *morra* with the scared eyes, the girl who ran away carrying a gym bag and a Double Eagle, has turned into one of those ghosts that float along behind me, looking at me with accusatory, or sad, or indifferent eyes. Maybe that's what life's like, and you breathe, walk, move so one day you can look back and see yourself back there. See yourself in the successive women—yours and others'—that every one of your steps condemns you to be.

She stuck her hands into the pockets of her raincoat—underneath, a sweater, jeans, comfortable boots with rubber soles—and took out the pack of Faros. She was lighting one at the flame of an altar candle when she saw don Epifanio Vargas silhouetted against the red and blue flashes at the door.

T eresita. It's been a long time."
He looked almost the same, she saw. Tall, heavyset. He had hung his raincoat on the rack next to the door. Dark suit, shirt collar open, no tie, pointed-toe boots. With that face that reminded her of old Pedro Armendáriz movies. He had a lot of gray in his moustache and at his temples, quite a few more wrinkles, a few more inches at the waist, perhaps. But he was the same don Epifanio.

"I hardly recognize you," he said, taking a few steps into the chapel after glancing suspiciously to one side and then the other. He was looking at Teresa fixedly, trying to relate her to the other woman he had in his memory.

"You haven't changed much," she said. "A little heavier, maybe. And the gray."

She was now sitting on the pew, next to the image of Malverde, and she didn't move.

"Are you carrying?" don Epifanio asked, ever cautious.

"No."

"Good. Those *hijos de puta* out there patted me down. I wasn't, either."

He sighed, looked up at Malverde in the trembling light of the candles, then back at her.

"The gray . . . I just turned sixty-four. But I'm not complaining."

He came closer, until he stood very close, studying her from above. She remained as she was, holding his gaze.

"I'd say things have gone well for you, Teresita."

"Haven't gone bad for you, either."

Don Epifanio nodded slowly, agreeing. Pensive. Then he sat down beside her. They were sitting exactly the way they had been the last time, except that she wasn't holding a Double Eagle.

"Twelve years, right? You and I on this very spot, with that notebook of Güero's . . ."

He paused, giving Teresa a chance to add a memory of her own to the conversation. But she said nothing. After a moment don Epifanio took a cigar out of the chest pocket of his jacket.

"I never imagined," he started to say as he took off the wrapper. But he stopped again, as though he'd just come to the conclusion that what he'd never imagined didn't matter now.

"I think we all underestimated you," he said at last. "Your man. Me. All of us." He spoke the words "your man" a little softer, as if trying to slip them in unnoticed among the rest.

"Maybe that's why I'm still alive."

Don Epifanio thought that over as he held the flame of his lighter to the cigar.

"Being alive is not a permanent state, or guaranteed," he said with the first puff. "A person stays alive until he's not anymore."

The two of them smoked for a while, not looking at each other. She'd almost finished her cigarette.

"What are you doing, Teresa, getting involved in all this?"

She took one last puff, then dropped the butt and carefully put it out with the toe of her boot.

"Well, I'll tell you," she replied, "it's to settle some old debts."

"Debts," Epifanio repeated. He took another puff on his Havana. "It's better to just let some debts go."

"No way to do that," said Teresa, "if they keep you from sleeping at night."

"You don't gain anything."

"What I gain is my business."

For a few seconds the only sounds were the sputtering of the candles at the altar and the rain beating on the roof of the chapel. Outside, the red and blue of the Federales' car was still flashing.

"Why do you want to screw *me*? . . . All you're doing is playing into the hands of my political enemies."

It was a nice tone, she had to admit. Almost affectionate. Less a reproach than a hurt question. He was the betrayed godfather. The wounded friend. And the fact is, she thought, I never saw him as a bad guy. He was often sincere with me, and maybe still is.

"I don't know who your enemies are, and I don't care," she answered. "You did wrong in killing Güero. And Chino. And Brenda and the kids."

If this was about affection, she could go that route, too. Don Epifanio looked at the ember of his cigar, frowning.

"I don't know what they've told you. But whatever it was, this is Sinaloa. . . . You're from here, and you know what the rules are."

"The rules," Teresa said slowly, "include collecting debts from people that owe you." She paused, and she heard the man's breathing as he concentrated on her words. "And besides the others," she added, "you tried to have *me* killed."

"That's a lie!" Don Epifanio seemed genuinely shocked. "You were here, with me. I protected you, I saved your life . . . I helped you escape."

"I'm talking about later. When you changed your mind."

"In our world," don Epifanio said, after thinking about it, "business is complicated." He studied her once he'd said this, like a man waiting for a tranquilizer to take effect. "Anyway," he added, "I can understand that you'd want to send me the bill. You're from Sinaloa, and I respect that. But to strike a deal with the gringos and those *cabrones* in the government that want to bring me down . . ."

"You don't have any idea what *cabrones,* if any, I've struck a deal with."

She said this somberly, with a firmness that left the man thoughtful. He held the cigar in his mouth, his eyes squinting from the smoke, the flashes from the street turning him alternately red and blue.

"Tell me one thing. The night we met you'd read the notebook, hadn't you? . . . You knew about Güero. . . . But I didn't realize that. You tricked me."

"My life was on the line."

"So why are you digging up all these old things?"

"Because until now I didn't know who asked Batman Güemes for a favor. And Güero was my man."

"He was a DEA *cabrón.*"

"*Cabrón* and DEA, he was my man."

She heard him swallow an obscenity as he stood up. His corpulence filled the small chapel.

"Listen," he said. He looked at the image of Malverde, as though calling the patron saint of drug lords as a witness. "I always behaved well. I was godfather to both of you. I loved Güero and I loved you. He double-crossed me, but despite that I saved your pretty ass. . . . The other was much later, when your life and mine took different paths. . . . Now time has passed, I'm out of that. I'm old, and I've even got grandchildren. I'm in politics, and I like it, and the Senate will let me do new things. That includes helping Sinaloa. . . . What do you gain by hurting me? Helping those gringos that consume half the world's drugs while they decide, depending on what's convenient to them at the moment, which narcos are good and which ones are bad? Helping the people that financed the anti-Communist guerrillas in Vietnam with drug money and then came to ask us Mexicans to pay for the Contras' weapons in Nicaragua? . . . Listen to me, Teresita, those people that are using you now once helped me earn a fuckload of money with Norteña de Aviación, and then launder it in Panama. . . . Tell me what those *cabrones* are offering you. . . . Immunity? . . . Money?"

"Neither one. It's more complex than that. Harder to explain."

Epifanio Vargas turned to her again. As he stood before the altar, the candlelight aged him.

"You want me to tell you," he insisted, "who's been trying for years to fuck me in the United States? . . . Who's pressuring the DEA? . . . A federal prosecutor in Houston, named Clayton, with close ties to the Democratic Party . . . And you know who he was before he became a federal prosecutor? . . . A defense lawyer for Mexican and gringo narcos, and a close friend of Ortiz Calderón, who was director of aerial interception in the Judiciales and who's now living in the United States in the Witness Protection Program after stealing millions of dollars. . . . And on this side, the people trying to bring me down are the same ones that were in bed with the gringos and me: lawyers, judges, politicians, all trying to take the heat off themselves by making me a scapegoat for the whole system. . . . You want to help those people fuck me?"

Teresa didn't reply. Epifanio regarded her for a while and then shook his head powerlessly.

"I'm tired, Teresita. I've worked hard all my life."

It was true, and she knew it. The campesino from Santiago de los Caballeros had worn huaraches and picked beans. Nobody had ever given him anything.

"I'm tired, too."

He was still watching her, probing her, searching for a chink through which to see what was going on in her head.

"There's no way for us to work this out, then, apparently," he concluded.

"I don't think so."

The cigar's ember flared, illuminating don Epifanio's face.

"I've come here to see you," he said, and now his tone was different, "to talk to you—to explain things to you. . . . Maybe I owed you that, maybe I didn't. But I came, like I came twelve years ago, when you needed me."

"I know, and I thank you for that. You never did anything that bad except when you killed Güero and when you tried to kill me. . . ." She shrugged. "Everybody has their own road to walk."

A very long silence. The rain was still pelting the roof. St. Malverde looked impassively into the void with his painted eyes.

"All those guns and cops outside don't guarantee a thing," Vargas said at last. "And you know it. In fourteen or sixteen hours a lot of things can happen. . . ."

"I don't give a shit," Teresa replied. "You're at bat now."

Don Epifanio nodded as he repeated, "At bat now"—a perfect summary of the situation. He lifted his hands, then dropped them to his sides in desolation.

"I should have killed you that night," he said. "Right here."

He said it without passion, calmly and objectively. Teresa looked at him from the pew, not moving.

"Yes, you should have," she said just as calmly. "But you didn't, and now I've come to collect."

"You're crazy."

"No." Teresa stood up in the flickering candlelight, in the flashes of red and blue. "What I am is dead. Your Teresita Mendoza died twelve years ago, and I'm here to bury her."

She leaned her forehead against the fogged-up second-floor window, the wetness cooling her skin. The spotlights in the garden reflected off the rain and turned it into millions of drops of silver falling across the yard, among the tree branches, or hanging on the tips of the leaves. Teresa held a cigarette between her fingers, and the bottle of Herradura Reposado sat on the table next to a glass, a full ashtray, the SIG-Sauer with its three extra clips. On the stereo, José Alfredo: Teresa didn't know whether it was one of the songs Pote Gálvez was always playing for her, on the cassette for cars and hotels, or whether it had come with the house:

Half my drink, I left on the table
to follow you—I don't know why.

She'd been up here for hours. Tequila and music, memories and a present with no future. María la Bandida. *Just put me out of my misery, don't let me die of a broken heart.* The night I cried. She finished her drink, half the glass, and refilled it before returning to the window, trying to keep the room's light from making her too conspicuous. She wet her lips on the tequila while she sang along: *Half my future you took with you, I hope it does you more good than it did me.*

"All of them have left, *patrona*."

She turned slowly, all at once feeling very cold. Pote Gálvez was at the door, in shirtsleeves. He never appeared to her like that. A walkie-talkie in one hand, his revolver in its leather holster at his waist, he looked very serious. Dead serious. His shirt stuck to his heavy torso with sweat.

"What does that mean— 'all of them'?"

He looked at her almost reproachfully. Why ask if you know the answer? his look seemed to say. "All of them" meant all of them.

"The Federales, the escort," he explained. "The house is empty."

"Where'd they go?"

He didn't answer. He just shrugged. Teresa read the rest in his suspicious norteño eyes. Pote Gálvez' rat detector didn't use radar.

"Turn out the light," she said.

The room went dark; now there was just the glow from the hallway and the spotlights outside. The stereo clicked and José Alfredo was cut off mid-word. Outside, behind the tall entrance gates, everything looked normal: she could see soldiers and jeeps under the streetlamps. In the garden, though, there was no movement. The Federales that had been patrolling it were nowhere to be seen.

"When was the relief supposed to come on, Pinto?"

"Fifteen minutes ago. A new group came and the old ones left."

"How many?"

"The usual: three ugly ones in the house and six in the garden."

"What about the radio?"

Pote hit the button on the walkie-talkie twice and then held it out to her. Nothing. "Nobody says anything. But if you want, we can talk to the *guachos*."

Teresa shook her head. She went to the table, grabbed the SIG-Sauer and stuffed the three reserve clips into her pants pockets, one in each back pocket and one in the right front. They were heavy.

"Forget them. Too far." She loaded the pistol, *click click,* one round in the chamber and fifteen in the clip, and stuck it in her waistband. "Besides, they could be in on it."

"I'm going to have a look," the bodyguard said. *"Con su permiso."*
He left the room, revolver in one hand and walkie-talkie in the other, while Teresa went to the window again. She stood to the side and peeked out. Everything looked to be in order. For a second she thought she saw two shadows moving among the shrubbery, under the big mango trees. That was all, and she wasn't even sure of that.

She tapped the butt of the pistol, resigned. Two pounds of steel, lead, and gunpowder—not much for what they must be organizing for her outside. She took the *semanario* off her wrist, put the seven silver bangles in her one empty pocket. No need to announce your position.

Her mind was working fast. Numbers pro and con, balances. The possible and the probable. Once again she calculated the distance from the house to the main gate and the walls, and reviewed what she had been recording in her memory these last few days: spots that had some protection and spots that were exposed, possible routes, potential traps. She'd thought about all this so much that even though she was going over it now point by point, she had no time to feel fear. Unless fear, tonight, was the sense of physical helplessness that had come over her—the sense that her flesh was vulnerable and that she was infinitely alone.

The Situation.

That's exactly what this is, she suddenly realized. The truth was, she hadn't come to Culiacán to testify against don Epifanio Vargas, she'd come to hear Pote Gálvez say, "We're on our own, *patrona*." She'd come to feel what she was feeling now—with the SIG-Sauer at her waist, ready to pass the test. Ready to step through the dark doorway that had stood before her for twelve years, stealing her sleep in the dirty gray dawns. And when I see the light of day again, she thought, if I do, everything will be different. Or won't be.

She stepped away from the window, went to the table and took a last swig of tequila. Half my drink, I leave on the table, she thought. For later. She was still smiling inwardly when Pote Gálvez appeared in the door. He was carrying an AK-47, and over his shoulder a heavy-looking canvas bag. Teresa's hand went instinctively to the butt of her pistol, but it stopped midway. Not Pinto, she told herself. I'd rather turn my back and let him shoot me than distrust him and have him see it.

"Ande, patrona," the *pistolero* said. "They've laid a trap for us worse than the Coyote's. *Pinches hijos de su madre."*

"Federales or *guachos*? . . . Or both?"

"I'd say it's the Federales, and that the others are just watching. But who knows. Should I radio for help?"

Teresa laughed. "Help from who? They all went off to Taquería Durango for vampire tacos and heads on stakes."

Pote Gálvez looked at her, scratched his head with the AK-47, and then managed a smile—simultaneously confused and ferocious.

"That's the truth, *mi doña*," he said, as the light dawned. "We'll do what we can." And at that, the two regarded each other, one in the light, one in shadow, in a way they never had before. Then Teresa laughed again, sincerely, inhaling air deep inside and with her eyes open, and Pote Gálvez moved his head up and down like a man catching a really good joke.

"This is Culiacán, *patrona*," he said, "and we're going to be laughing out loud in just a minute. I wish those *hijos de perra* could see you before we burn their asses—or vice versa."

"Well, maybe I'm laughing because I'm scared of dying," she said. "Or scared it'll hurt before I die."

Pote Gálvez nodded again. "You're just like everybody else, *patrona*, what did you think? But dying takes time, so while we're dying—or not—let's make sure we take some others with us."

L istening. Sounds, creaks, the pitter of rain on the windows and roof. Try to keep the pounding of your heart, the throbbing of the blood in the tiny veins that run through the inside of your ears from drowning out all the rest. Calculate every step, every movement of your eyeballs. Motionless, with your mouth dry and tension rising painfully in your thighs and belly to your chest, cutting off the little breathing you still allow yourself. The weight of the SIG-Sauer in your right hand, your palm tight around the butt. The hair you pull back from your face because it gets in your eyes. The drop of sweat running down your forehead to your eye, stinging, that you finally lick up off your lips with the tip of your tongue. Salty.

The waiting.

Another creak in the hall, or maybe on the stairs. Pote Gálvez' look from the door across the hall—resigned, professional. His misleading bulk kneeling, half his face peering around the door frame, the AK-47 ready, the stock removed to make it easier to handle, a clip with thirty shells clicked into place and another taped on with masking tape, upside down, ready to be turned over and changed the instant the other one empties.

More creaking. On the stairs.

Half my drink, Teresa whispers to herself, I leave on the table. She feels hollow inside, lucid outside. There are no reflections, no thoughts. Nothing but absurdly repeating the chorus of that song and focusing her senses, interpreting sounds and sensations. At the end of the hall, above the opening for the stairs, is a painting: Black stallions galloping over a broad green prairie. In front, a white horse. Teresa counts the horses: four black, one white. She counts them as she has counted the twelve balusters coming off the stairs, the five colors of the stained-glass window that opens onto the garden, the five doors on this side of the hall, the three sconces on the walls, and the one ceiling light. She also mentally counts the round in the chamber and the fifteen in the clip, the first shot double-action and a bit harder, and then the others just fire, one after another, the forty-five in the three reserve clips weighing down her jeans. There's enough, she thinks, although it all depends on what the bad guys bring in. Anyway, Pote Gálvez recommended that you squeeze them off one by one. No nerves, no rush, just one by one. They last longer and you waste less. And if the lead runs out, insult them—that hurts, too.

The creaking is footsteps. And they're coming up the stairs.

A head comes up over the landing, warily. Black hair, young. A torso and then another head. They're carrying weapons, and the barrels swing back and forth, looking for something to shoot at. Teresa puts out her arm, looks at Pote Gálvez out of the corner of her eye, holds her breath, and pulls the trigger. The SIG-Sauer recoils, spitting bullets like thunderclaps—*boom, boom, boom*—and before the third report, the hallway echoes deafeningly with the short bursts from Pote's AK-47—*ra-a-a-a-ka, ra-a-a-a-ka, ra-a-a-aka*—and is filled with acrid smoke.

Through the smoke she sees half the balusters shatter into fragments and splinters—*ra-a-a-a-ka, ra-a-a-a-ka*—and the two heads disappear, and from downstairs she and Pote hear voices yelling, and somebody running, and Teresa stops shooting and pulls back her weapon, because Pote, with unexpected agility for a man of his size, gets up and runs, bent over, toward the stairway. *Ra-a-a-a-ka, ra-a-a-a-a-ka*—he fires his AK-47 again, now with the barrel pointing down the stairs, not aiming. Another long burst, then he sticks his hand in the bag over his shoulder, feeling for a grenade, pulls the pin with his teeth—just like in the movies, thinks Teresa—tosses it down the stairwell, turns back, still hunched down, and throws himself down the hall on his belly while the stairs go *FMMMM!* Through the smoke and the noise and a blast of hot air that hits Teresa in the face, everything on the stairway, horses included, is blown to smithereens.

A la fucking chingada.

Now the lights suddenly go out all over the house. Teresa doesn't know whether that's good or bad. She runs to the window, looks out, and sees that the garden is also dark, and that the only lights are the streetlamps, on the other side of the walls and the gate. She runs, hunched over, back to the door, stumbles over the table and knocks it down, with everything on it—the tequila and the cigarettes, *shit!*—and throws herself down by the door again, sticking an eye and the pistol out. The hole that was the stairs is weakly lit by the glow from the broken stained-glass window.

"How are you, *mi doña*?"

It is just a whisper. "Okay," she whispers back. "Fine." The bodyguard says nothing else. She can see his form in the darkness, three paces away, on the other side of the hall. He is wearing a white shirt.

"Pinto," she whispers again. "Your shirt!" They'd be able to see it a mile away.

"Too late to change now," he says. "You're doing fine, *mi doña*. Make the ammo last."

Why don't I feel any fear? Teresa asks herself. Who the fuck do I think all this is happening to? She touches her forehead with a dry, ice-cold hand, and clutches the pistol with a hand wet with sweat. I wish somebody would tell me which one of these hands is mine.

"The *hijos de puta* are coming back," Pote Gálvez whispers, swinging his AK-47 out the door.

Ra-a-a-a-ka. Ra-a-a-a-ka. Short bursts, as before, with the 7.62 shells tinkling as they hit the floor, the smoke swirling in the darkness making Teresa's throat itch; blasts from Pote's AK-47, blasts from the SIG-Sauer she holds with both hands—*boom, boom, boom,* her mouth open so the noise doesn't burst her eardrums—blasts shooting toward the blasts that come from the stairs; the buzz of the bullets passing close by—*ziannng, ziannng*—and dull, sinister chuffs against the plaster of the walls and the wood of the doors; the clink and crash of breaking glass when the windows on the other side of the hall are hit. The carriage of her pistol locks to the rear, *click, click,* with no more rounds to shoot, and Teresa is confused for a second, until she realizes what's happened.

She pushes the button to release the empty clip and clicks in another, the one that was in the front pocket of her jeans, and when she frees the carriage it chambers another round. She aims to shoot but waits, because Pote has half his body in the hall and another grenade is rolling toward the stairs, and this time the blast is huge in the darkness, thunderous, truly deafening—*FMMMM. Cabrones!* When Pote stands up and runs hunched over down to the hole, the AK-47 ready, Teresa stands up too and runs beside him, and they arrive at the destroyed railing at the same time. When they peer over, ready to wipe out anybody that might still be standing, the muzzle flashes from their guns reveal at least two bodies lying in the rubble of the stairway.

C*híngale*. Her lungs hurt from the gunpowder and smoke. She muffles her coughing the best she can. She doesn't know how much time has passed. She is very thirsty. She is not afraid.

H ow much ammo, *patrona*?"
    ".Not much."
    "Here you go."
    In the darkness, she catches two of the full clips Pote Gálvez tosses to her, but misses the third. She gropes along the floor for it, then sticks it in one of her back pockets.
    "Isn't anybody going to help us, *mi doña*?"
    "Get real."
    "The *guachos* are outside. . . . The colonel seemed like a decent man."
    "His jurisdiction ends at the wall. We're going to have to make it out there."
    "No way. Too far."
    "Yeah. Too far."

C reaking and footsteps. She grips the pistol and aims into the shadows, clenching her teeth. Maybe this is it, she thinks. But nobody comes up. *Chale*. False alarm.

S uddenly they're there, and she hasn't heard them come up. This time the grenade rolling along the floor is aimed at the two of them, and Pote Gálvez has just enough time to see it. Teresa rolls inside, covering her head with her hands, and the explosion lights up the door and hallway like day. Deafened, she takes a few seconds to register that the distant murmur is the sound of the furious bursts of gunfire that Pote Gálvez is getting off. I ought to do something, too, she thinks. She gets up, staggering from the shock of the blast, grips the pistol, walks on her knees to the door, puts one hand on the frame for support, stands, steps outside, and starts firing blindly—*boom, boom, boom*—blasts of gunfire from both sides, the noise growing louder and louder, closer and closer, and all at once she sees black shadows rushing toward her, flashes of orange and blue, *boom, boom, boom,* and bullets zing past, *ziannnng,* and there are chuffs on the walls everywhere, even behind her, to one side, under her left arm, and Pote Gálvez' AK-47 joins in—*ra-a-a-a-ka, ra-a-a-a-a-ka*—this time not short bursts but long, endless ones. *Cabrones!* she hears him scream, *cabrones!* and she realizes that something is going wrong, maybe he's been hit, or maybe she has, maybe she herself is dying right now and doesn't know it. But her right hand keeps squeezing the trigger, *boom, boom,* and she thinks, *If I'm shooting I must be alive.* I shoot, therefore I am.

Her back against the wall, Teresa rams her last clip into the SIG-Sauer. She has checked herself all over and is amazed not to find a scratch. The sound of rain outside, in the garden. From time to time she hears Pote Gálvez groaning through his teeth.

Are you wounded, Pinto?"
     "I fucked up real bad, *patrona.* . . . I took some lead."
"Does it hurt?"
"Hurts like hell. Why would I tell you no if the answer's yes?"

Pinto."
     "*Sí, señora.*"
"Staying here won't cut it. I don't want them to hunt us down when we're out of ammunition, like rabbits."
"Say the word."

The porch, she decides. There's an overhanging roof with shrubbery underneath, at the other end of the hall. The window above it is no problem, because by now there won't be a pane of glass left. If they can make it there, they can jump down and then cut their way through, or try to, and make it to the entrance gate or the wall beside the street. The rain can save their lives as well as it can slow them down. And the soldiers can fire inside, too, she thinks, although that's another risk. There are reporters outside, and people watching. Not as easy as at home.

And don Epifanio Vargas can buy a lot of people, although no one can buy everybody.

C"an you move, Pinto?"
 "Yes, *patrona.* I can."
"The idea is the hall window, and then jump."
"The idea is whatever you say."

T"his has happened before, Teresa thinks. Something similar, and Pote Gálvez was there that time too.
"Pinto."
"*Señora.*"
"How many grenades are left?"
"One."
"Well, go for it."
The grenade is still rolling when they take off running down the hall, and the blast goes off just as they reach the window. Hearing the stutter of Pote's AK-47 behind her, Teresa puts one leg and then the other through the window, being careful not to cut herself on the splinters of glass, but when she puts her left hand down for support, she cuts herself. She feels the thick warm liquid run down the palm of her hand as she swings herself out, and the rain hitting her face. The tiles of the overhang creak under her feet. She sticks the pistol into her waistband before she drops, and she slides along the wet surface, braking at the downspout. Then, after hanging her feet over the edge, she kicks off and drops.

S"he splashes through the mud, the pistol once more in her hand. Pote Gálvez lands beside her. A thump. A groan of pain.
"Run, Pinto. Toward the wall."
There's no time. From the house, the cone of light from a flashlight is seeking them out, and the shooting starts again. This time the slugs make a dull sucking sound when they hit mud, a splash when they hit water. Teresa lifts the SIG-Sauer. I hope all this shit doesn't jam it, she thinks. She shoots single rounds, carefully, not losing her head, in an arc, and then throws herself facedown in the mud. Then she realizes that Pote Gálvez is not firing. She turns to look at him, and in the distant light from the street sees him sprawled against a porch column.

"I'm sorry, *patrona*," she hears him whisper. ". . . This time they fucked me good."

"Where?"

"In the gut . . . I don't know whether it's blood or rain, but there's a lot of it, whatever it is."

Teresa bites her muddy lower lip. She looks at the lights on the other side of the gate, the streetlamps that silhouette the palms and mango trees. It will be tough, she sees, to do it herself.

"Your gun?"

"Right there . . . between us. I put in a double clip, full, but it slipped out of my hands when I got shot."

Teresa lifts her head to see. The AK-47 is on the porch steps. A burst of gunfire from the house forces her to duck.

"I can't reach it."

"Well, I'm truly sorry."

She looks toward the street. There is a crowd of people on the other side of the gate. Police sirens are wailing and a voice is yelling through a megaphone, but she can't tell what it's saying. In the trees, to the left, she hears splashing. Footsteps. Maybe a shadow. Somebody trying to get around on the other side of them. I hope those *cabrones* don't have night-vision goggles, she thinks.

"I need the AK-47."

It takes Pote Gálvez a moment to respond. As if he were thinking about it.

"I can't shoot anymore, *patrona*," he finally says. "I don't have the strength . . . but I can try to push it to you."

"Get real, Pinto. They'll kill you if you so much as stick your nose out."

"Fuck 'em. When it's over it's over."

Another shadow splashing around in the trees. Time's running out, Teresa realizes. Two minutes more, and the only way out won't go anywhere anymore.

"Pote."

A silence. She has never called him by his name.

"*Señora.*"

"Pass me the *pinche* gun."

Another silence. Raindrops pitter in the puddles and on the leaves of the trees. Then, in the background, the muffled voice of the body-guard:

"It was an honor knowing you, *patrona*."

"*Lo mismo te digo.*" Same here, Pote.

Este es el corrido del caballo blanco, Teresa hears Potemkin Gálvez sing softly. And with those words in her ears, breathing great lungfuls of air in fury and desperation, she grips the SIG-Sauer, half stands, and begins to shoot toward the house to cover her man. Then the night bursts forth in gunfire again, and slugs rip into the porch and the tree trunks. And silhouetted against all that she sees the chunky mass of the bodyguard push itself up and limp toward her, heartbreakingly, anguishingly slow, while bullets come at him from every direction, one after another hitting his body, ripping it to pieces like a doll whose joints are being torn apart, until he falls to his knees next to the AK-47. And it is a dead man who, with the last strength of his body, lifts the weapon by the barrel and tosses it away from himself, blindly, in the approximate direction of Teresa, before he rolls down the steps and falls on his face into the mud.

Then she screams: *Hijos de toda su puta madre!* ripping that last howl up from her belly, emptying the pistol's last shells into the house. Then she throws it to the ground, grabs the AK-47, and takes off running, her feet sinking into the mud, toward the trees to the left, where she saw the shadows before, with the low branches and shrubbery lashing her face, blinding her with splashes of water and rain.

A shadow better defined than others—the AK-47 to her cheek, a short burst of fire that makes the gun hit her chin as it recoils, cutting her. Gunshots behind her and to the side, the gate and wall closer than before, figures in the lighted street, the megaphone still roaring incomprehensibly. The shadow isn't there anymore, and as she runs hunched over, with the AK-47 hot in her hands, Teresa sees a hulking mass. It moves, so without stopping she lifts the gun, turns the barrel, pulls the trigger, and shoots as she passes. I didn't hit it, she thinks when the blast fades away, crouching as much as she can. I don't think I hit it. More gunshots behind her and *ziannnng ziannnng* near her head, like lead mosquitoes. She turns and pulls the trigger again, and the AK-47 jumps in her hands with its *pinche* recoil. The flash of her own shots blinds her as she moves away, just as somebody sends a burst of fire where she'd been a second earlier. *Fuck you, cabrón.* Another shadow in front of her. The sound of footsteps running after her, behind her. The shadow and Teresa fire at each other at point-blank range, so close that she sees a face in the flash of the gunshots: a moustache, eyes wide open, a white mouth. She almost pushes him over with the gun barrel when she runs past, as he falls to his knees among the shrubbery. *Ziannnng.* More bullets fly past, she trips, rolls along the ground. The AK-47 goes *click, click.* Teresa rolls over onto her back in the mud and creeps along like that, the rain running down her face, as she pushes the lever, pulls the long double-curved clip out, and turns it around, praying that there's not too much mud in the mechanism. The weapon is heavy on her stomach. The last thirty rounds, she says to herself, sucking on those showing at the top of the clip, to clean them. She pushes the clip in. *Click.* She pulls back hard on the carriage and lets it go. *Click, click.* Then, from the nearby gate, comes the admiring voice of a soldier or a cop:

"*Órale, mi narca!* . . . Show 'em how a Sinaloa girl dies!"

Teresa looks toward the gate, bewildered. Unsure whether to curse or laugh. Nobody is shooting now. She gets to her knees and then stands. She spits out bitter mud that tastes like metal and gunpowder. She runs through the trees, zigzagging, but her splashing makes too much noise. More gunfire behind her. She thinks she sees other shadows slipping along next to the wall, but she's not sure. She fires off a short burst to the right and another to the left, *Hijos de puta,* she mutters, runs five or six yards more and crouches down again. The rain turns to steam when it hits the hot barrel of the gun. Now she is close enough to the gate and the wall to see that the gate is open. She can see people out there, lying in the street, crouching behind cars, and can hear the words being repeated through the megaphone:

"*Come this way, Señora Mendoza.* . . . *We're from the Ninth District.* . . . *We will protect you.* . . ."

You could protect me a little more over this way, she thinks. Because I've still got twenty yards to go, and they're the longest twenty yards of my life. Certain that she will never be able to cover that distance, she lies down in the rain and says good-bye, one by one, to the ghosts that have been by her side for so many years. See you there, guys. Fucking *pinche* Sinaloa, she says—one last parting word.

Another burst of gunfire to her right, and one to her left. Then she grits her teeth and takes off, stumbling in the mud. So tired she falls, or almost does, but then suddenly nobody is shooting. She stops abruptly, surprised, turns around, and sees the dark garden and the back of the house in shadow.

The rain is pelting the ground at her feet as she walks slowly through the gate, still carrying the AK-47, toward the people looking in from outside, *guachos* in ponchos gleaming with the rain, Federales in street clothes and uniforms, cars with red and blue lights, television cameras, people lying on the sidewalks, in the rain. Flashbulbs.

"*Put down the weapon, señora.*"

She looks into the spotlights that are blinding her, confused. She's unable to understand what the voices are saying. Finally she raises the

AK-47 slightly, regarding it as though she'd forgotten she was holding it. It's heavy. Really fucking heavy. So she drops it and starts walking again.

Híjole, she says to herself as she passes through the gate. I am so fucking tired. I hope some *pinche hijo de puta* has a cigarette.

Afterword

A t eight that morning, Teresa Mendoza was driven to the attorney general's office in the Ministry of Justice building, with military vehicles and soldiers in combat gear cutting off all other traffic to Calle Rosales. The convoy roared up with sirens screaming, lights flashing in the rain. Armed men in gray Federales uniforms and green combat fatigues stood guard on the roofs of neighboring buildings, and barriers were set up on Morelos and Rubí streets; the historic old section of the city looked like a city under siege.

From the gate of the law school, where a space for journalists had been cordoned off, we saw her get out of the armored Suburban with blacked-out windows and walk under the arch toward the neocolonial patio with wrought-iron lampposts and stone columns. I was with Julio Bernal and Elmer Mendoza, and we would get only a glimpse of her, lit by photographers' flashbulbs, in her short walk from the Suburban to the arch, surrounded as she was by agents and soldiers, and protected from the rain by an umbrella. Serious, elegant, dressed in black, with a dark raincoat, a black leather purse, and a bandaged hand. Her hair combed back with a part down the middle, gathered into a chignon at the nape of her neck, two silver earrings.

"There goes a girl with balls," Elmer said.

She spent an hour and fifty minutes inside, sitting before a commission consisting of the attorney general of Sinaloa, the commander of the Ninth Military District, an assistant federal attorney general who had come in from the Distrito Federal, a local representative to the House of Deputies, a federal representative, a senator, and a notary acting as secretary. And perhaps, as she took her seat and answered their questions, she could read on the table the headline from one of that morning's Culiacán newspapers: "Battle in Chapultepec: Four Federales Killed and Three Wounded Defending Witness—Gunman Also Killed." And another, more sensational: "Narca Slips Through."

Later I was told that the members of the commission, impressed, treated her from the first moment with extreme deference, and that the general commander of the Ninth District apologized for the security lapses, and that Teresa Mendoza listened and then inclined her head a little. And when she concluded her testimony and everyone stood up and she said, Thank you, gentlemen, and walked to the door, the political career of don Epifanio Vargas had been ruined forever.

W e saw her reappear outside. She walked under the arch and came out toward the street, surrounded by bodyguards and soldiers, photographers' flashbulbs popping, while the Suburban's engine started and the car rolled slowly forward to meet her. Then I saw her stop and look around, as though she was searching for somebody in the crowd. A face, or a memory. Then she did something strange: she put a hand in her purse, rummaged inside, and took something out, a piece of paper or a photograph, and looked at it for a few seconds. We were too far away, so I pushed forward through the reporters, trying to get a better view, until a soldier stopped me. It might, I thought, have been the old half-snapshot I'd seen her holding during my visit to the house in Colonia Chapultepec. But from that distance, I just couldn't tell.

Then she tore it up. Whichever it was, piece of paper or photograph, I watched her tear it into tiny pieces before letting them fall to the wet ground. Then the Suburban drove up between us, and that was the last time I ever saw her.

That evening, Julio and Elmer took me to La Ballena, Güero Dávila's favorite cantina, and we ordered three Pacíficos and listened to Los Tigres del Norte sing "Carne Quemada"—"Burned Flesh"—on the jukebox. We drank in silence, looking at other silent faces around us.

I later learned that Epifanio Vargas lost his political position shortly thereafter. He spent time in the Almoloya prison while his extradition to the United States was being processed—an extradition which, after a long and scandalous review, the attorney general denied.

As for the other characters in this story, they each went their own way. Tomás Pestaña, the mayor of Marbella, is still leading the city into the future. Former commissioner Nino Juárez is still head of security for a chain of department stores, now part of a powerful multinational corporation. Attorney Eddie Alvarez has gone into politics in Gibraltar, where a brother-in-law of his is the minister of labor and economy. And I was able to interview Oleg Yasikov while the Russian was serving a short sentence at Alcalá-Meco for a murky affair involving Ukrainian immigrants and arms trafficking. He was a surprisingly pleasant fellow, and he spoke about his old friend with great affection and almost no inhibitions; he even told me some things of interest that I was able to fit into this story at the last minute.

I have never been able to learn what happened to Teresa Mendoza. There are those who say that she changed her face and identity and now lives in the United States. Florida, they say. Or California. Others claim that she went back to Europe, with her daughter, or son, if she had the baby. They mention Paris, Mallorca, Tuscany, but the fact is, nobody knows anything.

As for me, that last day as I sat before my bottle of beer at La Ballena, in Culiacán, listening to songs on the jukebox with a bunch of moustached, silent Sinaloans, I was sorry I lacked the talent to sum it all up in three minutes of words and music. Mine, for good or ill, was going to be a corrido on paper, more than four hundred pages of it.

You do what you can with what you've got. But I was sure that somewhere near there, somebody was already composing the song that would soon be playing in Sinaloa and all of Mexico, sung by Los Tigres, or Los Tucanes, or some other legendary group. A song those tough-looking individuals with big moustaches, plaid shirts, baseball caps, and blue jeans who surrounded Julio, Elmer, and me in the same cantina—maybe at the same table—where Güero Dávila had sat would listen to, their faces stony, and each with a Pacífico in his hand, nodding in silence. The story of the Queen of the South. The corrido to Teresa Mendoza.

La Navata, Spain, May 2002

There are complex novels that owe a great deal to a great many. Besides César "Batman" Güemes, Elmer Mendoza, and Julio Bernal—my *carnales* from Culiacán, Sinaloa—*The Queen of the South* would never have been possible without the friendship of the best helicopter pilot in the world, Javier Collado, aboard whose BO-105 I spent many nights chasing down speedboats on the Strait. To Chema Beceiro, skipper of a Customs HJ turbocraft, I owe the detailed reconstruction of Santiago Fisterra's last trip, León Rock included. My debt of gratitude extends to Patsy O'Brian for her precise prison memories; to Pepe Cabrera, Manuel Céspedes, José Bedmar, José Luis Domínguez Iborra, Julio Verdú, and Aurelio Carmona for technical advice; to Sealtiel Alatriste, Óscar Lobato, Eddie Campello, René Delgado, Miguel Tamayo, and Germán Dehesa for their generous friendship; to my editors, Amaya Elezcano and Marisol Schulz for their enthusiasm; to María José Prada, for her implacable Holmesian mind; and to the protective shadow of the always loyal Ana Lyons. Nor must I forget Sara Vélez, who lent her face for the mugshot and youthful photo of her compatriot Teresa Mendoza on the cover of the Spanish edition. Except for some of the names above, which appear with their real identities in the novel, the rest—people, addresses, corporations, boats, places—is fiction or has been used with the liberty that is the privilege of the novelist. As for others who for obvious reasons can't be named here, they know who they are, how much I owe them, and how much this story owes them.

ABOUT THE AUTHOR

Internationally acclaimed and bestselling author Arturo Pérez-Reverte was born in 1951 in Cartagena, Spain; he now lives near Madrid. His five previous books, among them *The Nautical Chart* and *The Flanders Panel*, have been translated into nineteen languages in thirty countries and have sold millions of copies.